Praise for *Homeward Bound:*

"This fascinating book shows us that the Cold War took place in kitchens, bedrooms, and family rooms, as well as in the Pentagon. This is not just for historians—it's a good read for everyone."
—Linda Gordon, New York University

"May sets a new standard for social history by linking intimate family life of the 1950s with the larger imperatives of the Cold War. *Homeward Bound* should lay to rest forever the notion that the '50s represent some sort of benchmark for 'traditional values' . . . a fascinating look at this unique, even aberrant, decade."
—Barbara Ehrenreich, author of *Nickel and Dimed*

"*Homeward Bound* comes as a timely antidote to any nostalgia for the 'affluent' '50s or a revival of its domestic ideology."
—*San Francisco Review of Books*

"Required reading for anyone who wants to understand how the upheavals in family life of recent years could have happened so quickly after the baby-boom era of togetherness and stability."
—Arlene Skolnick, University of California, Berkeley

"A provocative, challenging, persuasive interpretation of the internal dynamics that shaped American family life in the postwar years."
—William Chafe, Duke University

"Elaine Tyler May's wise and humane book roots the contemporary women's movement in the unsuspected anxieties of the 1950s. This is a book for everyone who lived through the '50s—and for everyone who lives with its legacies." —Linda Kerber, University of Iowa

"In spotlighting the condition of 'contained' homemakers, May makes us see afresh how diabolical sexism is."
—Constance Perin, *Los Angeles Times Book Review*

"A provocative, always entertaining description of the inter-connections between the Cold War anticommunism of post–World War II America and the domestic ideology that Betty Friedan unmasked . . ." —*Signs*

"A provocative thesis that will stir debate." —*Library Journal*

"This book helps the Baby Boom generation understand its genesis."
—*Booklist*

"May offers a sensitive, nuanced reading of domestic ideology, judging but never blaming. Her men are not oppressors, her women not betrayers. . . . History has a long—and often dark—shadow in this book." —Beth Bailey, author of *Sex in the Heartland*

"Particularly refreshing is May's superb use of images taken from Civil Defense publications. . . . May's scholarship is superb."
—Joseph M. Hawes, *Journal of American History*

"May is fundamentally correct . . . that something was cooking under the surface of those placid 1950s families with their station wagons and their bomb shelters." —*Minneapolis Star Tribune*

HOMEWARD BOUND

ALSO BY ELAINE TYLER MAY

Barren in the Promised Land:
Childless Americans and the Pursuit of Happiness

Pushing the Limits:
American Women, 1940-1961

Great Expectations:
Marriage and Divorce in Post-Victorian America

Created Equal:
A Social and Political History of the United States
(with Jacqueline Jones, Peter Wood, Thomas
Borstelmann, and Vicki Ruiz)

Tell Me True:
Memoir, History, and Writing a Life
(co-edited with Patricia Hampl)

Here, There, and Everywhere:
The Foreign Politics of American Popular Culture
(co-edited with Reinhold Wagnleitner)

HOMEWARD BOUND

AMERICAN FAMILIES IN THE COLD WAR ERA

Fully Revised and Updated
20th Anniversary Edition,
With a New Post 9/11 Epilogue

ELAINE TYLER MAY

BASIC
BOOKS

New York
A MEMBER OF THE PERSEUS BOOKS GROUP

"13 Women," words and music by D. Thompson. Published by Danby Music.
Copyright © 1954, renewed 1962.

Quotations from letters written to Betty Friedan in response to *The Feminine Mystique*, in the archives of the Schlesinger Library at Radcliffe College, courtesy of Betty Friedan.

Published by
Basic Books, A Member of the Perseus Books Group
387 Park Avenue South
New York, NY 10016

Books published by Basic Books are available at special discounts for bulk purchases in the United States by corporations, institutions, and other organizations. For more information, please contact the Special Markets Department at the Perseus Books Group, 2300 Chestnut Street, Suite 200, Philadelphia, PA 19103, or call (800) 810-4145, ext. 5000, or e-mail special.markets@perseusbooks.com.

Library of Congress Cataloging-in-Publication Data
May, Elaine Tyler.
  Homeward bound : American families in the Cold War era / Elaine Tyler May.
— Fully rev. and updated 20th anniversary ed., with a new post 9/11 epilogue.
      p. cm.
  Includes bibliographical references and index.
  ISBN 978-0-465-01020-2 (alk. paper)
  1. Family—United States—History—20th century. 2. United States—Social conditions—1945- 3. Baby boom generation—United States. I. Title.

HQ535.M387 2008
306.850973'09045—dc22
                          2008015412

11

In Memory of Ken Edwards, who taught me the meaning of courage;
For Sue Tyler Edwards, who taught me the meaning of strength.

CONTENTS

Acknowledgments

After writing so many words for so many years, I never thought I would find myself at a loss for words when I finally reached this point. But I cannot find adequate words to express the gratitude I feel to all the friends, colleagues, and students who helped me along the way.

Generous financial support provided me with time free from teaching and with essential research assistance. I am grateful for a Mellon Faculty Fellowship in the Humanities at Harvard University in 1981–1982; Radcliffe Research scholarships funded by the Mellon Foundation in summer 1982 and fall 1984; a research fellowship from the American Council of Learned Societies, 1983–1984; a National Endowment for the Humanities summer research stipend in 1983 and a Travel to Collections Grant in 1984; and a research grant from the Rockefeller Foundation, from 1985 to 1987, under the program Exploring Long-Term Implications of Changing Gender Roles. My own institution, the University of Minnesota, generously provided essential leave time and research support. In 2006–2007, residencies at the Huntington Library in San Marino, California, and the Rockefeller Study and Conference Center in Bellagio, Italy, enabled me to work on this new edition.

Early versions of chapters were presented as papers at meetings of the American Historical Association, the Organization of American Historians, and the American Studies Association. Several fine research assistants contributed to this study: Jennifer Delton, Erin Egan, Cherry Goode, Steven Lassonde, Chris Lewis, Polly Martin, Kathryn Ratcliff, Charles Schneeweis, and Omri Shochatovitz. For help with the 1999 edition, I am grateful to Andrea Sachs, Mary Strunk, and Matt Basso. This new edition benefited from the able assistance of Jason Stahl, Peter Kizilos-Clift, and Drew Billups. Many excellent curators and archivists provided essential help. I want to thank in particular David Klaassen of the Social Welfare History Archives at the University of Minnesota, who found things for me I did not even know existed. Radcliffe College provided magnificent archival sources, splendid staff support, and an environment conducive for thinking, working, and sharing ideas with others. Anne Colby, Marty Mauzy, and Erin Phelps at the Henry Murray Research Center, and Barbara Haber, Patricia King, Karen Morgan, and Eva Moseley at the Arthur and Elizabeth Schlesinger Library, shared their time and expertise and answered my endless questions.

My year at Harvard University was enriched by the wisdom and assistance of Stephan Thernstrom and Richard Hunt, who did so much to make my time there productive and fun. I am especially grateful to Ellen Rothman, who helped me in the archives at Radcliffe.

Several friends and colleagues read drafts of chapters, shared ideas, and offered suggestions. They include Ron Aminzade, Harry Boyte, Winifred Breines, Tom Engelhardt, Lewis Erenberg, Roger Friedland, Gary Gerstle, Linda Kerber, Barbara Laslett, Doug Mitchell, Ruth Rosen, Joyce Seltzer, and Martin Sherwin. Special thanks to those who gave close critical readings to the entire manuscript: Nancy Cott, John D'Emilio, Estelle Freedman, Edward Griffin, George Lipsitz, Lary May, Mary Jo Maynes, and Judith Smith. This book was nourished start to finish by the members of my long-standing weekly research and writing group: Sara Evans, Amy Kaminsky, Riv-Ellen Prell, and Cheri Register. They provided criticism and encouragement chapter by chapter, draft after draft, and sustained me with their energetic collaborative spirit and precious friendship.

Steve Fraser, my initial editor at Basic Books, was helpful beyond words. From the time that this book was nothing but a vague idea to the final manuscript, he was supportive and involved. His insights and sharp critical eye made this a much better book than it would have been without his help. Amanda Moon, my editor for this new edition, has been tremendously helpful and supportive. Thanks also to photo sleuth Whitney Casser and eagle-eyed copy editor Margaret Ritchie. Whatever flaws remain after so much good advice from so many smart people are, of course, mine.

Writing about the family is always complicated by the fact that we each have at least one of our own. My family has influenced this project in many ways. My parents, the late Lillian Bass Tyler and the late Edward T. Tyler, imbued me with respect and admiration for their generation, whom I have tried to understand in this study. My children, Michael, Daniel, and Sarah, provided me with empathy for my parents and their peers who reared the baby boomers. When I wrote the book they were children, and they kept me grounded. Today they are young adults whose ideas and insights inspire me to think in new ways.

Finally, I am grateful to Lary May for his help at every step along the way, for prodding me with his criticism, for encouraging me with his enthusiasm, and most of all, as this new edition goes to press, for thirty-eight years of a loving partnership.

E.T.M.
Minneapolis, 2008

FIGURE I Atomic-age newlyweds prepare for their "sheltered honeymoon" in their new fallout shelter. Surrounded by consumer goods and other supplies, they pose for news cameras. At the rear of the photo, next to the portable toilet, is the entrance to the shelter. (*Steve Wever, Miami Herald.*)

INTRODUCTION

I N THE SUMMER OF 1959, a young couple married and spent their honeymoon in a bomb shelter. *Life* magazine featured the "sheltered honeymoon"
with a photograph of the duo smiling on their lawn, surrounded by dozens of
canned goods and supplies. Another photograph showed them descending
twelve feet underground into the twenty-two-ton steel and concrete 8-by-11-
foot shelter where they would spend the next two weeks. The article quipped
that "fallout can be fun" and described the newlyweds' adventure—with obvious
erotic undertones—as fourteen days of "unbroken togetherness."[1] As the couple
embarked on family life, all they had to enhance their honeymoon were some
consumer goods, their sexuality, and privacy. This is a powerful image of the
nuclear family in the nuclear age: isolated, sexually charged, cushioned by abundance, and protected against impending doom by the wonders of modern technology (see Figure 1).

The stunt was little more than a publicity device; yet, in retrospect it takes
on symbolic significance. For in the early years of the cold war, amid a world of
uncertainties brought about by World War II and its aftermath, the home
seemed to offer a secure, private nest removed from the dangers of the outside
world. The message was ambivalent, however, for the family also seemed particularly vulnerable. It needed heavy protection against the intrusions of forces
outside itself. The self-contained home held out the promise of security in an
insecure world. It also offered a vision of abundance and fulfillment. As the cold
war began, young postwar Americans were homeward bound.

Demographic indicators show that in this period, Americans were more
eager than ever to establish families. The bomb-shelter honeymooners were part
of a cohort of Americans who lowered the age at marriage for both men and
women and quickly brought the birthrate to a twentieth-century high after more
than a hundred years of steady decline, producing the "baby boom" (see Tables 1
and 2). Virtually everyone of childbearing age participated in the production of
the baby boom. Americans of all racial, ethnic, and religious groups, of all
socioeconomic classes and educational levels, married younger and had more

FIGURE 2   The honeymooners kiss as they descend into their backyard bomb shelter for two weeks of "unbroken togetherness." (*Courtesy of Bll Sanders, photographer.*)

children than at any other time in the twentieth century. Black and white, rich and poor, they all brought the marriage rate up and the divorce rate down. Although the nation remained divided along lines of race and class, and only members of the prosperous white middle and working classes had access to the suburban domesticity that represented the "good life," family fever swept the nation and affected all Americans. These young adults established a trend of early marriage and relatively large families that lasted for more than two decades (see Table 3). From the 1940s through the early 1960s, Americans married at a higher rate and at a younger age than did their European counterparts.[2]

Less noted but equally significant, the men and women who formed families between 1940 and 1960 also reduced the divorce rate after a postwar peak. Marriages forged in the late 1940s were particularly stable. Even those couples who eventually divorced remained together long enough to prevent

TABLE 1: MEDIAN AGE AT FIRST MARRIAGE, 1890–2005

SOURCES   U.S. Bureau of the Census, *Current Population Reports*, Series P20-514, "Marital Status and Living Arrangements: March 1998 (Update)"; U.S. Department of Commerce, Bureau of the Census, *Historical Statistics of the U.S., Colonial Times to 1970*, Part 1 (Washington, D.C.: Government Printing Office, 1975), p. 19; U.S. Dept. of Health and Human Services, Public Health Service, *Vital Statistics of the United States*, *1981*, Vol. 3 (Hyattsville, Md.: National Center for Health Statistics, 1985), Table 1-9, pp. 1–11; U.S. Census Bureau, *Current Population Survey, March and Annual Social and Economic Supplements, 2005 and Earlier* (Washington, D.C.: U.S. Census Bureau, September 21, 2006), Table MS-2, www.census.gov/population/socdemo/hh-fam/ms2.pdf).

the divorce rate from rising until the mid-1960s (see Table 5). Although the United States maintained its dubious distinction of having the highest divorce rate in the world, the temporary decline in divorce did not occur to the same extent in Europe. Contrary to fears of commentators at the time, the roles of breadwinner and homemaker were not abandoned; they were embraced.

Why did postwar Americans turn to marriage and parenthood with such enthusiasm and commitment? Scholars and observers frequently point to the family boom as the inevitable result of a return to peace and prosperity.[3] They argue that depression-weary Americans were eager to put the disruptions and hardships of war behind them and enjoy the abundance at home. There is, of course, some truth in this claim, but prosperity followed other wars in our history, notably World War I, with no similar increase in marriage and childbearing.

TABLE 2: FERTILITY RATE PER 1,000 WOMEN AGED 15–44

SOURCES   U.S. Bureau of the Census, *Historical Statistics of the U.S., Colonial Times to 1979*, Part 1, bicentennial ed., Series B 5-10 (Washington, D.C.: U.S. Department of Commerce, U.S. Government Printing Office, 1975) p. 49; U.S. Bureau of the Census, *Statistical Abstract of the U.S., 1986*, 107th ed. (Washington, D.C.: U.S. Department of Commerce, U.S. Government Printing Office, 1986), p. 57; Centers for Disease Control and Prevention, *National Vital Statistics Report*, Vol. 47, No. 18 (Hyattsville, Md.: Maryland National Center for Health Statistics, 1999), Table 1, p. 22.; U.S. Census Bureau, *Current Population Survey, Selected Years 1976–2004* (Washington, D.C.: U.S. Census Bureau, 2006), Table H1, www.census.gov/population/www/socdemo/fertility.html#hist).

Peace and affluence alone are inadequate to explain the many complexities of the post–World War II domestic explosion. The demographic trends went far beyond what was expected from a return to peace. Indeed, nothing on the surface of postwar America explains the rush of young Americans into marriage, parenthood, and traditional gender roles.

It might have been otherwise. The Great Depression of the 1930s brought about widespread challenges to traditional gender roles that could have led to a restructured home. The war intensified these challenges and pointed the way toward radical alterations in the institutions of work and family life. Wartime brought thousands of women into the paid labor force when men left to enter the armed forces. After the war, expanding job and educational opportunities, as well as the increasing availability of birth control devices, might well have led young people to delay marriage or not to marry at all, and to have fewer children

TABLE 3: BIRTHRATE, WHITE AND NONWHITE, 1909–2004

SOURCES   U.S. Department of Health and Human Services, Public Health Service, *Vital Statistics of the United States, 1990*, Vol. 1 (Hyattsville, Md.: National Center for Health Statistics, 1985), Table 1-1, pp. 1–2; National Vital Statistics System, National Center for Health Statistics, Centers for Disease Control and Prevention, *Birth Data Files*, "Birth, Fertility, and Total-Fertility Rates by Race: United States, 1980–2005" (Hyattsville, Md.: NCHS, 2005), www.census.gov/compendia/statab/vital_statistics).

if they did marry. Indeed, many scholars and observers at the time feared that these changes seriously threatened the continuation of the American family. Yet the evidence overwhelmingly indicates that postwar American society experienced a surge in family life and a reaffirmation of domesticity that rested on distinct roles for women and men.[4]

The demographic explosion in the American family represented a temporary disruption of long-term trends. It lasted only until the baby-boom children came of age. The parents, having grown up during the depression and the war, had begun their families during years of prosperity. Their children, however, grew up amid affluence during the cold war; they reached adulthood during the 1960s and 1970s, creating the counterculture and a new women's liberation movement. In vast numbers, they rejected the political assumptions of the cold war, along with the domestic and sexual codes of their parents. This generation

TABLE 4: MARRIAGE RATE PER 1,000 UNMARRIED FEMALES, 1920–2004

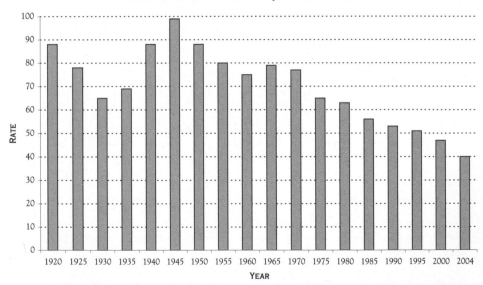

SOURCES   U.S. Department of Commerce, Bureau of the Census, *Historical Statistics of the United States, Colonial Times to 1970*, Part 1 (Washington, D.C.: Government Printing Office, 1975), p. 64; U.S. Department of Health and Human Services, Public Health Service, *Vital Statistics of the United States, 1981*, Vol. 3 (Hyattsville, Md.: National Center for Health Statistics, 1985), Table 1-3, p. 1-6; U.S. Department of Health and Human Services, Public Health Service, *Monthly Vital Statistics Report*, Vol. 44, No. 11 Supplement (Atlanta, Ga.: Centers for Disease Control and Prevention, National Center for Health Statistics, June 24, 1996), Table 1, pp. 7–8; U.S. Census Bureau, *2001 Statistical Abstract of the United States* (Washington, D.C.: U.S. Census Bureau, 2004), Table 117, p. 99; National Marriage Project, *The State of Our Unions* (Piscataway, N.J.: Rutgers University, 2006), Figure 1, p. a17, www.marriage.rutgers.edu/Publications/SOOU/TEXTSOOU2006.pdf).

brought the twentieth-century birthrate to an all-time low and the divorce rate to an unprecedented high.[5]

Observers often point to the 1950s as the last gasp of time-honored family life before the sixties generation made a major break from the past. But the comparison is shortsighted. In many ways, the youths of the sixties resembled their grandparents, who came of age in the first decades of the twentieth century. Like many of their baby-boom grandchildren, the grandparents had challenged the sexual norms of their day, pushed the divorce rate up and the birthrate down, and created a unique youth culture, complete with music, dancing, movies, and other new forms of urban amusements. They also behaved in similar ways politically, developing a powerful feminist movement, strong grassroots activism on behalf of social justice, and a proliferation of radical movements to challenge the status quo. It is the generation in between—with

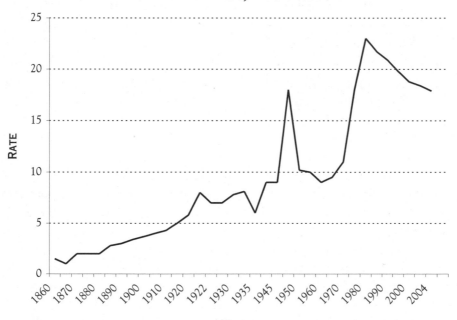

TABLE 5: ANNUAL DIVORCE RATE PER 1,000 MARRIED WOMEN, 1860–2004

SOURCES   Andrew J. Cherlin, *Marriage, Divorce, Remarriage* (Cambridge, Mass.: Harvard University Press, 1992), Figure 1-5, p. 21; National Marriage Project, *The State of Our Unions* (Piscataway, N.J.: Rutgers University, 2006), Figure 5, p. a19, www.marriage.rutgers.edu/ Publications/SOOU/TEXTSOOU2006.pdf).

its strong domestic ideology, pervasive consensus politics, and peculiar demographic behavior—that stands out as different.[6]

Observers normally explain the political activism and the demographic behavior of the baby-boom generation as the effects of affluence and the result of expanding opportunities for women in education and employment. Yet the same conditions existed twenty years earlier at the peak of the domestic revival. The circumstances were similar, but the responses were different. What accounted for the endorsement of "traditional" family roles by young adults in the postwar years and the widespread challenge to those roles by their children?

These questions stimulated the exploration that led to this book. Answering them requires entering the minds of the women and men who married and raised children during these years. The historical circumstances that framed their lives shaped the families they formed.

What makes the postwar demographic explosion even more curious and remarkable is its pervasiveness across all groups in the society. Americans of all backgrounds rushed into marriage and childbearing, even though many of these newly formed families—most notably large numbers of Americans of color—were excluded from suburbia, the site of the "American way of life." Racial and class divisions were concealed beneath an aura of unity in the aftermath of the war. Post–World War II America presented itself as a unified nation, politically harmonious and blessed with widespread affluence. Emerging triumphant from a war fought against racist and fascist regimes, spared the ravages of war-torn Europe and Asia, and prosperous from the booming wartime economy, the United States embraced its position as the "leader of the free world."

But major challenges lay ahead if the nation was to maintain its leadership in the world. The atomic blasts that devastated Hiroshima and Nagasaki marked both the end of World War II and the beginning of the cold war. The United States now faced its former ally, the Soviet Union, as its major foe. The cold war was largely an ideological struggle between the two superpowers, both hoping to increase their power and influence across the globe. The divisions in American society along racial, class, and gender lines threatened to weaken the society at home and damage its prestige in the world. In the propaganda battles that permeated the cold war era, American leaders promoted the American way of life as the triumph of capitalism, allegedly available to all who believed in its values. This way of life was characterized by affluence, located in suburbia, and epitomized by white middle-class nuclear families. Increasing numbers of Americans gained access to this domestic ideal—but not everyone who aspired to it could achieve it.

Poverty excluded many from suburban affluence; racism excluded others. Nevertheless, experts and officials insisted that the combined forces of democracy and prosperity would bring the fruits of the "good life" to all. Racial strife, they asserted, was diminishing. Workers, they argued, were prosperous. But anxieties surrounding these issues did not disappear. Policymakers perceived racial and class divisions as particularly dangerous, because dissatisfied workers and racial minorities might be drawn to left-wing political agitation, leading to socialism or even communism. According to the cold war ethos of the time, conflict within the United States would harm our image abroad, strengthen the Soviet Union, and weaken the nation, making it vulnerable to communism. The worst-case scenario was communist takeover and the defeat of the United States in the cold war. Although strategists and foreign policy experts feared that the Soviet Union might gain the military might and territorial expansion to achieve world domination, many leaders, pundits, and observers worried that the real dangers to America were internal ones: racial strife, emancipated women, class conflict, and familial disruption. To alleviate these fears, Americans turned to the family as a bastion of safety in an insecure world, while experts, leaders, and politicians promoted codes of conduct and enacted public policies that would bolster the American home. Like their leaders, most Americans agreed that family stability appeared to be the best bulwark against the dangers of the cold war.

These widely held beliefs and the public policies they generated led to some dramatic transformations in American society, beyond the rush into marriage, childbearing, and domesticity. Most important, they blurred class lines while sharpening racial divisions. The massive infusion of federal funds into the expansion of affordable single-family homes in suburban developments made it possible for white working-class families to achieve a middle-class lifestyle. Second-generation European immigrants moved out of their ethnic neighborhoods in the cities, leaving their kinship networks, along with their outsider status, behind. Postwar prosperity and the promise of assimilation made it possible for ethnic Americans with white skin to blend into the homogeneous suburbs. Jews and Catholics joined Anglo-Saxon Protestants in these all-white communities, even if they could not join their country clubs or social gatherings. Greeks, Poles, and Italians joined Norwegians and Swedes as members of the white middle class, reaping the benefits of affluence and the American way of life.

People of color were excluded from the vast majority of these suburban communities and were denied the benefits of American prosperity even if they could afford them. With very few notable exceptions, residential segregation defined the postwar suburbs. Persistent racial discrimination proved to be the nation's worst embarrassment throughout the cold war. It also proved to be a situation that African-Americans were unwilling to tolerate. It is no accident that the civil rights movement developed in the wake of World War II, as black soldiers returned from fighting a war against racism to face segregation, discrimination, and brutality at home. Black leaders and federal officials also understood that the national government needed to promote civil rights at home in order to save face abroad, as the Soviet Union and other communist countries pointed to American race relations as an indication of the hypocrisy and failure of the American promise of freedom for all.[7]

But the strategic alliance between the national government and civil rights leaders required that the movement remain limited to legal and political rights, which were consistent with principles of equal opportunity. Issues such as school desegregation and access to public transportation did not violate private property rights. Although most Americans approved of the U.S. Supreme Court's 1954 decision to desegregate public schools, as late as 1964, 89 percent of those polled in the North and 96 percent in the South believed that "an owner of property should not have to sell to a Negro if he doesn't want to." Anything that hinted of a redistribution of wealth evoked fears of socialism and a threat to American capitalism. These cold war principles precluded governmental efforts to strengthen the hand of those with less against those with more. Civil rights leaders understood these imperatives, and they limited their efforts to achieving political rights rather than economic justice. After all, the rallying cry of the United States in the cold war was "freedom," not "equality," and "freedom" became the rallying cry of the civil rights movement as well.[8]

The focus on political rights allowed the government to support certain aspects of the civil rights movement, such as the dismantling of the Jim Crow system in the South, while doing nothing to alleviate residential segregation or the widespread poverty that kept Americans of color at the bottom of the society. As a result, American leaders spoke loudly and often about the efforts the nation was making to eradicate institutionalized racism, claiming that the situation for black Americans was improving. At the same time, they allowed racial segregation to prevail in the suburbs, where the Federal Housing Authority and lending banks maintained redlining policies that prevented black Americans from obtaining home mortgages.[9]

These policies did little to challenge the racial attitudes of white Americans. In the late 1950s, in spite of widespread support for school desegregation, white Americans were less enthusiastic about bringing the races into closer contact in more private realms. Although 60 percent of whites outside the South said they would stay if a black family moved next door, only 45 percent said they would remain in the neighborhood if large numbers of people of color moved in. Disapproval of racial integration was strongest in the most intimate realm of life: the family. The vast majority of Americans—92 percent in the North and 99 percent in the South—approved of laws banning marriage between whites and nonwhites. As late as the mid-sixties, more than half of northern whites and over three-fourths of southern whites still opposed interracial marriage.[10]

The long-term effects of these policies and attitudes were devastating. Black Americans were excluded from most suburbs, even if they could afford suburban homes. That exclusion denied them the opportunity for capital accumulation and upward mobility that homeownership provided. So while white working-class Americans prospered and joined their middle-class peers as suburban homeowners, African-Americans lost ground economically. They were forced to reside in substandard urban housing, left out of postwar prosperity, and denied the government subsidies available to whites.

Out of these developments came a society with a rhetoric of classlessness, but sharply divided along racial lines. From a prewar nation made up of many identifiable ethnic groups, postwar American society divided rigidly along the color line. The children of immigrants identified as outsiders before World War II became "white" after the war, gaining access to the privileges and opportunities that whiteness bestowed, such as life in the suburbs.[11] Political leaders highlighted the nation's prosperous all-white suburbs, hid its poverty in rural and urban areas, and masked its racial oppression by promoting the civil rights movement. Nevertheless, the "American way of life" embodied in the suburban nuclear family, as a cultural ideal if not a universal reality, motivated countless postwar Americans to strive for it, to live by its codes, and—for black Americans—to demand it.

Scholars of the postwar era have begun to examine the connections among cold war politics, suburban development, race relations, and the domestic ideal. The context of the cold war points to previously unrecognized links between political and familial values. Diplomatic historians painted one portrait of a world torn by strife and a standoff between two superpowers that seemed to hold the fate of the globe in their hands. Sociologists and demographers provided a different picture of a private world of affluence, suburban sprawl, and the baby boom. This disconnect suggested the peculiar notion of domestic tranquillity in the midst of the cold war.[12] In *Homeward Bound*, public policy and political ideology are brought to bear on the study of private life, locating the family within the larger political culture, not outside it. This approach illuminates both the cold war ideology and the domestic revival as two sides of the same coin: post-war Americans' intense need to feel liberated from the past and secure in the future.

These cold war anxieties are most apparent in the anticommunist hysteria that swept the nation in the postwar years. Public opinion polls taken at the time illuminate the breadth and depth of anticommunist sentiment in the nation. The vast majority of those polled believed that members of the Communist Party in the United States were loyal to Russia, not to America, and that membership in the Communist Party should be forbidden by law. Although the Communist Party remained legal, it was extremely perilous to join. In the late 1940s, nearly three-fourths of those polled believed that members of the Communist Party should not be allowed to teach in colleges and universities. Fully one out of three said that communists should be killed or imprisoned. Only 16 percent believed they should be left alone. Americans expressed nearly as much hostility to communists in the United States after the war as they did to Nazi leaders in Germany during the war (one-third said Nazis should be executed, another third said they should be imprisoned, and 19 percent said they should be tried and punished). In 1950, at the height of the anticommunist crusade in the United States, 90 percent of Americans polled believed that communists should be removed from jobs in industries that would be important during wartime. When asked what should be done with Communist Party members in the event of a war with Russia, only 1 percent believed it was best to do "nothing, everyone [is] entitled to freedom of thought."[13] Although freedom of thought was one of the most cherished principles of the democracy that cold warriors were fighting to protect, most Americans in 1950 would deny this basic right to members of a small oppositional political party.

Political opportunists like Senator Joseph McCarthy preyed upon these anticommunist sentiments. McCarthyism targeted perceived internal dangers, not external threats. The Soviet Union loomed in the distance as an abstract symbol of what Americans might face if they became "soft." Anticommunist crusaders called on Americans to strengthen their moral fiber in order to pre-serve their freedom and their security. A society weakened by luxury and deca-dence would be vulnerable to subversion from within. Deviations from the norms of appropriate sexual and familial behavior might lead to social disorder and national vulnerability.

Fears of decadence and "softness" led to widespead purges of those whose political or sexual inclinations might make them security risks. The most severe censure was reserved not only for those suspected of ties to the Communist Party, but also for gay men and lesbians, who faced harsh repression and official homophobia. As anticommunist crusaders launched investigations to root out "perverts" in the government, homosexuality itself became a mark of potential subversive activity, grounds for dismissal from jobs, and justification for persecution. In what came to be known as the lavender scare, more people lost their jobs than those who were fired for being suspected "reds." To escape the status of pariah, many gay men and lesbians locked themselves in the stifling closet of conformity, hiding their sexual identities and passing as heterosexuals. As one lesbian recalled, "It has never been easy to be a lesbian in this country, but the 1950s was surely the worst decade in which to love your own sex."[14]

The domestic ideology emerged as a buffer against those disturbing political and sexual tendencies. Yet domesticity ultimately fostered the very tendencies it was intended to diffuse: materialism, consumerism, and bureaucratic conformity. This inherent tension defined the symbiotic connection between the culture of the cold war and the domestic revival. Rootless Americans struggled against what they perceived as internal decay. The family seemed to offer a psychological fortress that would protect them against themselves. Bolstered by heterosexual virility, scientific expertise, and wholesome abundance, it might ward off the hazards of the age.

This challenge prompted Americans to create a family-centered culture that was more than the internal reverberation of foreign policy, and that went beyond the explicit manifestations of anticommunist hysteria such as the "red" and "lavender" scares. It took shape amid the legacy of the depression, World War II, and the anxieties surrounding atomic weapons. It reflected the fears as well as the aspirations of the era. Prosperity had returned, but would there be a postwar slump that would lead to another depression, as there had been after World War I? Would the GIs be able to find secure positions in the postwar economy? Women had proved themselves competent during the war in previously all-male blue-collar jobs, but what would happen to their families if they continued to work? Science had discovered atomic energy, but would it ultimately serve humanity or destroy it?

The family was at the center of these concerns, and the domestic ideology that was taking shape provided a major response to them. The legendary white middle-class family of the 1950s, located in the suburbs, complete with appliances, station wagons, backyard barbecues, and tricycles scattered on the sidewalks, represented something new. It was not, as common wisdom tells us, the last gasp of "traditional" family life with roots deep in the past. Rather, it was the first wholehearted effort to create a home that would fulfill virtually all its members' personal needs through an energized and expressive personal life.[15]

To gain insight into this unique historical era, I have drawn on a wide range of sources, including evidence from the popular culture, especially movies, mass-circulation periodicals, and newspapers; the writings of professionals in numerous fields; and the papers and statements of those who influenced and formulated public policies. In addition, I have utilized a remarkable data collection—the Kelly Longitudinal Study (KLS)—which consists of several surveys of 600 white middle-class men and women who formed families during these years (see Appendix I).[16] E. Lowell Kelly, a psychologist at the University of Michigan, was interested in long-term personality development among married persons. The 300 couples who participated in the study were contacted through announcements of engagements in the late 1930s in New England local newspapers. Kelly sent questionnaires to them every few years and took his most detailed and extensive surveys in 1955. By that time, most of the respondents had been married for at least a decade and were rearing their baby-boom children in suburban homes.

The KLS questionnaires are a valuable source for finding out why white middle-class Americans adhered so strongly to a normative and quite specifically defined notion of family life at the time. Many respondents filled pages with their detailed testimonies, often attaching extra sheets to explain their answers more fully. They wrote about their lives, the decisions they made concerning their careers and children, the quality of their marriages, their family values, their sexual relationships, their physical and emotional health, and their major hopes and worries. They also reflected on their marriages, what they felt they had sacrificed, and what they had gained. In these open-ended responses, freed from Kelly's categories and concerns, they poured out their stories.[17]

The respondents to the KLS were among the cohort of Americans who began their families during the early 1940s, establishing the patterns and setting the trends that were to take hold of the nation for the next two decades. Their hopes for happy and stable marriages took shape during the depression, when many of their parents' generation struggled with disruption and hardship. They entered marriage when World War II thrust the nation into another major crisis, wreaking further havoc on families. They raised children as the cold war took shape, with its cloud of international tension and impending doom.

Yet these women and men were hopeful that family life in the postwar era would be secure and liberated from the hardships of the past. They believed that affluence, consumer goods, satisfying sex, and children would strengthen their families, enabling them to steer clear of potential disruptions. In pursuing their quest for the good life, they adhered to traditional gender roles and prized marital stability; few of them divorced. They represent a segment of the predominantly Protestant white population who were relatively well educated and who generally lived comfortable middle-class lives. In other words, they were among those Americans who would be most likely to live out the postwar American dream. Their poignant testimonies, however, reveal a strong undercurrent of discontent; their hopes for domestic happiness often remained unfulfilled.

The KLS participants, as well-educated, affluent, heterosexual, and married, represented the white Protestant men and women who were most likely to reap the benefits of postwar prosperity and achieve the ideal of "the American way of life." They may not have found the perfect contentment they hoped to realize in their comfortable suburban homes, but they had the best opportunity to pursue its promise. As long as they conformed to the prevailing norms of political and personal behavior, their virtue and patriotism would not be questioned, and they would have access to the suburban dream. It is important to keep in mind who was not represented in the sample. With very few exceptions, Americans of color had no such access. Nor did single women or men, because suburban homes were built for families. Those who divorced faced a powerful stigma that cast their personal virtue and even their status as mature adults into question. Childless couples were excluded from the child-centered culture of the suburbs and were regarded with either pity or scorn, depending on whether their childlessness resulted from chance or choice.[18]

Although all groups contributed to the baby boom, it was the values of the white middle class that shaped the dominant political and economic institutions that affected all Americans. Those who did not conform to them were likely to be marginalized, stigmatized, and disadvantaged as a result. So although the KLS sample included only a few individuals from other ethnic or socioeconomic backgrounds, it was made up of men and women who wholeheartedly and self-consciously attempted to enact cultural norms. These norms represented the ideal toward which upwardly mobile Americans strove and reflected the standard against which nonconforming individuals were judged. It is all the more important, then, to understand the standards of appropriate behavior established by the white middle class. During the postwar years, there were no groups in the United States for whom these norms were irrelevant.

The responses of individuals in the KLS breathe life into contemporary values and reveal how postwar Americans fortified the boundaries within which they lived. They wanted secure jobs, secure homes, and secure marriages in a secure country. Security would enable them to take advantage of the fruits of prosperity and peace that were, at long last, available. And so they adhered to an overarching principle that would guide them in their personal and political lives: containment. Containment was the key to security. The word had currency at the time in its foreign policy version, first articulated by George F. Kennan, the American chargé d'affaires in Moscow, in 1946. The power of the Soviet Union would not endanger national security if it could be contained within a clearly defined sphere of influence.[19] But the term also describes the response to other postwar developments. The terrifying destructive potential of the atomic bomb would not be a threat if it could be contained, first in the hands of the United States and later through peaceful applications. If the atom were "harnessed for peace," as the proponents of nuclear energy claimed, it would enhance, rather than threaten, our security. Domestic anticommunism was another manifestation of containment: If subversive individuals could be contained and prevented from spreading their poisonous influence through the body politic, then the society could feel secure.

In the domestic version of containment, the "sphere of influence" was the home. Within its walls, potentially dangerous social forces of the new age might be tamed, so they could contribute to the secure and fulfilling life to which postwar women and men aspired. Domestic containment was bolstered by a powerful political culture that rewarded its adherents and marginalized its detractors. More than merely a metaphor for the cold war on the homefront, containment aptly describes the way in which public policy, personal behavior, and even political values were focused on the home.

There were, of course, those who did not live in tune with the containment ethos. In addition to southern black civil rights activists, there were dedicated women and men who continued to work for liberal political causes such as peace and women's rights, often labeled as "pink" for their efforts. There were also increasing numbers of married women who worked outside the home, a few of them managing to juggle domestic responsibilities with full-time careers, although most worked in jobs or community volunteer efforts that were secondary to their responsibilities as homemakers. Rebellious youths and nonconforming Beats of the 1950s made it clear that not everyone or everything could be contained in the nuclear family ideal. But these were the exceptions. Vast numbers of American women and men during the early years of the cold war—more than ever before or since—got married, moved to the suburbs, and had babies. If they felt frustrated with their lot, the women were more likely to turn to tranquilizers, and the men to *Playboy* magazine, for escape. But few were willing to give up the rewards of conforming for the risks of resisting the domestic path.[20]

The familial ideology that took shape in these years helps explain the apolitical tenor of middle-class postwar life. With the notable exceptions of labor unions and black civil rights organizations, and the incipient antinuclear movement, the 1940s and 1950s did not foster the emergence of grassroots social movements whose leaders would challenge the system. Rather, professionals became the experts of the age, providing scientific and psychological means to achieve personal well-being. These experts advocated coping strategies to enable people to adapt to the institutional and technological changes taking place. The therapeutic approach that gained momentum during these years was geared to helping people feel better about their place in the world, rather than change it. It offered private and personal solutions to social problems. The family was the arena in which that adaptation was expected to occur; the home was the environment in which people could feel good about themselves. In this way, domestic containment and its therapeutic corollary undermined the potential for political activism and reinforced the chilling effects of anticommunism and the cold war consensus.

Ultimately, containment proved to be an elusive goal. But it held sway on the diplomatic and the domestic levels well into the 1960s, when it collapsed in disarray. The baby-boom generation abandoned the idea, shrugging off the obsession with security and the vision of the family in which their parents had placed their highest hopes. By the late 1960s, many among this new, "uncontained" generation had rejected the rigid institutional boundaries of their elders. They substituted risk for security as they carried sex, consumerism, and political activity outside the established institutions. Activism replaced adaptation as the strategy for changing the conditions of life. Despite their simultaneous assault on the cold war ideology and the imperatives of domesticity, the baby boomers did not abandon the therapeutic methods and personal values that had motivated their parents.[21] Rejecting familial security as the means but retaining individual freedom and fulfillment as the ends, they carried forward the quest for liberation through politics as well as their personal lives. When a powerful backlash emerged in the 1970s and 1980s in reaction to the assault on containment, the rhetoric of the cold war revived, along with a renewed call for the "traditional" family as the best means to achieve national and personal security. These tensions fueled the culture wars that continued to the end of the cold war and beyond, until the terrorist attacks of September 11, 2001, diverted Americans' attention to a new crisis.

The story of domestic containment—how it emerged, how it affected the lives of those who tried to conform to it, and how it ultimately unraveled—will help us come to terms with ourselves and the era in which we live. In the postwar years, Americans found that viable alternatives to the prevailing family norm were virtually unavailable. Because of the political, ideological, and institutional developments that converged at the time, young adults were indeed homeward bound. But they were also bound to the home. The chapters that follow explore the reasons why, in the cold war era, it was the vision of the sheltered, secure, and personally liberating family on which homeward-bound Americans set their sights.

CHAPTER ONE

CONTAINMENT AT HOME: COLD WAR, WARM HEARTH

> I think that this attitude toward women is universal. What we
> want is to make easier the life of our housewives.
>
> —VICE PRESIDENT RICHARD M. NIXON, 1959

IN 1959, the year the atomic-age newlyweds spent their honeymoon in a fall-out shelter, when the baby boom and the cold war were both at their peak, Vice President Richard M. Nixon traveled to the Soviet Union to engage in what would become one of the most noted verbal sparring matches of the century. In a lengthy and often heated debate with Soviet premier Nikita Khrushchev at the opening of the American National Exhibition in Moscow, Nixon extolled the virtues of the American way of life, while his opponent promoted the communist system. What was remarkable about this exchange was its focus. The two leaders did not discuss missiles, bombs, or even modes of government. Rather, they argued over the relative merits of American and Soviet washing machines, televisions, and electric ranges—in what came to be known as the "kitchen debate" (see Figure 3).

The "kitchen debate" was one of the major skirmishes in the cold war, which was at its core an ideological struggle fought on a cultural battleground. For Nixon, American superiority rested on the ideal of the suburban home, complete with modern appliances and distinct gender roles for family members. He

FIGURE 3   Vice President Richard Nixon and Soviet Premier Nikita Khrushchev spar verbally at the American Exhibition in Moscow in 1959. Here they engage in the "kitchen debate" as they fight the cold war over the commodity gap rather than the missile gap. (*Wide World Photo.*)

proclaimed that the "model" home, with a male breadwinner and a full-time female homemaker, adorned with a wide array of consumer goods, represented the essence of American freedom:

> To us, diversity, the right to choose, . . . is the most important thing. We don't have one decision made at the top by one government official. . . . We have many different manufacturers and many different kinds of washing machines so that the housewives have a choice. . . . Would it not be better to compete in the relative merits of washing machines than in the strength of rockets?[1]

Nixon's focus on household appliances was not accidental. After all, arguments over the strength of rockets would only point out the vulnerability of the United States in the event of a nuclear war between the superpowers; debates over consumer goods would provide a reassuring vision of the good life available in the atomic age. So Nixon insisted that American superiority in the cold war rested not on weapons, but on the secure, abundant family life of modern suburban homes. In these structures, adorned and worshipped by their inhabitants, women would achieve their glory and men would display their success. Consumerism was not an end in itself; it was the means for achieving individuality, leisure, and upward mobility.

The American National Exhibition was a showcase of American consumer goods and leisure-time equipment. But the main attraction, which the two leaders toured, was the full-scale "model" six-room ranch-style house. This model home, filled with labor-saving devices and presumably available to Americans of all classes, was tangible proof, Nixon believed, of the superiority of free enterprise over communism.

In the model kitchen in the model home, Nixon and Khrushchev revealed some basic assumptions of their two systems. Nixon called attention to a built-in panel-controlled washing machine. "In America," he said, "these [washing machines] are designed to make things easier for our women." Khrushchev countered Nixon's boast of comfortable American housewives with pride in productive Soviet female workers: In his country they did not have that "capitalist attitude toward women." Nixon clearly did not understand that the communist system had no use for full-time housewives, for he replied, "I think that this attitude toward women is universal. What we want is to make easier the life of our housewives." Nixon's knockout punch in his verbal bout with the Soviet premier was his articulation of the American postwar domestic dream: successful breadwinners supporting attractive homemakers in affluent suburban homes.

Although the two leaders did not agree on the proper social roles for women, they clearly shared a common view that female sexuality was a central part of the good life that both systems claimed to espouse. Noting that Nixon admired the young women modeling American bathing suits and sports clothes, the Soviet leader said with a wink, "You are for the girls, too." Later in the day, when the two leaders faltered over a toast in which Khrushchev proposed to drink to the removal of foreign bases and Nixon would drink only to the more general hope of "peace," Khrushchev smoothed over the impending confrontation by gesturing to a nearby waitress and suggesting, "Let's drink to the ladies." Relieved, Nixon chimed in, "We can all drink to the ladies."

American journalists who were present, however, viewed the appearance and situation of Soviet women as anything but feminine. An article in *U.S. News and World Report*, noted for its anticommunism and cold war militance, suggested that Soviet women, as workers and political activists, desexualized themselves. It described Moscow as "a city of women—hard-working women who show few of the physical charms of women in the West. Most Moscow women seem unconcerned about their looks. . . . Young couples stroll together in the parks after dark, but you see many more young women [stride] along the streets purposefully, as though marching to a Communist Party meeting."[2] The implied contrast was clear. American women, unlike their "purposeful" and unfeminine Russian counterparts, did not have to be "hard working," thanks to the wonders of American household appliances. Nor did they busy themselves with the affairs of men, such as politics. Rather, they cultivated their looks and their physical charms, to become sexually attractive housewives and consumers under the American capitalist system.

Of course, in reality, both American and Soviet women worked outside as well as inside the home; and in both countries women had primary responsibilities for housekeeping chores. But these realities did nothing to mitigate the power of gender ideologies in both countries. Assumptions about Soviet women workers versus sexually attractive American housewives were widespread. More than a decade before Nixon's trip to Moscow, for example, Eric Johnston, president of the U.S. Chamber of Commerce, wrote contemptuously of the claim that Soviet women were emancipated because they held jobs. He argued, "Russian women, like women in all undeveloped countries, have always done the . . . hardest work." He labeled as "simply Communist propaganda" the claim that Soviet women were "emancipated from housework" and noted sarcastically that they were "permitted the glory of drudgery in industry" in the Soviet Union. Like Nixon, he pointed to the home, where breadwinners supported their housewives, as the place where American freedom was most apparent.[3] The implication, of course, was that self-supporting women were in some way un-American. Accordingly, anticommunist crusaders viewed women who did not conform to the domestic ideal with suspicion.

With such sentiments about gender and politics widely shared, Nixon's visit was hailed as a major political triumph. Popular journals extolled his diplomatic skills in the face-to-face confrontation with Khrushchev. Many observers credit this trip with establishing Nixon's political future. Clearly, Americans did not find the kitchen debate trivial. The appliance-laden ranch-style home epitomized the expansive, secure lifestyle that postwar Americans wanted. Within the protective walls of the modern home, worrisome developments like sexual liberalism, women's emancipation, and affluence would lead not to decadence but to a wholesome family life. Sex would enhance marriage, emancipated women would professionalize homemaking, and affluence would put an end to material deprivation. Suburbia would serve as a bulwark against communism and class conflict, for according to the widely shared belief articulated by Nixon, it offered a piece of the American dream for everyone. Although Nixon vastly exaggerated the availability of the suburban home, he described a type of domestic life that had become a reality for many white working-class and middle-class Americans—and a powerful aspiration for many others.

The momentum began to build toward this ideal long before it became widely available. Those who came of age during and after World War II were the most marrying generation on record: 96.4 percent of the women and 94.1 percent of the men (see Table 6). These aggregate statistics hide another significant fact: Americans behaved in striking conformity to each other during these years. In other words, not only did the average age at marriage drop, but almost everyone was married by his or her mid-twenties. And not only did the average family

TABLE 6: MARITAL STATUS OF THE U.S. POPULATION, 1900–2005

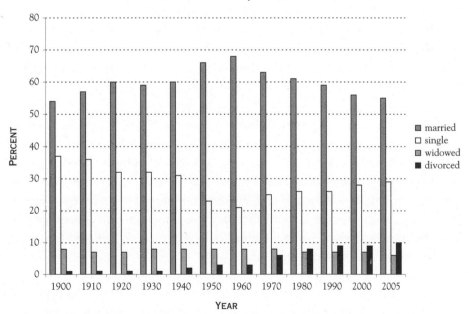

SOURCES   U.S. Department of Commerce, Bureau of the Census, *Historical Statistics of the United States, Colonial Times to 1970*, Part 1 (Washington, D.C.: Government Printing Office, 1975), pp. 20–21; U.S. Bureau of the Census, *Current Population Reports*, Series PLO-514, March 1998 (Update), and earlier reports; U.S. Census Bureau, *Current Population Survey, March and Annual Social and Economic Supplements, 2005 and Earlier* (Washington, D.C.: U.S. Census Bureau, September 21, 2006), Table MS-1, www.census.gov/population/www/socdemo/hh-fam.html#history).

size increase, but most couples had two to four children, born sooner after marriage and spaced closer together than in previous years.[4] At a time when the
availability of contraceptive devices enabled couples to delay, space, and limit
the arrival of offspring to suit their particular needs, this rising birthrate resulted
from deliberate choices. Nixon could, therefore, speak with some conviction
when he placed the home at the center of postwar ideals.

What gave rise to the widespread endorsement of this familial consensus in
the cold war era? The depression of the 1930s and World War II laid the foundation for a commitment to a stable home life, but they also opened the way for a
radical restructuring of the family. The yearning for family stability gained
momentum after the war, but the potential for restructuring the family withered
as the powerful ideology of domesticity was imprinted on everyday life.
Ironically, traditional gender roles became a central feature of the "modern"
middle-class home.

Since the 1960s, much attention has been paid to the plight of women in
the 1950s. But at that time, critical observers of middle-class life considered
homemakers to be emancipated and men to be oppressed. Much of the most
insightful writing examined the dehumanizing situation that forced middle-
class men, at least in their public roles, to be other-directed "organization men,"
caught in a mass, impersonal white-collar world. The loss of autonomy was real.
As large corporations grew, swallowing smaller enterprises, the number of self-
employed men in small businesses shrank dramatically. David Riesman recognized that the corporate structure forced middle-class men into deadening,
highly structured peer interactions; he argued that only in the intimate aspects
of life could a man truly be free. Industrial laborers were even less likely to
derive intrinsic satisfactions from their jobs. Thus, blue-collar and white-collar
employees shared a sense of alienation and subordination in the postwar corporate workforce. At work as well as at home, class lines blurred for white men in
the postwar era. Both Riesman and William Whyte saw the suburbs as extensions of the corporate world, with their emphasis on conformity. Yet they perceived that suburban homes and consumer goods offered material
compensations for organized work life.[5]

In spite of the power of the homemaker ideal, increasing numbers of married
women worked outside the home in the postwar years. But their job opportunities were limited, and their wages were low. Employed women held jobs that
were even more menial and subordinate than those of their male peers. Surveys
of full-time homemakers indicated that they appreciated their independence
from supervision and control over their work; they had no desire to give up

their autonomy in the home for wage labor. Educated middle-class women, whose career opportunities were severely limited, hoped that the home would become not a confining place of drudgery, but a liberating arena of fulfillment through professionalized homemaking, meaningful child rearing, and satisfying sexuality.[6]

While the home seemed to offer the best hope for freedom, it also appeared to be a fragile institution, subject to forces beyond its control. Economic hardship had torn families asunder, and war had scattered men far from home and drawn women into the public world of work. The postwar years did little to alleviate fears that similar disruptions might occur again. In spite of widespread affluence, many believed that the reconversion to a peacetime economy would lead to another depression. Even peace was problematic, since international tensions were palpable. The explosion of the first atomic bombs over Hiroshima and Nagasaki marked not only the end of World War II but the beginning of the cold war. At any moment, the cold war could turn hot. The policy of containment abroad faced its first major challenge in 1949, with the Chinese revolution. In the same year, the USSR exploded its first atomic bomb. The nation was again jolted out of its sense of fragile security when the Korean War broke out in 1950. Many shared President Harry Truman's belief that World War III was at hand.[7]

Insightful analysts of the nuclear age have explored the psychic impact of the atomic bomb. Paul Boyer's study of the first five years after Hiroshima showed that American responses went through dramatic shifts. Initial reactions juxtaposed the thrill of atomic empowerment with the terror of annihilation. The atomic scientists were among the first to organize against the bomb, calling for international control of atomic energy, and others soon followed suit. By the end of the 1940s, however, opposition had given way to proclamations of faith in the bomb as the protector of American security.

Along with that faith came fear. In 1950, 61 percent of those polled thought that the United States should use the atom bomb if there was another world war, but 53 percent believed there was a good or fair chance that their community would be bombed in the next war, and nearly three-fourths assumed that American cities would be bombed. Most agreed that since Russia now had the bomb, the likelihood of another war increased. By 1956, nearly two-thirds of those polled believed that in the event of another war, the hydrogen bomb would be used against the United States.

As support grew for more and bigger bombs, arguments for international control waned, and the country prepared for the possibility of a nuclear war by instituting new civil defense strategies. Psychologists were strangely silent on the issue of the fear of atomic weapons, and by the early fifties, the nation seemed to be apathetic. Boyer echoed Robert J. Lifton in suggesting that denial and silence may have reflected deep-seated horror rather than complacency. Indeed, in 1959, two out of three Americans listed the possibility of nuclear war as the nation's most urgent problem.[8]

Lifton argued that the atomic bomb forced people to question one of their most deeply held beliefs, that scientific discoveries would yield progress. Atomic energy presented a fundamental contradiction: Science had developed the potential for total technological mastery as well as for total technological devastation. Lifton attributed "nuclear numbing" to the powerful psychic hold that the fear of nuclear annihilation had on the nation's subconscious. He pointed to unrealistic but reassuring civil defense strategies as the efforts of governmental officials to tame or "domesticate" the fear.[9]

Americans were well poised to embrace domesticity in the midst of the terrors of the atomic age. A home filled with children would create a feeling of warmth and security against the cold forces of disruption and alienation. Children would also be a connection to the future and a means of replenishing a world depleted by war deaths. Although baby-boom parents were not likely to express conscious desires to repopulate the country, the devastation of hundreds of thousands of deaths could not have been far below the surface of the postwar consciousness. The view of childbearing as a duty was painfully true for Jewish parents, after six million of their kin were snuffed out in Europe. But they were not alone. As one Jewish woman recalled of her decision to bear four children, "After the Holocaust, we felt obligated to have lots of babies. But it was easy because everyone was doing it—non-Jews, too."[10]

In secure postwar homes with plenty of children, American women and men might be able to ward off their nightmares and live out their dreams. The family seemed to be the one place where people could control their destinies and perhaps even shape the future. Of course, nobody actually argued that stable family life could prevent nuclear annihilation. But the home represented a source of meaning and security in a world run amok. Marrying young and having lots of babies were ways for Americans to thumb their noses at doomsday predictions. Commenting on the trend toward young marriages, one observer noted, "Youngsters want to grasp what little security they can in a world gone frighteningly insecure. The youngsters feel they will cultivate the one security that's possible—their own gardens, their own . . . home and families."[11]

White working-class and middle-class women and men were not the only ones who hoped to embrace this vision of domesticity. Other groups of

Americans had their own particular reasons for aspiring to the nuclear family ideal. Postwar prosperity allowed African-Americans, for the first time, to imagine the possibility of a family life where the earnings of men would be ample enough to allow women to stay home with their own children, rather than tending to the houses and children of white families. Celebrating that possibility in 1947, *Ebony* magazine proclaimed, "Goodbye Mammy, Hello Mom." World War II "took Negro mothers out of white kitchens, put them in factories and shipyards. When it was all over, they went back to kitchens—but this time their own. . . . And so today in thousands of Negro homes, the Negro mother has come home, come home perhaps for the first time since 1619 when the first Negro families landed at Jamestown, Virginia." For the black woman, domesticity meant "freedom and independence in her own home."[12] People of color longed for the "good life," just like anyone else. But their exclusion from the opportunities most citizens took for granted intensified their desires. Black artists expressed this yearning for a new life. Lorraine Hansberry's powerful 1959 play, *A Raisin in the Sun*, articulated with great eloquence the importance of a home in the suburbs, not to assimilate into white America but to live as a black family with dignity, pride, and comfort.

Asian-Americans also had good reason to celebrate home and family life. With the end of the exclusion of Chinese immigrants during World War II, wives and war brides began to enter the country, transforming communities like New York's Chinatown from small societies of bachelors into thriving family-oriented communities. Japanese-Americans, after the humiliations, disruptions, and anguish of internment, were eager to put their families and lives back together. Children of European immigrants hoped to use the fruits of postwar abundance to escape the crowded ethnic neighborhoods of the cities and blend into white America, in spacious single-family homes in the suburbs.[13]

For all of these groups, thoughts of the family rooted in time-honored traditions may have allayed fears of vulnerability. Nevertheless, much of what had provided family security in the past became unhinged. For many Americans, the postwar years brought rootlessness. Those who moved from farms to cities lost a familiar way of life that was rooted in the land. Children of immigrants moved from ethnic neighborhoods with extended kin and community ties to homogeneous suburbs, where they formed nuclear families and invested them with high hopes. Suburban homes offered freedom from kinship obligations, along with material comforts that had not been available on the farm or in the ethnic urban ghetto. As Whyte noted about the promoters of the Illinois suburb he studied, "At first they had advertised Park Forest as housing. Now they began advertising happiness." But consumer goods would not replace community, and young mobile nuclear families could easily find themselves adrift. Newcomers devoted themselves to creating communities out of neighborhoods composed largely of transients. As Whyte noted, "In suburbia, organization man is trying, quite consciously, to develop a new kind of roots to replace what he left behind."[14]

Young adults aged twenty-five to thirty-five were among the most mobile members of the society, constituting 12.4 percent of all migrants but only 7.5 percent of the population. Higher education also prompted mobility; fully 45.5 percent of those who had one year of college or more lived outside their home states, compared to 27.3 percent of high school graduates. Overwhelmingly, these young educated migrants worked for large organizations: Three-fourths of all clients of long-distance movers worked for corporations, the government, or the armed services, with corporate employees the most numerous. In their new communities, they immediately endeavored to forge ties with other young transients that would be as rewarding and secure as the ones they left behind, but free of the restraints of the old neighborhood.[15]

Postwar Americans struggled with this transition. The popular culture was filled with stories about young adults who shifted their allegiances from the old ethnic ties to the new nuclear family ideal. When situation comedies shifted from radio to television, working-class ethnic kin networks and multigenerational households faded as the stories increasingly revolved around the middle-class nuclear family.[16] One of the most popular films of the 1950s was *Marty*, winner of the Academy Award for best motion picture in 1955 and first produced as a television play in 1953. In the film, Marty, a young man living with his mother, has a deep commitment to the ethnic family in which he was reared. The sympathy of the audience stays with him as he first demonstrates his family loyalty by allowing his mother to bring her cranky, aging sister to live with them and doing his duty as the good son. As the story unfolds, Marty falls in love and, to the horror of his mother and his aunt, decides to marry his sweetheart and move away from the old neighborhood. Far from his family and their obligations, the young couple can embark on a new life freed from the constraints of the older generation. By the film's end, the audience has made the transition, along with the main character, from loyalty to the community of ethnic kinship to the suburban ideal of the emancipated nuclear family.[17]

Whyte called the suburbs the "new melting pot," where migrants from ethnic working-class neighborhoods in the cities moved into the middle class. In the process, they lost much of their identity as ethnic outsiders and became simply "white."[18] Kin and ethnic ties were often forsaken as suburban residents formed new communities grounded in shared experiences of homeownership and child rearing, and conformity to the modern consumer-oriented way of life. Young suburbanites were great joiners, forging new ties and creating new institutions to replace the old. One such suburban community, Park Forest, Illinois, had sixty-six adult organizations, making it a "hotbed" of participation. Churches and synagogues, whose membership reached new heights in the postwar years, expanded their functions from prayer and charity to recreation, youth programs, and social events. Church membership rose from 64.5 million in 1940 to 114.5 million in 1960—from 50 percent to 63 percent of the population (100 years earlier only 20 percent of all Americans belonged to churches). Churches and synagogues provided social arenas for suburbanites, replacing, to some extent, the communal life previously supplied by kin or neighborhood.[19] Religious affiliation became associated with the "American way of life." Americans highlighted their religiosity, in contrast to the "godless communists." "In God We Trust" became the national motto, appearing on all paper currency; and the words "under God" became part of the Pledge of Allegiance. Religion offered to bind citizens to each other and to provide a sense of belonging.

Still, these were tenuous alliances among uprooted people. With so much mobility and with success associated with moving on to something better, middle-class nuclear families could not depend on the stability of their communities. As much as they tried to form ties with their neighbors and conform to each other's beliefs and lifestyles, they were still largely on their own. The new vision of home life, therefore, depended heavily on the staunch commitment of individual family members. Neither the world nor the newly forged suburban community could be trusted to provide security. What mattered was that family members remained bound to each other—and to the modern, emancipated home they intended to create.

The wisdom of earlier generations would be of little help to postwar Americans who were looking toward a radically new vision of family life and trying self-consciously to avoid the paths of their parents. Thus, young people embraced the advice of experts in the rapidly expanding fields of social science, medicine, and psychology. After all, science was changing the world. Was it not reasonable to expect it to change the home as well?

Postwar America was the era of the expert. Armed with scientific techniques and presumably inhabiting a world that was beyond popular passions, the experts had brought us into the atomic age. Physicists developed the bomb, strategists created the cold war, and scientific managers built the military-industrial complex. It was now up to the experts to make the unmanageable manageable. As the readers of *Look* magazine were assured, there was no reason to worry about radioactivity, for if ever the time arrived when you would need to understand its dangers, "the experts will be ready to tell you." Science and technology seemed to have invaded virtually every aspect of life, from the most public to the most private. Americans were looking to professionals to tell them how to manage their lives. The tremendous popularity of Benjamin Spock's *Baby and Child Care* reflects a reluctance to trust the shared wisdom of kin and community. Norman Vincent Peale's *The Power of Positive Thinking* provided readers with religiously inspired scientific formulas for success. Both these best-selling books stressed the centrality of the family in their prescriptions for a better future.[20]

The popularity of these kinds of books attests to the faith in expertise that prevailed at the time. One retrospective study of the attitudes and habits of over four thousand Americans in 1957 found that the reliance on expertise was one of the most striking developments of the postwar years. Long-term individual therapy, for example, reached unprecedented popularity in the mid-1950s. The authors concluded:

> Experts took over the role of psychic healer, but they also assumed a much broader and more important role in directing the behavior, goals, and ideals of normal people. They became the teachers and norm setters who would tell people how to approach and live life. . . . They would provide advice and counsel about raising and responding to children, how to behave in marriage, and what to see in that relationship. . . . Science moved in because people needed and wanted guidance.[21]

The Kelly Longitudinal Study (KLS) confirmed these findings. By the mid-fifties, one out of six respondents had consulted a professional for marital or emotional problems; yet fewer than one-third that number considered their personal problems to be severe.[22] It seems evident, then, that people were quick to seek professional help. When the experts spoke, postwar Americans listened.

Despite the public's perceptions of scientific mastery and objectivity, professionals groped for appropriate ways to conceptualize and resolve the uncertainties of the times. Like other Americans, they feared the possibility of social disintegration during this period. As participants in the cold war consensus, they offered solutions to the difficulties of the age that would not disrupt the status quo. In the process, they helped focus and formulate the domestic ideology. For these experts, public dangers merged with private ones, and the family appeared besieged as never before. The noted anthropologist Margaret Mead articulated this problem in a 1949 article addressed to social workers. The methods of the past, she wrote, offered "an inadequate model on which to build procedures in the atomic age." Children were now born into a world unfamiliar even to their parents, "a world suddenly shrunk into one unit, in which radio and television and comics and the threat of the atomic bomb are everyday realities." The task for helping professionals—psychologists, psychiatrists, family counselors, and social workers—would be especially complicated because conditions had changed so drastically. Each adult faced "the task of trying to keep a world he [sic] never knew and never dreamed steady until we can rear a generation at home in it."[23]

According to the experts, political activism was not likely to keep the world steady. They advocated adaptation rather than resistance as a means of feeling "at home." The modern home would make the inherited values of the past relevant for the uncertain present and future, but it had to be fortified largely from within. Married couples were determined to strengthen the nuclear family through "togetherness." They would have "well-adjusted" children—adjusting to the world as it was, rather than trying to change or adjust that world. With the help of experts to guide them, successful breadwinners would provide economic support for professionalized homemakers, and together they would create the home of their dreams.

The women and men who embraced this vision were not simply victims of an ideology foisted upon them by the power elite. Although political repression and institutional barriers constrained their options, many were deeply committed to the promise of domestic security and happiness. Marriage promised not only happiness, but also a positive alternative to the lonely life of a single person. In the postwar years, many agreed with the experts that single women would be doomed to an unfulfilled and miserable existence, and that bachelors were psychologically damaged and immature, locked into "primitive and infantile modes of thinking," in the words of one psychiatrist.[24] The respondents to the 1955 KLS survey articulated that fervent commitment to marriage. These white middle-class Americans were among the first to establish families according to the new domestic ideology. Relatively affluent, more highly educated than the average, they were able to take advantage of the fruits of postwar prosperity (see Appendix 1). They looked toward the home, rather than the public world, for personal fulfillment. No wonder that when they were asked what they thought they had sacrificed by marrying and raising a family, an overwhelming majority of them replied, "Nothing."

One of the striking characteristics of the KLS respondents was their apparent willingness to give up autonomy and independence for the sake of marriage and a family. Although the 1950s marked the beginning of the glamorization of bachelorhood, most of the men expressed a remarkable lack of nostalgia for the unencumbered freedom of a single life. Typical responses to the question "What did you have to sacrifice or give up because of your marriage?" were "nothing but bad habits" and "the empty, aimless, lonely life of a bachelor." One who gave up only "a few fishing and hunting trips" claimed that "the time was better . . . spent at home." Many of these men had been married for over a decade and had their share of troubles. The comment of one man was especially poignant. Although he described his wife as addicted to alcohol and "sexually frigid," he claimed that "aside from the natural adjustment, I have given up only some of my personal independence. But I have gained so much more: children, home, etc. that I ought to answer . . . 'nothing at all.'"[25]

Women were equally quick to dismiss any sacrifices they may have made when they married. Few expressed regrets for devoting themselves to the home-maker role—a choice that effectively ruled out other lifelong occupational avenues. Although 13 percent mentioned a "career" as something sacrificed, most claimed that they gained rather than lost in the bargain. One wife indicated how her early marriage affected the development of her adult identity: "Marriage has opened up far more avenues of interest than I ever would have had without it. . . . I was at a very young and formative age when we were married and I think I have changed greatly over the years. . . . I cannot conceive of life without him."[26]

Many wives who said they abandoned a career were quick to minimize its importance and to state that they "preferred marriage," a response suggesting that the pursuit of both was not viable. Many defined their domestic role as a career in itself. One woman defended her decision to give up her career: "I think I have probably contributed more to the world in the life I have lived." Another mentioned her sacrifices of "financial independence [and] freedom to choose a career. However, these have been replaced by the experience of being a mother and a help to other parents and children. Therefore the new career is equally as good or better than the old." Both men and women mentioned the responsibilities of married life as sources of personal fulfillment rather than sacrifice.[27]

Further evidence of the enormous commitment to family life appears in responses to the question "What has marriage brought you that you could not have gained without your marriage?" Although the most common answers of men and women included family, children, love, and companionship, other typical answers were a sense of purpose, success, and security. It is interesting to note that respondents claimed that these elements of life would not have been possible without marriage. Women indicated that marriage gave them "a sense of responsibility I wouldn't have had had I remained single" or a feeling of "usefulness . . . for others dear to me." One said marriage gave her a "happy, full, complete life; children; a feeling of serving some purpose in life other than making money." Another remarked, "I'm not the 'career girl' type. I like being home and having a family. . . . Working with my husband for our home and family brings a satisfaction that working alone could not."[28]

Men were equally emphatic about the satisfactions brought about by family responsibility. Nearly one-fourth claimed that marriage gave them a sense of purpose in life and a reason for striving. Aside from love and children, no other single reward of marriage was mentioned by so many of the husbands. Included in the gains they listed were "the incentive to succeed and save for the future of my family," "a purpose in the scheme of life," and "a motivation for intensive effort that would otherwise have been lacking." One man confessed, "Being somewhat lazy to begin with, the family and my wife's ambition have made me more eager to succeed businesswise and financially." A contented husband wrote of the "million treasures" contained in his family; another said that marriage offered "freedom from the boredom and futility of bachelorhood."

Others linked family life to civic virtues by claiming that marriage strengthened their patriotism and morals, instilling them with "responsibility, community spirit, respect for children and family life, reverence for a Supreme Being, humility, love of country." Summing up the feelings of many in his generation, one husband said that marriage

> increased my horizons, defined my goals and purposes in life, strengthened my convictions, raised my intellectual standards and stimulated my incentive to provide moral, spiritual, and material support; it has rewarded me with a realistic sense of family and security I never experienced during the first 24 years of my life.[29]

The respondents expressed a strong commitment to a new and expanded vision of family life, focused inwardly on parents and children and bolstered by affluence and sex. They claimed to have found their personal identities and achieved their individual goals largely through their families. Yet the superlatives ring hollow, as if these women and men were trying to convince themselves that the families they had created fulfilled all their deepest wishes. For as their extensive responses to other questions in the survey will show, they experienced disappointments, dashed hopes, and lowered expectations. Many who gave their marriages high ratings had actually resigned themselves to a great deal of misery.

As postwar Americans endeavored to live in tune with the prevailing domestic ideology, they found that the dividends required a heavy investment of self. For some, the costs were well worth the benefits; for others, the costs were too high.

Ida and George Butler were among those who felt the costs of marriage were worth the benefits. After more than a decade together, they both claimed that they were satisfied with the life they had built. When they first embarked on married life, they brought high hopes to their union. Ida wrote that George "very nearly measures up to my ideal Prince Charming." George, in turn, noted Ida's attractiveness, common sense, and similar ideas on home life and sex. He was glad she was not the "high stepping" type but had "experience in cooking and housekeeping." For this down-to-earth couple, the home contained their sexuality, her career ambitions, his drive for success, and their desires for material and emotional comforts.

Yet, like all things worth a struggle, it did not come easy. Ida's choices reflect the constraints that faced postwar women. She sacrificed her plans for "a professional career—I would [have] liked to have been a doctor—but we both agreed that I should finish college, which I did." Following her marriage, there were "obstacles" to her continuing to pursue a career in medicine. It was difficult to combine a professional life with a family. For one thing, the children were primarily her responsibility. She explained:

> My husband works very hard in his business and has many hobbies and friends. The care and problems of children seem to overwhelm him and he admits being an "only" child ill prepared him for the pull and tug of family life. We work closely together on discipline and policies, but he is serious minded and great joy and fun with the children [are] lacking.

If Prince Charming's shining armor tarnished a bit with the years, Ida was not one to complain. She had reasons for feeling contented with the family she helped build:

> I think a *stability* which runs through my life is important. I cannot recall any divorce or separation in my immediate family. We are a rural close-to-the-soil group and I was brought up to take the "bitter with the sweet"—"you made your own bed, now lie in it" philosophy, so it would not occur to me to "run home to mother."

Although marriage was not Ida's first career choice, it eventually became her central occupation: "Marriage is my career. I chose it and now it is up to me to see that I do the job successfully in spite of the stresses and strains of life." She felt that the sacrifices she made were outweighed by the gains: "children, a nice home, companionship, sex, many friends." George also claimed to be "completely satisfied" with the marriage. He wrote that it brought him an "understanding of other people's problems, 'give and take,' love and devotion." He felt that he sacrificed "nothing but so-called personal freedom." Her medical career and his so-called personal freedom seemed to be small prices to pay for the stable family life they created together.[30]

For couples like the Butlers, the gains were worth the sacrifices. But their claims of satisfaction carried a note of resignation. Combining a profession with a family seemed an unrealistic goal for Ida; combining personal freedom with the role of provider seemed equally out of reach for George. They both thought they faced an either/or situation and they opted for their family roles. At first glance, this case appears unremarkable: two people who made a commitment to marriage and made the best of it. But the Butlers' choices and priorities take on a larger significance because they were typical of their generation, which was unique in its commitment to family life. The costs and benefits articulated by the Butlers—and their willingness to settle for less than they bargained for—were conditions they shared with their middle-class peers.

Unlike the Butlers, Joseph and Emily Burns emphasized the costs of family life. Haunted by the legacy of the Great Depression and World War II, Joseph expected marriage to yield the "model home" described by Nixon, where affluence, intimacy, and security would prevail. But the worrisome state of the world was inescapable for him, even in the family. Nevertheless, he articulated the way in which the world situation contributed to the intense familism of the postwar years.

At the time of his engagement, Joseph Burns had high expectations for his future marriage. He had chosen his fiancée because he could trust and respect her, her "past life has been admirable," she did not drink or smoke, and "she is pleasing to the eye." If anything made him uneasy about their prospects for future happiness, it was the fear of another depression: "If the stock market takes another drop . . . business will be all shot." The depression had already made him wary, but his disillusionment would be complete by the end of World War II.

Looking back over his life from the vantage point of the 1950s, Joseph Burns reflected:

> As I review the thoughts that were mine at the time of my marriage and as they are now, I would like to give an explanation that should be considered. . . . A young couple, much in love, are looking forward to a happy life in a world that

has been held up to them by elders as a beautiful world. Children are brought up by their parents to love God and other children, honesty is a must, obedience to the Ten Commandments and to the golden rule is necessary.

With such training, I started out my life only to find out the whole thing is a farce. Blundering politicians lusting for power and self-glory have defiled what is clean and right, honesty is just a word in the dictionary, love of God—who really believes in God? Love of neighbor . . . get him before he gets you.

I agree it does sound cynical, but let us face the facts. Mankind has been slowly degenerating, especially since 1914, and today, what do we have to look forward to? Civil defense tests, compulsory military training, cold wars, fear of the atomic bomb, the diseases that plague man, the mental case outlook? . . . I submit these things to show how a marriage can be vitally affected as was ours and, therefore, many of my ideals, desires, and, most of all, my goal.

Joseph's cynicism toward the wider world made him place even higher hopes on the family to be a buffer. When world events intruded into that private world, he was devastated: "On December 7, 1941, the question burned in my mind, How can so-called Christian nations tear each other apart again?" Joseph resolved his personal anguish by becoming a Jehovah's Witness. But he continued to cling to the family as security in a chaotic world. Although he claimed that the world situation had dashed his ideals, he still rated his marriage happier than average and said it gave him "the opportunity to think and reason." As far as what he sacrificed for his marriage, he wrote, "Whatever [I gave] up, which probably would have been material possessions, has been offset by the things [I] gained." Joseph's rage at the world was tempered by the benefits of having a family. He believed that the family provided him with security and satisfaction, and fulfilled at least some of the hopes he originally brought to it.

Emily Burns had a different view of their marriage and found little comfort in her life with Joseph. Although his religious conversion was at the center of her dissatisfaction, her responses raise other issues as well. Emily complained about her husband's pessimism, coldness, aloofness, and lack of a love of beauty. She emphasized that her husband's change of religion had affected his whole life—"[his] attitude toward wife, children, home, friends, and world. Unless I become absorbed in [his religion], we [will come] to a parting of the ways, since I'm an outsider in my own home." In addition to the major rift over her husband's conversion, Emily enumerated her sacrifices as follows:

1. A way of life (an easy one).
2. All friends of long duration; close relationships.

3. Independence and personal freedom.
4. What seemed to contribute to my personality.
5. Financial independence.
6. Goals in this life.
7. Idea as to size of family.
8. Personal achievements—type changed.
9. Close relationship with brother and mother and grandmother.

Her complaints add up to much more than religious incompatibility. They suggest some of the costs of adhering to the domestic ideology of the postwar era: an emphasis on the nuclear family at the expense of other relatives and friends, as well as loss of personal freedom, financial independence, "goals," and "personal achievements." For Emily, like Ida Butler and others of their generation, marriage and family life led to a narrowing of options and activities. But it was a bargain she accepted because it appeared to be the best route toward achieving other goals in life. Although she claimed that she would not have married the same person if she had to do it over again, she never considered divorce. The benefits she gained in marriage offset her discontent with her spouse. Her list of benefits reveals why she chose the domestic path:

1. The desire to give up all for the love of one.
2. The placing of self last.
3. A harmonious relationship until religion . . . changed this.
4. Two ideal children even though the boy is cold and indifferent like his father. (They have strong religious ties in common.)
5. A comfortable home independent of others.
6. Personal satisfaction if all turns out well.
7. Personal satisfaction in establishing a home.

In this list, Emily mentioned practically all the major subjective compensations that made marriage such an important commitment for so many women at the time. Yet it was a qualified list. Her dissatisfaction was obvious even in her enumeration of her gains. So she struggled to improve her situation as best she could. While her husband used the last space in the questionnaire to brood over the world situation and explain his turn toward religion, Emily used it to reaffirm her faith in the potential for happiness in marriage. She wrote to Kelly and his research team, "Honestly wish this survey will help future generations to maintain happiness throughout marriage and that your book will become more than cold facts and figures. We have enough such now!"

Emily revealed a submerged feminist impulse that also surfaced in numerous testimonies of her peers. To help her formulate these ideas and influence her husband, she turned to experts:

> Have tried to arouse interest in the woman's point of view by reading parts of Dr. Marie Carmichael Stopes' works pertaining to marriage, to my husband. He says, "Oh, she is just a woman, what does she know about it?" and "How can such things [marriage relationship] be learned from a book?" I have ideas on marriage and when I see the same ideas expressed in print by a person of authority, at least I can see that I am not the only woman or person who thinks "such and such."

Recognizing that her husband was not sympathetic to her rebellion against female subordination, she predicted, "Because of a developing hard, slightly independent attitude on my part, I believe my husband's report on me will be anything but favorable."

Joseph and Emily Burns, in spite of their numerous complaints, stayed together. Through all their disillusionment and anger, they never wavered in their commitment to their imperfect relationship and insisted that their marriage was worth the struggle. Emily chafed against the limits to her freedom and turned to experts to bolster her status within the family. Joseph turned to the home to provide solace from the miseries that surrounded him in the public world. Both had invested a great deal of their personal identities in their domestic roles and were not willing to abandon them. Even if the home did not fulfill their dreams of an emancipated, fulfilling life, it still provided more satisfaction and security than they were likely to find elsewhere. For all their struggles and strains, Joseph and Emily Burns had created something together that met their needs. In 1980, they were still married to each other.[31]

Like the Butlers, the Burnses demonstrate the powerful determination and the considerable sacrifice that went into the creation of the postwar family. Even if the result did not fully live up to their expectations, these husbands and wives never seriously considered bailing out. It is important to consider the limited options and alternatives that these men and women faced. It was not a perfect life, but it was secure and predictable. Forging an independent life outside marriage carried enormous risks of emotional and economic hardship, along with social ostracism. As these couples sealed the psychological boundaries around the family, they also sealed their fates within it.

CHAPTER TWO

DEPRESSION:
HARD TIMES AT HOME

Economic conditions of the country appear to be wrecking
many marriages.

—DAVID SANDERS, 1938[1]

AS DAVID SANDERS contemplated marriage, hard times lingered at home
and war loomed abroad. Economic misfortune had already taken its toll
on American families, yet Sanders hoped that his marriage would succeed, even
in the face of hardship. His optimism rested on the belief that he could learn
from the past. He and his fiancée shared a vision of marriage based on togetherness and security, freed from economic and sexual restraints. He noted that they
had "worked and played together successfully for four years," were "sexually well
mated," and held "common social ideals as a unifying force." He believed that
their careful planning would guarantee the stability of their relationship: "The
common causes for divorce have been thoroughly discussed and if differences of
opinion ever exist, they will be eradicated, I hope, by discussion, not compromise." Sanders placed his faith in himself and his future wife, who he described
as "intelligent in matters of general interest." Like others of his generation, he
looked forward to a new type of marriage, one based on a partnership of two
rational, forward-looking individuals.[2]

For young adults like David Sanders, romantic love, combined with an awareness of the perils in the world, seemed to be the best formula for marital success. With adequate supplies of both, they thought they would be able to contend with any crisis that came their way. At a time when the economy appeared to be irrational and out of control, they were confident because, in the words of one young woman, "Our marriage should be rational and controllable. He has two legs and so do I; there is no insuperable burden on either side."[3] This view, they believed, would help them avoid the problems that had plagued the marriages of their elders. As one young man noted on the eve of his marriage, "I feel we've seen enough trouble in marriages to benefit our own."[4]

In tune with the nation's reformist politics, young adults would strive to restore health to the family, while policymakers struggled to restore health to the economy. Both situations called on Americans to abandon the constraints of the past and move forward, boldly, into the future. The 1930s was a time not only of misery, but of tremendous energy and radicalism. Populism, union organizing, and reform movements of all kinds flourished. Recovery in the family, as in the economy, would be achieved not simply by returning to ways of the past, but by adapting to new circumstances. The economic crisis, therefore, opened the way for a new type of family based on shared breadwinning and equality of the sexes. But it also created nostalgia for a mythic past in which male breadwinners provided a decent living, and homemakers were freed from outside employment.[5]

The depression thus paved the way for two different family forms: one with two breadwinners who shared tasks and the other with spouses whose roles were sharply differentiated. In the latter form, the father earned the "family wage" while the mother cared for the children, supplementing her husband's earnings with a job, if necessary. Young people like David Sanders and his fiancée could have chosen either path in their quest for the modern, liberated home life they desired. But by the time the depression was over and World War II had come and gone, it was clear that millions of middle-class American families, like that of the Sanders, would take the path toward polarized gender roles. What caused the overwhelming triumph of "traditional" roles in the "modern" home? The answer can be found in the seeds sown during the depression and how those seeds were cultivated in the 1940s.

Efforts to save the family from financial disaster began when the depression first gripped the nation, when communities and kin networks came together to provide mutual aid and support. Sometimes these informal modes of assistance were sufficient; often they were not. As a result, the state began to intervene in private life to an unprecedented extent. President Franklin D. Roosevelt not only told Americans that they had "nothing to fear but fear itself" but taught them not to fear the power of the national government, as it encroached on the home to alleviate the extreme hardships. From social security to the numerous public works programs, the New Deal brought the government directly into people's lives. Roosevelt's policies set new precedents for political innovation as well as governmental intervention. Although some people resisted this intrusion, most of the nation backed Roosevelt and his programs so overwhelmingly that the political coalition that came together around the New Deal retained national hegemony for three decades. While the depression lingered, unresolved, throughout the 1930s, Roosevelt's New Deal helped to create a spirit of optimism and a willingness for change that permeated the population.

The New Deal did a great deal to ease the suffering of many during the depression, but it did not eradicate poverty or solve the economic crisis. Among the hardest hit by the economic collapse were African-Americans. For every dollar earned by white men during the depression, white women earned 61 cents while black women earned only 23 cents. Nine out of ten employed black women were either domestics or agricultural workers and therefore exempt from most New Deal benefits, which blatantly discriminated against blacks, women, southerners, and rural laborers. As late as 1941, 40 percent of all American families lived below the poverty level, almost 8 million workers earned below the legal minimum wage, and the median income was only $2,000 per year.[6] Thus, although it was important that personal and national efforts support and reinforce each other, people could not expect the government to solve their problems. Americans had to fend for themselves, turning to federal agencies when necessary, or adapting to circumstances as best they could. The depression did not affect everyone in the same manner, but it created a general state of crisis that altered expected roles and rewards.

One role that changed was the role of marriage in people's lives. The marriage rate plummeted to an all-time low during the early 1930s, as young men and women postponed marriage or opted to remain single. Men were reluctant to marry if they thought they would not be able to provide for a family. Numerous educators, clergy, and observers from many professions worried that delayed marriage would lead to sexual transgressions. Many cautioned young people to keep their passions under control until they were able to marry, even though most experts doubted that these efforts would be effective. So another solution to the problem gained support: In spite of hard times, parents who could afford to do so should help young lovers with financial assistance to enable them to marry.

According to a 1937 Roper poll, so widespread was the concern about delayed marriage that over one-third of Americans favored the extraordinary idea of governmental subsidies to help young couples marry; only half those polled rejected the idea. Young marriage with financial dependence was considered preferable to sexual involvement prior to marriage. This was the first expression of an idea that would become much more widely advocated during the war and postwar years: early marriage as an antidote to illicit sex. As the well-known marriage counselor Paul Popenoe wrote, "In heaven's name, why wait? . . . If you are sincerely in love, old enough to know what you are doing, understand what marriage means and are free to enter into it, you have no right to let anything, least of all money, bar you from happiness."[7]

In spite of such exhortations, the marriage rate limped along during the 1930s, below the rate of the 1920s. It was not until 1940 that it began to rise significantly. The birthrate also declined more sharply in the 1930s than previously, and divorces increased as families collapsed under the financial strain. At the same time, the depression created opportunities for a growing number of single women to be self-reliant. These working women were able to support themselves and their families through their own efforts.[8]

For young single working women in the 1930s, the experience of some form of economic independence, even if it was to help support their families, inhibited them from marrying young and offered an alternative to the role of dependent housewife. As Judith Smith pointed out in her study of Providence, Rhode Island, many of these young women were not inclined to hurry into marriage. One young working woman in Smith's study remarked about her decision not to marry, "It's not that I didn't want to get married, but when you are working and have your own money" she did not feel compelled. She had many young male and female peers who made similar decisions. One explained, "During all the years I worked, I had a boyfriend, but we both had responsibilities at home. . . . Now they say 'career woman' but at the time you wouldn't call yourself that. It's just because you felt you had a responsibility at home, too."[9]

These women felt a sense of obligation to their parents, but they also took pride in their economic contributions. In spite of the discrimination women faced in the paid labor force, many achieved some measure of independence that they were not so eager to relinquish to become dependent in someone else's home—especially with men's employment as precarious as it was. As a result, over 6 million single women in the 1930s were making it on their own and contributing to the support of their parents' households.[10]

The popular culture at the time, particularly movies and fan magazines, glamorized single working women and affirmed their active role in public life.

Since the advent of the Hollywood star system in the 1910s, film stars had provided role models for men and women, reflecting as well as helping to shape popular values, styles, and behavior. In the 1930s, young women and men watched the films and read the stories about Hollywood celebrities in record numbers. The motion picture industry was one of the few economic enterprises that did not suffer serious losses during the depression. Rather, it expanded, gaining wider audiences in urban and rural areas all over the country. Furthermore, most of the viewers were young; movie patrons were primarily aged fifteen to thirty-five, with the largest concentration under twenty-five. Although few lived like the Hollywood stars, they identified with the personal dramas enacted on and off the screen. Movies and fan magazines reflected and stimulated strategies for coping with the depression. As both a barometer and a beacon, Hollywood was a focal point for the nation's mass culture.[11]

The way in which heroes and heroines were portrayed on the screen and the stars off the screen indicates that Hollywood encouraged the independence of women and the equality of the sexes. The popular culture bolstered the side of the 1930s that challenged traditional gender arrangements. Polls taken at the time reveal that the Hollywood stars believed in the message of gender equality that permeated the films and fan magazines. Representing a cultural vanguard, 93 percent of the female stars and 78 percent of the male stars thought that women were entitled to a career after marriage, in contrast to the population at large, which frowned on wives holding jobs. These responses are not surprising, considering that at the time, the movie industry was perhaps the only place in which women could achieve status and income equal to those of men. Nevertheless, the film celebrities agreed that there was a tension between love and ambition, and that love must come first if a marriage was to last.[12] Ultimately, it was this last message from Hollywood that resounded the loudest.

A survey of the most popular fan magazine, *Photoplay,* provides powerful evidence of the emergence of these themes from the 1930s onward. The twenties had witnessed a shift away from Victorian models of womanhood. Stars of the 1910s, such as Lillian Gish and Mary Pickford, with their childlike innocence, declined in popularity as new stars emerged. The more exciting women of the 1920s, like Clara Bow or Greta Garbo, experimented with new moral styles and sexual ethics. The plots of the most popular films in the 1920s centered on the romance between two young moderns leading to marriage, or on stagnant marriages that were revitalized through recreation, sensuality, and excitement. Cecil B. DeMille became one of the most successful directors of the 1920s by making films that celebrated marriages based on consumerism and sex. Couples were prominent, although these screen marriages rarely included children. The focus of their private lives was on the potential for finding personal fulfillment through modern marriage.[13]

By the 1930s, however, a new image of female stars—strong, autonomous, competent, and career-oriented—had gained momentum. Even the physical appearance of the stars had changed. For example, by the mid-1930s, Hollywood columnists were urging Loretta Young to gain weight, "more flesh and physical strength. . . . She seems to lack vitality." Mae West was applauded for her sensuality and power, as well as her spunky aggressiveness. In an era when single women were coping with a national crisis and making it on their own in a "man's world," the stars were admired for their independence and strength of character. During the war and postwar years, single women would be viewed with suspicion as potential corruptors of the home, but during the 1930s, they were glorified.[14]

Yet for all its affirmation of the emancipation of women, Hollywood fell short of pointing the way toward a restructured family that would incorporate independent women. These strong and autonomous women of the 1930s no longer represented ideal wives, as had their counterparts in the twenties who brought their emancipated selves into revitalized marriages. Rather, these tough and rugged career women were admired as *women*, not as wives.

Photoplay frequently portrayed marriage as problematic for the career woman; the tensions between successful female stars and their husbands filled the pages of the magazine. Like ordinary men and women who struggled with shifting power relations in the home when wives became breadwinners during the depression, Hollywood celebrities presented strategies for coping with that situation, but they did not endorse new domestic roles. Rather, the message emanating from Hollywood was that although career women were viable models for the population, a career does not easily mix with marriage or having children. In other words, women who held jobs and pursued careers were applauded for choosing positive alternatives to the role of wife and mother, but combining both roles was clearly difficult.

Hollywood offered few suggestions for how successful career women who happened to be married could achieve a workable family life. Instead, the popular culture began to condone divorce. No longer advocated merely as an escape for women married to brutal or irresponsible men, or for men wed to less-than-virtuous wives, divorce became a solution for difficult circumstances caused by disrupted power relations in the home. This justification represented a major shift from earlier themes. In the 1920s, the primary message in the movies was to join in a modern fun-filled marriage. The major threat to happiness was the vestiges of Victorian formality and restraint. But in the 1930s, giving up the past for modernity would not provide the solution.

As early as 1931, *Photoplay* began to carry articles stating that divorce was acceptable if love had vanished and a husband and wife were incompatible. Although the divorce laws still rested on the guilt of one party or the other, Hollywood began to endorse the concept of irreconcilable differences. Popular articles stressed that women should struggle to succeed in their careers as much as men do, even if marriage is the casualty. As one article (pondering the question "Why Can't the Stars Stay Married?") concluded, "There is a pretty big conflict between a career in pictures and our unconscious longing for domestic life."[15] Women were torn between wanting both a career and a home and not being able to have both.

The women, it is important to note, were not condemned if their marriages fell apart as a result. They certainly were *not* encouraged to give up their ambition. Hollywood applauded successful female stars and frowned on those who relinquished a career for marriage. *Photoplay* explicitly chastised one young starlet for attempting to save her marriage by becoming a subservient wife. The writer chided Lupe for saying, "Yes darling," whenever Johnny spoke. "Johnny's socks . . . are far more important to Lupe than the biggest screen role in Hollywood." To save their marriage she had become "a little give-in mama. . . . Now peace and Johnny reign."[16]

Upward mobility in Hollywood was not the exclusive preserve of men. Women were encouraged to be ambitious and individualistic, too. One star, giving advice to other women hoping to get ahead, claimed that her secret of success was to "stand before the glass and say very earnestly and sincerely to yourself, 'I will be a beautiful and successful woman. I will.' Say it over and over and watch the confidence stealing over you." Female stars were frequently described, with admiration, as being "abrupt, blunt, frank and stubborn." Joan Crawford, a major star of the era noted for her characterizations of strong, independent women, was featured in *Photoplay* for her self-sacrifice, courage, and persistence as she struggled for success.[17]

Typical of this emphasis on the autonomous woman was Carole Lombard's 1937 article, "How I Live by a Man's Code," in which she urged her female readers to "be efficient . . . play fair (men do) . . . obey the boss, take criticism, love is private, work—and like it! (All women should have something worthwhile to do and be efficient at it.) . . . Pay your share (no one likes a man who is always fumbling when it's time to pay the check. . . . You don't have to surrender your femininity to pay your share of the bills.)"[18] These tips for success did not necessarily

FIGURE 4   In this scene from *Blonde Venus* (1931), the domesticating influence of the child tames the wayward tendencies of the mother (Marlene Dietrich). Family harmony is restored when the mother quits her job and the father goes back to work. (*The Museum of Modern Art/Film Stills Archive. Courtesy of Photofest.*)

mesh with matrimony. The independent woman glamorized in Hollywood could not always be expected to have a smoothly functioning marriage.

Hollywood in the 1930s saw itself as promoting the equality of the sexes. But it did not provide a new model of marriage that incorporated equality. Individual women and men were simply urged to be flexible and somehow find a way to avoid competition and jealousy in marriage—a message that was relevant not only to stars but to couples of modest means trying to survive the depression and the tensions inherent in the two-earner household.

Major films of the decade illustrate this ambivalent stance toward emancipated women who married. *Blonde Venus*, a popular film of 1931, charts the story of a "new woman" (Marlene Dietrich) who gives up her career as an actress to marry a young chemist and have a child. The husband becomes ill and, like many men in the 1930s, is unable to support his family. The young mother goes back to acting, and her sexual allure attracts a "sugar daddy" who secretly supports her family while the sickly father tends to the home and child. The role reversal destroys the family; the husband discovers what has come of his wife's sexual and economic emancipation. The story is resolved when the child restores unity to the family: The mother gives up her job and her rich lover, and the now-healthy husband goes back to work to support them (see Figure 4). The moral of the story is clear: Emancipated women pose a danger to the family at a time when men are weakened and unable to provide. If the man is strong, however, the domesticated emancipated woman can bring excitement and new intimacy to the home.[19] Films of the 1920s first introduced the "new woman" as the modern wife, but films of the 1930s emphasized her subordination and need to be "tamed" by a strong man and the domesticating influence of a child.

By the end of the decade, films were still pessimistic about the possibility of happiness in marriage for untamed, autonomous women. The 1940 box office hit *His Girl Friday*, a remake of the 1931 film *Front Page*, begins after the feisty reporter, Hilde Johnson (Rosalind Russell), has divorced her work-obsessed boss (Cary Grant) (see Figure 5). In a curious twist on role reversals during the depression, Hilde Johnson, a man in the 1931 version, is a woman in the 1940 rendition. The name of the character remained the same, as did much of the dialogue. In the 1940 version, the star reporter is a divorced woman determined to marry a devoted, sappy fellow who promises her domestic bliss. In the end, she gives up her doting fiancé and realizes that she cannot bear to give up either her career or her rough and rugged ex-husband boss. In the film's finale, the spunky reporter proclaims her deep wish for a home and babies and agrees to remarry her boss. She expresses her hope that this time, the two journalists will be able to combine their fast-paced careers with serene domesticity. Even though romance triumphs, the heroine is once again headed toward an unsteady marriage, one that has already ended in divorce and may indeed do so again, since nothing has changed between the couple.[20]

An unsteady marriage involving a tough and independent woman appeared again in the most popular movie made during the 1930s. *Gone with the Wind* is the story of Scarlett O'Hara (Vivien Leigh), who survives hard times as a shrewd businesswoman through her grit, determination, and intelligence. Her marriage to Rhett Butler (Clark Gable), however, does not work out. Domesticity flourishes briefly when Scarlett and Rhett have a child and Scarlett becomes sexually and economically subordinate to her husband. But when their daughter dies, the marriage dies, too. In the end, successful marriage eludes the heroine, as Rhett

FIGURE 5   In the 1940 film *His Girl Friday*, the tough reporter (Rosalind Russell) vies with her ex-husband boss (Cary Grant) in the rough-and-tumble world of journalism. (*The Museum of Modern Art/Film Stills Archive. Courtesy of Photofest.*)

departs, claiming that he does not "give a damn." Scarlett, forlorn but not defeated, turns her back on the past, claiming that "tomorrow is another day."[21]

The message of domestic tension in these films came through loud and clear. If emancipated women could be tamed by domesticity, with a man to support them and children to nurture, the family would be rejuvenated. But if husbands were weak or if wives took their independence and sexuality out into the world, disaster would strike the home. Although audiences found validation for single working women, movies and stars seemed to present female viewers with a choice between pursuing careers as single women or giving up careers to achieve stable marriages. Most young female viewers probably hoped to marry at some point in their lives. They also realized that as poorly paid members of the labor force, they were not likely to achieve the success, fame, and fortune of the film stars. Female celebrities may have faced a difficult choice between their glamorous careers and their lives as housewives, but for the average overworked and underpaid young working woman, the choice was not likely to be so difficult. These women may have admired the stars, but they knew that their own choices were different. Because it continually presented marriage as problematic for career women, Hollywood ultimately, and perhaps unwittingly, came down on the side of traditional domestic roles.

These ideas prevailed in the world beyond Hollywood as well. Even the most radical measures of the New Deal, created to alleviate hardship, failed to promote the possibility of a new family structure based on gender equality. Although female unemployment was a severe problem, and many families depended on the earnings of both spouses, federal policies supported unemployed male breadwinners but discouraged married women from seeking jobs. Section 213 of the Economy Act of 1932 mandated that whenever personnel reductions took place in the executive branch, married persons were to be the first discharged if their spouse was also a government employee. As a result, sixteen hundred married women were dismissed from their federal jobs. Many state and local governments followed suit; three out of four cities excluded married women from teaching, and eight states passed laws excluding them from state jobs. The government provided relief for families in need, but not jobs for married women.[22]

The New Deal also failed to alleviate the wage differentials that persisted during the depression; by ignoring the plight of working women, it actually contributed to the deterioration of their economic status. The state might provide employment or even take over as breadwinner for an unemployed head of a household, but it would not provide well-paying jobs for women, day care facilities, or any other measures that would help alleviate women's economic dependence on men. In accord with these policies, vocational counselors endeavored to minimize competition between women and men over scarce jobs by steering women toward low-level "pink-collar" occupations that rarely threatened men's employment. Therefore, when young women looked to the future, most of them had little trouble choosing between their ill-paying jobs and the prospect of marriage to a promising provider, because institutional constraints made only one "choice" viable. Although the need for women's earnings brought more wives into the paid labor force during the depression, the disincentives were so powerful that by 1940 only 15 percent of married women were employed. The government thus reinforced the idea that the best way to strengthen the family was to keep women home and give men work.[23]

These efforts to curtail women's employment opportunities were directly related to the equally powerful imperative to bolster the employment of men.

Although most Americans experienced some form of hardship, it was the nation's male breadwinners—fathers who were responsible for providing economic support for their families—who were threatened or faced with the severest erosion of their identities. Those who lost income or jobs frequently lost status at home and self-respect as well. Between 1933 and 1935, one out of every five male wage earners accepted federal relief, and even more received local aid. The "dole" was a public badge of defeat. One survey of unemployed middle-class men found that nearly one-third lost status with their wives. Economic hardship placed severe strains on marriage. Surveys taken at the time indicated that the rate of sexual intercourse among married couples declined during the 1930s. Going on relief may well have helped the family budget, but it would do little for the breadwinner's feelings of failure.[24]

Advertisers during the depression years played on men's guilt at a time when many men felt responsible for placing the security of their families in jeopardy. Although advertising tableaux in popular magazines featured cozy nuclear families in soft focus surrounded by a hazy glow of intimacy and togetherness, other advertisements were harsher. They pointed to the personal failures of men, rather than to the problems of the economy, and urged fathers to take measures so that the same fate would not befall their sons. Life insurance companies exhorted men to invest in their childrens' future, because of "the lonely uphill struggle you would like to save your boy." Even consumer goods could be an investment in a child's future during hard times, according to an ad for Lionel Electric Trains addressed "to fathers who want to be proud of their sons." More damning was the harsh picture above an advertisement for Ethyl gasoline that portrayed an angry child, fist clenched, admonishing his bewildered and chagrined father in the driver's seat next to him, "Gee, Pop—they're all passing you."[25]

With the breadwinner role undermined, other family roles shifted dramatically. Frequently, wives and mothers who had never been employed took jobs to provide supplemental or even primary support for their families. Their employment often meant facing intense social condemnation as well as miserably low wages. While men suffered the stigma of failure if they were unemployed, working wives faced intense pressure to relinquish their jobs even if their families depended on their earnings. Although women rarely displaced male workers— the vast majority held "women's jobs" that men would not take in any case— they were considered selfish if they were employed when men were out of work. Women also suffered the hardships of low wages and poor working conditions. Despite the needed income these jobs provided, employed wives were not likely to resist pressures to quit if they could be certain of adequate support from their husbands. A 1936 Gallup poll indicated that 82 percent of those surveyed (including three-fourths of the women) believed that wives of employed husbands should not work outside the home. By 1939, nearly 90 percent of the men who were polled believed that "women should not hold a job after marriage," and most women still agreed. Public praise was reserved for self-supporting single women, or for frugal and resourceful homemakers whose domestic endeavors helped their families through the crisis.[26]

These pressures, combined with federal policies that favored the employment of men, made it difficult for women to be self-supporting. Yet most women had one or more dependents; even if married, they were often the sole wage earners in their families. Female unemployment rose during the decade as male unemployment declined, a reflection of the fact that an increasing number of women actively sought jobs.

By 1940, nearly 30 percent of all women were employed. Most of these women clustered in such low-paying occupations as light manufacturing, service, and clerical work. Hard-won gains by middle- and upper-middle-class feminists who had fought for the right to pursue careers were eroded during the 1930s as professional opportunities for women shrank. Although many women held key positions in the federal government and formed a network that concerned itself with women's issues, feminism took a backseat to what appeared to be the more pressing issue of general economic recovery. By the end of the decade, the employment rate of married women had risen only 3 percent in ten years. According to the historian Peter Filene, who charted the erosion of earlier feminist gains during the depression era, "It was as if the twenties had never happened."[27]

Given the need for women's earnings, the widespread employment of women might have been one of the most important legacies of the depression era. But discriminatory policies and public hostility weakened that potential. As women's paid work increased only slightly, their domestic roles expanded considerably. Often it was in the home, rather than in the underpaid female labor force, that married women could make the most dramatic economic contribution to their families' resources. Women usually controlled about 80 percent of the family income, and their spending practices determined how far the wage earners' wages would stretch. At the same time, they made significant financial contributions by taking over tasks and providing services that had previously been purchased. They expanded their unpaid labor, did more things manually without the conveniences of technology or appliances, and substituted previously purchased goods, such as food and clothing, with items they made themselves. Because of these efforts, many families with reduced incomes were able to maintain their predepression standard of living.[28]

The depression thus created a tension between traditional domestic roles and challenges to those roles. The prevailing familial ideology was gravely threatened during the 1930s, when women and men adapted to hard times by shifting their household responsibilities. But in the long run, these alternatives were viewed as temporary measures caused by unfortunate circumstances, rather than as positive outcomes of the crisis. Young people learned, on the one hand, to accept women's employment as necessary for the family budget; on the other hand, they saw that deviations from traditional roles often wreaked havoc in marriages, among successful Hollywood stars as well as among their own kin. Children who grew up in deprived families during these years watched their parents struggle to succeed as breadwinners and homemakers and suffered along with their parents if those expectations proved impossible to meet. The realities of family life combined with institutional barriers to inhibit the potential for sustained radical change.

Glen Elder, Jr., in his sociological classic, *Children of the Great Depression*, studied a sample of white, largely Protestant, working- and middle-class individuals who were youths during the depression. He found that when hardship caused parents to abandon traditional gender roles, children saw the changes as unfortunate consequences of the crisis, not positive alternatives with intrinsic merit. Although low-income families faced the severest economic deprivation, middle-class households also experienced a significant loss in status and material well-being. For the children, unfortunate reversals in parental roles yielded certain advantages. Boys who took jobs to help support their families gained a greater degree of social independence; girls, however, were less likely to do so. Although some girls entered the paid labor force along with their brothers, they were more likely to take over domestic responsibilities at an earlier age, especially if their mothers held jobs outside the home. In other words, although hard times encouraged children to accept adult responsibilities, the depression nevertheless propelled young men and women to adopt the roles of breadwinner and homemaker at an earlier age and to view those roles in a positive light. Elder concluded that this situation, especially in the more severely deprived homes, led to "a conducive environment for traditional sex roles and an accelerated movement toward adulthood."[29]

Elder's findings would no doubt have been different if viable employment opportunities had been available to married women, or if the government had provided public works jobs for women to the same extent that it did for men. But public agencies supported the idea of a "family wage" for men and economic dependence for women. As a result of their limited employment opportunities and heavy responsibilities at home, it is no wonder that many mothers in the 1930s struggled to keep their families afloat and longed for "normal" circumstances that would enable their husbands to support them. As one daughter of immigrants recalled:

> The emigrant mother often had to work not only in her home, but outside as well, under the most harrowing conditions. . . . For the son, it was important and necessary to obtain an education, so he could escape the sweatshop labor of his father. For the daughter, however, the most precious legacy was an escape from the hard work and drudgery of her mother and the attainment of leisure—the very leisure this emigrant mother never knew herself, and which she so desperately needed. . . . To this emigrant mother, education was only necessary for her son to get a better job, and the daughter, with nothing else besides her femininity, would, with luck, marry well and thereby achieve the leisure her mother never knew.[30]

Because male authority was widely associated with a man's ability as a provider, the more a family's traditional gender roles were disrupted, the more likely the children were to disapprove of the shift in the balance of power in their homes. As Elder noted about the increased influence of mothers in these families, "Mother's power seemed to be an accepted adaptation to economic hardship . . . but it is clearly a major source of negative sentiment in the adult years." When surveyed in the 1950s, fewer than half these daughters had positive views of their mothers if they had been dominant in the home during the 1930s, while 86 percent approved of their mothers' roles if their fathers had been equal or superior to them in decision making. Elder concluded that "the primary effect of economic loss occurs through mother's power and its negative implication to daughters," who were to become mothers themselves in the 1950s. The more role reversal their parents had experienced, the more likely the daughters were to aspire to normative roles with traditional power relationships in the families they established themselves. If a woman's earnings helped keep the family afloat without weakening the man's authority, however, it was seen as necessary and acceptable. In this way, the 1930s helped set the stage for a major change in the 1950s: the widespread employment of wives whose earnings as well as domestic authority remained secondary to those of their breadwinner husbands.[31]

These attitudes were adopted early and held firmly by the people in Elder's Oakland sample. Homes in which traditional roles were undermined appeared "deviant" to these young white women and men. Children of deprived homes who assumed adult roles so early lacked the frivolity normally associated with the life of a "teenager." This seriousness appeared to be a theme of the 1930s, in contrast to the noted youth culture of the 1920s. As *Life* magazine noted in 1938, "U.S. youths today are a sober lot." Elder noted that young men were distinctly work-centered and sensitive to the emotional significance of a secure home. Women, mindful of the limited employment opportunities open to them and aware of the stigma facing working wives, were likely to embrace the homemaker role as significant, important, and fulfilling. The adults of the 1950s would thus be eager to establish secure families with the traditional gender roles that had been so seriously threatened during their childhoods in the 1930s.[32]

The KLS respondents were contemporaries of those studied by Elder. Unlike Elder's sample, however, most of them came from comfortable homes; few experienced severe hardship during their childhood and young adulthood. Nevertheless, they shared many of the attitudes and values that Elder found were characteristic of individuals from deprived homes, and they articulated numerous concerns reflected in the popular culture. They admired the ability of women to take care of themselves but were committed to traditional gender roles within marriage. Like the Hollywood stars, they recognized that two careers in a marriage could lead to tension, but unlike the stars, most of the women intended to relinquish their ambitions for a career, to achieve a happy marriage. They also recognized that the circumstances brought about by the depression might well affect their futures, and they endeavored to minimize the risks.

Most of the respondents were native-born white Americans, and two-thirds had native-born parents. Financially, they fell somewhere between the wealthy stars of Hollywood and the members of Elder's Oakland sample who had been impoverished during the depression. Most described their childhoods as happy and said that their parents were happily married. Only 6 percent had parents who were separated or divorced. Most of their families had incomes well above the national average in the late 1930s. Although they had few savings at the time of their engagement, they had almost no debts. By the 1950s, most fell into the comfortable end of the middle class.[33]

When the respondents filled out their first questionnaires, they explained why they chose their particular partners and what made them believe their marriages would be successful. They also stated whether they could foresee any problems ahead. Their responses reflect the widespread admiration for single women who supported themselves. One man explained that he chose his future wife "because she was the only one that I had met while unemployed who asked me to go to a social function, knowing that I could not return the invitation, because of a lack of funds, so I felt that under those circumstances she would be true under any circumstances."[34] This favorable attitude toward independent women stopped short of marriage, however. The respondents believed that a successful marriage depended on a committed partnership between a successful breadwinner and his helpmate.

Sexual and economic independence were appreciated as positive attributes of a future spouse. One respondent said his fiancée was "refreshingly independent; no clinging vine," and went on to describe her other appealing attributes: "physically attractive as any woman I have known and decidedly more extroverted; passionate (and how) on occasion." His fiancée was equally enraptured, saying that he was "more attractive physically and more compatible than any man with whom I have had experience. I enjoy his company immensely and am usually with him from morning till night without any feeling of restraint or boredom." Still, their euphoria was tempered by a certain soberness and a realization that life was hard and would need to be faced with determination. She explained why she thought their marriage would be successful: "I am interested in the same type of career so that two heads will be better than one."[35]

The young woman's last remark suggests a theme that recurred throughout the responses: If a woman was interested in her husband's work, that interest would strengthen the marriage. If she became a helper to her husband, even better. Jonathan Morell listed the reasons why he felt his marriage would be a success: "My profession will bring in a favorable income and my work is interesting to both of us. My wife will be invaluable as an assistant in my office and has undertaken a keen interest in our way of earning a living." Similarly, Stephan Houser chose his partner in part because "she is a trained nurse and can understand the life of an M.D., which makes for congenial relations." As long as the husband was the primary provider, he welcomed his wife's assistance. But if a wife had her own career or even a job, it became a potential problem, especially if she earned more than he did. Although Stuart Petersen was glad that his future wife had "financial independence," he anticipated problems because the "source of our financial support for a few years will be mainly from my fiancée."[36]

Several women in the sample gave up careers precisely because they did not wish to compete with their husbands. At the time of their engagement, 70 percent of the women were employed, but only a third intended to continue their employment after marriage. It was no doubt easier for these women to give up their low-paying jobs than for the highly successful film stars who struggled to combine their careers with marriage. Fewer than half the women were earning over a thousand dollars a year, compared to nearly 90 percent of the men.[37] Nevertheless, many had ambitions that they sacrificed to avoid any marital tensions in the future. Vivian Lester, for example, noted that she gave up "opportunities of leadership in certain areas in order not to compete with my husband."[38]

Others felt that even the strain of poverty would be preferable to the ill effects of the wife earning an income. Janet Farrell noted that hardship might even be a virtue: "We are going to be very poor for some time, but that may be an asset rather than otherwise." Whatever difficulties they had to endure, most of the KLS respondents believed that the success of their marriages would rest largely on the ability of the husband to provide for his wife and children, and for the wife to help the breadwinner establish himself. Frederick Hall wrote that the success of his marriage was "only a question of my future advancement and income." Lawrence Olson was grateful because "my fiancée is willing to start with a little and not expect too much." Stanley Morris also worried about his future financial situation but believed that he would prevail through sheer will. He was confident that his marriage would be a success because "I have decided to make it so."[39]

Although men were expected to be the heads of their households, depression-bred women envisioned more egalitarian unions than did women in the past: 60 percent of women polled by the *Ladies Home Journal* objected to the word *obey* in the vows, 75 percent believed in joint decision making, and 80 percent believed an unemployed husband should keep house for a working wife. Yet 60 percent said they would lose respect for a husband who earned less than his wife, and 90 percent believed a wife should give up employment if her husband wanted her to do so. This vision of modern marriage, then, included a measure of equality within the relationship but distinct roles for breadwinners and homemakers.[40]

The acquiescence of women to their domestic roles makes more sense if one keeps in mind the constraints they faced in the work world and the difficulties encountered by their parents. As Elder noted, for depression-bred women who formed families during prosperous years, "successful husbands made economic dependence a viable option for women who learned, as children, the value of a woman's role in the home." The economic crisis legitimated employment for single women and for married women whose earnings supplemented the male breadwinner's income. But their jobs remained in the pink-collar sector of the economy, yielding lower pay and status than did men's jobs. The women in Elder's Oakland sample who faced these limited choices were "members of a cohort which tends to prize family roles (mother, wife, homemaker) far more than any other activity." Elder was aware of the role that institutional barriers played in the stated goals of these women, for he noted that this preference was underscored in the postwar years, when "bona-fide occupational careers which have a measure of autonomy and equality relative to the husband's worklife [were] practically nonexistent."[41]

If the paid labor force had been a more hospitable place, and if public policies had fostered equal opportunities for women, young people in the 1930s might have been less inclined to aspire to prevailing gender roles. After all, many families managed to survive the depression because women as well as men earned incomes. But in the long run, those contributions were applauded only if they supported and upheld traditional power arrangements in the home. The number of employed women did increase—and judging from the high female unemployment rate, many more were seeking jobs. If opportunities had expanded, the number of women holding jobs would have risen dramatically. Viable long-term job prospects for women might have prompted new ways of structuring family roles. In the face of persistent obstacles, however, that potential withered. The popular culture reflected widespread admiration for independent women, but even the cultural vanguard in Hollywood fell short of affirming an alternative to the traditional family arrangement.

And so the potential for radically altered gender roles in the family never reached fruition in the 1930s. As the depression continued, the path toward traditional domestic arrangements appeared to be the one most likely to bring Americans toward the secure homes they desired. The obstacles to gender equality might have lifted with the end of hard times. With full employment, women's jobs would no longer be seen as contributing to men's unemployment and loss of status. When World War II brought a sudden end to the depression, yielding full employment and a booming economy, many of the obstacles to a fundamental restructuring of public as well as private roles would be removed. The national response to this new crisis would determine which of the two paths that were forged in the depression Americans would ultimately pursue.

CHAPTER THREE

WAR AND PEACE:
FANNING THE HOME FIRES

> We had as a nation emerged from a great war, itself following upon a long and protracted Depression. We thought, all of us, men and women alike, to replenish ourselves in goods and spirit, to undo, by exercise of collective will, the psychic disruptions of the immediate past. We would achieve the serenity that had eluded the lives of our parents, the men would be secure in stable careers, the women in comfortable homes, and together they would raise perfect children. . . . It was the *Zeitgeist*, the spirit of the times.
>
> —JOSEPH ADELSON, A PSYCHOLOGIST[1]

REMINISCING about life in the United States after World War II, Joseph Adelson aptly described the "spirit of the times" as profoundly domestic. The utopian vision included "replenished" families with male providers "secure in stable careers" and female housewives "in comfortable homes," who would "raise perfect children." It was a dream that Americans had carried with them since the depression. Like the depression, World War II brought new challenges and new disruptions to families. For many who looked forward to building stable and secure homes after the depression, the war put their hopes on hold. When thousands of men were called to war, their unquestionably manly responsibilities as soldiers took precedence over their roles as breadwinners. While the men vanished to foreign shores to fend off the enemy, the women were left to fend for themselves.

The war emergency required the society to restructure itself and opened the way for the emancipation of women on an unprecedented scale. The potential for gender equality, thwarted during the 1930s, now had a chance to reach fruition. The depression ended abruptly. The unemployment rate fell from 14 percent to nearly zero. In response to the needs of an expanding wartime economy, public policy shifted dramatically from barring women from jobs to recruiting them. Married women were not only tolerated in the paid labor force but actively encouraged to take "men's jobs" as a patriotic duty to keep the war economy booming while the men went off to fight. Public opinion followed suit. During the depression, 80 percent of Americans objected to wives working outside the home; by 1942, only 13 percent still objected.[2]

As a result of the combined incentives of patriotism and good wages, women began streaming into jobs. By 1945, the number of employed women had leaped 60 percent. Three-quarters of these new workers were married, and a third had children under age fourteen.[3] War production needs might have led to a restructuring of the labor force along gender-neutral lines, ending sex segregation in the workplace and bringing about a realignment of domestic roles. The dislocation of wartime might have led to the postponement of marriage and child rearing, continuing the demographic trends of the thirties toward later marriage, a lower marriage rate, and fewer children. But nothing of the kind took place. The potential for significant alterations in gender arrangements was, once again, thwarted. In spite of the tremendous changes brought about by the war, the emergency situation ultimately encouraged women to keep their sights set on the home, and men to reclaim their status as the primary breadwinners and heads of households.

Instead of deterring Americans from embarking on family life, the war may have sped up the process. Women entered war production, but they did not give up on reproduction. The war brought a dramatic reversal to the declining marriage rate of the 1930s. Over 1 million more families were formed between 1940 and 1943 than would have been expected during normal times, and as soon as the United States entered the war, fertility increased. Between 1940 and 1945, the birthrate climbed from 19.4 to 24.5 per one thousand population. The marriage age dropped and the marriage rate accelerated, spurred, in part, by the possibility of draft deferments for married men in the early war years and by the imminence of the men's departure for foreign shores. Thus, a curious phenomenon marked the war years: a widespread disruption of domestic life accompanied by a rush into marriage and parenthood.[4]

Tangible as well as intangible factors spurred this increase in the formation of families. Economic hardship was no longer a barrier to marriage, as it had been in the 1930s, and dependents' allowances eased the burdens of families if the breadwinners were drafted. But perhaps more important was the desire to solidify relationships and establish connections to the future when war made life so uncertain. Widespread war-propaganda efforts called on the nation to support the men who were fighting to protect their families back home. To Americans who were steeped in an isolationist tradition, suspicious and not sure about the stakes in Europe, these appeals were more than clichés. They provided tangible reasons to live, and even to die. Men at war were well aware of the possibility that they might never return. As an American fighter pilot wrote to the woman he had married before he left, "Our love will never die. . . . I love you more than anything in life. . . . A million kisses, darling, I'll see you again—sometime, somewhere." Shortly after writing this declaration of undying love, he died in a flight over France.[5]

With losses and tragedies pervading the national consciousness, Americans were receptive to emotional appeals to home and hearth. The popular culture carried many such appeals. Under the sponsorship of the Office of Facts and Figures, all the major radio networks aired a series of programs in 1942 to mobilize support for the war. One highly acclaimed segment, "To The Young," included this exhortation:

> YOUNG MALE VOICE: "That's one of the things this war's about."
> YOUNG FEMALE VOICE: "About us?"
> YOUNG MALE VOICE: "About *all* young people like us. About love and gettin' hitched, and havin' a home and some kids, and breathin' fresh air out in the suburbs . . . about livin' an' workin' *decent*, like free people."[6]

Movies carried similar messages, and their sponsorship by the government did nothing to dampen their popularity. The 1943 war propaganda film *This Is the Army*, starring Ronald Reagan, was the most successful film of the war years. The plot revolves around the efforts of the central character's sweetheart, a Red Cross volunteer, to persuade her reluctant soldier to marry her. She finally succeeds, and the duo wed just before the hero leaves to fight on foreign shores. As

FIGURE 6   This scene from the 1943 war propaganda film *This Is the Army* shows a GI dressed in drag for an army dance routine, proving that he's just as tough as the next guy. The scene uses humor to deflect wartime anxieties about altered gender roles. (*The Museum of Modern Art/Film Stills Archive. Courtesy of Photofest.*)

he marches off with his buddies, she remains at home. For the remainder of the war, she would provide the vision of what the men were fighting for: home and hearth. In addition to its affirmation of the family, the film also reveals a discomfort with the disrupted gender roles brought about by war. Soldier-comedians joke about their female superior officers, and a group of he-men in drag do a clumsy chorus-line routine showing their hairy legs beneath their skirts (see Figure 6). Ironically, while the film was intended to make light of gender role reversal, as well as to defuse fears about the very real potential for wartime to foster homosexual communities, *This Is the Army* became a hugely popular cult film among gays and lesbians.[7]

The popular culture reflected widespread admiration for the many thousands of female war workers but also affirmed the primacy of domesticity for women. Wartime films presented these contradictory messages to their female viewers, who constituted two-thirds of the movie audience. Numerous popular movies portrayed tough heroines who took on previously male responsibilities and survived on their own or with the support of other women. Whether in military situations, as in *Here Come the Waves* or *So Proudly We Hail*, or as war workers, in films such as *Swing Shift Maisie* or *Government Girl*, women displayed courage and independence. Major stars of the decade, such as Katharine Hepburn, were noted for their dignity and strength, both on and off the screen.

Other popular media also emphasized women's capabilities, most notably the invincible "Wonder Woman," who made her comic strip debut in 1941. But the independent heroine did not replace the familial image of women. Often the spunky career woman married her ardent suitor in the end, as did the nurse in *This Is the Army*. In popular magazine fiction, women remained devoted to their homes and families rather than to careers. One study found that although female characters were more likely to hold jobs in the 1940s than in the 1930s or the 1950s, the stories of the war decade represented "the strongest assault on feminine careerism." Heroines who gave up a career for marriage were portrayed favorably, while those who combined a career and family were condemned as poor wives and mothers.[8] As in the depression, wartime gave rise to two different popular images of women: one independent, the other domestic.

The emancipated heroine did not survive in peacetime, however. After the war, less positive images of women began to appear in films. These movies portrayed female sexuality as a positive force only if it led to an exciting marriage; otherwise, it was dangerous. The popular and aesthetically compelling film noir genre, which evolved during and after the war, explored themes of personal anxiety and alienation. Films in this genre often portrayed female sexuality as both powerful and dangerous. Barbara Stanwyck played an evil wife who plotted to kill her husband in *Double Indemnity* (1944), and Rita Hayworth's sexy character destroyed her man in the 1947 film *The Lady from Shanghai*. Perhaps the most telling saga of the transformation of female sexuality in the popular culture is the career of Marilyn Monroe. The future sex goddess first achieved notice when *Yank* magazine published a picture of her working in a war production plant, and she became popular as one of the noted "pinup girls" of wartime. Like the other famous pinups, including Betty Grable, Rita Hayworth, and Lena Horne (the most popular African-American pinup for the black troops), Monroe served as an inspiration to the fighting men. After the war, she appeared in many film noir movies that portrayed her sexuality as a destructive force.[9]

In the popular media, women's sexuality became increasingly central to their identity. The promising as well as the troublesome potential of female eroticism found expression in the plots and genres of the decade. From the late forties to the fifties, subordination made the difference between good or bad female sexuality. Sexy women who became devoted sweethearts or wives would contribute to the goodness of life; those who used their sexuality for power or greed would destroy men, families, and even society. Some of Marilyn Monroe's films demonstrate this dichotomy. In *Niagara*, made in 1953, Monroe portrayed a woman whose aggressive sexuality ultimately leads to the deaths of her husband, her lover, and herself. *Niagara* was one of the last films to portray Monroe's sexuality as dangerous; in most of her films in the 1950s, she portrayed a harmless "sex kitten" whose childlike innocence and sexual allure contributed to men's power and enjoyment, without threatening them.[10]

In their off-screen lives, female film stars began to portray a new model of womanhood. During the war, popular magazines suddenly featured them chiefly as wives and mothers. Joan Crawford, for example, evolved from the embodiment of female independence and overt sexuality to become a paragon of domesticity (see Figure 7). The shift began even before the United States officially entered the war; 1940 marked a change from the dominant themes of the depression. A typical 1940 *Photoplay* featured film star Claudette Colbert. In a stance different from that of the 1930s, in which popular writers criticized women for submerging their identities in marriage, the magazine stated approvingly, "Step over this charming threshold and meet—not a star and her husband—but a doctor and his wife."[11]

No longer urged to follow their own ambitions, women were now offered tips on how to keep a husband interested. Colbert gave advice to a woman whose husband had grown indifferent to her emotional needs and who ran after other women. With not a word of criticism toward the errant man or even a suggestion that the wife should leave him, Colbert wrote that although it is difficult to keep house all day, "take care of three children and be a bundle of charm at the day's end, . . . that is what man has expected of a wife since the world began—and if you love your husband and want to keep him it would be worth your effort to try this. . . . Try to be gay and interesting when he is home."[12]

The actress Ann Sothern echoed the same theme. She urged her readers to read up on "what he is doing, what we're fighting for, what will come afterward. . . . [We] began planning our house—our 'perfect house.' Then we began to think about the nursery . . . and that became the most important room in the house-to-be, the most important thing in our plans for the future and it made us feel our sense of responsibility to that future." Here was the essence of their vision of togetherness: "I know that a lot of men are dreaming of coming back

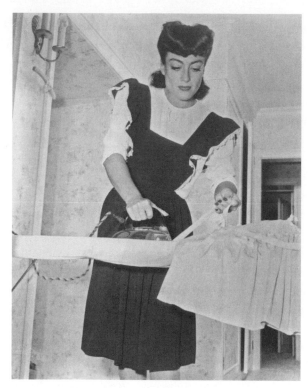

FIGURE 7   Here is Joan Crawford in the 1940s portrayed as a happy housewife. The studio made a point of noting in the caption that this is the "real" Joan Crawford, off screen, tending to her domestic duties. *(The Museum of Modern Art/Film Stills Archive. Courtesy of Photofest.)*

not only to those girls who waved good-by to them. They are dreaming of coming back to the mothers of their children!"[13]

During the war, advice givers were mindful of the psychological dislocation that returning veterans would face. Much of the healing process would fall to women. Sothern continued, "When he comes back it may take a few years for him 'to find himself'—it's [your] job—not his—to see that the changes in both of [you] do not affect the fundamental bonds between [you]. . . . I won't bother to remind you of the obvious, to keep up your appearance—to preserve for him the essence of the girl he fell in love with, the girl he longs to come back to. . . . The least we can do as women is to try to live up to some of those expectations."[14]

Sothern articulated a theme that would carry through the advice literature and characterize many postwar marriages: Women should adapt to men's interests and needs.

The wifely focus of the 1940s marked a shift from the flamboyant sexuality exhibited by stars of the 1930s, like Mae West, to a prudent respectability. Bette Davis, noted for her strong-minded independence in the 1930s, proclaimed in 1941 that "men and women are equals today in business, politics and sports—women are as brave, intelligent and daring collectively as are men." But in a statement that seemed to run counter to her image and experiences, she warned her fans that it's still "a man's world in spite of the fact that girls have pretty much invaded it. And because it is a man's world, women must protect the most precious thing they have: their reputations." She claimed that modern women still want what grandma wanted: "a great love, a happy home, a peaceful old age." Do not be afraid to be termed a "prude," said Davis. "Good sports get plenty of rings on the telephone, but prudes get them on the finger. Men take good sports *out*—they take prudes home . . . to Mother and Dad and all the neighbors."[15]

When the war came to an end, the domestic messages that prevailed throughout the conflict now focused on the needs of the returning veterans. The 1946 film *The Best Years of Our Lives* charts the story of three returning veterans who come home broken in mind, body, and spirit. They need the care and tending of strong, courageous women who restore their emotional and psychological health, as well as their manhood. The film was a huge box-office success and swept the Academy Awards, winning seven Oscars including best picture.

Advice writers urged women to be sensitive to the needs of the returning veterans, since the men's battles were not all behind them. Warning of the white-collar world in which many postwar men found their manliness at risk, *Photoplay* exhorted women to take responsibility for building up the male ego: "Think about [men's] problems for a minute. [They] spend their lives fighting a competitive world. . . . They may fight sitting behind a big mahogany desk, or they may fight in a lesser job. . . . They need to escape the doubts the best of them entertain about themselves. So they seek a girl who . . . soothes their ego because, attractive enough to have other men, she chooses them. Who by virtue of her own good spirits leads them to relax and have fun." Added Wanda Hendrix, the movie-star wife of a veteran, "Anyone who really loves a war veteran will try to understand him and do everything she can to make his adjustment easier."[16]

Popular magazines advised women to cultivate "that romantic look. . . . Will you be like the ideal the boys carried in their hearts when they were overseas, a girl softly feminine, wistful and gay?" Tough, gritty women were no longer idealized; softness was back. "Listen to your laughter . . . let it come easily, especially if you're with boys who have had little to laugh at for too long. Laugh at the silly things you used to do together. . . . And if you hear your laugh sound hysterical, giddy or loud, tone it down. . . . Serenity is the wellspring of the romantic look. . . . This Christmas, with our men home, surely we should know serenity. So let us look happy and contented and starry-eyed."[17]

These themes represent a dramatic departure from the advice prevalent in the 1930s, which urged women to follow their own ambitions, even if it put their chances for a happy marriage at risk. These messages suggested that Hollywood couples in the 1940s no longer competed in their careers, like their 1930s counterparts whose marriages eroded. The prototypical happy marriage in the 1940s was that of Ronald Reagan and Jane Wyman. In a prophetic 1946 feature article that hinted at Reagan's future political career, *Photoplay* pointed to what seemed to be the key to their success: "First of all there is no professional jealousy." Jane teased Ronnie at their poolside: "Go away, you bother me. Go get the world straightened out and then maybe I'll talk to you." The writer commented, "Rest assured, if it were up to Ronnie, he's the one man who could do it!" A few years later, however, as Wyman's career soared while Reagan's faltered, the duo divorced. Reagan then married Nancy Davis, an actress who promptly agreed to give up her career to be a full-time wife and mother.[18]

Overall, then, Hollywood's professed advocacy of gender equality evaporated during the forties. Two positive images of women had shared the limelight during wartime: the independent heroine and the devoted sweetheart and wife. After the war, as subservient homemakers moved into center stage, emancipated heroines gave way to predatory female villains. Even Wonder Woman lost some of her feminist characteristics and became more dependent on men. The dramatic shift in the popular culture raises a fundamental question: Why did the emphasis on domesticity emerge in the era of Rosie the Riveter? Clues to this apparent irony are found in what some historians consider to be the most substantial change of the 1940s: the entry of an unprecedented number of women into the paid labor force. In examining who these women were and what they did—particularly their long-term opportunities—one can see that the possibilities for employed women were much more limited than they seemed.[19]

Women entered jobs at the beginning of the 1940s with tremendous disadvantages. In 1939, the median annual income of women was $568—and

$246 for black women—compared to $962 for men. By 1940, only 9.4 percent of union members were women, although women were 25 percent of the operatives. Women had few bargaining levers with which to improve their working conditions. Considering the strong sentiment against female employment that had prevailed in the 1930s, it is not surprising to find that even feminist organizations stressed women's need to work over their right to employment—a strategy that underscored women's responsibilities to their families.[20]

Moreover, young married women, those most likely to have children at home, made the smallest gains in employment over the decade—less than pre-war predictions would have indicated. Because single women had been the largest proportion of paid female workers before the war, the demands of production during the 1940s quickly exhausted the supply. Few young single women were available, for with the war came a rapid drop in the marriage age and a rise in the birthrate. Thus, young women who might have been expected to spend a few years holding a job were now marrying and having children; once they had small children, they were encouraged to stay home.

Although some day care centers were established for the children of employed mothers, they were generally considered harmful to a child's development. Public funds were not allocated for day care centers until 1943, and even then, the centers provided care for only 10 percent of the children who needed it. Americans were reluctant to send their children out of the home for care. Most no doubt shared the sentiments of the public official who proclaimed that "the best service a mother can do is to rear her children in the home."[21]

The decline in the number of employable young women led to the employment of numerous older married women. These women were the fastest-growing group among the employed, a trend that would continue after the war. During the war, the proportion of all women who were employed rose from 28 percent to 37 percent, and women were 36 percent of the civilian labor force. Three-fourths of these new female employees were married. By the end of the war, fully 25 percent of all married women were employed—a huge gain from 15 percent at the end of the 1930s. Because most of these workers had spent their early adult years as homemakers, they were unlikely to enter careers that required training and experience and that had a significant potential for good pay, advancement, or job security. As a result, their large number contributed to the increasing segregation of women into low-level "female" jobs.[22]

Rosie the Riveter was the notable exception, but the women she represented were a temporary phenomenon. Nearly all the "men's jobs" filled by women went back to men when the war ended. Even during the war, both the popular literature and the politicians exhorted married women to return to their domestic duties, and single women to relinquish their jobs and find husbands when the hostilities ceased.[23] This advice reflected not only the affirmation of home and family, but the prevailing suspicion of women—especially unmarried women—who entered the world of men.

During the war, commentators often portrayed single women as potential threats to stable family life and to the moral fiber of the nation. A typical wartime pamphlet warned, "The war in general has given women new status, new recognition. . . . Yet it is essential that women avoid arrogance and retain their femininity in the face of their own new status. . . . In her new independence she must not lose her humanness as a woman. She may be the woman of the moment, but she must watch her moments."[24] This theme echoed through the prescriptive literature written during the war. One textbook explained why women had to watch their moments so carefully: "The greater social freedom of women has more or less inevitably led to a greater degree of sexual laxity, a freedom which strikes at the heart of family stability. . . . When women work, earn, and spend as much as men do, they are going to ask for equal rights with men. But the right to behave like a man [means] also the right to misbehave as he does. The decay of established moralities [comes] about as a by-product."[25] In this remarkable passage, the authors stated their opinion, as if it were a scientific formula, that social freedom and employment for women would cause sexual laxity, moral decay, and the destruction of the family. Such assumptions were widely shared. Many professionals and observers agreed with the sociologist Willard Waller that women had "gotten out of hand" during the war.[26]

The independence of wartime women gave rise to fears of female sexuality as a dangerous force on the loose. The iconography that decorated thousands of fighter planes, for example, reflects the association between sexy women and aggressive power (see Figure 8). But if such erotic force were unleashed within the nation (rather than against its enemies), the results could be disastrous. An increase in "promiscuity" was one of the greatest fears surrounding women's wartime independence. The term itself applied to women's sexual behavior, not to men's. This worry extended beyond the traditional fear of prostitutes and "loose women" to include "good girls" whose morals might unravel during wartime. Men were to avoid such women, as if they were predators. "She is more dangerous to the community than a mad dog," warned a federal committee. Men would "succumb" unless they were wary and controlled. Women in wartime suddenly appeared as aggressors, threatening to weaken the war effort and the

FIGURE 8   This example of World War II "nose art"
adorns the front end of a B-29 bomber, as the man on top
adjusts the ammunition in the gun turret. Thousands of
similar erotic motifs adorned fighter planes during the
war, suggesting that the iconography, like the machine of
war it decorated, held the potential for aggressive,
destructive force. (*Courtesy of National Archives, photo
no. NWDNS-342-FH-3A45736-557b3AC.*)

family. Soldiers and happy homes would be the sorry victims of female sexuality
on the loose.[27]

To keep their behavior and aspirations focused on the home, experts urged
women to remain "pure" for the soon-to-be-returning men. At the same time,
they warned men to avoid contact with single women for fear of catching venereal diseases. As historian Allan Brandt has shown, wartime purity crusades
marked a revision of the germ theory: Germs were not responsible for spreading
disease, "promiscuous" women were. Widely distributed posters warned soldiers
that even the angelic "girl next door" might carry disease. "She may look
clean—but . . ." read one caption next to a picture of everybody's sweetheart.[28]

These sentiments reflect widespread fears that single women might not be willing to settle down into domesticity once the war ended. Perhaps the anxieties stemmed from the fact that, unlike the 1930s, the war years brought a noticeable number of women out of their homes and traditionally sex-segregated jobs into occupations previously reserved for men. In addition, the war removed men from the home front, demonstrating that women could manage without them. Single women now became targets of government-sponsored campaigns urging women back into their domestic roles.

Although wartime did contribute to intimacy, romance, and sexual encounters with or without marriage, there is no evidence that these relationships dampened Americans' enthusiasm for marriage. In fact, more families were formed than torn asunder during the war. Even in 1946, the most disruptive year for families, the marriage rate increased more precipitously than did the divorce rate. Nevertheless, many observers continued to fret about the new economic and sexual independence of women and its potential effect on the family. Wartime ushered in a fear of all forms of nonmarital sexuality, a fear that had been dormant since the Progressive Era and that continued in the postwar years. This preoccupation ranged from a concern about prostitution and "promiscuous" women to fierce campaigns against homosexuals and other "deviants" in military as well as civilian life.[29]

The employment of women during the war, then, created a great deal of ambivalence. While officials encouraged women to enter the paid labor force, their public presence gave rise to concerns about the long-term effects of the changes that were taking place while the men were overseas. These concerns were eased by viewing women's jobs as temporary extensions of patriotism and domestic responsibilities that resulted from the emergency situation. Above all, women were expected to remain "feminine"—a term that implied submissiveness and allure along with sexual chastity—and to embrace domesticity after the war.

Nowhere was this ambivalence more obvious than in the military. For the first time, the armed forces actively recruited women to enlist, and to enter every part of the military service except combat. As Oveta Culp Hobby, director of the Women's Army Auxiliary Corps (WAACS), proclaimed, women "are carrying on the glorious tradition of American womanhood. They are making history! . . . This is a war which recognizes no distinctions between men and women." To the female Americans she hoped to recruit, she said, "This is YOUR war." Women of "excellent character" who could pass an intelligence test could join the WAACS, provided they had no children under age fourteen; and unmarried, healthy women with no dependents under age eighteen could enlist in the WAVES (Women Appointed for Voluntary Emergency Service, a U.S. Navy organization). A WAVE who married might remain in the service, as long as she had finished basic training and her husband was not in the service. The birth of a child brought an "honorable discharge."[30]

At first glance, it appears that the armed forces offered dramatic new opportunities for women. But on closer examination, it is clear that these wartime endeavors were temporary. It was impossible to combine jobs in the service with family life. Moreover, to dispel prevailing notions that military work would make women "masculine" or ruin their moral character, the armed services portrayed female recruits as "feminine" and domestically inclined. For example, the caption to a photograph of a young WAVE in a guidebook for women in the armed services and war industries described her as "pretty as her picture . . . in the trim uniform that enlisted U.S. Navy Waves will wear in winter . . . smartly-styled, comfortable uniforms . . . with a soft rolled-brim hat." Women in the military were needed for their "delicate hands" and "precision work at which women are so adept," and in hospitals, where "there is a need in a man for comfort and attention that only a woman can fill." Women's corps leaders did little to challenge prevailing notions about female domesticity; they assured the public that after the war, enlisted women would be "as likely as other women to make marriage their profession."[31]

These publicity measures met with only partial success amid public sentiment that was suspicious of women in nontraditional roles. In fact, rumors about the supposedly promiscuous sexual behavior and scandalous drunkenness of female recruits were so widespread that the armed forces had to refute the charges publicly. One result was the institutionalization of the double standard in the military: Men were routinely supplied with contraceptives and encouraged to use them to prevent the spread of venereal disease, but women were denied access to birth control devices. In the rare cases in which sexual transgressions were discovered, women were punished more severely than were men.

Wartime also revived a long-dormant concern about lesbianism. The mobilization encouraged female camaraderie in military as well as civilian life, raising suspicions that were translated into public policy. Although enlisted women could be dismissed for lesbianism, few were. The armed services were reluctant to enforce such policies because they did not want to acknowledge that military life fostered the development of lesbian relationships and communities. Calling attention to this fact would be more detrimental, they believed, than looking the other way, especially since they were making such strenuous efforts to portray the women's military corps as the training ground for future wives and mothers. Yet the repressive measures established during the war carried over into the postwar years, when the marital-heterosexual imperative became even more intense, contributing to increasing persecution of gay men and lesbians.[32]

Women who took wartime jobs in the industrial sector, like those in the armed forces, were assured that their domestic skills would suit them well in industrial production. Women war workers "have special capacities for work requiring 'feel,' that is minute assembly work and adjustments. Women are especially capable in grinding where fine tolerances are necessary."[33] Automation had reduced the amount of physical strength needed for most jobs, and women's "nimble fingers" were well suited to the tasks at hand. Propaganda efforts launched by the War Manpower Commission and the Office of War Information to draw women into the labor force presented war work as glamorous and exciting, but its main appeal was to patriotism. Patriotism, along with altruism and self-sacrifice, were less threatening motives for women to take jobs because they implied impermanence. Although women had many other reasons for taking war production work—not the least of which was good pay— government propaganda during the war laid the groundwork for the massive layoffs of female employees after the war.[34]

Women's tasks in the home also gained a patriotic purpose. Millions of women were involved in volunteer efforts during the war, such as canning, knitting, saving fats, and making household goods last longer. Just as women's homemaking skills were critical for the survival of their families during the depression, so their domestic work made important contributions to the war effort.

Wartime elevated another female task to a patriotic level: purchasing. Purchasing power has been rooted in patriotic ideals since the days of the Revolution, when Americans joined ranks to boycott English goods and wear homespuns.[35] During World War II, the management of personal finances became a problem of national concern. Bank deposits were at a record high, and spending was frustrated by shortages and rationing. The 6.5 million women who entered the labor force during the war acquired $8 billion more to spend. Since women usually did most of the purchasing for their families, much of the literature on the need for cautious consumerism was directed toward them. One typical example was a 1942 public affairs pamphlet, *How to Win on the Home Front*. The pamphlet addressed the problem of "more money to spend, less to buy." In a section entitled "Mrs. America Enlists," the author encouraged frugality: "In 1942 alone . . . the cost of the war to the consumers of the country is estimated at 3,500,000 automobiles, 2,800,000 refrigerators,

11,300,000 radios, 1,650,000 vacuum cleaners, and 1,170,000 washing machines. . . . The government is taking from the people what is needed to win the war. Consumers . . . must get along with what is left." Housewives were called on to be "militant consumers. . . . Their weapons are intelligent buying, conservation, and cooperation. . . . Their budget is their battle plan."[36]

More important than resourceful homemaking and careful consuming was parenting during wartime. Experts warned working mothers "to see that their physical absence from home does not carry over into a mental absence after working hours." War should not undermine women's primary task: "If they carry out their pregnancies successfully, this is the most important patriotic job they can do." If these priorities shifted, "the whole structure of civilization may become undermined." No public official was more adamant on this issue than J. Edgar Hoover, director of the Federal Bureau of Investigation. In a 1944 article entitled "Mothers . . . Our Only Hope," he pointed to "parental incompetence and neglect" as the causes for "perversion" and "crime." War jobs were not appropriate for mothers, Hoover claimed: "She already has her war job. Her patriotism consists in not letting quite understandable desires to escape for a few months from a household routine or to get a little money of her own tempt her to quit it. *There must be no absenteeism among mothers.* . . . Her patriotic duty is not on the factory front. It is on the home front!"[37]

Mothers were praised for doing their job well, but if they were not attentive enough or were too attentive, they became the decade's villains. It was in 1942 that Philip Wylie coined the term "Momism" in his best-selling book *Generation of Vipers*.[38] "Momism," according to Wylie and his many followers, was the result of frustrated women who smothered their children with overprotection and overaffection, making their sons, in particular, weak and passive. As a fervent patriot during the war and a virulent anticommunist after the war, Wylie argued that the debilitating effects of Momism would seriously weaken the nation and make it vulnerable to an enemy takeover.

Wartime posed particular problems, warned one of Wylie's contemporaries, because when husbands are overseas "and the days stretch to twice their normal length, it is a natural temptation to pour all your extra energy and affection into Peter and Polly. After all, you rationalize, I have to take the place of two parents now. . . . This is a dangerous assumption." Another argued that "[a] mother should be a beacon, not a barnacle" and condemned a woman who was "on the verge of a nervous breakdown" because her son received a letter from his draft board. Similar concerns were expressed after the war; a psychiatrist writing in the *Saturday Evening Post* warned that "moms" were responsible for "the appalling number of young Americans whose rearing made them unfit for military service." A mother was criticized for discouraging her daughter's suitors and telling her, "'You have plenty of time for marriage' . . . and Martha foolishly believed her" until she "subsided into genteel spinsterhood." This author warned that during wartime, "increased doses of maternal anxiety and sentimentality will not give [children] the sense of security they need." Above all, according to these writers, a mother was to avoid turning to her children to compensate for her missing spouse. Female sexuality, repressed and frustrated, would become warped and misdirected toward sons in a dangerous Oedipal cycle. The cure was sexual satisfaction in marriage. Until the servicemen returned, women were to busy themselves in healthy ways. When the war ended, husbands were expected to take over their rightful place in the home.[39]

The vast changes in gender arrangements that some feared and others hoped for never fully materialized. Actually, the war underscored women's tasks as homemakers, consumers, and mothers just as powerfully as it expanded their paid jobs. For all the publicity surrounding Rosie the Riveter, few women took jobs that were previously held exclusively by men, and those who did earned less than men. Developments in the female labor force foreshadowed a pattern that continued after the war: the numerical expansion of opportunities flowing into an increasingly limited range of occupations. Although women demonstrated their eagerness for nontraditional work and proved themselves competent, few were able to retain those jobs after the war. As a result, wartime ultimately reinforced the sex segregation of the labor force.

After the war, nearly all the Rosies who had riveted had to find something else to do. Government propaganda urged women to go home as wives and mothers, not only to release jobs for returning veterans, but also to promote the notion that the nuclear family was the foundation of democracy and had to be protected. This effort extended abroad, as American occupation officials in Japan urged the production of romantic movies and other cultural messages encouraging egalitarian marriage in order to foster American-style democracy.[40] In the United States, although women war workers embraced marriage and family life along with nearly everyone else, they did not simply give up employment for full-time homemaking. Even if the potential for a restructured workforce withered when the men reclaimed their old jobs, the promise of altered domestic roles still remained alive. Three out of four employed women hoped to keep working after the war, including 69 percent of the working wives. Somehow, home life would have to respond to the increasing number of married women who would be employed. Family routines as well as power relations would shift if women became breadwinners along with men. But the policies of the government, private sector employers, and even unions made it difficult for women to avoid economic dependence, even if they continued to hold jobs. Although it was still possible for most women who wanted a job to find one, the economic status of employed women deteriorated significantly after the war. Women's average weekly pay declined from $50 to $37—a drop of 26 percent, compared to a national postwar decrease of only 4 percent. Three-fourths of the women who had been employed in war industries were still employed in 1946, but 90 percent of them were earning less than they had earned during the war.

The range of jobs for women in the military also shrank considerably after the war, owing in part to negative public opinion that would no longer tolerate "unfeminine" military occupations for women in peacetime. As a result, women left the armed services. Fewer than half, however, were able to find jobs that made use of the skills they had learned in the military. To make matters worse, these female veterans were considered dependents rather than providers in their homes and therefore were ineligible for many of the important veterans' benefits that were available to their male counterparts.

All female employees found it increasingly difficult to combine the responsibilities of a family with employment. The few child care facilities that had been established by the federal government during the war closed, and mothers of small children faced even more intense pressures to stay home. Two million women left their jobs after the war. The number of employed women aged twenty to thirty-four dropped to one million below the prewar predictions. The retreat of these women made room for more older women to enter the paid labor force in the expanding pink-collar sector. Therefore, the actual number of women in gainful employment continued to rise after the war, even though the range of employment available to them narrowed. Black women were hit especially hard by the restructuring of the female labor force. Although they experienced a slight overall gain, their income was still less than half that of white women at the end of the decade.[41]

The jobs available to these older women did little to challenge domestic power relations. A wife's wages and status were almost certain to be lower than those of her husband; consequently, she posed little threat to his role as breadwinner. Her earnings were more likely to be seen as a welcome supplement, enabling the family to purchase extra consumer goods, especially during postwar inflation, that would increase or even simply maintain the family's standard of living. By 1960, 10 million wives were employed—triple the number in 1940—but fewer than half worked full time. The largest growth was among white-collar workers. Most of these positions were jobs, not careers. In spite of the return to prosperity, the proportion of women in the professions remained below 1930 levels. Polls of employed wives revealed that half were working "to buy something"; a mere one-fifth were working to fill "a need for accomplishment." Only 60 percent said they found self-esteem in their jobs. The limited nature of most women's jobs legitimated employment for married women, while reinforcing women's subordinate position in the occupational hierarchy. For young married women, then, the strain of holding a job may not have been worth the meager rewards. For older married women, however, a job was an acceptable alternative to the full-time homemaker role.[42]

The narrowing opportunities for female employment during and after the war reflected more than mere efforts to keep women "in their place." Just as important was the need to preserve a place for men. The depression had barely lifted before men who were in the prime of their working lives were again wrenched from their jobs. Many of the more than 16 million Americans who served in the armed forces during the war wondered if they would be unemployed when they returned. Wartime surveys revealed a deep insecurity about postwar economic prospects: Seven out of ten Americans expected to be personally worse off after the war, six out of ten anticipated lower wages, and three-fourths assumed there would be fewer jobs. The majority of fifteen hundred business leaders who were polled expected that there would be a major depression with large-scale unemployment within a decade. Enlisted men were equally pessimistic. As *Fortune* magazine noted, "The American soldier is depression conscious . . . worried sick about post-war joblessness."[43]

These dire predictions were not entirely unfounded. By June 1946, the nearly 13 million former soldiers who returned to civilian life faced many difficulties. During one month in 1947, close to 8 million unemployment claims were filed with the Veterans Administration (VA). By the end of 1947, the government had paid nearly $2.5 billion to unemployed veterans. As families doubled up in the face of a severe housing shortage, the government granted more than 800,000 housing loans to veterans in 1947 alone. Along with these economic difficulties were the physical and psychic scars of war. In 1946, VA hospitals treated 37,000 former soldiers as inpatients. An additional million utilized outpatient services, including 144,000 who saw social workers for counseling— double the number in 1944. More than half these veterans were treated for neuropsychiatric conditions.[44]

Under the circumstances, few balked at the advantages given to former ser-vicemen in the way of housing loans, educational benefits, or medical care. Returning soldiers were the nation's heroes, and they represented the collective experience of a generation of American men: After Harry Truman left office, the next seven presidents were World War II veterans. Most of the veterans' benefits were geared toward men, not to formerly enlisted women. Like their civilian sisters, female veterans were expected to become wives and mothers after the war. There they would best serve the needs of the returning soldiers, rather than competing with them for jobs and training programs.

After the war, colleges and universities experienced tremendous growth, largely as a result of the GI Bill and the entry of millions of returning veterans into the schools. The GI Bill, which paid veterans' tuition, along with a living allowance, funneled over 6 million men (and a much smaller number of women)—nearly half the veteran population—into colleges, universities, and other training programs. By 1947, veterans constituted nearly half the college enrollments. Higher education often made a critical difference in occupational opportunities, especially for men. One study noted that regardless of a man's family background during the depression, a college education would ensure his upward mobility.[45]

College enrollments also increased for women during the postwar years, but not at the same rate as for men. Although more women were enrolled than previously, they represented a smaller percentage of the student population. These numerical differences increased the gap between men and women in higher education and contributed to the polarization of the sexes in terms of educational content and achievement. Furthermore, college degrees did not guarantee the same entry into well-paying jobs and careers for women as they did for men. As a result, white women were likely to drop out of college in order to marry.

One study showed that young women in an all-white sample were twice as likely to enter college as their mothers had been but were much less likely to complete degrees. Rather, they were much more likely than were their mothers to marry highly educated men. In other words, college enabled these white women to achieve upward mobility not through their own occupations but by attaching themselves to well-educated men who had good occupational prospects. For black women, the pattern was different. Since most black women expected to be employed, like their mothers and grandmothers before them, college degrees would greatly improve their occupational prospects. Thus, although they were much fewer in number, more than 90 percent of the black women who entered college completed their degrees.[46]

A survey of five thousand women who graduated from college between 1946 and 1949 found that two-thirds had married within three to six years after graduation. Only half these women had been able to find the kind of work they had wanted and for which they had been prepared. Those who had chosen such traditional female occupations as teaching, nursing, and secretarial work were largely successful, but fewer than half who sought work in science, psychology, music, personnel work, or journalism were able to find jobs—2.5 times as many of these women were in clerical work as had planned to be. It is not surprising that these professionally trained clerical workers were the least satisfied with their jobs.[47]

For white middle-class women, then, college was often an entry into affluent domesticity. Many no doubt believed that if they found a suitable mate at college, it made good sense to quit school and marry. By 1956, one-fourth of all urban white college women married while still in college. To do otherwise was a gamble. A woman who decided to postpone marriage, complete her education, and attempt to pursue a career during these years was likely to find it difficult, if not impossible, to gain access to a professional school or to find a job in the occupation of her choice. She might also find her chances for marriage reduced if she waited too long.

College life encouraged women to marry young. As a result of the influx of returning veterans, many of whom were married, the living atmosphere of the colleges changed. Before the war, most colleges had forbidden students to marry. After the war, however, the GIs with wives needed places to live, and the universities were forced to provide living accommodations for married students and to accept them as a natural part of campus life. As a result, young women could marry when they were in school. While their husbands remained enrolled, the wives could drop out and have children. Women were urged to take advantage of their college years to find a mate. As one postwar text advised, "Nothing is to be gained by women's trying to imitate men." With regard to female students, it stated, "chances for marriage are greatly reduced if they do not make a permanent attachment during the college years." Men were also encouraged to marry while they were in school. Wives could be a help to male college students by taking care of their housekeeping needs or working to support them until they finished school. As the *Ladies Home Journal* advised in 1949, "Many young men find that they can do much better work if they get the girl out of their dreams and into their kitchens."[48]

Dropping out of college did not necessarily mean that women lacked ambition or were unable to handle the academic burden. Rather, given the limited advantages that higher education would offer them, especially if they intended to marry—as most did—abandoning college may have resulted from a rational consideration of options, similar to those facing young women who contemplated careers. Postwar Americans believed wholeheartedly that the happiness of men and women depended on marriage. According to one study, only 9 percent believed that a single person could be happy. While higher education and career aspirations would enhance the potential for a man to be happily married, that might not necessarily be the case for women. During these years, women were frequently "leading a contingent life," in which their husbands' aspirations determined their fate as well as their material security. Young women ordinarily had to bend their own potential plans to suit their husbands'.[49] Because of the severely limited opportunities for women in the paid labor force, women who hoped to marry may have believed that continuing with higher education would lead them to career aspirations that would ultimately be frustrated.

Professionals in various disciplines reinforced these expectations. A postwar guidebook provided women with a means of testing their suitability for marriage. The book included a "Test of Neurotic Tendencies" that contained a series of multiple-choice questions. Each question presented the reader with a situation and asked how she would behave. One question described a situation in which a college-educated woman with career ambitions might have found herself: "You are a clerk in a large bank." A new clerk, a man "who is intelligent and ambitious," comes to work beside you. The choices for the reader were as follows: "A. Work harder to show that you are superior to him. B. Be friendly and helpful, since he may be your boss someday. C. Help him as little as possible since that's the way you had to learn." Obviously, neither her ambition nor her seniority counted for anything. The man was expected to move up the ladder and become the female clerk's boss—or perhaps her husband, if she conducted herself properly. It is clear that "B" was the correct answer; the other choices reflected "neurotic tendencies." In keeping with this theme, a marriage counselor summed up the postwar mood in a statement addressed to wives and future brides of returning veterans: "Let him know you now want him to take charge."[50]

Vocational guidebooks and career counselors echoed these messages. They urged women to prepare themselves to earn a living in case of an emergency, or to earn enough money to enhance their families' standard of living. This may have been realistic advice, given the meager employment opportunities for women. Nevertheless, it caused many college-educated women to resent their college training for raising their expectations, and to feel frustrated and bored because their desire for intellectual and creative work, which had been sparked while in college, was unfulfilled. The frustration led many of these female graduates to call for efforts to tailor the college curriculum for women so it would prepare them more properly for their future lives, namely, the role of mother and homemaker. As one female university graduate later recalled, "An appalling number of graduates apparently felt that they should be more adequately prepared for their 'roles as wives and mothers' and suggested courses and reading lists to that end. I was horrified."[51]

She was not the only one who was horrified. Older professional women watched helplessly as early feminist gains were eroded. One woman, who was born in 1885 and was a professor of English at the University of Illinois until her retirement in 1954, wrote this about the college women of the late forties and early fifties: "For those last ten years I felt increasingly that something had gone wrong with our young women of college age. . . . I noted it all with growing alarm and anger. . . . I thought when I started teaching that since the battle to open doors to women had been won, all that was needed was for us to buckle down and show what stuff we were made of. I think I was confident the will was there—I knew the capacity was. But I was mistaken about the will."[52]

Another woman who worked in a campus office while her husband was on the faculty also noticed the pervasive domestic orientation of the female students. By the mid-fifties, she "realized the apathy of the whole campus, compared with the first years of all kinds of political and social questionings, meetings, picketings. . . . It was a total thing." Her sociologist husband polled his advanced undergraduates and "found out that all the girls wanted to have 'four children.' And that he was no longer able to find a girl under-graduate assistant who was interested in preparing for graduate school. Nice girls, smart girls, girls able to do fairly complex statistical work and think clearly. All going to be married right after graduation."

When she and another woman tried to warn these students against early marriage, the two were soon

characterized as bitter, unromantic old witches, in an affectionate kind of way, . . . because we were anti-early marriage. We're both quite satisfactorily married, and I have two boys—it's only in recent years that I've had to go through the ridiculous business of explaining that I love them, that they 'come first' even though I've always worked at some kind of other job. . . . We did try to explain that we weren't unromantic—that was the funniest part, because our whole objection to this all-exclusive domesticity on the campus was that *it* was unromantic! Settling down, boy and girl in the library, making out lists of toasters, washing machines, towels. It seemed to us about the most unromantic thing we could think of, but we never got it across, and settled for being witches.

Domesticity had not been the stuff of romance when she watched the screen heroines of the 1930s: "We considered a movie no good if Joan Crawford was already married to Clark Gable."[53]

The young women of the day would not be dissuaded: They were homeward bound and hoped their college experience—academically as well as socially— would foster their domestic aspirations. Accordingly, educators and counselors during these years endeavored to refashion women's education to fit domestic tasks and advised female students to gear their programs to traditional women's fields. Home economics courses and programs proliferated. Advisers urged women to attend college to become interesting wives for educated husbands, to gain essential training for their future role as expert homemakers and mothers, and perhaps to have "something to fall back on." A 1942 study of higher education argued that the traditional liberal arts curriculum failed to prepare women for their most likely future occupation: motherhood and homemaking.[54] In 1949, *Time* quoted Lynn White, president of Mills College, who bemoaned the fact that "women are educated to be successful men. Then they must start all over again to be successful women." It also quoted a faculty member at Stephens College, Columbia, Missouri, who defended his institution by claiming that "a high proportion of our graduates marry successfully" as a result of the school's "emphasis on marriage and appearance" and their efforts to curb the "directness, aggressiveness, and forcefulness" of their female students.[55]

The education that was fashioned for women during these years prompted a critical response from professional women at the time. A political scientist at Syracuse University, who was a member of the Syracuse Business and Professional Women's Club, complained about the trend toward redesigning college curricula for women "to meet distinctively feminine needs in accordance with the biological role women are destined to play." Nevertheless, even she acknowledged that "colleges could do far more to prepare women for their important tasks as mothers and homekeepers."[56]

Dissenting voices were unable to turn the tide. It would be decades before feminists in great number would protest, "What the universities are offering is an education designed to turn out efficient little suburban housewives with minor marketable skill so they can enrich their children's lives and not disgrace themselves in front of husband's business associates."[57] But at the time, those who bemoaned the trends were overshadowed by those who welcomed the domestication of women's education as a way of meeting a need expressed by many educated women who found few opportunities for careers.

In the long run, preparation for homemaking did not solve the problems of frustration and boredom. The wives in the Kelly Longitudinal Study (KLS) revealed the difficulties these overeducated housewives would encounter. At a time when only 16 percent of all Americans had attended institutions of higher education, two-thirds of the wives in the KLS had attended college, with half graduating and another 18 percent going to graduate school. These women were not far behind their husbands in education; two-thirds of the men had graduated from college and half of those had gone beyond. Most of the men had worked steadily in professional or managerial positions with few interruptions and few job changes. But most of the women had worked only intermittently outside the home. By the mid-fifties, only 40 percent of the wives were employed; 20 percent held professional jobs, 8 percent were skilled workers, 10 percent were unskilled workers, and 2 percent were businesswomen.[58]

After a decade of marriage, many of these women found that professionalized homemaking was not enough to keep their minds alive. Yet they faced few alternatives, other than unpaid community volunteer work or menial, subordinate jobs in the sex-segregated paid labor force. One explained her frustration this way: "This problem of the 'educated woman' learning to accept the monotony of housework and child training with cheerfulness and happiness, has plagued me. I find much greater happiness now that the children are older." Like many other women of her generation, she considered outside work only when her children were in school. But her choices were limited: "I realize now that I probably should have taken outside work the first year or two of marriage—then I might have been able to afford some things not possible on my husband's salary, and I would have appreciated staying at home more. . . . Having been trained in the same field as my husband I have had a close bond of interest with him; however, I feel there might have been richer and more varied interests if I had been trained in another field."[59] These comments reveal the bind in which educated women found themselves. This woman was glad she had training in her husband's field but now wished she had some avenue of endeavor that was her own. Her training geared her toward being his wife, not his colleague.

Several factors inhibited women from entering the same profession as their husbands. The prospects for women in male-dominated fields were slim, especially if they hoped to pursue a career and a family at the same time. Charles and Margaret Rogers, for example, had planned to work together in bio-chemistry.[60] But Margaret decided not to pursue a career with Charles. Charles expressed his "resentment at the way my wife has wasted a fine technical education. . . . I had fully expected she would be a research partner, but she had no real interest in biochemistry or research or even steady work. God knows she works hard enough at volunteer stuff to be worth $7–8,000 a year, but she doesn't use and has forgotten most of her science." Margaret may have been daunted by the limited opportunities for women to excel in scientific professions at the time. She may also have assumed that the partnership would not be an equal one, since Charles believed that he was the smarter of the two. He admitted his surprise when he discovered that he was wrong: "I peeked at her report and found our I.Q.'s were the same, which gave me more respect for her." Margaret Rogers may have found that a separate and autonomous role as a homemaker, including dedication to volunteer work, was a more satisfying alternative than the prospect of being her husband's junior partner or even research assistant.

Margaret's responses to the questionnaire indicate other difficulties in the marriage. She revealed what her husband's responses did not: that he was an alcoholic who was sober only two of the fifteen years of their marriage. Yet, like so many others, she was determined to make the best of the situation and focused on what she had gained. Putting her troubles aside, she rated her marriage highly and wrote that it had given her "a husband and child and the chance to make a home for them. . . . I always wanted marriage more than a career, and I have found the community activities one gets involved in (PTA, Girl Scouts, League of Women Voters, Women's Club, Church) keep you just as busy as a job and are equally stimulating."[61]

In contrast to Charles Rogers, Leon Shaw resented his wife Mildred's pursuit of a career. Before their marriage, Leon delighted in sharing academic interests with his fiancée: "We are both studious and like to study the same things together." But later, that mutuality turned sour, and he complained, "My wife is a 'scholar'—has won her M.A. since marriage and is now working on her Ph.D. in addition to teaching mornings. I feel she spends too much time outside [the] home because our 4 children are all under 11—yet she is miserable when confined to home activity with only social activity outside the home." Leon thought Mildred was "too independent" and had "too much ambition."[62]

Clearly, Mildred Shaw was restless with the role of full-time homemaker. But outside jobs were also a problem, since most employed wives were stressed and exhausted because they were responsible for homemaking tasks as well. As Helen Faber explained, "Having worked since I was 12, always working, never having 2 weeks vacation at once, I've gotten used to my way. Frankly, I don't brood over the condition. There *are* times when I get tired (who doesn't?) when I'm inclined to wish for more money, more time for myself, and a little less tension brought on by my husband's ulcers (he had this condition before our marriage). I'm never sorry for myself just a little worried there is so little time left. And have I done what I wanted?" Obviously, the job did not provide her with the creative outlet she desired: "I've always liked acting (had a few successful years in an amateur group in Hartford), but I couldn't be a mother, run a house, act, and go to work so I gave up the theater. Now my pleasure is taking my daughter to plays, and she seems quite interested. What is to be gained by lamenting what might have been?"

In spite of her disappointments, Helen Faber found contentment in the rewards of family life. Expressing what must have been true for many of her peers, she wrote philosophically about the difficulties of the past and the high priority she placed on stability. If some of her personal needs went unmet, if some of her expectations lowered over time, at least she had achieved a secure and tranquil family life. "We lived through the depression with no financial help from anyone; what we own, where we've gone has been done by ourselves. I love people. My husband can get along without them. It used to annoy me—now, no more. Life is too short and I don't want ulcers. Perhaps my sense of humor helps me. I have many friends and so manage. I also love to read. My husband is kind and considerate and respects me. Our home is neat, congenial, quiet and relaxed. No tension. I think it reflects in our daughter. I have worked to help with doctor and hospital bills when my husband had attacks."[63]

For married women, the choice to hold a job or pursue a career required decisions based on the recognition of real needs and trade-offs. One wife explained her decision this way: "I gave up a promising career as advertising manager in a department store for children. I could have continued it with a leave of absence and had my first child, but I felt I should be a full-time mother. I might have been a garret artist if I didn't marry, but I doubt that, whatever talents I have, I could have lived a true artist's life." She turned her interests into community work: "Now I paint as a hobby and help run an Art League." What she felt she gained, however, was "a much fuller life, emotionally and physically. An aim, a feeling of accomplishment and greater happiness." Another wife explained her commitment to the homemaker role by claiming that she sacrificed "nothing. I gained and gained. [My husband] gave me things I longed for. Social position, nice family, background, the kind of home I wanted, money." It is worth restating that many of the gains she listed would have been difficult for a single woman to attain through the opportunities available at the time in the paid labor force.[64]

These attitudes were shared by other women in the KLS sample. Many who held outside jobs to contribute to household income articulated the stresses of "double duty." One wife poignantly expressed this difficulty. Since her work as homemaker was expected to be her major and most important career, her employment got in the way of that primary responsibility. She reflected, "Working denies me the privilege of being a good housewife and, shall we say, a more patient mother, but I guess we will manage." Almost as an afterthought, she added, "We gals are never satisfied, or are we?"[65]

Postwar women, many of whom had lowered their expectations, came to accept their domestic role as the center of their identity. Given the limited job and career opportunities available to them, it is understandable that many would have chosen to become homemakers and to invest that role with heightened importance. But what about the men who waxed eloquent about the centrality of home and family in their lives? Why did so many husbands insist that their families gave their lives meaning and stimulated their motivations and ambitions? These white middle-class men were the ones who faced few obstacles in their pursuit of higher education and career goals. Yet, on closer inspection, it is obvious that men's opportunities for self-fulfillment at work were also limited by the nature of the jobs they held.

As historian Peter Filene observed, men who had lived through the depression and war wanted "'the good life,' by which they meant security."[66] The trade-off was the loss of autonomy. Men had to "get along" in organizations; work no longer provided arenas for the display of aggressive, "manly" individualism. The public world in which they worked was more "feminized" in that they now had to rely on interpersonal skills. Like their wives, men placed a high premium on security. After the upheavals of the recent past, they were reluctant to take risks for uncertain rewards or advancement and were more likely to settle for lower-paying but secure jobs. They were less likely to turn to industrial society for the promise of happiness and more likely to turn to the family. Even professionals and businessmen were not immune to the forces of impersonalization and diminishing authority at work.

Men's anxieties about security were exacerbated by the postwar reconversion process. In spite of the advantages offered by the GI Bill, thousands of veterans felt dislocated or suffered from the aftereffects of a long and violent war. Concerns about their adjustment were widespread. Many contemporaries feared that returning veterans would be unable to resume their positions as responsible citizens and family men. They worried that a crisis in masculinity could lead to crime, "perversion," and homosexuality. Accordingly, the postwar years witnessed an increasing suspicion of single men as well as single women, as the authority of men at home and at work seemed to be threatened.[67]

Where, then, could a man still feel powerful and prove his manhood without risking the loss of security? In a home where he held the authority, with a wife who would remain subordinate. It is no wonder, then, that many men who hoped their wives would help them in their work resisted equal partnerships and chafed if their spouses insisted on pursuing outside interests. These men had survived the depression and war and struggled to achieve secure jobs to provide a lifestyle of abundance. The mark of success went to those who were good providers. Women, too, endorsed these priorities. In one survey of middle- and upper-middle-class women, two-thirds considered their husband's most important role that of "breadwinner." Family life promised to provide men with the sense of power they were not likely to experience at work. At home, they could see tangible results of their efforts and achieve a measure of respect. It was important for these men to be the unchallenged heads of their households. In spite of the togetherness ethic that stressed mutual decision making and "companionate marriages," postwar Americans believed wholeheartedly that men should rule the roost.[68]

Accordingly, a majority of both men and women in the KLS believed that men should "wear the pants" in the family, with more women than men in strong agreement. Fewer than 10 percent thought it was important that a wife "should have money of her own or should earn her own living by paid employment, and not be financially dependent on her husband." Similarly, only 17 percent of the women and 6 percent of the men thought it was "very important" for a wife to find an outlet for her interests and energies in paid employment; more than half the husbands and wives said it was not important at all. The vast majority, however, believed it was essential for women to devote the major part of their interests and energies to their homes and families. Reflecting women's high stake in the homemaker role, 70 percent of the wives rated this concern at the top of a five-point scale, compared to 54 percent of the husbands. Men were more emphatic about the importance of their authority: Close to half the men and over a third of the women agreed with the statement that it was "unnatural" for women to be placed in positions of authority over men.[69]

In the wake of World War II, then, the short-lived affirmation of women's independence gave way to a pervasive endorsement of female subordination and domesticity. Ironically, the sudden emancipation of women during wartime gave rise to a suspicion surrounding autonomous women that had not been present during the depression. In the 1930s, while single women carved out a respected niche in the public arena, joined by married women who had to seek employment as a result of economic misfortune, the sex segregation of the paid labor force was never violated. Moreover, although gender roles were unavoidably reversed in many homes, such reversals were often experienced as negative results of the disaster. During the war, however, even though the paid labor force remained predominantly sex-segregated, women began to fill many jobs previously defined as "male." Not only were these female war workers accorded widespread publicity, but they were praised for their skills and patriotism. Their war work, however, also appeared threatening because it demonstrated that women could do "men's work" and survive without men. The sexual independence of women also raised fears; many believed it would weaken the nation during wartime and threaten the family later.

In addition to the ambivalence surrounding new roles for women, postwar life in general seemed to offer mixed blessings. Americans had postponed and pent up their desires to create something new and liberating, but unleashing those desires could lead to chaos as well as security. During the war, savings reached an all-time high as people banked one-fourth of their disposable income—more than triple the proportion saved during the decades before and since.[70] People looked forward to spending their money when the war ended, in much the same way as they looked forward to delayed gratifications in other areas of life. While Rosie riveted, men far from home hung pictures of sweethearts and sexy film stars on their walls and looked ahead to going home to sexually charged relationships. But according to widely expressed concerns, too much money, strong women, and too much sex might destroy the dream of the good life unless they were channeled in appropriate and healthy ways. Many hoped that women would be emancipated from their jobs and into the home, which would be enhanced by sex as well as consumer goods. But if all went awry, happiness and security would remain out of reach. The nightmare side of the postwar dream included "domineering" women and economic insecurity, all waiting to overwhelm the returning veterans hoping to get their jobs and their "girls" back.

And so the potential for a new model family, with two equal partners who shared breadwinning and homemaking tasks, never gained widespread support. In the long run, neither policymakers nor the creators of the popular culture encouraged that potential. Instead, they pointed to traditional gender roles as the best means for Americans to achieve the happiness and security they desired. Public policies and economic realities during the depression and the war limited the options of both women and men and reinforced traditional arrangements in the home. Even during the war, Americans were heading homeward toward gender-specific domestic roles. But it was not until after the war that a unique domestic ideology fully emerged.

The end of World War II brought a new sense of crisis. "Peace" was ushered in by nuclear explosions that engulfed two Japanese cities in massive fireballs. Over the debris and destruction, the United States and the Soviet Union glared at each other with suspicion and hostility. It was not the kind of peace that brought confidence in a secure future. As the chill of the cold war settled across the nation, Americans looked toward the uncertain future with visions of carefully planned and secure homes, complete with skilled homemakers and successful breadwinners. The fruits of postwar America could make the family strong; the family, in turn, could protect the nation by containing the frightening potentials of postwar life.

So when Secretary of State Dean Acheson spoke in 1947 of the need to formulate "a mood" to deal with the cold war, he mentioned the "long, long job" the country faced in "getting itself together" to confront the Russians. "The country is getting serious," Acheson said to a country that had been serious for some time. Americans reared amid the depression and the war now had to accept national security as "a perception, a state of mind. . . . The nation must be on permanent alert." The national security state he envisioned would require "money, imagination, American skill and technical help, and many, many years."[71] Such sober prescriptions were not likely to stun a generation that had grown up with emergency as a way of life.

From the Great Depression of the 1930s through World War II and now the cold war, extraordinary national circumstances had created the boundaries within which these Americans made the choices that determined their lives. Their responses to the cold war would be shaped, in large measure, by the experiences of their youth. They looked toward home as a way to bolster themselves against potential threats. One postwar husband, describing this defensive domesticity in unmistakable cold war terms, claimed that his family gave him "a sense of responsibility, a feeling of being a member of a group that in spite of many disagreements internally always will face its external enemies together."[72] As the cold war took hold of the nation's consciousness, domestic containment mushroomed into a full-blown ideology that hovered over the cultural landscape for two decades.

CHAPTER FOUR

EXPLOSIVE ISSUES:
SEX, WOMEN, AND THE BOMB

Last night I was dreamin', dreamed about the H-bomb
Well, the bomber went off and I was caught
I was the only man left on the ground
There was thirteen women and only one man in town
And as funny as it may be, the one and only man in town was me
Well, thirteen women and me the only man around

I had two gals every morning, seein' that I was well fed
And believe you me, one sweetened my tea
While another one buttered my bread
Two gals gave me my money, two gals made me my clothes
And another sweet thing bought me a diamond ring
About forty carats I suppose

I had three gals dancin' the mambo
Three gals ballin'-the-jack
And all of the rest really did their best
Boy, they sure were a lively pack

I thought I was in heaven, and all of these angels were mine
But I woke up and I head for the train
'Cause I had to get to work on time . . .

—BILL HALEY AND HIS COMETS, 1954[1]

B ILL HALEY'S rock-and-roll ballad was one among many examples of the popular culture during the cold war that connected the unleashing of the atom and the unleashing of sex. But the connections went beyond these atomic age sexual fantasies into more frightening scenarios. In 1951, for example, Charles Walter Clarke, a Harvard physician and executive director of the American Social Hygiene Association, published a major article in the *Journal of Social Hygiene* on the dangers of atomic attack. "Following an atom bomb explosion," he wrote, "families would become separated and lost from each other in confusion. Supports of normal family and community life would be broken down. . . . There would develop among many people, especially youths . . . the reckless psychological state often seen following great disasters." The preparedness plan that Clarke devised to cope with this possibility centered not on death and destruction or psychological damage, but on the potential for sexual chaos. "Under such conditions," he continued, "moral standards would relax and promiscuity would increase." Clarke predicted that postbomb rampant sexual activity would lead to a "1,000 percent increase" in venereal disease unless "drastic preventive measures" were taken. He then called on public health professionals to help ensure that, in the event of an atomic attack, there would be adequate supplies of penicillin in potential target areas and "strict policing, . . . vigorous repression of prostitution, and measures to discourage promiscuity, drunkenness, and disorder."[2]

Clarke's preoccupation with sexual chaos may seem absurd in the face of the incomprehensible horror of a nuclear holocaust. Clearly, he did not represent mainstream medical opinion, since his organization had been preoccupied with venereal disease for decades. Nevertheless, his ideas struck a responsive chord among many fellow professionals who shared his concern about sexual order in the atomic age. When he sent a draft of the article to over seventy experts in medicine and public health around the country, most applauded his idea and endorsed his plan.[3] By linking fears of out-of-control sexuality with the insecurities of the cold war, Clarke articulated a symbolic connection that found widespread expression in professional writings, anticommunist campaigns, and the popular culture.

Fears of sexual chaos tend to surface during times of crisis and rapid social change. The depression and the war years were two such times when concern over the impending doom of the family surfaced. Clarke's article and the response it generated suggest that these concerns continued into the cold war era. Much of the anxiety focused on women, whose economic and sexual behavior seemed to have changed dramatically.[4] By articulating the unique form this anxiety took during the postwar years, professionals in numerous fields, government officials, and creators of the popular culture revealed the powerful symbolic force of gender and sexuality in the cold war ideology and culture. It was not just nuclear energy that had to be contained, but the social and sexual fall-out of the atomic age itself. Many contemporaries believed that the Russians could destroy the United States not only by atomic attack but through internal subversion. In either case, the nation had to be on moral alert. Clarke was one of many postwar experts who prescribed family stability as an antidote to these related dangers.

Nonmarital sexual behavior in all its forms became a national obsession after the war. Many high-level government officials, along with individuals in positions of power and influence in fields ranging from industry to medicine and from science to psychology, believed wholeheartedly that there was a direct connection between communism and sexual depravity. The Republican Party national chairman, Guy Gabrielson, claimed that "sexual perverts . . . have infiltrated our Government in recent years," and they were "perhaps as dangerous as the actual Communists." The logic went as follows: National strength depended upon the ability of strong, manly men to stand up against communist threats. It was not simply a matter of general weakness leading to a soft foreign policy; rather, sexual excesses or degeneracy would make individuals easy prey for communist tactics. According to the common wisdom of the time, "normal" heterosexual behavior culminating in marriage represented "maturity" and "responsibility"; therefore, those who were "deviant" were, by definition, irresponsible, immature, and weak. It followed that men who were slaves to their passions could easily be duped by seductive women who worked for the communists. Even worse were the "perverts," who had no masculine backbone.[5]

Armed with this questionable logic, anticommunists turned their wrath on homosexuals. After the war, which had fostered the emergence of same-sex communities and the increasing visibility of gay men and lesbians, the postwar years brought a wave of officially sponsored homophobia. The word *pervert* was used to describe a wide range of individuals, from adults who engaged in same-sex consensual relationships to violent criminals who raped and murdered children. The persecution of homosexual men and women became more intense than ever before. Gay baiting rivaled red baiting in its ferocity, destroying careers, encouraging harassment, creating stigmas, and forcing those who "confessed their guilt" to name others with whom they associated. In 1950, the Senate issued a report on the *Employment of Homosexuals and Other Sex Perverts in Government*, which asserted that "those who engage in overt acts of perversion lack the emotional stability of normal persons. . . . Indulgence in acts of sex perversion weakens the moral fiber of the individual." Like communists, who would infiltrate and destroy the society, sexual "perverts" could spread their poison simply by association. "One homosexual can pollute a Government office," claimed the Senate report.[6]

The Federal Bureau of Investigation (FBI) mounted an all-out effort to discover the personal sexual habits of those under suspicion of subversive behavior, as well as all those who were seeking government employment. State and local governments followed the lead of the federal government in demanding evidence of moral probity as well as loyalty. From private industry to the military, the sexual behavior of employees was considered a legitimate focus of investigation. Sexual "deviants" were allegedly security risks because they could be easily seduced, blackmailed, or tempted to join subversive organizations, since they lacked the will and moral stamina to resist. A former employee of the State Department recalled his job interview, in which he was closely questioned about his sexual habits as well as those of his roommate. His interviewer explained that the information was necessary because homosexuals were easy prey for communists, who used seduction to gain secrets. Once he gained his security clearance and began work as a file clerk, he found huge files detailing the personal sexual histories of numerous individuals suspected of potential anti-American activity.[7]

Historian John D'Emilio articulated the dubious assumptions beneath this sexual side of anticommunism:

> Allegedly slaves to their perverted desires, [homosexuals] stopped at nothing to gratify their sexual impulses. The satisfaction of animal needs dominated their lives until it atrophied all moral sense. Communists taught children to betray their parents; mannish women mocked the ideals of marriage and motherhood. Lacking toughness, the effete, overly educated male representatives of the Eastern establishment had lost China and Eastern Europe to the enemy. Weak-willed, pleasure-seeking homosexuals—"half-men"—feminized everything they touched and sapped the masculine vigor that had tamed a continent.[8]

With such ideas widely endorsed, individuals who chose personal paths that did not include marriage and parenthood risked being perceived as perverted, immoral, unpatriotic, and pathological. Neighbors shunned them as if they were dangerous; the government investigated them as security risks. Their chances of living free of stigma or harassment were slim. As a result of this "lavender scare," hundreds of government employees and many more in other areas of work lost their jobs—far more than those who were fired for being "red."

The persecution of homosexuals was the most blatant form of sexual paranoia linking "perversion" to national weakness, but it was not the only form. The media focused attention on "sexual psychopaths," who, like communists and homosexuals, might be lurking anywhere. The hysteria whipped up by the publicity surrounding an alleged wave of sex crimes reached grotesque proportions in the postwar years. The respondents to the Kelly Longitudinal Study (KLS) were vehement on this matter. A majority agreed, and one-fourth strongly agreed, that "sex crimes, such as rape and attacks on children, deserve more than mere imprisonment; such criminals ought to be publicly whipped or worse."[9]

The specific targets of these crusades were usually men, but women were nevertheless implicated. As temptresses who seduced men into evil or as overprotective mothers guilty of "Momism," women were blamed for men's sexual transgressions that could lead them down the path to communism. Behind every subversive, it seemed, lurked a woman's misplaced sexuality. Psychologists fueled these connections by asserting as scientific fact the theory that the causes of "abnormality" were rooted in early childhood. Mothers who neglected their children bred criminals; mothers who overindulged their sons turned them into passive, weak, and effeminate "perverts." Sons bred in such homes, according to psychologists and psychoanalysts, would find it difficult to form "normal" relationships with women. Experts continued to give advice to mothers to help their sons "develop normally." First on the list was to be a loving wife, rather than a domineering mother: "Which are you first of all, Wife or Mother?" asked *Parents Magazine*. A man is quoted as telling a friend, "But women all get that way after children come—too much mother, too little wife." One young wife discovered her folly just in time and confessed, "My babies were becoming an obsession. . . . And as for Jim, I didn't have any time or energy left for him. He'd become a part of the furniture."[10]

Most theorists believed that women married to strong men who assumed their rightful economic and sexual dominance in the home would channel their sexual energy into marriage. These sexually fulfilled and submissive wives would lavish care on their children and sexual affection on their husbands. Sexually frustrated mothers whose husbands were not in command might turn their perverted desires toward their sons, thwarting the boys' natural masculine development.[11] As political theorist Michael Rogin has shown, films, novels, and popular journals were filled with these themes. Philip Wylie, who gained fame in 1942 as the creator of the theory of Momism, wrote *Smoke across the Moon*, in which a sexually liberated left-wing woman encourages communist infiltration and destroys men. In 1954, Wylie wrote *Tomorrow*, in which he proposed civil defense as a protection against Momism. Wylie's influence extended beyond his popular writings; he also became a special consultant to the Federal Civil Defense Administration.[12]

These sources of popular and official ideology insisted that male power was as necessary in the home as in the political realm, for the two were connected. Men in sexually fulfilling marriages would not be tempted by the degenerae seductions of the outside world that came from pornography, prostitution, "loose women," or homosexuals. They would be able to stand up to the communists. They would be able to prevent the destruction of the nation's moral fiber and its inevitable result: communist takeover from inside as well as outside the country. At the same time, women had to turn their energies toward the family in healthy ways. As long as they were subordinate to their husbands, sexually and otherwise, they would be contented and fulfilled wives devoting themselves to expert child rearing and professionalized homemaking. As loving, erotic mates, they would prevent their husbands from straying from the straight and narrow. And they would raise healthy children to be strong, vital citizens.[13]

The alternative scenario was frightening. The popular culture gave full play to the fears of sex and communism running amok. Millions of avid American readers made Mickey Spillane one of the most successful writers of the decade, with his anticommunist thriller mysteries. In novels like *Kiss Me Deadly* and *One Lonely Night*, foolish or evil women working for the communists try to steal atomic secrets from hapless men who are unable to resist their seduction. In *One Lonely Night*, the hero boasts of his delight in the grisly murders he commits, all in the name of destroying a communist plot to steal atomic secrets. After a night of carnage, the triumphant murderer gloats, "I shot them in cold blood and enjoyed every minute of it. I pumped slugs in the nastiest bunch of bastards you ever saw. . . . They were Commies. . . . Pretty soon what's left of Russia and the slime that breeds there won't be worth mentioning and I'm glad because I had a part in the killing. God, but it was fun! . . . They figured us all to be soft as horse manure and just as stupid." The hero was not "soft as horse manure" because he was able to resist the advances of the female secret-snatchers. Never mind that he was a bloodthirsty murderer; he had the moral stamina to say no to seductive spy women. As he proclaimed with patriotic zeal, "I want to make sure this country has a secret that's safe." Of course, Mickey Spillane's hero was a loner. He channeled his sexual energy into righteous violence. He had to save the nation from its own moral failings because other men were unable to contain their sexual passions. If they had been able to resist temptation and if the women had behaved themselves, there would have been no need for the hero's bloody deeds.[14]

In the postwar years, these sexual-political assumptions did not seem far-fetched. Foreign policy itself rested on well-articulated assumptions about masculine power—a power drawn from sexual potency as well as the moral strength to resist temptation. Consensus academics articulated the need for tough men of will in politics, using prose laden with metaphors of sexual prowess. Arthur Schlesinger, Jr., for example, wrote that postwar leaders in the "Vital Center" brought "a new virility into public life" in contrast to the "political sterility" of leftists and the "emasculated" ruling class. Softness would lead to subversion, "which is why the Doughface so often ends up as the willing accomplice of Communism." Ideologues were "soft, not hard," and displayed "the weakness of impotence," compared to tough-minded American capitalists. Communism was "something secret, sweaty and furtive like nothing so much, in the phrase of one wise observer of modern Russia, as homosexuals in a boys' school."[15] Real Americans were not like that. Husbands, especially fathers, wore the badge of "family man" as a sign of virility and patriotism. There is no question that the social pressure to appear mature, responsible, "normal," and patriotic contributed to the rush into marriage. Even gay men and lesbians used marriage as a cover during these years to escape stigma and persecution.[16]

At the same time, when anticommunism began to destroy careers in Hollywood, a community notorious for its lack of attention to sexual propriety, the screen stars trumpeted their hometown as a paragon of family virtue. Film celebrity Ronald Reagan spoke enthusiastically about Hollywood's high level of church attendance, low divorce rate, and child-centered homes. A Hollywood studio executive told a reporter in the midst of the red scare, "Why, I suddenly find myself beating my breast and proclaiming my patriotism and exclaiming that I love my wife and kids, of which I have four with a fifth on the way. I'm all loused up. I'm scared to death, and nobody can tell me it isn't because I'm afraid of being investigated."[17]

From the Senate to the FBI, from the anticommunists in Hollywood to Mickey Spillane, moral weakness was associated with sexual degeneracy, which allegedly led to communism. To avoid dire consequences, men as well as women had to contain their sexuality in marriage, where masculine men would be in control with sexually submissive, competent homemakers at their side. Strong families required two essential ingredients: sexual restraint outside marriage and traditional gender roles in marriage. The issue of sexuality was central to both.

The 1951 meeting of the Massachusetts Society for Social Health (MSSH), for example, featured a panel discussion of "Social Hygiene in Total Mobilization." Bringing together physicians, clergy, social workers, military officers, and civil defense administrators, the Advisory Committee on Defense Activities of MSSH outlined several areas for discussion, including "promiscuity and prostitution." The MSSH saw the increasing expression of female sexuality, along with the entrance of women into the paid labor force, as two sides of the same dangerous coin. The criticism of women's sexuality and employment was aimed at married as well as single women. These public health professionals argued that inside as well as outside the home, women who challenged traditional roles placed the security of the nation at risk. The experts warned that young women were drawn to public amusement areas that would lead them to sexual promiscuity, while the employment of married women led to "unsupervised homes where both parents are working." The MSSH cited both trends as major causes for the decline of sexual morality among youths and a weakening of the nation's moral fiber at a time when the country had to be strong.[18]

Despite such warnings, the vast number of employed married women did not leave the labor force. Anxiety continued to surround this issue, since an essential ingredient in winning the cold war was the rearing of strong and able offspring. The influx of women into jobs revived not only fears of sexual promiscuity and neglected children, but also the old eugenic cry of "race suicide." Numerous observers expressed concern over an anticipated decline in the birthrate but failed to notice that the baby boom was well under way among all segments of the population. One scholar at Stanford University reported that the most "talented" Americans were reproducing at a very low rate.[19] Presumably, in the next generation, there would be a critical shortage of the scientists and experts needed to sustain American technical superiority and leadership in the world.

A writer in the *Ladies Home Journal* complained that the perceived failure of the educated to reproduce adequately

> undoubtedly has to do with the so-called "emancipation" of women. Every field of life and activity is open to women today, and every year thousands of women leave our colleges and universities determined to make careers for themselves. They marry, but find reasons to postpone having children. Often Nature, as well as birth control measures, assist [sic] them in this. Women who lead very active lives, under conditions of nervous stress and strain, often do not conceive, and when they do, they miscarry. These women are violating their own biological natures; and for this they pay a heavy price. . . . The feminist movement was an attempt to break into "a man's world"—and in the process, through envy, accepted to an alarming extent the values of men.[20]

The alleged dangers of race suicide, sexual promiscuity, and careerism might be avoided by adhering to family values. The containment of premarital sex was central to this effort. Although the ideal of chastity was certainly not new in these years, the behavior advocated for achieving it was. Since the 1930s, when moralists worried that delayed marriage would lead to an increase in premarital sex, many experts had argued for the removal of impediments to marriage. But they still urged restraint for the unmarried. Wartime, however, had caused such a massive unleashing of sex in all its forms that postwar experts realized that repression was no longer possible. They believed that premarital sexual experimentation was taking place to such an extent that calls for abstinence would be futile. The goal now was to teach young people already indulging in "petting" how to keep sex under control.[21]

But sex was already out of control. Alfred Kinsey, with meticulous scientific detail, shocked the nation in 1948 and 1953 with his documentation of widespread premarital intercourse, homosexual experiences, masturbation, and extra-marital sex among American men and women.[22] As if to prove his point about the American interest in sex, the public made his tedious treatises instant best sellers. (Some accused Kinsey of aiding world communism because of his sex research.)[23] In the face of Kinsey's evidence, efforts to achieve sexual repression gave way to new strategies for sexual containment. Marriage was considered the appropriate container for the unwieldy American libido.

Even the most outspoken advocates of healthy sexual expression, such as the noted physician Mary Calderone, advised young people to avoid premarital intercourse. According to Calderone and other sexual liberals, sex education would be the most effective means of channeling sex into marriage. (It is also worth noting that for her advocacy of sex education, Calderone, too, was labeled a "communist.")[24] One method of containing sex was through elaborate courtship etiquette. Dating, a ritual that first emerged in the 1920s, had become an integral part of the youth culture by the 1950s. Before mid century, few articles on courtship appeared in the popular press. After that time, however, articles proliferated telling the dos and don'ts of dating. Experts repeatedly explained that it was up to young women to "draw the line" and exercise sexual restraint, thereby safeguarding the stability of their future families.[25]

Nevertheless, public health professionals, social workers, and popular writers realized that appeals to moral rectitude and patriotism were not likely to eradicate sexuality among young people. They argued that the best way to contain sex was through early marriage. In the postwar years, writers of the prescriptive literature began to advocate early marriage as the prerequisite for a healthy family and sexual life. As one professional explained:

> Psychologists observe increasing difficulties of sexual abstinence for those who have not trained themselves in self-control and filled their lives with absorbing purposes and activities to the exclusion of sexual experience. . . . Marriage is better late than never. But early marriage gives more opportunity for happy comradeship, mutual development and physical adjustment, for having and training children, building a home, promoting family life as a community asset, and observing one's grandchildren start their careers.[26]

Most guidelines gave twenty-one as a healthy age for marriage, and public opinion polls indicated that most Americans agreed. Moreover, it was the woman's responsibility to achieve it. One typical guidebook, *Win Your Man and Keep Him*, stressed the need for young women to cultivate good looks, personality, and cheerful subservience. The authors advised, "If you are more than 23 years old . . . perhaps you have begun to wonder whether Mr. Right would ever come along for you. Your chances are still good; you can increase them appreciably by taking actions which this book advocates." Another text offered a similar rational, scientific formula: "A girl who reaches the middle twenties without a proposal ought to consider carefully whether she really wishes to remain single. If she does not, she should try to discover why marriage hasn't come her way, and perhaps take steps to make herself more interesting and attractive."[27]

The ideological connections among early marriage, sexual containment, and traditional gender roles merged in the context of the cold war. Experts called upon women to embrace domesticity in service to the nation, in the same spirit that they had come to the country's aid by taking wartime jobs. A team of sociologists called for a "new family type for the space age." Women's domestic roles needed to be infused with a sense of national purpose. It was not the first time that motherhood provided the female version of civic virtue. Indeed, as historian Linda Kerber has shown, ever since the era of the American Revolution, the nation's political ideology has held a special place for women as the nurturers and educators of future citizens. This notion of republican motherhood held unique power in the nineteenth century, when women were not allowed to vote but were encouraged to exercise their civic responsibility through enlightened motherhood.[28]

Although at first glance the "new" family type looked like the "old" traditional home with mother as moral guardian, the "space age" mother needed to go beyond inherited wisdom by cultivating professional skills to meet the challenges of the modern era. In addition, unlike Victorian mothers, who were expected to be reluctant sexual partners who tolerated sex for reproduction only, wives in the postwar era were recognized as sexual enthusiasts whose insistence on conjugal satisfaction would contribute to erotically charged marriages. Sexual containment—unlike sexual repression—would enhance family togetherness, which would keep both men and women happy at home and would, in turn, foster wholesome child rearing.

In the years after World War II, female domesticity took a new form to fit the cold war. In addition to sexual recreation, women's homemaking duties would also be purposeful. One new requirement for the professional homemaker was expertise in dealing with the possibility of nuclear war. This new function might fuse women's domestic role to the larger national purpose, as had occurred during the war. The Federal Civil Defense Administration (FCDA), created by President Harry Truman in 1950, was actively involved in developing the concept of professionalized homemaking for the atomic age.

By 1950, the immediate postwar call for international control of the bomb had given way to advocacy of civil defense planning. Now that Russia had the bomb, atomic war could occur "whenever the fourteen evil men in Moscow decide to have it break out," warned the governor of New York.[29] Preparedness was now the key to survival in the nuclear age. The FCDA coordinated the nation's efforts in this regard. Several women, including Jean Wood Fuller and Katherine Graham Howard, held key positions in this agency. Their task was to help formulate and promote the role of American women in civil defense.[30]

Since broad-based governmental programs for evacuation of the population and for public shelters were quickly abandoned as impractical, the focus of the FCDA centered on local and private efforts. Fuller, director of women's activities, played an important role in these civil defense plans, for she was responsible for educational programs to be implemented in localities across the country. Born in Los Angeles, Fuller had been in the retail trades in Beverly Hills prior to World War II. During the war, she served in the Red Cross and the Home Services Corps, and from 1950 to 1954, she was president of the California Federation of Republican Women.

Fuller claimed that women had special skills and qualities that enabled them to cope with atomic war. Her stance fit the increasingly widespread belief that atomic warfare could be waged and survived. During the 1955 test of the atomic bomb in the Nevada desert, Fuller served, as she put it, as a "female guinea pig" in the trench thirty-five hundred yards from ground zero. After the blast, the Los

Angeles *Times* quoted her as saying it was "terrific, interesting and exciting. . . .
My experience this morning shows conclusively that women can stand the
shock and strain of an atomic explosion just as well as men. . . . It also proved
that with the proper precautions, entire communities can survive an atomic
bombing." Glowing from the experience, she spoke of "the beauty of [the mush-
room cloud] . . . the colors and just before dawn you could get a sort of lovely
background."[31]

Fuller's observation of the blast led her to develop a program of "home protection and safety." With chilling cheerfulness, she called for "positive action" to
overcome anxiety about the new age. She was critical of women's groups who
opposed the tests, such as the American Association of University Women, and
urged women to draw on their unique domestic expertise to find new roles suited
to the cold war. Home nursing, including first aid, was one important area; in
the event of a nuclear attack, well-trained women would be equipped to tend to
injured family members. Another skill to cultivate was the power of persuasion.
Fuller urged women to convince public officials to become interested in civil
defense by approaching them "in your own feminine way—but never be belliger-
ent, please." She appealed to rural as well as urban housewives, particularly to
church women: "It's second nature for them to put on large dinners. Aren't they
just perfect naturals for our mass feeding groups?" Along with learning how to
feed the survivors of a nuclear attack, women had to teach the children as well:
"Civil defense training is almost akin to religious training. . . . We must teach
our children protection. . . . A mother must calm the fears of her child. Make a
game out of it: Playing Civil Defense."[32]

One of Fuller's most ardent campaigns was for women to prepare their homes
for a nuclear attack. Radiation, she claimed, was not so dangerous as it used to
be. "Our chances of living through the worst that the enemy can do are greater
than his. . . . We must have a strong civil defense program . . . to help us get up
off the floor after a surprise attack, and fight back and win."[33] Along with other
civil defense experts, Fuller devised several campaigns that drew on women's traditional domestic functions to equip them for a nuclear emergency.

One of the most extensively publicized campaigns was "Grandma's Pantry"—
the home bomb shelter. With the help of the National Grocer's Association,
several pharmaceutical houses, and the American National Dietetic
Association, Fuller drew up guidelines for withstanding a nuclear holocaust. The
campaign appealed to time-honored values and rested on conservatism and nostalgia. Evoking memories of a simpler past, the official government brochure
contained the slogan "Grandma's pantry was always ready. She was ready when

the preacher came on Sunday or she was ready when the relatives arrived from Nebraska. Grandma's Pantry was ready—Is Your Pantry Ready in Event of Emergency?" (see Figure 9). The brochure featured a picture of an old-fashioned and well-supplied kitchen and included a long list of foods, canned goods, medical supplies, and other helpful items, such as first aid kits, soap, candles, buckets, and pet foods. It taught women to rotate canned goods regularly, change bottled water every three months, wrap items stored in glass for protection, and concluded, "With a well-stocked pantry you can be just as self-sufficient as Grandma was. Add a first aid kit, flashlight, and a portable radio to this supply, and you will have taken the first important step in family preparedness."[34]

Many widely publicized disaster feeding drills also took place around the country. Women were instructed how to cook with makeshift utensils, "how to use this and that to make do with bricks and rubble and grates that you might find so that you could cook." They were assured that if they learned first aid, home nursing, firefighting, and how to supply a bomb shelter, they need have no fear of an atomic attack. Fuller taught women how to construct simple shelters in their basements from a large board leaning against a wall. To underscore the importance of this project, she showed detailed photographs of the atomic test in Nevada that depicted child-sized mannequins under shelters still standing after the blast, while those outside the lean-tos were maimed.[35]

A major goal of these civil defense strategies was to infuse the traditional role of women with new meaning and importance, which would help fortify the home as a place of security amid the cold war. Even in the ultimate chaos of an atomic attack, appropriate gender roles would need to prevail. A 1950 civil defense plan put men in charge of such duties as firefighting, rescue work, street clearing, and rebuilding, while women were to attend to child care, hospital work, social work, and emergency feeding.[36]

It is not known how many people equipped their basements according to the plan of "grandma's pantry," but it is known that by the 1950s, civil defense strategies focused on the home had become a major means of simultaneously calming the nation's atomic fears while reinforcing hostility toward the Soviet Union. Experts in nearly every field, from education to medicine, contributed their advice. Even schoolchildren were taught how to protect themselves in case of a surprise attack; teachers would command, "Drop," and children would duck under their desks, close their eyes to avoid blindness from the flash, and clasp their hands around their heads to keep their skulls intact. Once the "all clear" sounded, these children would run home to join their parents in basement fallout shelters. Simple measures such as these were attempts to reassure the public

GRANDMA'S PANTRY WAS READY

Is Your "Pantry" Ready in Event of Emergency?

FIGURE 9   The Federal Civil Defense Administration evoked comforting images of traditional domesticity in its campaign for home bomb shelters, "Grandma's Pantry."
(*Federal Civil Defense Administration.*)

that they could protect themselves against nuclear annihilation. Yet, at the same
time, they intensified the nation's consciousness of the imminence of nuclear
war, raising the specter of sudden carnage. In virtually all the civil defense publicity, safety was represented in the form of the family.[37]

Fuller and the civil defense establishment were not the only ones preoccupied with family bomb shelters. Contractors commercialized the idea by creating
a variety of styles and sizes to fit the tastes of consumers, from a "$13.50 foxhole
shelter" to a "$5,000 deluxe 'suite' with telephone, escape hatches, bunks, toi-
lets, and geiger counter."[38] Moments of increased tension in the cold war, such as
the Cuban missile crisis, sparked flurries of shelter construction. Although relatively few Americans actually built them, private shelters symbolized family
security and togetherness in the face of a frightening world. Whether con-

structed of concrete or created out of well-stocked basements, family shelters contributed to homeowners' pride and became "an important source of reassurance . . . with considerable symbolic value as an anxiety-reducing feature of the environment," argued a Yale psychologist in a RAND Corporation study.[39] Popular magazines poured out numerous articles on the uses of home bomb shelters during peace as well as war. Peacetime uses for the shelters reinforced women's roles as homemakers. As one woman said of her new shelter, "It will make a wonderful place for the kids to play in. And it will be a good storehouse, too. I do a lot of canning and bottling, you know." Other promoters offered shelters to the "harried housewife," who would be able to send her children off to play in sheltered safety.[40]

Rural areas also offered the combined appeals of escape from the threat of nuclear attack and a retreat into a vision of old-fashioned family life—much like Grandma's Pantry. In 1950, the *New York Times* reported that a boom in rural real estate was directly linked to civil defense concerns. While government-sponsored dispersal plans never achieved widespread support, individual families turned to country life for protection. Numerous realtors across the country noted that rural sales had increased dramatically, in some places as much as 100 percent, and that buyers frequently wanted to be far from a city—at least fifty miles from any likely nuclear target. Brokers advertised "country properties for this Atomic Age" and described them as "protected country settings" and "retreats." Buyers came from all socioeconomic levels and ranged from those who placed small down payments on abandoned farms to wealthy purchasers of country estates.[41]

In these ways, civil defense merged with widespread popular wishes for family security. Frequently, marriage itself symbolized a refuge against danger. One of the most explicit symbolic representations of this fusion was the *Life* magazine story mentioned in the Introduction, which featured a couple who descended into their own new bomb shelter just after their wedding. With powerful associations of family togetherness as the first positive step toward survival in the atomic age, *Life* noted that the sheltered honeymoon was purposeful: "Mr. and Mrs. Melvin Mininson this month subjected their budding marriage to the strain of 14 days (the crucial period of fallout danger) of unbroken togetherness. . . . When they emerged last week the Mininsons were in fine spirits and the stunt had produced some useful evidence on underground survival."[42]

Ultimately, bomb shelters were not nearly as widespread as the particular form of family life they symbolically contained. Americans did, however, opt for early marriage, traditional gender roles, domesticated sexuality, and a home life centered on security. Even the ranch-style suburban houses that proliferated across the country seemed to evoke protection. As historian Clifford Edward Clark, Jr., showed, low-pitched roofs, attached carports, and fences surrounding yards gave these structures "a sheltered look. . . . [The] 1950s design standards conceived of the natural world in a simplified and controlled way that eliminated anything that was wild or irregular." Neither the Victorian homes of the nineteenth century, with their bold, stately, and public facades, nor the informal bungalows of the early twentieth century exuded this sense of isolation, privacy, and containment.[43]

In keeping with these images, much of the postwar social science literature connected the functions of the family directly to the cold war. In one study funded by the Ford Foundation, two Harvard sociologists examined sixty thousand "successful American families" to determine what made them successful. Success was defined as the ability to keep children in school through high school. The authors explained the reason for this concern as follows:

> Early in January, 1957, Russia exploded an atomic bomb, and American scientists monitored its fallout of fission products. Non-stop simulated bomber flights in the upper atmosphere were now reported by the U.S. as traveling around the world in about forty-five hours. Trouble arose in the Middle East. Hungary broke into revolution. Then came *Sputnik*, space vehicles, ICBM's and crash programs for training more scientists. The world is like a volcano that breaks out repeatedly. . . . The world approaches this critical period with a grave disruption of the family system. . . . The new age demands a stronger, more resolute and better equipped individual. . . . To produce such persons will demand a reorganization of the present family system and the building of one that is stronger emotionally and morally.[44]

The heart of these professionals' concern was not just the cold war, but "grave disruption of the family system." The key to successful families, they concluded, was stable homes in which men and women adhered to traditional gender roles. Parents should set good examples for their children, stay together and not divorce, and associate with like-minded families that shared common values and moral principles. In keeping with the American tradition, it was up to women to achieve successful families. If women fulfilled their domestic roles, as adapted to the atomic age, they would rear children who would avoid juvenile delinquency (and homosexuality), stay in school, and become future scientists and experts to defeat the Russians in the cold war.

In this vision of the atomic age family, women were the focus of concern. It was important to recognize their increasing sexual and economic emancipation, but to channel those energies into the family. Outside the home (or even inside the home without a strong male authority), they would become a dangerous, destructive force. This message was overtly expressed in the literature surrounding the cold war, civil defense, and the family. So pervasive and lasting was the connection between taming fears of the atomic age and taming women that as late as 1972, a civil defense pamphlet personified dangerous radioactive rays as sexy women. To explain the dangers of fallout, the authors wrote, "Radioactivity is also energy—but this time the rays come invisibly; alpha, beta, and gamma rays cause varying degrees of silent damage. Alpha's cannot penetrate, but can irritate the skin; betas cause body burns; and gammas can go right through you— and thus damage cells, which can make you ill, or kill you. Like energy from the sun, these rays are potentially both harmful and helpful."[45]

Beside this explanation was a drawing of the three types of rays, personified as large-breasted bathing beauties in seductive poses (see Figure 10). Other illustrations in the pamphlet indicated how to find safety by avoiding and containing

FIGURE 10   This illustration from a civil defense pamphlet personifies the three deadly rays of radiation. The pamphlet explained that "these rays are potentially both harmful and helpful," like the sexy women who represent them. (*Your Chance to Live*, Defense Civil Preparedness Agency.)

FIGURE 11   Domesticity represents the safest haven in the face of the dangers of the atomic age. Here Mom, Dad, and Baby huddle in coziness as chaos reigns outside. (*Your Chance to Live*, *Defense Civil Preparedness Agency*.)

these dangers: Mom, dad, and baby huddled together in a home bomb shelter as chaos reigns above, and a detailed drawing of a well-equipped shelter with "Home Sweet Home" tacked on the wall (see Figures 11 and 12). These illustrations made explicit the message that sexually liberated women, like the alpha, gamma, and beta rays, were potentially destructive creatures who might be tamed and domesticated for the benefit of society. Even though the fervor of the cold war had waned considerably by 1972, the images in these illustrations are powerful testimony to the symbolic connections between the fears of atomic power, sex, and women out of control.

These images also surfaced in the wider culture. During these years a slang term for a sexy woman outside the home was a *bombshell*. (Other terms connoting the devastating power of female sexuality included a *knockout* and a "dynamite" woman.) The use of the term *bombshell* to describe a woman first emerged during the 1930s, with the increasing recognition of female sexuality as powerful and explosive. During World War II, pilots named their bombers after their sweethearts and decorated their planes with erotic portraits. The wartime emergency, calling for fashion adaptations that would conserve fabric, gave rise to the two-piece bathing suit, which also appeared dangerous. The *Wall Street Journal* noted ominously that "the saving has been effected in the region of the

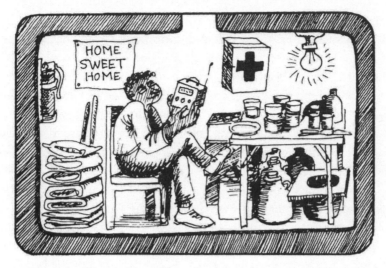

FIGURE 12 "Home Sweet Home" inside a bomb shelter. Note the reassuring effects: the sign on the wall, the first aid kit, consumer goods, and the inexplicably lit lightbulb. (*Your Chance to Live, Defense Civil Preparedness Agency.*)

midriff. . . . The difficulties and dangers of the situation are obvious."[46] In the postwar era, female sexuality continued to represent a destructive and disruptive force. A photograph of Hollywood sex symbol Rita Hayworth was actually attached to the hydrogen bomb dropped on the Bikini Islands. The island itself provided the name for the abbreviated swimsuit the female "bombshells" would wear. The designer of the revealing suit chose the name *bikini* four days after the bomb was dropped to suggest the swimwear's explosive potential.[47]

Similar images infused the popular culture. The words of the 1954 recording by Bill Haley and His Comets, "Thirteen Women (and Only One Man in Town)," quoted at the beginning of this chapter, express the sexual fantasy of a young man dreaming of being the sole male survivor of an H-bomb explosion, with thirteen women to do his bidding. Filled with sexual puns and double entendres typical of rhythm-and-blues lyrics, the song expresses its eroticism in terms of the women's domestic subservience. In keeping with visions of the modern home, the women make his food and clothes, provide consumer goods, and entertain him with leisure pursuits such as dancing. And of course, there is the implicit suggestion of sexual adventures with this "lively pack" of bombshells—a vision that would no doubt cause Charles Walter Clarke and his colleagues in the American Social Hygiene Association to shudder. Yet, like other potentially explosive forces in postwar America, the female bombshell could be "harnessed for peace" within the home. It was widely believed during these years that atomic energy could foster a better lifestyle through nuclear power, which would be achieved by taming the atom.[48] Female sexuality could also be contained and domesticated. Knockouts and bombshells could be tamed, after all, into harmless *chicks*, *kittens*, and the most famous sexual pet of them all, the Playboy bunny.

Symbols of sexual containment proliferated during these years. Even the fashions reflected this image. Gone was the look of boyish freedom that characterized the flapper of the 1920s and the shoulder-padded styles evoking strength of the 1930s and early 1940s. In the late 1940s and 1950s, quasi-Victorian long, wide skirts, crinolines, and frills were back, along with exaggerated bust lines and curves that created the aura of untouchable eroticism. Female sexuality was, once again, contained in stays and girdles that pinched waists and padded brassieres that made women appear to have large breasts. But the body itself was protected in a fortress of undergarments, warding off sexual contact but promising erotic excitement in the marital bed. According to a 1947 poll, women did not like this style but said they would wear it anyway.[49]

At home, sexuality could be safely unleashed by both men and women, where it would provide a positive force to enhance family life. It is no wonder, then, that professionals attempted to promote a vision of the family that would contain the social, sexual, and political dangers of the day and would root the revitalized home in time-honored traditional values. Although conditions had irreversibly changed, Americans refused to abandon the values of the past. So they contained the new realities within the boundaries of old structures, such as Grandma's Pantry. For policymakers concerned with domestic as well as diplomatic issues, containment was the order of the day. Subversives at home, Communist aggressors abroad, atomic energy, sexuality, the bomb, and the "bombshell" all had to be "harnessed for peace."

Containment at home offered the possibility that the modern family would tame fears of atomic holocaust and tame women as well. With their new jobs and recently acknowledged sexuality, emancipated women outside the home might unleash the very forces that would result in a collapse of the one institution that seemed to offer protection: the home. For women, the rewards offered by marriage, compared to the limited opportunities in the public world, made the homemaker role an appealing choice. So women donned their domestic harnesses. But in their efforts to live according to the codes of domestic containment, they were bound to encounter difficulty. Only later did they discover how uncomfortable those harnesses could be.

CHAPTER FIVE

BRINKMANSHIP: SEXUAL CONTAINMENT ON THE HOME FRONT

> Intercourse prior to marriage may have played a deeper psychological part than we then believed.
>
> —GEORGE PETERSON, 1955[1]

IN THE 1940s, Maria Kimball defied the code of sexual containment by engaging in sexual intercourse before marriage. In so doing, she went against the advice of experts who wrote prescriptive literature, anticommunist crusaders, and the teachings of churches and synagogues, which called for the containment of sex in marriage. Yet her behavior was hardly unique. In spite of time-honored taboos and the heavy stigma associated with premarital sex, nearly half Kimball's contemporaries did the same. In an age when the ideology of sexual containment carried such power, what were the implications for individual lives? This chapter explores how sexual containment affected postwar men and women, those who adhered to the codes of proper conduct and those who violated them.

For Maria Kimball, premarital sexual adventures took their toll. Years later, she reflected on the experience:

The freedom of our relations before marriage saved us many stresses and strains we might otherwise have had. On the whole, however, I would say it was unfortunate. Despite his failure to recognize it then—or now, for that matter—I have concluded that my husband has deep emotional conventionality such that the attitudes our "free love" experience fostered undermined his respect and admiration for me. This is pure guesswork—but I think we established a set of "mistress patterns" that had far-reaching unhealthy effects for our marital adjustment. Also it was stupid of me not to anticipate that his oft-expressed philosophy of the desirability of sexual freedom indicated that he would be prone to infidelity. I didn't expect it, and it came as a severe blow. An even worse blow was his amazement at this, and his statement that faith in a partner's constancy is sheer stupidity. I have been faithful, but doubt if he believes this.

This couple, before marriage, freely deviated from prevailing sexual mores. Yet, Maria would suffer for her transgression for years to come. In the eyes of her husband, she became morally suspect, even though he, as well as she, willingly participated in their premarital sexual activity. She believed that his lingering suspicion of her provided him with justification for his own philandering and ultimately poisoned their relationship.[2]

The foregoing account suggests the power of postwar taboos against premarital sexual activity for women. Maria Kimball came of age during a time when the sexual containment ethos was in full force, even though it was widely violated in practice. When Alfred Kinsey published his exhaustive studies of the sexual behavior of thousands of white American men and women in the late 1940s and early 1950s, Americans discovered that some of their most deeply held beliefs about proper sexual conduct were honored more in the breach than in fact.[3] This situation makes it difficult to determine what the "norms" actually were in postwar America. Widely expressed values represented the ideal, while documented sexual behavior indicated the reality. Some critics responded to Kinsey's findings by calling for an effort to bring behavior into conformity with prevailing codes. Others claimed that the studies themselves were subversive of the nation's moral fiber. Critical responses notwithstanding, the unassuming zoologist who authored these best-selling tomes quickly joined the ranks of postwar experts who became household words. Yet Kinsey's "count and catalog" approach to sexual behavior did little to reveal the emotional and psychological dimensions of sexuality.[4]

Maria Kimball's story illustrates the difficulty that scholars face in trying to understand sexuality in its fullest context. Most research investigates behavior alone, which reveals little about the quality of the sexual experience. Even those surveys that attempt to explore attitudes are likely to yield partial or even misleading conclusions.[5] For example, the lengthy KLS questionnaire that Maria Kimball filled out gives the initial impression that she and her partner (later her husband) had a positive sexual relationship. Kimball checked off responses indicating that she was sexually satisfied, well prepared for marriage, and free of guilt about her behavior. It was only in the open-ended questions at the end of the survey that she revealed the complex and troubled nature of her marriage. Hundreds of cases like hers yield insights into the difficulties experienced by postwar couples. Whether or not women and men actually conformed to the containment prescription, they were likely to be affected by its power.

During the postwar years, sexual values as well as sexual behavior were in flux. According to historians Estelle Freedman and John D'Emilio, these years marked the widespread acceptance of "sexual liberalism," which included tolerance for noncoital forms of premarital sex, some measure of "intimacy with affection," a heightened expectation for erotic fulfillment in marriage, and an explosion of sexual images in the media.[6] At the same time, the taboos against premarital intercourse, homosexuality, and other forms of nonprocreative sex remained central tenets of sexual morality. Sexual liberalism notwithstanding, it was in marriage that sexuality was expected to culminate and flourish and to provide fulfillment to both partners.

Sexual satisfaction would safeguard marriage against unhealthy developments that would weaken the family from within. If parents were sexually frustrated, the impact on children might be disastrous. A professor of education at Whittier College warned that "children need happily married parents. . . . When there are lacks in the sharing of satisfaction in sexual relations, some sort of deep and fundamental disappointment occurs. Each partner goes his [sic] way feeling unfulfilled and thwarted, and both find themselves incomprehensibly irritable and tense in situations [in] which the child has a part. . . . The matter, then, of sexual adjustment between the parents was found to be related to children's difficulties and maladjustments to a very important degree." Although the author ended the article with this statement, the postscript could have been written by Philip Wylie or any number of psychologists at the time who warned against the "Momism" that would result from sexually frustrated mothers, who would turn their sons into passive weaklings, "sissies," potential homosexuals, "perverts," or easy prey for communists. Nearly all postwar experts agreed with the advice writer who claimed that "wholesome sex relations are the cornerstone of marriage."[7]

The sexual containment ideology was rooted in widely accepted gender roles that defined men as breadwinners and women as mothers. Many believed that a violation of these roles would cause sexual and familial chaos and weaken the country's moral fiber. The center of this fear was the preoccupation with female "promiscuity," despite the lack of evidence of any significant increase in premarital sexual intercourse at the time. These rates remained stable from the 1920s to the 1960s.[8]

This is not to say, however, that nothing had changed. Rather, the statistics reflect widely held attitudes at the time concerning sexual legitimacy. Most studies measured the frequency of *premarital* sex. The critical factor in these studies was whether the sexual partners were married. If the figures are determined instead according to age, one finds that men and women were engaging in intercourse at a younger age and that many of these young couples were married. It appears, then, that the rates of premarital intercourse remained stable because early marriage legitimated the widespread practice of sexual intercourse among young adults.[9] Teenage sex was rampant, but most of these teenagers were married.

Early marriage was one way to bring changing behavior into conformity with the codes prohibiting premarital sex. In addition, the taboo against premarital sexual intercourse, along with the double standard, continued to place on women the burden of "holding out" until marriage.[10] Why did young people accept these sexual taboos? The preconditions for large-scale challenges to them were certainly present during the postwar years. Contraceptive devices were increasingly available, job and educational opportunities for women expanded, and dating was a means of gaining privacy and intimacy before marriage. Given these circumstances, young women and men might have chosen to establish sexual relationships more frequently and to postpone marriage, but they did not. Rather, they turned to marriage earlier, with heightened expectations for sexual fulfillment.[11]

Sexual attraction was an important component in the choice of a mate—too important, according to some observers at the time. One postwar sociologist and marriage counselor, reflecting the current faith in science and expertise, called for the rational selection of a mate: "[When] the methods of science are applied to . . . the way men and women interact in marriage, we have the means for greater personal development than ever before in history."[12] Another writer provided a formula for "real love" that reflected the trend toward the increasing sexual expectations for marriage. The exact proportions he recommended were "60 percent profound affection and respect [and] 40 percent intense sex attraction." He said this was a rare mixture but if found, "you can be fairly sure that you'll get the happy, fantastic, fairy-tale result." Unfortunately, he said, most unions were based on 70 percent sexual attraction and 30 percent genuine affection, which would be more likely to lead to divorce. His speculation reveals his recognition of the long-term twentieth-century trend toward sexual attraction as a basis for marriage. It is interesting to note that although he thought this trend had gone too far, he devoted a substantial proportion of his formula for marital success to sexuality—affirming the postwar concern with the importance of sex as long as it was contained in marriage.[13]

These ideals found support not just among experts and journalists, but among their audiences. Men and women in the KLS shared the belief that sexual fulfillment was central to a successful marriage. The study itself attests to the heavy weight placed on sexual matters at the time. The questionnaire included over sixty items on sexual attitudes and behavior, such as premarital experience, sex education, conjugal relations, and extramarital affairs. When the respondents were first surveyed before their marriages, they were asked why they chose their particular mates and why they believed their marriages would be successful. Physical attraction was listed frequently as a reason for choosing a mate, and sexual compatibility was considered a major criterion for a successful marriage— even among couples who had refrained from intercourse.[14] One man wrote, "I like particularly her size and form and think she is an attractive and sweet girl. . . . She attracts me strongly, physically." Others wrote that "sexual desire" was a major factor, that the two were "passionately attracted to each other," or that they were "attracted to one another sexually and spiritually in a very satisfactory manner." Women were also likely to mention physical appeal as a reason for choosing a mate; one noted that her fiancé was "easy on the eyes."[15]

The respondents agreed on the importance of sexual compatibility and exclusiveness within marriage. Yet there was no consensus on how compatibility should be determined before marriage. As one wife explained, "Looking back on it, I do not believe I gave the matter [of sex] anywhere nearly enough thought or consideration. Appreciating, as I do now, the importance of a normal, satisfying sexual relationship between husband and wife, I marvel at my good fortune in being lucky enough to have married a man who *is* suited to me, sexually, and vice versa. On further thought, I don't really know how I would have gone about finding out, had I been concerned."[16] Most couples expected to engage in a limited amount of sexual experimentation before marriage, provided it was kept in check—usually by the woman—and stopped short of intercourse. This delicately balanced intimacy with restraint was supposed to lead to a sexually satisfying marriage.

The path toward marriage began at a young age. High school provided an important institutional framework for dating rituals. Students established an elaborate, peer-enforced code of dating as early as the 1920s. As high school enrollments increased in the 1930s and 1940s, dating became nearly universal among teenagers. By the post–World War II period, as historian John Modell noted, "the whole schedule of dating was accelerated."[17] For women, training in the art of attracting dates began early. The *Ladies Home Journal* offered advice to fourteen-year-old girls who had not yet dated. The "Late Dater" was encouraged to develop social skills, poise, and charm. The article reassured young readers that it was not yet too late to attract a beau. Once caught, he was to be held at bay, while she gave all the appropriate signals to promise sexual excitement in marriage.[18]

The key was allure. Everywhere they turned, young women found instructions on "how to catch a husband" or "how to snare a male." But this catching and snaring was to be accomplished passively, with bait rather than a net. Never "give a man the idea you are running after him; pretend to let him catch you" was the rule. Young women were encouraged to "concentrate on your companion's feelings instead of your own" and "learn to talk about things that interest men." Above all, it was essential to "arouse and hold a man's interest."[19] A psychologist at Pennsylvania State University offered his professional expertise to readers of the *Ladies Home Journal* who "don't get dates." He asked "hundreds of single men" on campus and reported that dateless girls were guilty of careless grooming (grooming was a "consolation and challenge to the girl who feels her unattractive face or figure prevents her getting dates"), unsuitable clothes, poor dancing, coldness, unattractive appearance, or aggressive behavior.[20]

Youthful attractiveness held the promise of conjugal bliss. Marriage manuals of the 1920s and 1930s turned away from the old ideal of restraint in marriage; by 1940, experts had fully articulated the "cult of mutual orgasm."[21] Yet that sublime state of mutuality was not to be entered until after the wedding. The system of dating was supposed to provide the boundaries within which young people could find a suitable marital match. But it was an imperfect system that left many contradictions unresolved. With such a highly charged youth culture and sex permeating the media, it is no wonder that so many Americans broke the rules and engaged in sexual intercourse before marriage. Ideology and conduct were at odds. To understand the persistent power of sexual codes in the face of such challenges, it must be examined as part of the prevailing domestic ideal.

The KLS data illuminate the centrality of the dating system as a prelude to marriage, as well as its problematic aspects. Over one-third of the women and one-fifth of the men in the sample were dating by age fourteen; 75 percent and 65 percent, respectively, were dating by age sixteen. Few said that their spouses had been the "one and only"; most said they dated a number of people, and about half said they had loved at least one other person before becoming engaged. Ideally, this sort of relatively informal "shopping around" would lead to ease and familiarity between young women and men, which would enable them to make a wise marital choice. But dating did not always yield that comfortable familiarity. Only about one in five of the men and the women said they had been "very comfortable and relaxed" in relationships with the opposite sex before their engagements; half said they were "pretty much at ease," and the rest said that they were ill at ease.[22] Much of this discomfort no doubt resulted from sexual tensions, as couples struggled to define the line between appropriate expressions of affection and "going too far."

The majority of the KLS respondents experienced "much intimacy" but no intercourse, indicating that most couples "held the line" until marriage. Nevertheless, more than 40 percent reported they had intercourse with their future spouse, although fewer than 20 percent said they had engaged in "frequent intercourse" prior to their marriages. Nearly three times as many men as women had intercourse with someone other than their future spouse. When the women did do so, it was usually with persons for whom they "felt considerable affection"; fewer than 1 percent of the women, compared to 22 percent of the men, said they had intercourse with "casual dates or acquaintances." When asked about the extent of their physical relationships with all the people they had dated, including their future spouses, 62 percent of the men but only 44 percent of the women said they had intercourse. In other words, nearly 20 percent of the men in the sample admitted to intercourse with someone other than their spouses-to-be but waited until marriage before having intercourse with their fiancées.[23]

These statistics are consistent with Kinsey's findings that 50 percent of the women in his study had experienced premarital intercourse, regardless of educational level attained, as had 68 percent of the college-educated men. Kinsey's studies provide useful comparisons, for like the KLS respondents, Kinsey's samples were all white. Unlike the KLS, however, Kinsey's study included respondents from a wide range of socioeconomic and educational levels. Kinsey noted that men frequently engaged in premarital intercourse with women of a lower social class, rather than with partners from their own class, which would explain some of the discrepancy between the responses of college-educated women and men in both the KLS and the Kinsey studies.[24] At the same time, Kinsey noted an increase in petting among all groups and associated it with efforts to contain premarital intercourse. As one contemporary observer noted, the "ideal girl" on the college campus "has done every possible kind of petting without actually having intercourse. This gives her savoir-faire, while still maintaining her dignity."[25] This sexual brinkmanship provided a means for women to engage in sexual activity without "going too far." "To some extent," reported Kinsey, "petting is the outcome of the . . . attempt to avoid premarital intercourse. . . . In a number of cases, the specific record indicates that there would have been intercourse if petting had not supplied an outlet."[26]

The findings by scholars such as Kinsey and Kelly indicate that although there was widespread premarital intercourse, marriage was likely to follow very soon after, especially for women. Sexual pressure or guilt may have encouraged sexually active young people to marry sooner than they might have otherwise. It may even have affected their choice of a marriage partner, for if a relationship culminated in marriage, the stigma softened. As one study concluded, "Values have probably changed . . . at least to the extent that more girls accept premarital coitus *if* there is an emotional involvement with the partner and some commitment by him to marriage in the future."[27] The data indicated that these pressures may well have encouraged sexually active or sexually frustrated couples to hurry into marriage. If sexual intercourse took place, the couple—or at least the woman—might be inclined to legitimate the behavior by marrying her sexual partner. If intercourse was postponed, the couple might hurry their marriage in order to engage in sex. The KLS data suggest that the effort to legitimate sex within marriage was a major factor in the drop in the marriage age during these years. The findings support Modell's conclusion that "there can be little question that the success of the dating system placed a downward pressure on the age of marriage."[28]

The account of one woman illustrates this connection. This wife mentioned that because of her "background from Puritanical training," she was very uncomfortable about her premarital sexual experience: "The fact that we had been intimate, I am certain, made my mind set for marriage to him." It was not a good enough reason, for later she lamented her "poor choice of mate," whom she subsequently divorced. Nevertheless, it was clear that sexual activity propelled the relationship toward marriage. Kinsey found a similar trend: Women felt less guilt if they married the man with whom they had been intimate. Of those who married their premarital sexual partner, only 9 percent said they regretted having had intercourse prior to marriage, compared to 28 percent of those whose relationships did not result in marriage.[29]

All the evidence, from the popular culture to experts like Kinsey and Kelly, indicates that postwar Americans expected to find sexual enjoyment and legitimacy once they married. But marriage did not always provide total fulfillment of this expectation. Guilt and the stigma of "promiscuity" combined to make premarital sexual activity a particular problem for women, even if the relationship culminated in marriage. One researcher explained the subtle ways in which prevailing attitudes could ultimately undermine a relationship: "The double standard male usually wants the girl to whom he is committed to be 'good,' and he may feel he has to redefine her as 'bad' if his relationship with her becomes sexual."[30] So in spite of the increasing emphasis on sexual gratification, the double standard of sexual morality was still alive and well in the postwar era.

Premarital sex was, therefore, much riskier for women than for men. A woman's reputation was so deeply tied to her sexual behavior that fear of exposure was often intense. One wife confessed, "I was afraid that someone might have learned that we had intercourse before marriage and I'd be disgraced." Of those women in Kinsey's study who indicated why they were reluctant to engage in premarital intercourse, equal proportions attributed their reluctance to fear of pregnancy and fear of public opinion. But since most of them said that only their partners would know, "public opinion" most likely reflected their and their partners' attitudes toward the activity. Kinsey concluded that guilt was the major factor inhibiting premarital sexual activity: "Behavior which is accepted by the culture does not generate psychologic conflicts in the individual or unmanageable social problems. The same behavior, censored, condemned, tabooed, or criminally punished in the next culture, may generate guilt and neurotic disturbances in the nonconforming individual and serious conflict within the social organism."[31] Kinsey's observations were echoed by one husband, who noted that he did not realize the importance of sexual relations before his marriage. "Our civilization," he said, "is not in harmony with early sexual intercourse. This is something in which the primitive civilizations excel ours."[32]

Since women were the ones who suffered the stigma of violating the taboo, not to mention the possibility of pregnancy, they had the most difficult time walking the tightrope between sexual allure and the emphasis on virginity that permeated the youth culture. Kinsey found that nearly half the men surveyed wanted to marry a virgin, even though most men did not think that premarital intercourse was morally wrong. The exception was college-educated men, 61 percent of whom disapproved of premarital coitus. Among women, fully 80 percent had moral objections, even though 50 percent had themselves experienced premarital intercourse. Kelly also asked his respondents to indicate their level of agreement with prevailing sexual mores. When asked how important it was for couples to remain chaste prior to marriage, 21 percent of the women compared to 14 percent of the men said it was "essential," and 24 percent of the men and 30 percent of the women said it was "desirable." Only 12 percent of the women and 14 percent of the men thought it was undesirable to wait, yet nearly four times that many had actually waited themselves.[33]

When the responses to these questions were correlated with individual experiences, it is interesting to note that many of the respondents disapproved of their own behavior. As one man wrote, "Experiences before marriage showed we were sexually compatible and did not unfavorably affect relations after marriage at all. . . . I would not, however, recommend the general habit of premarital coitus in our society at the present day." Of those who believed it was *essential* to wait until marriage before engaging in intercourse, only two individuals failed to hold the line, but nearly all the rest had experienced a great deal of physical intimacy before marriage. Over a fourth of those who felt it was desirable (but not essential) to wait had not waited themselves. Of those who believed that premarital intercourse *was* desirable, 60 percent had experienced it, but 40 percent had not. Regret, then, was not uncommon even among those who had abstained.[34]

With so much tension and such high stakes surrounding premarital sex, it is no wonder that marriage did not always measure up to the expectations brought to it. Disjunctions between attitudes and behavior were at times so profoundly disturbing that they could fester for years within a marriage, as was the case with Maria Kimball, quoted at the beginning of this chapter. Her sense of disappointment and loss was not unique. Another woman whose marriage ended in divorce said that her husband "was exceedingly jealous of me and any friendly attentions from either men or women to me for which there was no foundation. I think he felt that because we had been intimate before marriage that I could be as easily interested in any man that came along."[35]

Similarly, Margaret Brown traced the failure of her marriage to her one experience of premarital sex and her husband's lack of any other sexual encounters. Her husband felt a deep need to "even the score," but when he finally did, he was consumed with guilt and unable to continue in the marriage. She wrote:

> My husband felt his lack of sexual experience, with other than myself was a great loss to him. All through our marriage, he occasionally bemoaned his lack of other experiences in a joking fashion. During the last year of marriage he talked seriously about his regrets and said he wanted other experiences. I think the fact I had had one love affair before ours bothered him considerably as well as his own

regrets being in large measure a major cause of our marriage breakdown. Once he began extramarital sexual experiences, he was filled with guilt feelings and felt he should not stay married.[36]

Guilt also affected the marriages of several women who had engaged in premarital sexual activity. Many were unable to achieve satisfying sexual relationships as a result. Betty Moran was one wife who suffered the effects of guilt for years. Although her husband noted simply that their marriage was "favorably affected by premarital sexual experiences with my wife," she disagreed:

> Our courtship did not result in marriage for over six years for educational and financial reasons. Our engagement had no definite beginning but was taken for granted after perhaps a year or two. Complete sexual experience therefore developed gradually and naturally after two or three years. (Without the moral codes of our civilization to which I tried to be loyal, it would have happened much earlier.) I feel this gradual introduction to sex experience has advantages over being plunged into it suddenly on the wedding night. However, it carried with it for me a high sense of guilt which still bothers me after all these years. I am forever grateful that we did finally marry because I probably would never have felt free to marry anyone else. This feeling of guilt may be why I am unable to respond sexually as I wish I could. I am glad I never indulged in petting with anyone but my husband.[37]

A husband in another case had a similar perception: "I have a persistent feeling that the sexual experiences in which my wife and I indulged *prior* to marriage has had an unfavorable effect upon our mutual enjoyment therefrom *since* our marriage. I believe it is a 'guilt block' which has produced what I will call her 'frigidity.'"[38]

Women in the sample were inclined to describe their feelings in more depth than did their husbands. As Lucy Owen explained, premarital sexual experience was "very definitely the most important factor" affecting her marriage: "Early parental discipline implanted a typical guilt feeling, as well as unusual interest in sex. During teenage [years], conflict between ideal and instinct was acute, resulting in a tendency to be inhibited. Puritan ideas of sex have caused great difficulties in adjustment on the mental, but not the physical level." This woman had so internalized prevalent notions about female sexuality that she described her own natural sexual responses as "abnormal." It is significant that she used psychological terminology popularized by professionals and measured her normality against an average that had been determined by a scientific expert, Kinsey:

"Early sex experience made me abnormally responsive, if Kinsey's statistics are accurate." In a revealing answer to a question asking respondents to rate their anticipation regarding sex at the time of their marriage on a scale from "extremely pleasant" to "extremely unpleasant," she ignored the ratings and wrote in, "Nasty but nice."

Chester Owen had his own perception of his wife's problem. He noted that her "adolescent training apparently left a rather deep scar: that sex was disgusting and available for peasants primarily—this was strenuously taught by her mother who was unhappily married. So . . . early premarital experiences, because they were rather unsatisfactory, quickly dispelled the earlier 'anticipations.' However, as the experts say, sex isn't everything." Despite the differences between the two spouses' perceptions of their sexual relations, they recognized the importance of early sexual training and attitudes, and they both referred to experts to bolster their views. But experts could not resolve their differences; the couple eventually divorced in 1967 and went on to new spouses.[39]

For many, sex in marriage was not the big thrill they had anticipated it to be before the wedding. One wife remarked, "Early sexual relations in marriage were not too good. Both of us lacked technique." A disappointed husband who remarked before his marriage that he and his fiancée were "passionately attracted to each other" later complained about his wife's "indifferent sexual desire."[40] Another who described his fiancée as "passionate (and how) on occasion" before their marriage later lamented, "If I had had intercourse experience before marriage, I believe I would have made a much more skilled lover and have been more successful in setting aside some of my wife's taboos which I've almost given up hope of doing." Apparently, the effort it took for his wife to contain her passion before marriage left a lasting pattern of restraint.[41] Still, the mystique of the wedding night prevailed. Pent-up desire was expected to explode in wonderful passion on the honeymoon. Some who did not wait for the wedding felt they missed something. As one husband explained of his perfectly comfortable but not quite magical sexual relationship with his fiancée, "Intercourse was immediate, was easy, and was thoroughly satisfactory to us both from the start; however, probably it never meant to us quite what it could have meant had we been continent before marriage."[42]

For some, sex was more pleasurable before the wedding than after. Whether the furtive quality of premarital intercourse, the newness of the relationship, or the freedom from the daily responsibilities of married life contributed to this relatively high level of excitement before marriage is impossible to determine. But the effect of diminished pleasure after marriage was devastating to at least a few couples. One man claimed that his wife was "frigid" after marriage but not before. He complained that the "warmth and response elicited by [my fiancée] during several years prior to marriage led to expectations that were sharply curtailed after marriage." The couple ended up divorced.[43]

Another divorced man complained bitterly about his wife's apparent loss of sexual desire for him: "I consider the turn of events a true tragedy. I don't believe there was ever a more wonderful woman." His wife's comments, however, suggest that he may have believed her original feelings were stronger than they were: "Although I knew before marriage that sex relations did not give me great satisfaction with him, I told myself it was *not* important." At the time of their engagement, she wrote a revealing comment: "I am not sure we are sexually better mated than I [would be] with other men, but I think I can make him happier than other women, in that way." Unfortunately, it did not work out, and they, too, divorced.[44]

Not all such problems, however, ended in divorce. Some just ended in unhappiness. One wife explained, "I found out that sex was a very pleasant experience with my husband . . . before marriage. . . . If we hadn't seemed so well adjusted before it would be easier to understand his attitude now. It makes life harder now. If I didn't know what I'm missing it wouldn't be so bad."[45] For these couples, then, satisfying but illicit premarital sex did not foster a pleasurable sexual relationship in marriage.

What about noncoital forms of premarital sexual activity? Many young women realized that it was possible to have a fairly active sex life and still remain a "virgin."[46] The taboo, after all, only applied to intercourse. To some extent, the emphasis on "drawing the line" at intercourse had the effect of liberating other forms of sexual expression. Kinsey and others documented an increase in noncoital forms of premarital sexual activity during these years. Dating, necking, and petting became almost universal. "Going steady" became a mechanism for sexual exploration in the context of intimacy and an accepted means for women to engage in behavior that would have previously damaged their reputations.[47]

Steady dating was a prelude to engagement and marriage and furthered a trend toward "permissiveness with affection." All these developments widened the boundaries of permissible sexual activity and softened the stigma associated with such behavior for unmarried women. Yet, because all "normal" forms of sexual behavior were assumed to culminate in penetration, erotic activities other than intercourse were considered steps along the way. Women were still responsible for "drawing the line," which meant that noncoital forms of sexual activity were a problem. Thus, in the elaborate sexual rituals that went along with dating, couples developed their own version of "brinkmanship": moving dangerously toward the edge of acceptable behavior, but not going "too far."

Petting was virtually universal among the KLS respondents. Those who thought it essential to refrain from premarital intercourse engaged in considerable physical intimacy before marriage. Only 10 percent of the women and 7 percent of the men entered marriage with experience limited to hugging and kissing; the majority engaged in further physical intimacy but refrained from intercourse. Because Kelly did not fine-tune the questionnaire to determine levels of mutual satisfaction or frequency of petting to orgasm, it is impossible to know to what extent frustration and tension characterized these premarital encounters. But the responses to the open-ended questions reveal that these relations were often filled with problems and created lasting effects on the marriages that followed.

Sexual brinkmanship was most difficult for women, since they were usually responsible for putting the brakes on lovemaking. As a result, women often had the most trouble adjusting to marital sex. Kinsey noted that patterns established prior to marriage often continued for many years. He emphasized "the importance of early experience in the establishment of habits of thought and attitudes which are very difficult to alter or counteract in later years. . . . When there are long years of abstinence and restraint, and an avoidance of physical contacts and emotional responses before marriage, acquired inhibitions may do such damage to the capacity to respond that it may take some years to get rid of them after marriage, if indeed they are ever dissipated."[48]

The accounts of numerous couples in the KLS illustrate how patterns and attitudes established before marriage affected the marital relationship. One divorced woman blamed premarital sexual patterns for the problems that eventually led to the breakup of her marriage. She explained, "My sexual experience *being with* my to-be husband succeeded in conditioning me to utter subservience to *his* satisfaction and he never thought mine could be other than automatic upon his (else I was 'frigid' or wrong somehow). And he is . . . a psychoanalyst! I remain as I was—unfulfilled."[49] Another couple had a different history but the wife had a similar complaint. They had waited until marriage before engaging in sexual intercourse, and their marriage was still intact. The husband believed that their premarital chastity affected the marriage favorably; his wife, however, complained about her inadequate preparation for the sexual side of marriage. She concluded, "I cannot say whether the lack of sexual experience before marriage marred our early days of marriage but I believe that a better understanding of woman's nature on the part of [my husband] could have helped considerably. After 17 years this understanding is still lacking."[50]

It was not uncommon for husbands and wives to perceive their sexual relationships differently. One couple illustrated this poignantly. Leon Shaw had no idea that the premarital sexual patterns they established had a devastating effect on his wife's ability to enjoy marital sex. Instead, he attributed her sexual reluctance to her defiance of the proper role for women. In keeping with the domestic ideology articulated by the experts, he believed that women would achieve personal and sexual fulfillment if they adhered to the homemaker-mother role. If his wife focused her attention on her home and family, he reasoned, she would be sexually responsive and satisfied. But she was working on a doctorate, and he resented her spending time outside home while her four children were young. Because of her professional aspirations, he concluded, "She is proud that she does not need physical love or sex. I need both. She has never had an orgasm. I feel both a failure as a lover and piqued at her refusal to lower herself to the 'physical' level. She does, however, try to do her duty as a wife."

In another part of the questionnaire, however, Leon listed "much sexual satisfaction" as one of the things he gained in his marriage. He said that in spite of his frustration, he was glad they had refrained from premarital intercourse because sex was "special" to the marriage. Mildred Shaw made it clear that her sexual difficulties had nothing to do with her educational or career aspirations, but that they dated back to the days of premarital restraint. She described the effects of their premarital sexual containment in this way: "I believe that our practice of letting my fiancé ejaculate between my legs into a handkerchief may have resulted in some frigidity on my part. I had accustomed myself to keep under control when he was so excited. To this day I have great difficulty in breaking this pattern."[51]

Along with premarital restraint, the double standard also took a toll, since many men entered marriage with much more sexual experience than their wives. One wife believed that if she had had "a better understanding of the part sex plays in marriage and also the part it plays in a man's life we could have avoided some of the trouble we had."[52] Another complained about her "incomplete knowledge and instruction mated to [her husband's] vast experience."[53] Several men also recognized this problem. One complained about his wife's "lack of interest in love" and blamed it on their premarital sexual restraint. He believed that lack to be "an extreme handicap, which . . . has caused tensed relations several times."[54]

Most of the respondents claimed that men were more adequately prepared for marital sexual relations. Nevertheless, it is curious to note that more women than men thought that the husband was more prepared, while more men than women believed that the wife was more prepared. One husband described the ill effects he experienced after years of fantasy combined with chastity: "Because such experiences had been the subject of day-dreaming for years, it was, at first, not easy to put these past images out of my mind and concentrate on the real experience."[55] Another couple found that sexual pleasure in marriage took some time to achieve, even though they were both glad they waited. As the wife recalled, "We had been engaged for over two years and together a great deal of the time as students in the same institution, so we both looked forward to the final consummation of our feelings for each other. Naturally there had been considerable longing for sexual intercourse, but we refrained until marriage." Her husband noted that in spite of the "considerable longing," mutual sexual pleasure was not immediate. "I would say that my marriage was helped by my continence before marriage, because this unique sharing with my wife was viewed by both as a thing to be treasured. Since she had some misgiving about sex and men it helped her to accept me, I believe. On the other hand, my shyness and lack of experience may have left her unaroused for some time."[56]

Although Kinsey ascertained that premarital sexual experience fostered the achievement of frequent orgasm in marital intercourse, he did not reach a definite conclusion about its impact on marriage.[57] Robert Bell, who examined the Kinsey findings as well as those of other studies, distinguished between sexual adjustment and overall marital adjustment. He concluded, "In general, premarital chastity may be favorable to overall adjustment in marriage, but premarital coitus appears favorable to sexual adjustment in marriage. However, the interpretation of these two levels of adjustment must be made with care because factors that make for good sexual adjustment may have little to do with overall marital adjustment."[58] Indeed, the KLS responses suggest that sexual adjustment and marital adjustment may be different. Norman Kimball, whose suspicion of his wife marred their marriage, noted that he liked his wife's "sexual ability," but Maria Kimball's questionnaire showed that premarital sex effectively destroyed their relationship.[59]

The KLS data, overall, suggest that no single formula worked for everyone. When the responses to open-ended questions are divided according to whether or not premarital intercourse occurred and how it affected the marriage, the data show that men were much more likely than were women to mention the positive effects of premarital intercourse and the negative effects of restraint. The men's combined responses indicate that 32 believed premarital intercourse enhanced marriage and 25 thought that it did not, while 22 women thought it had negative effects and 12 believed it had a positive effect.

Comments from the respondents provide some insight into these figures. One wife noted, "My lack of sexual relationship [prior to marriage] made no difference. We have both grown with our living together, learning from each other. I want to say we are completely compatible." Another wished her husband "had had some experience in order to take the lead. But it has been wonderful learning together," she added. (Her husband, however, felt that their waiting had no effect on the marriage.) Several men also prized their own as well as their wives' premarital restraint. One husband was "deeply grateful that I had no previous sex experience before marriage. Together we have explored unknown country." Another wrote that the "lack of sexual experience has made our marriage very pleasant and enjoyable—no comparisons, good or bad—no guilty conscience." The wife of still another husband who thought that their premarital chastity had a positive effect agreed, saying, "Our sexual life has been completely satisfying in all phases. We mutually agreed to save it for marriage—I am a very warm and affectionate person but strict in personal ideals. It has made for a warm, close and deeply satisfying relationship through the years."[60]

One wife noted that what mattered most was her husband's strong feelings about the matter: "The fact that I was a virgin when married was and still is an important factor in my husband's feelings for me. . . . As for possible repressions, frigidity and the other consequences that are said to go along with controlling the strong urges for intercourse before marriage, I feel I made a quick and easy adjustment in spite of my lack of sexual experiences." Her husband was less reflective on the subject, saying merely that their sexual experience prior to marriage was "probably of little moment."[61] A male respondent explained his philosophy: "I believe it very important to reserve the physical union for the one true love whom I married. . . . However, I did my share of necking before meeting my bride-to-be."[62]

There were also those couples who engaged in premarital intercourse with no apparent harm to their marriage. As one wife explained, "I enjoyed sex and was most anxious to be married and I'm sure my marriage has been happier because I had no fear or worry about sex in marriage."[63] But her attitude was rare among the women. Men were more likely to express this belief. They reported that it "helped me to understand it better and accept it in its proper perspective," or that it contributed to sexual compatibility: "I learned to pay much attention to the satisfaction of the other party, and unless hers is achieved mine is not complete."[64]

This final comment reflects a significant finding in the KLS data: Pleasing one's spouse physically seemed to be even more important than pleasing oneself. Both husbands and wives generally believed it was more important to have intercourse when their spouses wanted it than when they wanted it. Most of the respondents said that their spouses were considerate of their feelings about sexual relations; only 12 percent felt otherwise. Perhaps these responses help explain why 84 percent of wives said that their sexual relations were pleasant, while only 66 percent experienced orgasm regularly. Nearly one in five, then, enjoyed sex in spite of her lack of orgasms. Other items in the questionnaire provide further insight into this apparent disjunction. Both men and women, but more emphatically women, thought it was "very important" that their sexual relationships be "closely bound up with love and affection." Men and women alike also believed that it was desirable for husbands and wives to express their love for each other frequently in words. These responses indicate that many women found satisfaction in sex as an expression of closeness and affection, even if it did not provide physical release.[65] The responses also reflect the widely shared belief that providing sexual pleasure for one's spouse is a central requirement for a happy marriage. According to marriage manuals, sexual technique is an important skill to acquire, something akin to a "sex as work ethic."[66]

Whether they had to work at pleasure or not, in their own various ways the KLS respondents conformed to the spirit of sexual containment, even if not always to the letter of the law. Both the men and women reported feeling strong sexual attraction for their future spouses soon after they met and looking forward to sex within marriage. Most indicated that they had a fairly active sexual relationship during marriage. Few men reported experiencing impotence more than once in a while; only 10 percent said impotence was a regular occurrence. A majority of the wives indicated that they had orgasms regularly, even though fully one-third said that they rarely or never achieved orgasm. These findings are consistent with Kinsey's data on men of a similar age group and women who had been married ten to fifteen years.[67] In spite of all the sexual difficulties that surfaced in their testimonies, the KLS respondents, overall, chose to define their sexual relationships as satisfactory.

Their commitment to sexual containment is nowhere more evident than in the extent to which these women and men agreed on the importance of sexual exclusiveness within marriage. In spite of the existence of the double standard in premarital sexual behavior, both the men and the women agreed that the same standard of sexual morality should apply to both marital partners. Their behavior was fairly consistent with these attitudes: 89 percent of the wives and 85 percent of the husbands reported that they never had a love affair with anyone else during their marriage. Of those who did, however, some managed to keep the fact from their spouses, for when asked if their partners had ever had a love affair, 93 percent of the men and 87 percent of the women said never. When the question was phrased differently, there were some significant disparities between the men's and women's responses. Asked about the frequency of sexual relations outside marriage, rather than "love affairs," 91 percent of the women said never, compared to only 77 percent of the men.[68] It appears, then, that some of the women had what they considered love affairs without sex, and some of the men had sexual affairs without love. Here, again, the women were likely to emphasize the importance of the affectionate bond, while men more often focused on the physical.

By the time the KLS respondents filled out their questionnaires in 1955, sex had become far more than the carefully regulated marital duty that Victorian couples were expected to share. Postwar couples looked toward marriage for sexual fulfillment. If there was a sexual awakening taking place, it was focused on the promise of an eroticized marriage. Sex was expected to strengthen the marriage, enhance the home, and contribute to each partner's sense of happiness and well-being. Healthy families were built upon the bedrock of good sex. But this ideal often worked better in theory than in practice. The tension surrounding premarital sex, combined with highly inflated expectations for sublime marital sex, often led to disappointment and difficulty.

Despite these problems, many of the KLS respondents were able to settle into a sexual routine that they considered more-or-less satisfactory by scaling down their own expectations and concentrating on pleasing their spouses. Most of them were inclined to make the best of the situation, rather than turn to divorce or extramarital affairs for the magic that was missing at home. These reactions illustrate the ambiguous legacy of sexual containment, which promised fulfillment in an erotically charged marriage and security against sexual chaos. Although neither security nor fulfillment was guaranteed by adhering to containment, most people were unwilling to risk the loss of reputation, the stigma and economic hardship of divorce, or the destruction of "togetherness" that was likely to result if they strayed from the prescribed code. Keeping relationships intact and defining them as successful were apparently more important than actually achieving the promise of conjugal bliss. Many couples simply learned to live with sexual incompatibility or frustration. As one husband remarked, "Sex isn't everything." Yet there had to be some compensation. Another man explained that "satisfaction with [my] wife as a homemaker and mother makes up for the lack of complete sexual satisfaction."[69] This final comment gives a hint of where postwar Americans might have looked for happiness if sex turned out to be less than sublime. After all, with such a heavy emphasis on the "cult of mutual orgasm," married couples would need to find other ways to achieve the fulfillment that sexual containment promised but did not necessarily deliver.

CHAPTER SIX

BABY BOOM AND
BIRTH CONTROL: THE
REPRODUCTIVE CONSENSUS

On that day in August 1945, when the first atomic bomb fell on Hiroshima, new concepts of civilized living, based on the obligations of world citizenship . . . were born. Out of the smoke and smoldering ruins arose a great cry for leadership equipped to guide the stricken people of the world along the hazardous course toward peace. On that day parenthood took on added responsibilities of deep and profound significance. . . . Surely, in all history, the parents of the world were never so challenged! However, there is a defense—an impregnable bulwark—which lies in meeting the world's desperate cry for leadership. Upon the shoulders of parents, everywhere, rests the tremendous responsibility of sending forth into the next generation men and women imbued with a high resolve to work together for everlasting peace. . . . The new philosophy of child guidance makes of parenthood not a dull, monotonous routine job, but an absorbing, creative profession—a career second to none.

—LOUISA RANDALL CHURCH, 1946[1]

PROCREATION in the cold war era took on almost mythic proportions. The writer just quoted articulated the fundamental principle of postwar parenthood: Children were a "defense—an impregnable bulwark" against the terrors of the age. For the nation, the next generation symbolized hope for the future. But for individuals, parenthood was much more than a duty to posterity; the joys of raising children would compensate for the thwarted expectations in other areas of their lives. For men who were frustrated at work, for women who were bored at home, and for both who were dissatisfied with the unfulfilled promise of sexual excitement, children might fill the void. Through children, men and women could set aside the difficulties of their sexual relationships and celebrate the procreative results. In so doing, they also demonstrated their loyalty to national goals by having as many children as they could "raise right and educate and be a benefit to the world," in the words of one postwar father.[2] Rather than representing a retreat into private life, procreation was one way to express civic values.

Louisa Randall Church was one of the countless advocates of parenthood as the key not only to responsible citizenship and a secure future but to a personally fulfilling life. Sounding like those who blamed sexual degeneracy for the nation's problems, she railed against the parents of the past who "failed to produce the quality of leadership needed to harmonize world factions" because they were too preoccupied with "superficial culture, refinements and polish, luxury and ease . . . which nurtured flabby, apathetic, indifferent, irresponsible members of society." With such high stakes placed on the next generation, "Complacent, indifferent, ignorant, lazy or selfish parents have no place" in today's world.[3] What better way for postwar adults to demonstrate their potency, in contrast to the sloth of the past, than in prolific procreation and vigorous child rearing?

The postwar consensus was nowhere more evident than in the matter of having children. While sexual ideals and behavior often diverged, reproductive ideals and behavior fused. The baby boom was not the result of the return to peace, or of births to older parents postponed because of the war. Rather, the baby boom began *during* the war and continued afterward because younger couples were having babies earlier. Part of the boom can be explained by the drop in the marriage age, which was encouraged by sexual pressures. But a lower marriage age would not necessarily result in a higher birthrate. In fact, during the first few decades of the twentieth century, the marriage age *and* the birthrate both declined steadily. In the 1940s, however, the birthrate skyrocketed, reversing a decline in fertility that had lasted for nearly two centuries. How did this reversal happen? Demographers have shown that the baby boom did not result from women suddenly having a huge number of children; the number of children per family went up modestly. Women coming of age in the 1930s had an

FIGURE 13   Typical postwar baby-boom family, early 1950s. (*Courtesy of Judy Tyler.*)

average of 2.4 children; those who reached adulthood in the fifties gave birth to an average of 3.2 children. What made the baby boom happen was that *everyone* was doing it—and at the same time (see Figure 13).[4]

The birthrate rose among all social groups. One demographic study of the sources of the baby boom concluded, "The vast changes in fertility and fertility-related behavior since World War II . . . are pervasive; that is, those social and economic variables that we have been able to examine with census data, such as race, ethnic status, education and residence, do not indicate differences with respect to trends in fertility."[5] In addition, Americans behaved with remarkable conformity during these years. They married young and had an average of at least three children in a few years. Most couples who married in the 1940s and 1950s completed their families by the time they were in their late twenties. Thus, the smallest birth cohort of twentieth-century women, those born in the 1930s, had the largest birth cohort of children: the baby boom.[6]

Along with the baby boom came an intense and widespread endorsement of pronatalism—the belief in the positive value of having several children. A major study conducted in 1957 found that most Americans believed that parenthood was the route to happiness. Childlessness was considered deviant, selfish, and pitiable. Twenty years later, these pronatal norms began to break up. But in the 1940s and 1950s, nearly everyone believed that family togetherness, focused on children, was the mark of a successful and wholesome personal life.[7] One study of nine hundred wives in the 1950s found that the desire for children was second only to companionship in stated marriage goals.[8]

In spite of these widespread beliefs, and the fact that the baby boom was well under way, numerous postwar observers expressed fears that women might be inclined to shirk their maternal role—to the nation's detriment, as well as to their own. J. Edgar Hoover, director of the Federal Bureau of Investigation, spoke to "homemakers and mothers" about their unique role in fighting "the twin enemies of freedom—crime and communism." Hoover was careful to address these housewives as "'career' women. . . . I say 'career' women because I feel there are no careers so important as those of homemaker and mother."[9] Many agreed with Hoover that women should focus their talents and expertise on the home and argued that the new opportunities for education and employment would reduce a woman's reproductive potential. A 1946 study reported in the *American Journal of Sociology* concluded that the increase in women's employment "is related to the secular decline in the birth rate" and predicted (wrongly) that since the proportion of women in the paid labor force was likely to increase even more, the birthrate would continue to decline.[10]

That same year, *Newsweek* reported that education was equally detrimental to procreation: "For the American girl books and babies don't mix. Long ago scientists concluded that the American family's reproduction rate is in inverse ratio to the educational attainment of the parents. Now, analyzing facts collected for the first time in the 1940 United States Census, they have discovered that it is the higher-educated wife, rather than the husband, who brings down the birth rate."[11] *Newsweek* was careful to point out that the husband's educational attainment would not inhibit fertility—only the wife's. Therefore, there was no danger in men taking advantage of the GI Bill and going to college; women, however, ought to tend to their reproductive responsibilities instead.

As late as 1956—the peak of the baby boom—*U.S. News and World Report* echoed this concern: "America's college women are marrying earlier than they did, having more children." Nevertheless, the article continued with the misperception that college-educated women "are failing to keep up with the baby boom. It is the relatively uneducated women who keep the U.S. population on the rise."[12] The report was inaccurate. Although women with less education continued to have a higher overall birthrate, as had been the case for decades, the increase in the birthrate among these women during the baby-boom years was relatively modest. Actually, the sharpest increase in the birthrate was among the most highly educated women.[13] Nevertheless, distorted observations like these reports suggested that "inferior" groups were overpopulating the nation.

These sentiments echoed the elitist and nativist attitudes that fueled the eugenics movement popularized by Theodore Roosevelt in the early years of the twentieth century. At that time, proponents of eugenics urged the "better" classes, meaning white Anglo-Saxon Protestants, to reproduce at a rate equal to or higher than that of the "lower orders." They feared that white native-born Americans were committing "race suicide." After World War II, these concerns fed the controversy surrounding new educational and employment opportunities for women. The *Ladies Home Journal* entered the debate by asking, "Is College Education Wasted on Women?"[14] Some observers answered in the affirmative: College was good for women only if they found husbands there. As one writer proclaimed, "Certainly the happiest women have never found the secret of their happiness in books or lectures. They do the right thing instinctively."[15]

The "maternal instinct" was the point at which sexual and reproductive ideology fused, giving rise to a revival of the cult of motherhood. Of course, idealized motherhood was nothing new in the United States. It had its heyday in the nineteenth century when Victorian values were at their zenith. During that era, the declining birthrate contributed to the idealization of motherhood, for women could then spend more time and energy nurturing each child. In the twentieth century, the Victorian notions of motherhood were recast in the form of powerful sentiments encouraging women to have more, rather than fewer, babies. This new glorification of motherhood reflected the twentieth-century idea of the sexualized home.

The notion that motherhood was the ultimate fulfillment of female sexuality surfaced suddenly and visibly in the media at the beginning of World War II. Female film celebrities began to offer a new maternal model for identification and emulation.[16] In mass circulation magazines such as *Photoplay*, the shift in the portrayal of female stars was dramatic. Celebrities who were noted for their erotic appeal suddenly appeared in these magazines as contented mothers, nestled comfortably in their ranch-style suburban homes with their husbands and children. The most striking thing about the new image of women was the sudden introduction of babies. While children almost never appeared in stories or photographs of female stars in the 1930s, they became featured along with their famous moms in the war years.

One issue of *Photoplay* in 1940 ran a story headlined "Hollywood Birth Rate—Going Up! A Bumper Crop of Babies Brings a Message of Renewed Faith and Courage." By 1943, babies had taken center stage. Significantly, it was the sex symbols who were now featured as mothers. "Hollywood's Newest Pin-up Girl" was none other than the infant of Lana Turner, noted World War II "pin-up" herself. The article accompanying the picture stated approvingly that Lana Turner was giving up her film career to raise her daughter, suggesting that her sexual energy and her ambition now found fulfillment through motherhood. Joan Crawford, featured in the 1930s for her independence and ambition, became "another incredibly devoted and capable mother. . . . Every time she talked of her children I knew a sense of unreality. . . . It is a wonderful thing that these glamor girls insist upon being mothers."[17]

In "Should War Wives Have Babies?" actress Carole Landis Wallace answered in the affirmative and offered a lengthy lament:

> It is a great disappointment to me that I am not expecting along with several other of my married friends. Both my husband and I feel that it is time to forget about the superficial things in life. It is the natural, wholesome way of living— having children and establishing a home—that counts. Having a child makes a soldier realize that he has something very real to fight for. With a home and a family waiting for him, he has an incentive to give everything he has. When the war is over, we intend to buy a large ranch in Nevada. Lots of space, several children, simple living is our dream. Although my career is secondary, it will be necessary for me, and a lot of other wives, to help financially until my husband gets back into civilian life.[18]

Echoing this theme, Maureen O'Hara shared her maternal sentiments during her wartime pregnancy: "I am waiting for my baby. . . . I am aware of the power [my body] holds. It's a kind of spiritual awareness, a reverence, because within me I feel the gentle movement of another body. . . . Today I know the completeness of being a woman, a warm human being " She revealed her earlier illness and the anguish she felt when she had difficulty conceiving: "Everything in life for me focused on my determination to have a baby." How she envied a friend who was pregnant, "How empty . . . I felt inside myself because it wasn't happening to me!" After she told her husband the news of her pregnancy, "he walked more briskly, like all prospective fathers. His eyes sparkled. His voice had a new ring of authority."[19]

Protesting the popular image of Hollywood as corrupt and decadent, Rosalind Russell wrote an article for *Look* magazine proclaiming that "the glamour era" was over. Gone were the "sins of the fathers who helped their fans to sin vicariously"; gone were the "Commies." Hollywood inhabitants, she insisted, were early-to-bed churchgoing folk who doted on their children. Illustrating her point were photographs of Dorothy Lamour hosting her son's fifth birthday party, Loretta Young at a backyard family gathering, and Russell herself with her son and his toys.[20]

The message in the popular culture was clear: Motherhood was the ultimate fulfillment of female sexuality and the primary source of a woman's identity. Even during the war, when families were disrupted and women entered the workforce in massive numbers, maternal themes flourished. Female readers of *Life* magazine were assured that motherhood would enhance their physical attractiveness. In a 1944 feature article entitled "Model Mothers," *Life* focused on several professional models who had babies. The article began, "Here are family poses of some professional beauties who have found that having a baby is fine for their careers. . . . Having babies is no hindrance to the careers of the professional models who make a good living displaying their pretty faces and fine figures for photographers and illustrators. Motherhood, in fact, seems to help them. According to John Robert Powers and Harry Conover, heads of the leading model-booking agencies in New York, being a mother usually improves a girl's disposition, her attitude towards her work, her looks and even her figure." The article was illustrated with several photographs of glamorous models with their babies. One posed with her infant in front of a poster of war planes; the caption noted that her "husband is a seabee." In this twist on Rosie the Riveter, the female reader was assured that having a child could actually enhance her beauty as well as her ability to earn money while her husband was off fighting the war.[21]

Children promised to fulfill both sides of the postwar domestic equation: security as well as fulfillment. Nothing better tamed the wayward tendencies of postwar Americans than the arrival of a child. Popular stories and films at the time articulated this message in no uncertain terms. The editor of *Better Homes and Gardens*, for example, wrote about the moralizing and harmonizing effects of children:

> The young fellow who lives in the little house with the vines . . . used to be quite a "stepper." He didn't change his ways much when he married his little redhead. Nor, for that matter, did she. Her bright mop of hair was a danger signal, all right. . . . We don't worry about this couple any more. There are three in that family now. The little fellow['s] mother lives every moment for his comfort and welfare. His father is thinking, not about an evening with the "boys," but away off

in the future—about the kid's schooling, about the sort of country and the sort of world in which the lad will live someday.

The editor concluded, "Perhaps there is not much more needed in a recipe for happiness. . . . We become complete only thru our children."[22]

In 1941, as the depression gave way to wartime and the declining marriage rate and birthrate began to turn around, *Penny Serenade* captivated film audiences around the country. Virtually every anxiety of the early 1940s appears in this film, with one solution offered to all the problems of the age: children (see Figure 14). The film begins with Roger (Cary Grant), the restless newspaperman, wooing Julie (Irene Dunne), the young working woman. The night before the hero is transferred overseas (not to war but to become a foreign correspondent in Japan), the couple wed. Three months later, Julie joins Roger in Tokyo, where he has leased a luxurious house with Japanese servants (who have three cherubic children). Julie tells Roger she is pregnant, obviously since their wedding night. For Julie, it is a dream come true, but she worries about Roger's reckless extravagance. With the depression fresh in the mind of the audience, Julie chastises Roger for giving up a steady job to chase a dream of owning his own newspaper, and for buying her fancy clothes and planning an international vacation when they should be saving for the child. But all the plans are thwarted when an earthquake strikes, causing Julie to miscarry and rendering her permanently infertile. When Roger promises to give up his foolish ways and to settle down in a nice home of their own, Julie tells him that nothing matters to her anymore, since "the only thing that would have made me happy I can't have."

But happiness comes their way when they adopt a baby daughter. Long scenes focus on the mundane routines of feeding, diapering, and bathing the baby, with endless close-up shots of the face of the angelic girl. No romantic encounter between Dunne and Grant receives as much cinematic attention as the face of the child. After a year of tender, loving parenting, Roger's newspaper goes out of business just as the adoption probation period comes to an end. Roger goes to court, but the judge rules that the baby must be returned to the orphanage. In a tearful speech before the judge, the father articulates the resolutions of postdepression men. He vows to give up everything for the family and promises that his love for his child will make him a responsible provider. "Look, Your Honor," Roger pleads, "she's not like an automobile or a piece of furniture or something you buy on time and then when you can't keep up the payments they take it away from you. . . . Anyone can give up those kinds of things; but I ask you, Judge, how can you give up your own child?"

FIGURE 14   Dad (Cary Grant) dotes on his daughter as mom (Irene Dunne) confers with the adoption agency representative in a scene from *Penny Serenade*. In this 1941 film, as in the nation at large for the following two decades, babies entered center stage. (*The Museum of Modern Art/Film Stills Archive. Courtesy of Photofest.*)

As the baby whimpers, Roger continues, "I'm sorry, Judge, but . . . you don't know how badly my wife wanted a child. It wasn't so important to me. I—I dunno, I suppose most men are like this but children never meant a great deal to me, but the first time I saw her . . . she just sort of walked into my heart, Judge, and she was there to stay. I didn't know I could feel like that." The child transforms the man into a responsible citizen: "I'd always been, well, kinda careless and irresponsible, I wanted to be a big shot. I couldn't work for anybody; I had to be my own boss—that sort of thing. . . . Look, I'm not a big shot now. I'll do anything—I'll work for anybody—I'll beg, I'll borrow—Please, Judge, I'll sell anything I got until I get going again—she'll never go hungry and she'll never be without clothes not as long as I've got two good hands to help me." Roger proves his case. Although his wife had been employed before marriage, the man would clearly "beg or borrow" before he would suggest that she go back to work.

Joy fills the screen as father and baby return to mother waiting at home. But the joy does not last. Just after the child enters school, she becomes ill and dies. We never see the dying child, only the miserable parents, whose meaning in life, and in their relationship, has been destroyed. Roger withdraws into silence, and Julie prepares to leave. Just as Julie heads out the door, the phone rings. It is the adoption agency, with another child for them. Instantly the two burst into smiles and embrace. They will have another chance to renew their purpose in life and to find meaning in their marriage.[23]

Penny Serenade won an Oscar nomination for Cary Grant and for the writers of the screenplay, Garson Kanin and Ruth Gordon. It was an ideal film to inaugurate the 1940s. Like the hero, men would need to accept positions of subordination in large organizations rather than risk insecurity by going into business for themselves. Compensation for the loss of independence and creativity would be provided in the family, where fatherhood gave life meaning. The arrival of the child tamed the husband's extravagance and recklessness, making him a responsible provider. For the woman, the child meant everything. Without the child, even the marriage was worthless.

Just at the time when *Penny Serenade* drew crowds at the theaters, film magazines began to feature former sex symbols as wives and mothers, and former studs as dads. The dangerous potential of female sexuality found its safest expression in motherhood. Within a few years, Marynia Farnham and Ferdinand Lundberg would write a best-selling volume, *The Modern Woman: The Lost Sex*, insisting that the true fulfillment of female sexuality was in motherhood.[24] In spite of the increasing use of birth control devices, which had increased the time between marriage and parenthood before the war, the time gap began to shrink during the 1940s, clearly as a result of personal choice. People were marrying and having children right away. As for Julie in *Penny Serenade*, who became pregnant on her wedding night, the very meaning of marriage began to be identified with children.[25]

Penny Serenade also introduced the new theme of fatherhood. Once the child arrives, gone from the screen are the whirring presses and the impressive headlines emerging from the workplace. In fact, viewers do not know what the father does for a living once the baby arrives and his effort to create a thriving paper fails. He no doubt has a job, but he is not seen doing it. Within a decade, family dramas would take place primarily in the home. Particularly on television, the home entertainment, fatherhood became the center of a man's identity. Viewers never saw the father of *Father Knows Best* at work or knew the occupation of the Nelsons' lovable dad, Ozzie. They were fathers, pure and simple. Whatever

indignities and subordination they might suffer at their unseen places of employment, fathers on television exercised authority at home. The only time men's
occupations were mentioned was in working-class situation comedies, like *The
Honeymooners* or *Life of Riley,* in which the men were portrayed as buffoons.

The possible exception was Ricky Ricardo of *I Love Lucy,* who played a Cuban
bandleader married to the American Lucy, who yearned for a career in show business only to be continually thwarted. Ricky was a successful breadwinner, but he
was outside the middle-class mainstream as a result of his foreign and ethnic
background and his occupation as an entertainer. Full assimilation arrived in the
form of parenthood: Ricky and Lucy's greatest triumph was Lucy's pregnancy and
the announcement of the arrival of their television and real-life child on the
show itself—an event witnessed by one of the largest television audiences ever
assembled. On television, upward mobility into respectable middle-class life
emerged in the form of fatherhood, when men ceased to be workers and became
"dads." In fatherhood, a man could exert true authority and manliness.[26]

Fatherhood became a new badge of masculinity and meaning for the postwar
man, and Father's Day a holiday of major significance. Men began attending
classes on marriage and family in unprecedented numbers. In 1954, *Life* magazine announced "the domestication of the American male."[27] Fatherhood was
important not just to give meaning to men's lives, but to counteract the over-
abundance of maternal care. Although mothers were, of course, expected to
devote themselves full time to their children, excessive mothering posed the
danger that children would become too accustomed to and dependent on female
attention. The unhappy result would be "sissies," who allegedly were likely to
become homosexuals, "perverts," and dupes of the communists. Fathers had to
make sure this would not happen to their sons. "Being a real father is not 'sissy'
business," a male psychiatrist wrote in *Parents Magazine* in 1947. "It is an occupation . . . the most important occupation in the world."[28]

The outpouring of attention to fatherhood in the popular media belies an
undercurrent of uncertainty: Were fathers really involved in child rearing? A
writer in *Better Homes and Gardens* asked, "Are we staking our future on a crop
of sissies? . . . You have a horror of seeing your son a pantywaist, but he won't get
red blood and self reliance if you leave the whole job of making a he-man of him
to his mother." The author recounted an incident in which a well-meaning
mother tried to stop her small son from a harmless frolic. Her husband restrained
her gently, saying, "Let him go, he'll be all right." The author explained that the
mother was exercising her "perfectly normal and necessary instinct to protect
her children from harm," but the father "knew that a boy has to have chances to

try things on his own, to go off on new adventures. He understood that it is a father's job to encourage his son to adventure."[29] Even in parenting, strict gender roles applied: It was as inappropriate for the man to protect the child as for the wife to encourage the adventure.

An English anthropologist stated that worry about children becoming "sissies" was "the overriding fear of every American parent." The foreign expert apparently saw this as a uniquely American obsession. Professionals in the fields of psychology, education, sociology, and child development interviewed by the author believed that "the fears are well grounded. Millions of American boys and girls, they say, are so far on their way to being sissies that only professional help will save many of them." The expert suggested that one problem was weak men overshadowed by strong women: "Many fathers are not fully grown up and self-reliant themselves. . . . Too often the early years of a boy's life are dominated by women. . . . But the biggest single reason is absent fathers. . . . Even if you are away from home all day, you can make it up to your children during the hours you are home."[30]

Parents had to know what a "sissy" was to prevent their child from becoming one. Dr. Luther E. Woodward, psychologist and coordinator of the New York State Mental Health Commission at that time, provided the following definition: "A sissy is a boy (or girl) who gets too much satisfaction from what his mother does for him and not enough from what he does for himself [sic]." Fathers were told to start prevention early, by helping care for the child as a baby: "Any father who works an 8-hour day is around the home enough to do it."[31] *Parents Magazine* joined in, giving "A Build-Up for Dad." The article began with the basics, assuming that men knew virtually nothing about how to interact with children. Fathers should describe what they do at work, so their youngsters could be proud of them. Another article told men to do carpentry projects or play sports with their children. Men should venture into previously female realms as well: "It's a brave father who attends a parents' meeting, but he belongs there." Still, it was the woman's job to begin this "masculine regeneration. . . . The women of the country . . . may really have to work at it." It was up to the women to offset the imbalance, since they were responsible for "the overfeminization of schools and households."[32]

For those who needed help, the same issue of the magazine included a full-page advertisement for a fourteen-volume *Childcraft* guide, with four volumes of "expert advice" covering "every phase of your child's development. . . . You know what is normal behavior and what is not. You know how to . . . direct your child's growth and character." And just in case some questions were not answered in the guidebooks, "To help you solve any unusual or different prob-lems . . . *Childcraft* offers a FREE, confidential Advisory Service of expert per-sonal advice." *Woman's Home Companion* noted that "Fathers Are Parents, Too," and offered a fully illustrated "do's and don'ts" guide for fathers, including photo-graphs of dad in an apron, feeding his children, helping them make a box car, and teaching them about cars. *Parents Magazine* ran a feature, ". . . Specially for Fathers," giving tips on parenting to men. Another expert, writing in the *Ladies Home Journal*, encouraged women to get their husbands involved with the chil-dren in an article entitled "Making Marriage Work." It was important not only for the child but for the marriage. The writer assumed that fathers were inept with children unless coached by their wives: "Point out specific things he can do which you cannot. Tell him how much it means to you as his wife for your chil-dren really to know the man you love. If he's a husband worth having, he will try to cooperate." Then came a number of suggestions, such as "provide things to do" and "make the time short."[33]

An article in *American Home* had the title "Are You a Dud as a Dad?" The author argued that parenthood provides men with the opportunity for achieve-ment free from all the impediments that might obstruct success in the world of work: "Here is one area in your life which doesn't depend on 'breaks' or ability, or education or money. A man can be a success as a father, a real 'dad,' if he cares enough to try. . . . Share your small son's hobbies, laugh at his jokes, lend a lis-tening ear to his problems, the kind of things a fellow wants to talk over with a man."[34] In the face of the highly organized world of work that stripped men of their autonomy, fatherhood could be a substitute source of meaning and creativ-ity. Nowhere else was it easier for a man to be his own boss than in fatherhood.

Of course, women were also expected to achieve their greatest fulfillment in parenthood.[35] So prevalent was the assumption that women were naturally ful-filled in motherhood that anxiety or ambivalence surrounding pregnancy was actually considered a pathological condition. In 1953, a Cornell University obste-trician reported to the American Academy of Obstetrics and Gynecology his find-ings that repeated miscarriages might be caused by emotional factors and that a miscarriage might be the result of "an unconscious rejection on the mother's part of repeated pregnancies and of motherhood. Worry, tension, fear and other psy-chological stresses . . . may bring on the miscarriage." The researcher concluded that "psychiatric treatment will do more to help these women achieve happy motherhood than such prescriptions as vitamin E, sex hormones, or complete bed rest." The doctor reported "successful maternal psychotherapy" with "psychiatric care, aimed to relieve anxieties and possible fear of motherhood." The women in the study stopped having miscarriages, seemed to gain confidence, and "once these patients develop a pattern of success, they continue to do so time and again."[36] Although the conclusion that stress is unhealthy is sound and hardly surprising, the conditions that may create real stress in a woman embarking on motherhood were not at issue in the medical study. The point was not to address the sources of stress. Rather, the stress itself was considered pathological.

Given the strong connections among female sexuality, marriage, and motherhood, one might expect the birth control movement to have withered during these years. On the contrary, the movement gained momentum. Under the leadership of Margaret Sanger, birth control had gained a significant amount of liberal support during the 1920s and 1930s, with roots in feminism and socialism. The number of birth control clinics in the nation grew from fifty-five in 1930 to over eight hundred in 1942.[37] In 1942, the Birth Control Federation of America changed its name to the Planned Parenthood Federation of America (PPFA), signaling a major shift in the movement's direction. New goals included the strengthening of the family through the liberation of female sexuality in marriage. As historian Linda Gordon noted, "Part of the PPFA program of family stability was the recognition of mutual sexual enjoyment as an important cement in marriages, and of women's sexual repression as a dangerous, explosive frustration."[38] By eliminating the fear of pregnancy, birth control would contribute to women's sexual satisfaction and would tame and channel the power of female sexuality into rationally planned families.

The effect of the new direction was to bring contraception under professional control, making birth control devices more widely available and ultimately more effective. Most of all, PPFA gave the birth control movement "a clean image," emphasizing not women's rights, individual freedom, or sexuality, but as *Scientific American* noted, "the need for individual couples to plan their families and for nations to plan their populations."[39]

The focus on population planning emerged during World War II. At first, planning was geared to domestic needs, particularly the ideal of the postwar family. A 1943 PPFA pamphlet stated that "victory cannot be won without *planning.* . . . Planned Parenthood . . . can . . . be made to mean that more healthy children will be born to maintain the kind of peace for which we fight." Margaret Sanger herself called for "national security through birth control." At the same time, the war gave rise to the first direct connections between the American birth control movement and population control abroad. As the organization looked toward the postwar era, it became more concerned with the international implications of contraception. In a mass mailing sent to lawyers and businessmen, the PPFA argued, "Any sound peace plan must take into consideration population trends and natural resources, when we face such divergencies as the population of India." Healthy markets abroad were also an important consideration: "Sound planning for business expansion on a national scale must also consider carefully not only the numerical growth of people, but their purchasing power."[40]

These international issues fed directly into the postwar increase in support for research on contraception. Historian James Reed showed how the major funding for research that ultimately led to the development of intrauterine devices and oral contraceptives resulted directly from cold war concerns: "Nations newly liberated from colonial status wanted to share the prosperity of the West. Failure to develop their economies would lead to more bitter internal divisions and rejection of Western alliances in favor of communist models of development. Thus, political stability depended on rapid economic development and that development in turn could only succeed if the rate of population growth did not eat up the capital needed to finance development."[41] The anticommunist thrust of the funding for contraceptive research was obvious at the time. The Hugh More Fund distributed a pamphlet, frequently reprinted through the fifties and early sixties, entitled *The Population Bomb*. It claimed, "There will be 300 million more mouths to feed in the world four years from now—most of them hungry. Hunger brings turmoil—and turmoil, as we have learned, creates the atmosphere in which the communists seek to conquer the earth."[42]

Scientific, rational procreation at home and abroad fit the needs of the cold war and justified the acceptance of contraception by many liberal institutions. *Ebony* magazine assured its black readers that contraception "helps parents space babies to make them a blessing rather than a burden." Throughout the 1950s, religious groups, with the notable exception of the Catholic church, began to sanction birth control for family planning. The Very Reverend James Pike, a leading Episcopal spokesman, advocated contraceptive measures as "a positive duty" if a married couple, whether for reasons of health, emotional instability, or financial straits, did not want a child at a certain time. It was assumed, of course, that these circumstances were unusual and extraordinary, as well as temporary, and that the couple would procreate when these unfortunate conditions no longer existed. Under happier circumstances, the duty of parents was unquestionably to have children: "If the answer at a particular time is that they should be having a child, then they have a positive ethical responsibility to . . . carry out this intent, including medical assistance toward fertility." Pike's advocacy of birth control, then, was toward planned families: having children at the right time. Planned-parenthood workers, he urged, should be just as concerned with "planned procreation" as with the "limitation of birth."[43]

By 1961, the National Council of Churches of Christ had approved the use of contraceptives. Nonorthodox Protestant and Jewish organizations, according to one study, moved "from uncompromising hostility to birth control to fervid endorsement of its use, even making it a moral obligation to control family size."[44] The medical establishment concurred. At the same time, legislatures were loosening their restrictions on birth control. Before the war, most states banned the dissemination of contraceptive information and materials, even for doctors. But by the late 1950s, only two states, Connecticut and Massachusetts, still had these statutes on the books. Within the space of a few decades, major institutions shifted their perceptions of birth control from a threat to the social order to a positive tool for the nation's benefit. Throughout the 1950s, proponents of contraception continued to promote it as a means of controlling fertility abroad and spacing children at home.

Increased availability and legitimation led to the widespread use of birth control devices among married couples. American society was certainly ready to accept birth control as a means of improving marital sex and family planning. But it was not ready to accept its potential for liberating sex outside marriage or for liberating women from childbearing to enable them to pursue careers outside the home. As a result, contraception in the postwar years encouraged scientific family planning, rather than premarital sexual experimentation or alternatives to motherhood for women. American public opinion, legislative bodies, and the medical establishment all did their part to make sure that the birth control technology would encourage marriage and family life.[45]

In the early postwar years, the contraceptive technology actually reinforced existing mores and further encouraged the drop in the marriage age. It was widely argued that responsible young people could now marry young, even if they were in college or still economically dependent on their parents, because they could postpone the responsibilities of parenthood until they were ready. As late as 1968, one physician who was concerned about premarital sex stated, "I would certainly rather see a young couple marry early and postpone having babies than have them stumble into a sexual liaison in which they inadvertently start an unwanted life." He continued by endorsing sexual containment: "The sex drive, like hunger and aggressiveness, can be controlled in socially acceptable ways until marriage is possible."[46]

By enabling couples to marry young, postpone childbearing, and space their children, contraception fostered the modernization and professionalization of domestic roles. Like labor-saving appliances, birth control devices could con-tribute to enjoyment at home and heighten the standards for domestic conduct. Both kinds of products, however, placed the burden of responsibility on women and rooted them more securely as the custodians of the scientific home. Contraception thus reinforced the imperative to contain sex within marriage, and it underscored the ideology of modern domesticity that included reproduc-tive responsibilities and traditional roles for women. Consequently, one of the most explosive technological developments of the postwar years, which held the promise of freeing sex from marriage and marriage from procreation, did neither. That potential was not realized for two decades.

Advocates of family planning endorsed contraception but drew the line at abortion. Unlike contraceptives, which were promoted as a means of strength-ening the family, abortion was considered a threat to sexual morality and family life. While contraception was the reward for the virtuous, abortion was the pun-ishment for the immoral. Public health pamphlets published by the American Social Hygiene Association (ASHA), a conservative group of health profession-als, contained implicit warnings that sexual transgression could lead one to a dangerous abortionist's door. ASHA placed itself in the vanguard of the sex edu-cation movement, but the education it promoted was based on fear. One chapter of ASHA requested a cover design for a pamphlet on abortion that would pic-ture a frightened-looking woman walking up a dingy stairway in an obvious slum.[47] Illegal abortions were indeed dangerous, but ASHA urged individual caution rather than legalized abortion.

Legal abortions had been available for several decades at the discretion of physicians, but they became more difficult to obtain in the 1940s and 1950s. "Therapeutic" abortions could be performed legally in hospitals only if the physicians decided that continuing the pregnancy would present a danger to the life or health of the woman, and criteria were haphazard and arbitrary. In most states, physicians were able to interpret the danger as they saw fit, and some women were able to have safe operations. Legal abortions, however, accounted for only part of the terminated pregnancies. A thriving underground business provided illegal and often dangerous abortions to an estimated two hundred and fifty thousand to 1 million women each year during the postwar years. These illegal abortions were also responsible for an estimated 40 percent of all maternal deaths. Kinsey reported that among his sample, fully 24 percent of the wives had had abortions by the time they were forty, and that almost 90 percent of premarital pregnancies were aborted. Most of these operations were illegal.[48]

Clearly, illegal abortions were a serious health problem. But the problem was not new. In fact, Kinsey's evidence suggests that fewer abortions were performed in the postwar era than in the 1930s. Even though the actual number of abortions may have been going down, articles in the popular press increased.[49] Sensationalist coverage of illegal "abortion rings" were warnings to young women. Although these articles condemned the illegal abortionists, they also condemned the women who died at their hands.

Although many abortions were performed in safe and hygienic conditions by physicians who risked their reputations and even their licenses by doing so, it was the illegal abortionists who attracted the most attention. One who gained public notoriety was a "Dr." Faiman, who allegedly deluded young women with his "look of respectability." *Time* described Faiman as "living in an exclusive section of Dallas. . . . He has been supported in his pleasant position by panicky pregnant girls." Faiman was portrayed in much the same way as the "white slavers" of the Progressive Era: predatory, dark, sly, and foreign. He was believed to be an immigrant, "apparently born in Riga."[50]

Despite the publicity surrounding abortion scandals, most Americans still advocated restricted access to legal operations. Even physicians did not call for increasing the availability of legal abortions, which would minimize the risks involved. Rather, by the end of the 1940s, the medical establishment systematically reduced the number of abortions performed in hospitals by denying a greater proportion of the requests for therapeutic abortions. Moreover, hospitals began to change their policies by removing the discretionary power from individual physicians and requiring a hospital committee to rule on each abortion request. As a result, requests for legal abortions were more frequently denied than granted. A few voices called for legalized abortion, but they were faint compared to the roar that condemned the practice. The weight of public opinion was on the side of reproduction: Women who have sex should be married, and married women should have babies.[51] Medical advances in contraception might assist that effort, but abortion represented a threat to the family-planning ideal.

The behavior of the respondents to the Kelly Longitudinal Study (KLS) would have pleased those who advocated the use of contraceptives for family planning. Reflecting the concerns of the day, the KLS asked respondents to provide information about their plans for having children, their experiences with pregnancies and births, and their use of birth control. (The KLS questionnaire had forty-seven questions on reproduction alone.) Like most of their middle-class peers, the KLS respondents were conscientious family planners; 98 percent reported using some form of birth control, and nearly all used contraceptives to delay having children at the beginning of their marriage and to space their children afterward. There were, however, some accidental, unplanned pregnancies. Since the methods used at the time were less effective than the oral contraceptives and intrauterine devices that were available later, 30 percent said that at least one child was conceived while they practiced some form of birth control. Nevertheless, nearly all the 30 percent reported no negative effects from these accidental pregnancies. Although the KLS did not ask about premarital abortions, fewer than one in ten reported any "intentional termination of pregnancies" during the marriage.[52]

The KLS respondents' use of contraception is consistent with findings from other studies. Kinsey found that among white women born between 1920 and 1929, 94 percent used contraceptive devices; 57 percent used diaphragms and 37 percent of their husbands used condoms. National fertility studies in the 1950s showed that 81 percent of the white wives of childbearing age used birth control and 7 percent more planned to do so. The trend was toward using birth control earlier in marriage to plan first births and space the rest. By 1957, the peak year of the baby boom, a University of Michigan survey found that nearly all American couples were planning the size of their families. But they were planning for more children than in the past. Between 1940 and 1960, the "ideal" number of children went from two to four. In addition, planned children were born to young parents. In the 1950s, women had their first child at a younger age than did their grandmothers. Compared to white middle-class Protestant couples, blacks, Catholics, and those with less education were less likely to use contraception or to use it early in marriage. But by the 1960s, when oral contraceptives became available, these differences among groups were shrinking.[53]

The KLS respondents fit the national pattern: 70 percent of the couples had two to four children. Most began having children during the war; a small number in 1955 said they still would like more children. The majority had given birth to all their children within six or fewer years, and 80 percent within ten years. It seems clear that these respondents used birth control to postpone conception at the beginning of their marriage (most did not have children in the first year of marriage) but then chose to have children in rapid succession, ending their childbearing in most cases by their late twenties or early thirties. Birth control methods allowed them to plan their families according to their wishes, which matched the prevailing norms.[54]

As time went on, the couples in the KLS desired larger families, and there was 90 percent agreement between spouses about the number of children they wanted. Before the couples married, only 20 percent wanted four or more children. By the mid-1950s, 39 percent wanted at least four children. As one wife recalled, "Children were not discussed [during the engagement]. That was a time of depression and our desire was to afford marriage. . . . After the first baby, I wanted company for her and had a second daughter. A miscarriage left me with such a feeling of failure that I wanted the third child. The fourth was a happy accident. So now we're really 'happy' to be blessed with our 2 boys and 2 girls."[55] Miscarriage meant "failure"; unplanned pregnancy was a "happy accident." This woman articulated the widely held belief that a large family was a successful family and a happy one.

Only 14 percent of the KLS respondents said they had more children than they had originally desired. In contrast, 48 percent had fewer than they had hoped, and 61 percent said their family was smaller than they wished. More than 25 percent reported some difficulty in conception, and nearly 40 percent had lost at least one baby through a miscarriage or stillbirth. Those couples who had fewer children than they had wished did so primarily for financial reasons or physical difficulties, usually the health or age of the mother or infertility problems.[56] As the mother of an only child explained, "If able to carry them I would have wished to have four." Some women suffered at the hands of the medical profession. Explaining why she ended up with two children instead of the four she and her husband originally wanted, one woman blamed "the assembly line method . . . in hospitals when babies are born. Due to carelessness by a well known (woman's) specialist the after-birth was removed one week after 1st child was born. Before then 5 blood transfusions and many saline solutions were administered. . . . Usual rush and hasty use of forceps broke collar bone of 2d healthy child. Doctor denied anything wrong but 20 days later when dismissed from hospital X-ray showed broken collar bone mended and to this day child has not proper use of arm."[57] In those days, before the boom in lawsuits for medical malpractice, this mother kept her bitterness to herself and decided to stop having children.

The desire to provide a college education for each child was another major reason why some parents limited the size of their families. The comment of one woman was typical: "I think if money had not been such a worrisome thing and if we had not had so many periods of unsteady jobs, we might have had more children." Another woman had similar concerns but still considered the possibility of having more children: "After the first two were born and we appreciated the joys of parenthood it was mutually desired to have more children. We have stopped at 4 only because we feel the financial burden of educating more than 4 is more than we can see our way clear to assuming. We would both like six children. And it is not too late to change our minds about stopping at 4!"[58]

A few women in the sample who admitted that they believed there was more to life than constant child care gave personal reasons for limiting the size of their families. Joan Morey, for example, explained why she stopped at two children: "The expenses of raising a child made us feel 2 would be enough. For we wanted to give a college education, music lessons, etc. to each child, if he showed interest. Also the interests I have had in church and community activities made me discontent with constant baby or child care."[59] This final comment suggests another issue that surfaced: the stresses of motherhood. Although it was unfashionable to complain about these stresses, given the widely shared belief that children provided women with happiness and fulfillment, some of the women expressed their dissatisfactions in the privacy of the anonymous questionnaire.

Joan Morey wished to devote more of her time and energy to voluntary activities, which were an important route to public life for many homemakers at the time. Other women were more explicit about the burdens of full-time motherhood. Carol Hubbard was one mother for whom the strain became unbearable. Joseph Hubbard claimed that he and his wife modified their original desire for six children because of the costs involved in raising them. But his wife gave another explanation. She claimed that the reason was "my nervous condition after the third and my husband's indifference to my problems and his lack of assistance." Carol's perception of Joseph's denial of her trouble was confirmed in his responses to the questionnaire. When asked if his wife had experienced any emotional disturbances, he checked "a little" and noted, "General nervousness during menstrual period." His wife, however, described her emotional difficulties differently. Checking the highest category, "a great deal," she went on to explain, "Due to loss of sleep for 5 months with third baby and care of 2 other small children, I believe I had a nervous breakdown but did not realize a doctor could have helped me. Cried frequently, 'boiling' sensation inside would rise up to my head and then caused shrill screams. Inability to concentrate. Could not read or even sit down for long."[60]

The stresses of parenting did little to dampen the enthusiasm for having children, however. The desire for large families exhibited by wives in the KLS sample was shared by younger women as well. John Modell and John Campbell's study of 192 single women aged eighteen to twenty-one in 1955 found that they had a strong desire to have several children. These women were at least a decade younger than the KLS respondents, but they had many similar views. They were much more likely to express their desire for children than their eagerness for marriage (a much higher proportion associated pleasure, love, and joy with having children than with getting married). They also gave more reasons for having children than for getting married.

The researchers found few differentials by class, although the sample was all white. Their respondents expressed unromantic notions of marriage but saw children as providing a means of personal fulfillment. Many more among all classes rated children—rather than the marriage itself—as the most important aspect of married life. In addition, they strongly believed in planning for several children, a finding that suggests that the continued baby boom was the result not of a "baby binge," but of rational planning and a continued adherence to a pronatalist ideology. Economic well-being had only a minor impact on child-bearing aspirations; the respondents were more likely to decrease their fertility expectations if their financial circumstances became reduced than to increase them in flush times. The attitudes of these young single women suggest that by the mid-1950s a strong ideology prevailed that would keep the birthrate booming for nearly another decade.[61]

The baby boom was accompanied and reinforced by a widespread ideology favoring large families, reflected in everything from media images and medical theories to public policies. The popular press practically deified parenthood, while such measures as tax exemptions for dependent children and financial incentives for suburban home ownership encouraged postwar couples to have large families.[62] Still, one needs to ask why parents—especially women—wanted large families. Clearly, affluence alone cannot explain the baby boom. As one study concluded, the evidence "provides no support at all for the hypothesis that income bears a positive relation to fertility." Nevertheless, fertility fit "the consumer choice model," indicating that numerous children, like numerous commodities, reflected an abundant home. The desire for many children expressed widely shared societal norms: "The basic idea is that couples pick out a reproductive target and then are more or less successful at hitting it. The target chosen reflects the reproductive norms they have internalized." The researchers who documented this trend were at a loss to explain it. They concluded, "The level of fertility [went] up for every subgroup and then it [came] down for every subgroup, and we are far from an understanding of why that happened and whether it will happen again."[63]

An examination of the cultural factors offers some clues to this phenomenon. For instance, many educated women "professionalized" homemaking and made it their career, investing it with skills, prestige, and importance. Considering the difficulties women faced in combining a family with an occupation outside the home, it is not surprising that many women poured their creative energies into their families. The same impulses that promoted college training for homemakers would seek to elevate child rearing to fit a quasiprofessional model, complete with guidebooks and standards. Women whose aspirations for personal achievement had little chance of realization in the wider world put their energies into full-time motherhood. As the *Ladies Home Journal* noted, "Increasing numbers of women, disillusioned with their present roles or with what the workaday world can offer, will turn toward motherhood as the happiest road to fulfillment." But motherhood could only be full time as long as there were young children at home. Once the children entered school, full-time motherhood was not possible unless the women had more children. In addition, since widely read experts like Dr. Benjamin Spock stressed the vital importance of the early years, women could increase their sense of usefulness and importance by increasing the number of small children at home. In that way, they could extend their commitment to the "absorbing, creative profession" of parenting.[64]

It is no wonder that women responded to Dr. Spock's call for professionalized child rearing and propelled his guide to baby and child care to the top of the best-seller list.[65] If the occupational achievement of men was reflected in the income they brought home, that of women might be reflected in the number of children they raised successfully. Large families were an indication of a man's potency and ability to provide, and of a woman's success as a professional homemaker.

Thoughtful observers have suggested that the baby boom was a response to feelings of impotence in the wider world, which fostered the greater privatization and isolation of the family. As one team of scholars concluded, "If [men and women] lacked the hope to affect congressional decisions, they could still hope to influence their children and the local school board."[66] Although there is some truth to this view, procreation was not simply a "reaction to their loss of hope for significant influence on the world," as the authors claimed. Rather, child rearing was one of the few ways of *exerting* influence on the world. Domesticity was not so much a retreat from public affairs as an expression of one's citizenship. Postwar men and women were endorsing and affirming, through their families, the goals expressed by major political leaders and experts. With the support of public policies and institutions, and in conformity with widely shared political goals, they joined in the affirmation of planned families, took advantage of contraceptive techniques to space their children scientifically, accepted governmental benefits, and followed the prescriptions of the medical establishment. Rather than retreating from public life, baby-boom parents joined forces with government officials and professionals who called for bigger and better "successful American families."[67]

The rising birthrate, then, was not just a demographic phenomenon. It was the result of a fully articulated baby-boom ideology that found expression in Hollywood, in the political culture, in the prescriptive literature, and in the thoughts and aspirations of women and men at the time. Postwar Americans wholeheartedly endorsed this reproductive consensus. It fit their belief in abundance, progress, and productivity. As one man declared in 1955, "I'd like six kids. . . . It just seems like a minimum production goal."[68] Although many people experienced confusion and discord over sexuality, most had the same procreative ideals and followed the same procreative behavior. They used contraception, spaced their children, and created large families.

Children provided tangible results of a successful marriage and family life; they gave evidence of responsibility, patriotism, and achievement. They would tame the wayward tendencies of men and fulfill the sexual energies of women. Even when child rearing led to stress and exhaustion, parents still pointed to their offspring with a sense of accomplishment.

Like other elements of the postwar domestic ideal, however, the children in whom mothers and fathers invested so much of themselves could not possibly satisfy all their parents' expectations. Adults would wring their hands over their children's behavior, playmates, and social circles; authorities would fret about the alleged rise in juvenile delinquency; and those treasured children would become the rebellious youths of the 1960s and, eventually, grow up.[69] As the years wore on, the investment in child rearing would take its toll, especially on the women who found themselves stuck in an "empty nest" at a relatively young age, with little else to give purpose to their lives. But in the years of the baby boom, these parents were unaware of the potential disappointments that might result from placing such high hopes for personal fulfillment in child rearing. As they moved into the expanding suburbs and settled in with their growing families, they put their best efforts into living out the postwar version of the American dream. This was the way of life that spread a beacon to the free world; this was the family ideal worth protecting against hostile outside forces.

CHAPTER SEVEN

THE COMMODITY GAP: CONSUMERISM AND THE MODERN HOME

As a normal part of life, thrift now is un-American.

—WILLIAM H. WHYTE, JR., 1956

No man who owns his own house and lot can be a Communist. He has too much to do.

—WILLIAM J. LEVITT, DEVELOPER OF LEVITTOWN, 1948[1]

THE SEXUALLY charged, child-centered family took its place as the embodiment of the postwar American dream. The most tangible symbol of that dream was the suburban home—the locale of the good life, the evidence of democratic abundance. It did not take long for this consumer-laden dream house to land squarely in the middle of cold war politics. One remarkable example demonstrates the direct link between the suburban American dream and the international dynamics of the cold war. In 1948, when Europe was still recovering from World War II, American officials worried that political instability might lead some nations to embrace communism. Leaders in the United States were particularly worried that Italy might go communist. A critical election was approaching, and there were several "hot spots" in the country where impoverished Italians appeared to be leaning toward voting for the Communist Party. At that time, Richard Moore, an aide to California congressman Richard Nixon, was trying to figure out a way to influence the Italian election. Prior to joining Nixon's congressional staff in Washington, Moore had worked in the television industry in California. So he contacted John Guedel, creator of several early television shows, and asked for help.

Guedel came up with an idea: the "Win a Future" contest. Anyone who entered the contest had a chance to "win a future," which included a house in the newly completed suburban development of Panorama City, in the San Fernando Valley. The house would contain the finest new appliances and furnishings, and the lucky winner would also receive a new car and a job. According to Guedel, anyone could enter the contest by writing a letter stating in 100 words or less why it is better to live under capitalism than communism, enclosing ten cents, and sending it to the television station. Each week, one contestant was selected to appear on the television show *People Are Funny* and have an opportunity to solve a riddle in order to "win a future." Six hundred and forty thousand Americans entered the contest. The letters were collected and sent to Italy, along with CARE packages of food. The United States Army translated the letters and distributed them with the CARE packages to Italian voters in key areas at risk of electing communists. Apparently, the effort worked: The communists were defeated in the 1948 election in Italy. Meanwhile, contestant Vivienne George finally solved the riddle and "won a future." As it turned out, the future she won was not so bright. She and her husband, a disabled World War II veteran, only lived in the house for a few months. They were the first residents to move into Panorama City, and they were too isolated, especially considering his medical needs. The promised job never materialized, and the national notoriety left the Georges vulnerable to the demands of many people who believed that the couple were now fabulously wealthy.[2]

Although Vivienne George was the only one to "win a future," like many other Americans she discovered that the American dream did not fully live up to its promise. But the suburban home, complete with modern appliances and furnishings, continued to serve as a tangible symbol of the American way of life, and as a powerful weapon in the cold war propaganda arsenal. A decade after the "Win a Future" contest, Richard Nixon was no longer a congressman. He was now vice president under Dwight D. Eisenhower. In 1959, Eisenhower sent Nixon to represent the United States at the American Exhibition in Moscow, where a "model home," similar to the one in Panorama City won by Vivienne George, was on display. Let us now return briefly to the site of the famous "kitchen debate," where Vice President Richard M. Nixon articulated the essence of American superiority by pointing to the consumer-laden suburban home. The ideal home Nixon described was one that obliterated class distinctions and accentuated gender distinctions. The "model home" he extolled was not a mansion but a modest ranch-style structure, "within the price range of the average U.S. worker," complete with modern appliances that would "make easier the life of our housewives." Although Vivienne George had to solve a riddle to win her house in the suburbs because she couldn't otherwise afford it, for Nixon, the most important feature of the suburban home was its availability to Americans of all classes.

"Let us start with some of the things in this exhibit," Nixon began. "You will see a house, a car, a television set—each the newest and most modern of its type we produce. But can only the rich in the United States afford such things? If this were the case, we would have to include in our definition of rich the millions of America's wage earners." Nixon felt certain that the possibility of homeownership would defuse the most dangerous potential of class conflict. As he explained to Soviet premier Nikita Khrushchev, "Our steel workers, as you know, are on strike. But any steel worker could buy this house. They earn $3 an hour. This house costs about $100 a month to buy on a contract running twenty-five to thirty years." Khrushchev countered, "We have steel workers and we have peasants who also can afford to spend $14,000 for a house." But for Nixon, homeownership represented even more than a comfortable way of life; it was the validation of the free enterprise system.[3]

Nixon's frame of reference was the family: "There are 44 million families in the United States. Twenty-five million of [them] live in houses or apartments that have as much or more floor space than the one you see in this exhibit. Thirty-one million families own their own homes and the land on which they are built. America's 44 million families own a total of 56 million cars, 50 million television sets and 143 million radio sets. And they buy an average of nine dresses and suits and 14 pairs of shoes per family per year."

Nixon then described other miracles of domestic technology. Pointing to a television screen, he said, "We can see here what is happening in other parts of the home." Khrushchev, scorning the American obsession with gadgets, chided, "This is probably always out of order. . . . Don't you have a machine that puts food into the mouth and pushes it down? Many things you've shown us are interesting but they are not needed in life. . . . They are merely gadgets." Yet both leaders took the commodity gap seriously. The Soviet premier continued, "Newly built Russian houses have all this equipment right now. Moreover, all you have to do to get a house is to be born in the Soviet Union. So I have a right to a house. In America if you don't have a dollar, you have the right to sleep on the pavement. Yet you say that we are slaves of communism."

Khrushchev further accused Americans of building houses to last only twenty years, so builders could continually sell new ones. "We build firmly," said the Soviet leader. "We build for our children and grandchildren." But Nixon argued that after twenty years, the older home or kitchen would be obsolete. Linking consumer aspirations to scientific expertise, he explained that the American system was designed to take advantage of new inventions and new techniques. Unimpressed, Khrushchev replied, "This theory does not hold water." But for Nixon the theory did hold water, for it reflected his belief in the potential for individualism and upward mobility.

The metaphor that prevailed throughout the debate was that of a race. But it was not the arms race or the space race; it was the consumer race—centered on the home. Khrushchev estimated that it would take only seven years before the USSR would reach the American standard of living. Already in eight years, grain and milk output had nearly doubled, and television sets were up from sixty-seven thousand to a million. The terms of the cold war were set in these figures. Nixon was willing to concede Russian successes in the space race, but he argued that domestic consumer goods were the most meaningful measure of American superiority over the Soviet Union: "There are some instances where you may be ahead of us, for example in the development of the thrust of your rockets for the investigation of outer space; there may be some instances in which we are ahead of you—in color television, for instance." Not to be outdone, Khrushchev claimed, "No, we are up with you on this, too." Nixon remarked, "We welcome this kind of competition because when we engage in it, no one loses, everyone wins." Thus, the commodity gap took precedence over the missile gap.

In Nixon's vision, the suburban ideal of homeownership would tame two potentially disruptive forces: women and workers. In appliance-laden houses across the country, working-class as well as business-class breadwinners could fulfill the new American work-to-consume ethic. Homeownership would lessen class consciousness among workers, who would set their sights toward the middle-class ideal. The family home would be the place where a man could display his success through the accumulation of consumer goods. Women would reap rewards for domesticity by surrounding themselves with commodities; they would remain content as housewives because appliances would ease their burdens. For both men and women, homeownership would reinforce aspirations for upward mobility and diminish the potential for social unrest.

Nixon was not the only one who believed that the American preoccupation with procurement would be a safeguard against the threat of class warfare and communism. Mayor Joseph Darst of St. Louis, expressing the views of liberal anticommunists, wrote to the city's board of aldermen in 1951 that if everyone had good housing, "no one in the United States would need to worry today about the threat of communism in this country. Communists love American slums. Our clearance of these slums and erection of adequate housing is one of the most effective answers we can give communism locally."[4]

For those who agreed that economic optimism was essential to keep the free enterprise system alive and well, there were reasons to rejoice. The postwar years witnessed a huge increase in discretionary spending power, an increase that surpassed gains in income or prices. Between 1947 and 1961, the number of families rose 28 percent, national income increased over 60 percent, and the group with discretionary income (those with money for nonnecessities) doubled. Rather than putting this money aside for a rainy day, Americans were inclined to spend it. A 1946 Gallup poll indicated that in spite of persistent pockets of poverty and fears of another depression, the desire to spend was much stronger than the desire to save. This is not to say that the concern for future security was tossed to the wind; on the contrary, security remained a high priority. Americans were only slightly more hopeful about the economic future in 1945 than they had been in 1937 at the depth of the depression. Fears of another depression were widespread, and one-third of the population was still in poverty.[5] But the increase in income for the middle and working classes, combined with new governmental supports, encouraged Americans to invest their money in purchases. Social Security no doubt eased their fears of poverty in old age, and veterans' mortgages facilitated expenditures for homeownership. Americans responded with guarded optimism by making purchases that would strengthen their sense of security. In the postwar years, investing in one's own home, along with the trappings that would enhance family life, seemed the best way to plan for the future.

Instead of rampant spending for personal luxury items, Americans were likely to spend their money at home. In the five years after World War II, consumer spending increased 60 percent, but the amount spent on household furnishings and appliances rose 240 percent. In the same five years, purchases for food rose only 33 percent, and for clothing a mere 20 percent. From the depression onward, the trend in spending was striking. Between 1935 and 1950, the money income of Americans increased 50 percent. But this increase was not divided evenly among purchasing categories. Expenditures for food and drink increased only 30 percent; for clothing, 53 percent; for personal care, 69 percent; and for education, 73 percent. These increases were modest compared to the increases in expenditures for household operation (108 percent), recreation (185 percent), and automobiles (205 percent). In the four years following the end of the war, Americans purchased 21.4 million cars, 20 million refrigerators, 5.5 million stoves, and 11.6 million televisions and moved into over 1 million new housing units each year. The same patterns extended into the 1950s, a decade in which prosperity continued to spread.[6]

The locale for this consumer-oriented family life was suburbia. The suburban home caught the imagination as well as the purse strings of postwar Americans. A study of the psychology of spending noted, "The impact of suburbia on consumer behavior can hardly be overstated. . . . Young people chose to marry early, to have several children in the early years of marriage, to live in . . . nice neighborhoods, and to have cars, washing machines, refrigerators, television sets, and several other appliances at the same time." Americans channeled their spending accordingly. With the exception of the very poor, those of ample as well as modest means exhibited a great deal of conformity in their consumption attitudes and behavior. Spending patterns reflected widely shared beliefs about the good life, which seemed within reach of many, even those of the lower-middle and working classes.[7]

Consumer patterns, then, reflected one more aspect of containment behavior as the nation's affluent majority poured their income into homes and family pursuits. The old version of the virtuous home was a much more ascetic one. Still, the values associated with domestic spending upheld traditional American concerns with pragmatism and morality, rather than opulence and luxury. Purchasing for the home helped alleviate traditional American uneasiness with consumption: the fear that spending would lead to decadence. Family-centered spending reassured Americans that affluence would strengthen the American way of life. The goods purchased by middle-class consumers, like a modern refrigerator or a house in the suburbs, were intended to foster traditional values.[8]

Pragmatism and family enrichment were the keys to virtuous consumerism. The commodities that people bought promised to reinforce home life and uphold traditional gender roles. After all, American women were housewives; their lives were functional, not merely ornamental. In general, male breadwinners provided the income for household goods, and their wives purchased them.

Public opinion polls taken after the war indicate that both men and women were generally opposed to employment for women and believed that a woman who ran a home had a "more interesting time" than did a woman with a full-time job. There were, however, circumstances in which employment for women was approved—especially if the income it generated fostered family life. For example, one poll showed that postwar women and men believed that if a young couple could not marry because the man was not earning enough to support them both, "the girl should take a job so they can get married right away."[9] By and large, however, employment for married women was discouraged. Given these prevailing attitudes, it is no wonder that Nixon continually interchanged the words *woman* and *housewife* as he extolled the American way of life at the Moscow exhibition.

Yet that equation should be examined closely, since not all married women were full-time homemakers during the 1950s. In fact, the postwar years brought more wives into the paid labor force than ever before. Americans felt a great deal of ambivalence toward women's employment—a legacy of the depression and the war. On the one hand, it was unfortunate if a wife had to hold a job; on the other hand, it was considered far worse if the family was unable to purchase what were believed to be necessities for the home.

During these years, the very definition of household needs changed to include many more consumer items. Since it was the homemaker's responsibility to purchase these items, women sought employment, ironically, to promote their role as consumers. The economic importance of women's role as consumers cannot be overstated, for it kept American industry rolling and sustained jobs for the nation's male providers. Nearly the entire increase in the gross national product in the mid-1950s was due to increased spending on consumer durables and residential construction.[10] Many employed wives considered their jobs secondary to their role as consumers and in tune with the ethic of togetherness and subordination that characterized their marital relationships. This was one legacy that depression-bred daughters inherited: Women sought employment to bolster the family budget but not to disrupt domestic power relationships. As long as their employment provided a secondary source of income and did not undermine the authority of the male breadwinner, it was acceptable to the family.[11]

The house and commodity boom also had tremendous propaganda value, for it was those affluent homes, complete with breadwinner and homemaker, that provided evidence of the superiority of the American way of life. Since much of the cold war was waged in propaganda battles, this vision of domesticity was a powerful weapon. Although they may have been unwitting soldiers, women who marched off to the nation's shopping centers to equip their new homes joined the ranks of American cold warriors. As newscaster and noted cold warrior George Putnam said in 1947, shopping centers were "concrete expressions of the practical idealism that built America . . . plenty of free parking for all those cars that we capitalists seem to acquire. Who can help but contrast [them] with what you'd find under communism?"[12]

Consumers no doubt had fewer global concerns in mind. They had saved their money for specific purposes. During the war, a survey of bank depositors indicated that 43 percent were eager to spend their money on "future needs," and half of those specified purchases for the home. Leading architects helped give tangible form to these desires by publishing plans for "dream houses" in leading magazines like the *Ladies Home Journal*. Construction companies also fed consumer longings by selling scrapbooks for saving ideas for future houses, with sections divided into the various rooms of the home. The Andersen Window Company, for example, which was well aware of the potential market, distributed three hundred and fifty thousand embossed scrapbooks before the end of the war. By June 1944, appliances topped the list of the most desired consumer items. When asked what they hoped to purchase in the postwar years, Americans listed washing machines first, then electric irons, refrigerators, stoves, toasters, radios, vacuum cleaners, electric fans, and hot water heaters. Advertisers claimed that these items constituted the American way of life that the soldiers were fighting for.[13]

The pent-up desires for homes and appliances represented something more than mere fantasies of luxurious living. The need for wartime housing was great. Dislocated war workers needed $100 million worth of new housing, which prompted a construction boom during the war. By 1943, residential real estate buying reached levels unknown since the 1920s. But wartime building was inadequate to meet the increasing need. The housing shortage reached crisis proportions after the war. In 1945, 98 percent of American cities reported shortages of houses, and more than 90 percent reported shortages of apartments. By 1947, 6 million families were doubling up with relatives or friends. The housing industry gained tremendous momentum after the war in the face of these immediate needs, and it took advantage of the conversion of production technology for peacetime use.[14] Supply and demand came together to foster an explosion in residential housing after the war. But the expansion did not take place equally in all types of housing; nor were the new dwellings available to all Americans. Largely as a result of governmental policies, massive suburban developments of single-family houses took precedence over apartments and inner-city dwellings.

The Servicemen's Readjustment Act of 1944 (the GI Bill of Rights) created a Veterans Administration (VA) program of guaranteed mortgage insurance, expanding the Federal Housing Authority (FHA) program dating back to 1934. The new programs, which provided federal insurance for loans to white veterans, encouraged private investors to enter the housing mortgage market. In addition, the tax benefits for homeowners became substantial in the 1940s. The government also financed large suburban tracts, such as those built by William Levitt. With all these incentives for building and purchasing suburban residences, it soon became cheaper to buy than to rent. Provided they were white, veterans could buy homes in Levittown, with a thirty-year mortgage and no down payment, by spending only $56 per month. At the same time, the average apartment rental in many cities was $93. These overpriced, often substandard apartments were left to Americans of color, who were excluded from the suburbs. When asked why black families were not allowed to purchase homes in Levittown, William Levitt claimed that he was in the business of building houses, not solving social problems. As a result of such racist attitudes and the policies they generated, social problems that did not exist at the time emerged in the years to come.[15]

Postwar governmental policies fostered the construction of the vast majority of new housing in the suburbs. Housing starts went from 114,000 in 1944 to an all-time high of 1,692,000 in 1950. The cold war made a profound contribution to suburban sprawl. In 1951, the *Bulletin of Atomic Scientists* devoted an issue to "defense through decentralization" that argued in favor of depopulating the urban core to avoid a concentration of residences or industries in a potential target area for a nuclear attack. Joining this effort was the American Road Builders Association, a lobbying group second only to the munitions industry. As a result of these pressures, Congress passed the Interstate Highway Act in 1956, which provided $100 billion to cover 90 percent of the cost for forty-one thousand miles of national highways. When President Dwight D. Eisenhower signed the bill into law, he stated one of the major reasons for the new highway system: "[In] case of atomic attack on our key cities, the road net must permit quick evacuation of target areas."[16]

Many people believed that the suburbs also provided protection against labor unrest, which might lead to class warfare and its presumed inevitable result, communism. The report of a 1948 meeting of a San Francisco businessmen's association, chaired by the ex-president of the National Association of Home Builders, argued for the dispersion of industry outside central cities: "Conditions under which employees live, as well as work, vitally influence management-labor relations. Generally, large aggregations of labor in one big [central-city] plant are more subject to outside disrupting influences, and have less happy relations with management, than in smaller [suburban] plants."[17]

The suburban growth that resulted from these policies was neither universal nor inevitable; in Europe, centralization rather than decentralization predominated. In the United States, the FHA and VA mortgage policies, the highway system, the financing of sewers, the government subsidies for suburban developments such as Levittown, and the placing of public housing in the center of urban ghettos facilitated the dispersal of the white middle class into the suburbs and contributed to the decay of the inner cities. Furthermore, blacks were excluded from the suburbs by de facto segregation and the FHA's redlining policies that denied mortgages to black families, more than by poverty. Although there were a small number of black as well as racially integrated suburbs, the vast majority of suburban neighborhoods were restricted to whites.[18]

In 1946, as a result of all these supports for homeownership, for the first time a majority of the nation's white families lived in homes they owned. Over the next fifteen years, 12 million more families became homeowners. By the 1950s, most of those who purchased homes did so to buy a better house or move into a better neighborhood. Loans available to homeowners favored purchase over repair, which further spurred the movement of the white population into newly constructed suburban developments. Between 1950 and 1970, the suburban population doubled, from 36 million to 74 million; 83 percent of the nation's growth during those years took place in the suburbs.[19]

Although the suburbs were clearly designated for whites only, they offered a picture of domestic comfort available to those with modest incomes. These homes represented the American way of life, democratic and affordable, that Nixon would extoll in Moscow. Confirming Nixon's assertion of the American desire for change and newness, upgrading was a widespread motive for spending. The nation's consumers continually replaced, improved, or expanded their homes, appliances, and cars, long before those items had worn out. Federal policies, combined with increased affluence, made it possible for white Americans of moderate means to indulge their desires for newness and mobility.[20] In these ways, the cold war goal of defusing class conflict succeeded in the suburbs, where families of white-collar and blue-collar workers lived side by side.

Federal programs did more than simply blur class lines and spur a trend toward homeownership in the expanding suburbs. Policies that reflected and encouraged the American domestic ideology fostered and reinforced a particular kind of family life. In effect, these federal programs provided subsidies and incentives for couples to marry and have several children. Houses were designed to accommodate families with small children. Builders and architects assumed that men would be away at work during the day and houses would be occupied by full-time homemaker-mothers. In the first Levittown, a standardized suburban development built by William Levitt, 17,400 houses accommodated 82,000 residents. The structures were mass-produced and inexpensive, with a flexible interior design that was easily expandable if the family increased in size. Kitchens were near the front entrance, so mothers could keep an eye on their children as they cooked. Living rooms featured picture windows facing the backyard, also to facilitate the supervision of children. Appliances were included in the purchase price. The one-story design gave the home an informal look and was practical for families with young children, since there were no stairs, which could be dangerous. As young parents of the baby boom moved into these homes, it is no wonder that the first Levittown quickly earned the nicknames "Fertility Valley" and "The Rabbit Hutch."[21]

By stimulating these particular kinds of suburban housing developments and providing subsidies to homeowners, the federal government effectively underwrote the baby boom, along with the lifestyle and community arrangements that fostered traditional gender roles in the home. The government, along with the National Association of Home Builders, provided plans in the 1950s for smaller, inexpensive ranch-style homes that would allow for openness, adequate room for appliances and other consumer goods, and the easy supervision of children. Appliances were intended not to enable housewives to have more free time to pursue their own interests, but to help them achieve higher standards of cleanliness and efficiency, while allowing more time for child care. The suburban home was planned as a self-contained universe. Technological advances made housework efficient and professional; lawn mowers and cake mixes guaranteed a perfect result. In addition, homes were designed for enjoyment, fun, and togetherness. Family members would not need to go out for recreation or amusements, since they had swing sets, playrooms, and backyards with barbecues at home.[22]

Leisure pursuits encouraged a further infatuation with commodities. One of the most powerful of all postwar entertainments—the television set—sat squarely in people's living rooms. By the 1950s, televisions were selling at a rate of over 5 million a year. Television also fostered the classless ideal. Commercials extended the reach of advertising into people's homes, as did the abundant lifestyles portrayed on the screen. As historian George Lipsitz noted, situation comedies in the postwar years, especially those aimed at ethnic or working-class audiences, eased the transition from a depression-bred psychology of scarcity to an acceptance of spending. In shows like *I Remember Mama* or *The Honeymooners*, dramas of daily life often revolved around the purchase of consumer goods for the home. Characters in these programs urged each other to buy on installment, "live above our means—the American way," and spend rather than save. Commodities would solve the problem of the discontented housewife, foster pride in the provider whose job offered few intrinsic rewards, and allow children to "fit in" with their peers. Consumerism provided a means for assimilation into the American way of life: classless, homogeneous, and family-centered.[23]

The desire for the single-family home as a refuge against a chaotic world was not a postwar creation. Indeed, it dates back to housing reformers of the nineteenth century who first articulated the suburban family ideal. But it achieved new vigor in the postwar years, largely because the ideal was now within reach of most middle-class and many working-class Americans. In its modern manifestation, the suburban ranch-style home was to blend in with nature. As historian Clifford Edward Clark, Jr., observed, "The ranch house . . . was . . . seen as creating a unity with nature, but it was a unity that pictured nature as a tamed and open environment. . . . The 1950s design standards conceived of the natural world in a simplified and controlled way that eliminated anything that was wild or irregular."[24] (See Figure 15.)

The contained, natural style, enhanced by modern technology and design, offered a sense of security as well as privatized abundance. The natural look was more personal and even sensual than the formalized structures of public life and business. And although most ranch-style tract homes were relatively small, standardized one-story structures, the flexible interior space allowed for individuality—something increasingly lacking in the highly organized and bureaucratic world of work.[25]

Who purchased these homes, and did they satisfy their owners' needs and desires? According to surveys at the time, about half those who purchased houses in 1949 and 1950 were white World War II veterans in their mid-thirties with young children. The second half were about ten years older; their housing needs or financial resources had changed, prompting them to buy larger homes in the suburbs. Both groups were parents of the baby-boom generation. The second group included Americans of the age and circumstances of the respondents to the Kelly Longitudinal Study (KLS). The residents of Levittown, however, were more likely to belong to the first group: younger, less affluent, and largely working class. In his study of Levittown, Herbert Gans found that most of the residents claimed to be satisfied with their living arrangements.[26]

FIGURE 15   Ranch-style suburban home, built circa 1950. The style exudes a sheltered look of protection and privacy, surrounded by a tamed and controlled natural world. (*Courtesy of Judy Tyler.*)

Nevertheless, there were frustrations. Like expectations for exciting sexuality or fulfilling child rearing, the suburban ideal often promised more than it delivered. Many homeowners wished for more space but had to make do with smaller houses because of financial constraints. If spaciousness was an elusive goal for many suburbanites, so was the life of the happy housewife. Women in Levittown often complained about feeling trapped and isolated, facing endless chores of housekeeping and tending to children. For them, suburban life was not a life of fun and leisure but of exhausting work and isolation. In addition, since houses and neighborhoods were created with young children in mind, adolescents often chafed against the small rooms, lack of privacy, constant supervision, and absence of stores, restaurants, and other public gathering places where they could socialize in their neighborhoods. And although parents frequently mentioned the benefits of togetherness and the ability to spend more time with their families, the time-consuming commute for the men, and for the 25 percent of suburban women who were employed, actually reduced the amount of time available for families to share. Nevertheless, most homeowners expressed contentment with their residences, largely because they were significantly more spacious and comfortable than their previous dwellings, even if they did not

measure up to one's "dream house."[27] Once again, postwar Americans lowered
their expectations and expressed satisfaction with their suburban lot.

Although these suburban tracts have borne the brunt of scorn for their lack
of individuality and mass-produced sameness, they did offer a modicum of
comfort and convenience to growing families of modest means. Most of the
contract-built houses, like those in Levittown, had central heating, indoor
plumbing, telephones, automatic stoves, refrigerators, and washing machines—
conveniences that most middle-class Americans would not like to sacrifice. Yet
these isolated enclaves also weakened extended-family ties, promoted homo-
geneity in neighborhoods, intensified racial segregation, encouraged conformity,
and fostered a style of life based on traditional gender roles in the home.[28]

With the exception of avant-garde intellectuals and a small number of politically active feminists, few Americans articulated viable alternatives to the suburban lifestyle. Those who complained that life did not fit the ideal, like
overworked housewives in Levittown, generally tried to alleviate their miseries
with more money or goods. The ideal itself was rarely called into question, at
least not publicly. Nevertheless, it was difficult to achieve, even for those who
could afford it. These were by and large affluent middle-class Americans, well
educated and ambitious, who believed in the American dream and belonged to
the postwar consensus. The men worked in a highly organized and bureaucra-
tized economy, struggling to earn enough to afford the trappings of the good life.
Fully one-fourth of their wives entered the paid labor force, often in part-time
jobs when the children were at school, to help pay for the appliances and furnishings they desired. Whether or not they were employed, the women focused
their energies on the home, and together both husbands and wives sought personal fulfillment in their families, surrounded by children and consumer goods.
They entered marriage with a utopian vision that included happiness as well as
security. Did the "good life" in consumer-laden houses fulfill their expectations?
The responses of the couples in the KLS provide some answers.

These men and women were among the comfortable group of white middle-
class Americans able to take advantage of the fruits of prosperity. Eighty-five
percent had a family income of over $5,000 a year, although only thirteen per-
cent earned over $15,000. Most had never been heavily in debt; 98 percent had
never received any kind of public assistance and only 30 percent had received
aid from relatives or friends. Their purchasing habits reflected a national pattern: Personal extravagance was rare, but consumption for family enrichment
was a high priority. They exhibited a desire for consumer goods combined with a
concern for future financial security. About 70 percent of the sample spent
between $1,000 and $3,000 in housing expenses per year; 63 percent had one

car and 33 percent had two cars. Slightly more than half had purchased their cars new.[29]

Reflecting the values of the time, which linked status to consumer purchases as well as to occupational level, Kelly rated the "prestige value" of the cars each family owned. He determined that 45 percent fell into the "low prestige" category; 30 percent, the middle; and 22 percent, the high. Only 3 percent owned cars in the "super-high prestige" range, such as a Cadillac. Most said they had one or two thousand dollars to spend per year above basic needs and rarely, if ever, purchased anything on the installment plan. These, then, were well-to-do but conservative people, not extravagant consumers.[30]

Like the rest of the middle class, the KLS respondents sought an expansive, affluent life within the security of their suburban homes. They spent their money in ways that would achieve that goal. The most important spending priority for 60 percent of the respondents was future financial security; for 23 percent, it was "increasing day-to-day living for family members"; and for 15 percent, it was "providing special opportunities for children." Clearly, security and family-oriented pursuits, not personal luxuries, were their major concerns.[31]

These women and men reveal how deeply domestic aspirations were rooted in the postwar success ethic. The increasing emphasis on familial rewards as validation for work found expression in the popular literature as well. Elizabeth Long's study of best-selling novels in the decade after World War II reveals a dramatic shift. In 1945, popular novels celebrated a vision of entrepreneurial success. But by 1955, themes had shifted toward more personal rewards. Heroes now made choices between work and leisure, family and the public world. They were more likely to accommodate themselves to the job and accept a secure place in the organizational hierarchy. According to Long, in these later novels the individual depends on others for happiness, and on the organization merely for a job. She called this theme the "corporate suburban" model, in contrast to the entrepreneurial model that prevailed a decade earlier. A typical mid-fifties best seller was Sloan Wilson's *The Man in the Grey Flannel Suit*, in which the protagonist is the new type of corporate hero who accommodates himself to bureaucratic constraints and wants to get ahead without sacrificing his family. Success is defined not by being at the top, but by having a secure, balanced life. In all these novels, successful career women are portrayed as "selfish"; female ambition is associated with sexual promiscuity. Suffering is the final lot for most such women in these stories.[32]

Husbands in the KLS sample reflected the values expressed in these novels. The family, rather than the workplace, was the arena in which men demonstrated their achievement. Work appeared relatively meaningless without the family to give purpose to men's efforts. When the men responded to an open-ended question asking what marriage had brought them that they could not have gained if they had remained single, many referred to the motivation it provided them to work hard and succeed. One husband wrote that his marriage gave him "the incentive to succeed and save for the future of my family." Others mentioned "greater incentive to succeed in business career," "feeling of accomplishment," "a family to work for," and "greater financial security." Echoing Nixon's remarks, many of these husbands wanted to make life better for their wives. In return, they expected to be appreciated. One husband complained that the "chief weakness of our marriage seems to be her failure to feel any . . . accomplishment from mutual efforts—particularly the family increases in net worth—house and car, furniture, insurance and bank accounts."[33]

What is interesting about all these responses, particularly their frequency of occurrence, is that these husbands claimed that they would have had neither the motivation nor the success without marriage. Clearly, the provider role itself—and an economically dependent wife's recognition and appreciation of it—often offered a greater source of satisfaction than the actual work a man performed. Men were likely to place this aspect of their role in the center of their feelings of marital satisfaction. Ten husbands mentioned a better financial position as a benefit of marriage, another thirteen listed security and stability, and eleven others included social position; forty-three said marriage gave them a sense of purpose and responsibility. Together, these responses made up the third largest category of answers to the question of what marriage gave them that they would not have had without it, following closely after love and children.

The potential tragedy in this situation was that in spite of widespread prosperity, the provider role was a heavy burden, and not all men could be successful at it. Nor was the status of family breadwinner always adequate compensation for an otherwise monotonous or dissatisfying job. Just as material goods could contribute to marital harmony or even compensate for unhappiness to some extent, the failure to achieve or appreciate the fruits of prosperity could cause tension. One case illustrates how this could happen. Charlotte Oster complained that her aspirations for the good life were continually thwarted by her husband Brad's failure to achieve what she thought was an appropriate standard of living. "Having been forced to buy, after three wartime evictions, in a section which was not quite up to the social standards we were used to, we found it hard to accept the choice of friends of our oldest daughter. . . . It has been very hard to keep her within the boundaries of what we consider the proper social standards."

Charlotte's dissatisfaction was not lost on Brad, who was acutely aware of his inability to provide adequately for a wholesome family environment. Charlotte noted that he "is often upset because he thinks he hasn't provided for us as well as he would like to, and considers himself rather a failure." Nevertheless, she said that marriage brought her "four wonderful children, a home of our own, and always something better to look forward to and strive for." In the last section of the survey, in which respondents were asked to add anything that had not already been covered, Charlotte wrote the saga of her and Brad's marriage:

> We were married during the depression years on a shoestring; my husband lost his job soon after, and went into business for himself, also with no capital. Though he was excellent in his field (photography), he didn't have the drive necessary to sell himself, and we had very meager living for several years, till he got a factory job during the war. Though he did well, he liked having his own independence, and after quitting at several factory jobs because he didn't like the unfairness or domination, he started another business with a partner, in aerial photography. Then a series of unfortunate setbacks began . . . eviction . . . hurricane damage to his place . . . injuries. . . . Now my husband is back working for another aerial concern, but he dislikes the work, feels he is too old to start at the bottom in another line, and therefore is inwardly upset a good deal of the time. . . . I have always felt that he shouldn't cater to his feeling of having to be independent, and that he should take any kind of a good job with a steady pay . . . which would give us all a much stronger feeling of security.

Charlotte's words demonstrate the centrality of the provider role and the difficulties it could create when it conflicted with a man's effort to achieve independence and personal fulfillment through work. The Osters' marriage lasted until 1961, when the couple divorced.[34]

Although some husbands in the sample were content to be "organization men" as long as they could bring home the fruits of material success, others shared with Brad Oster a need for autonomy at work. But like him, they were likely to find that this need placed in jeopardy their ability to be good providers and, in turn, created marital friction. In a similar case, Maureen Gilford complained, "My husband is a tireless worker but insists on working *in his own business* and has made so many changes, it has been a constant struggle for 18 1/2 years with just one short period of success. I don't feel my standards are the cause of his hard work. So he is always tired and has little time for enjoyment. I feel badly about this, preferring that he get a modest *but steady salary* and work for someone else. It has made me pinch pennies for years. Also, I have to work *hard* to increase our income and have little time for my own use. Too much house-work, *too much work* altogether."

Maureen longed for more leisure, more planned activities together, and more regular hours for her husband: "He is always tired and overworked." She said he had some emotional disturbances from worry about business and too many job changes: "I wish he had *more time* for the children and for himself." George Gilford wrote little in his report. He said marriage brought him "a good way of life." He sacrificed "nothing material" and rated his marriage as generally satisfying, although he, too, worried about providing for his family's needs, par-ticularly a college education for both his children. Nevertheless, the fulfillment of the provider role would not necessarily satisfy George's need for meaningful work.[35]

The men in these cases faced the double anguish of failure to earn an ade-quate living in work they enjoyed and failure to be successful providers. For oth-ers, the breadwinner role, if performed successfully, might offer compensation for dissatisfaction at work. For women, marriage offered the possibility of material comforts and social standing—something a single woman earning a meager wage was not likely to achieve. Women also might gain some measure of autonomy in their domestic responsibilities—something that neither they nor their husbands were likely to find easily in the paid labor force. In addition, as wives of produc-tive breadwinners, women might be able to gain the trappings of success unavailable to them in the work and public arenas. Suburban houses, after all, were not built with single working women in mind.

Some women focused their personal ambitions vicariously on their husband's careers. One husband noted that this focus contributed to his own drive. "Being somewhat lazy to begin with," he wrote, "the family and my wife's ambition have made me more eager to succeed businesswise and financially." Other wives were explicit about the centrality of material possessions to their marital and family satisfaction. One equated marriage with keeping up with the Joneses while at the same time expressing individuality: "We feel that our possessions are as good as if not better than our neighbors as they are different, antique as to modern, and we hold that thought to us dearly."[36]

Another woman, Lucille Windam, elaborated on this theme more fully, offer-ing a shopping list of name-brand consumer items as evidence of a successful marriage. Yet her testimony also provides a glimpse of the difficulties that might arise even if—or perhaps because—one lived fully in accord with the domestic consumer ethic. She wrote:

One fortunate thing which is important in our marriage is our fortunate change in income bracket. When we were married my husband earned $30 a week. We rented a five room flat, . . . had a baby, etc. Now we have five children and an income of over $25,000 a year. We own our 8 room house—also a nice house on a lake. We have a sailboat, a Cris Craft, several small boats. We own our own riding horse which we keep at home. Our oldest child goes to a prep school. We have a Hammond organ in our home. . . . Our two sons at home own expensive instruments. We have and carry a lot of life insurance. Unless some disaster hits us, we see our way clear to educate all our children thru prep school and college.

It is important to note the kind of consumerism Lucille mentioned: All the goods were geared toward home, family leisure, education, and recreation. She did not mention diamonds, mink coats, or other personal luxuries. Yet here again is the potential hazard of domestic consumerism becoming the center of personal identity, for this woman's pride in her shopping-list definition of marital success was tempered by the complaint she added, almost as an afterthought: "My reaction to all this is that my husband doesn't seem content to save. He continually seeks something new to own; he doesn't keep his interest in any one thing very long." Her final remark is most telling, since it reflects the connection between success, consumerism, and domestic power relations: "He has terrific drive and aggressiveness, and I feel he tries to own all of us in the family too much." It is clear from Lucille's bitter words that the domestic consumer ethic, even at its most opulent, might be rife with tension. For her, family-oriented consumerism was the measure of successful married life and provided some compensation for her obvious disappointment in her relationship with her husband. For her husband, ambition and drive for power were expressed through his acquisition of goods and his total domination at home. Together they created an imperfect domestic relationship; nevertheless, that relationship clearly offered them both enough reasons for staying married.

Consumerism and children were the rewards that made the marriage worthwhile for Lucille Windam. In dedicating herself to the task of raising her children, she gained a sense of achievement that she believed she would not have found elsewhere. Her husband's ample income made her homemaking career possible. Even though she felt he was "overbearing, expects too much of me, and is inconsiderate of me," she appreciated his "ability to do almost anything he tries, his popularity, and his generosity to me financially." That financial generosity meant that she could devote herself to her children and provide them with all the finest things that money could buy: "I've worked hard at making my marriage work—for my own and for my children's sake. . . . Certainly—materially—I never could attain the things I have now. Of course, the children are a great satisfaction. My job seems to swamp me sometimes but I am really very fond of my family and I do try to treat each as a special individual so each personality is important and each child can have every advantage we can possibly give. I can't imagine my life without children. I have no special talents so as a career person I'm sure I would not be a great success. As a mother and homemaker, I feel I am quite successful." Although she blamed her lack of "talent," rather than the lack of viable opportunities, she turned her creative efforts toward homemaking with the dedication and high standards of a professional.

Yet this domestic success was gained at a price: "Because of the size of our family, we have very little personal fun—I mean no clubs or activities. I used to be very active in PTA, church (taught Sunday school), and garden club, but my last two children now 4 and 2 years old changed all this. I just stay home with them and taxi my oldest boys around. Our oldest boy, almost 15, is away at prep school, but in our rural community I have to drive someone somewhere every day. I expect to get back into community life when my younger children are in school all day. I feel quite stale as though I don't use my mind enough." Still, she claimed to be satisfied with her marriage, in spite of a "stale" mind and an "overbearing, inconsiderate" husband. The children, apparently, made it all worthwhile; the affluence made it all possible.

Ronald Windam also claimed to be satisfied with their life together. He took pride in his role as provider. He wrote that marriage had brought him "stability, a family which I very much admire and enjoy doing my best to provide for." As for sacrifices, he wrote, "There is nothing other than Utopia, and a little give and take in sexual relationship. Other than that, there has been no sacrifice." Like so many of their peers, Ronald and Lucille Windam resigned themselves to their disappointments and looked on the bright side. Although their affluent suburban lifestyle fell short of their dreams, they were determined to make the best of it.[37]

Consumerism in the postwar years went far beyond the mere purchase of goods and services. It included important cultural values, demonstrated success and social mobility, and defined lifestyles. It also provided the most vivid symbol of the American way of life: the affluent suburban home. There can be no doubt that the gender roles associated with domestic consumerism—homemaker and breadwinner—were central to the identity of many women and men at the time. It is also evident, however, that along with the ideology of sexual containment, postwar domestic consumerism required conformity to strict gender assumptions that were fraught with potential tensions and frustrations. Suburban homes filled with material possessions could not always compensate for the dissatisfactions inherent in the domestic arrangements consumerism was intended to enhance and reinforce. In fact, those very domestic arrangements, although idealized and coveted at the time, were the source of countless miseries. As one looks through the "window of vulnerability" in the cold war era, one sees families inside their suburban homes struggling to achieve the postwar dream of abundance and security. Many men and women made heroic efforts to live according to the ideal of domestic containment. Some were able to carve out meaningful and rewarding lives within its limits. For others, the rewards remained elusive.

CHAPTER EIGHT

HANGING TOGETHER:
FOR BETTER OR FOR WORSE

[Marriage has given me] my place in life. I feel I am doing exactly as I am fitted—with an occasional spurt of independence growing less all the time. I am settling down to a way of things. I am happy or content much more of the time than I am not.

—CAROL SEARS, 1955

When I'm crabby, she can handle me very nicely and soon has me smiling. . . . She looks to me for the answers of most responsible questions [*sic*].

—ROBERT SEARS, 1955[1]

CAROL SEARS described her independence as if it were a chronic disease or allergy that flared up now and then to bother her. But most of the time, she was able to keep it under control, even if she could not cure it. Independence was an uncomfortable condition for women like Carol Sears. It did not fit well with domestic containment. Independence might have led to a rebellion against the domestic role, or an active rejection of the status quo. But in the cold war era, such challenges to the prevailing ideology were highly risky ventures. Defying the consensus could lead to a loss of economic security, social reputation, or community support. Adaptation was clearly safer than resistance. Those who chafed against domestic containment, like Carol Sears, buried their discontent and sought therapeutic, rather than political, solutions to their problems.

For women and men like Carol and Robert Sears, a successful family life was a major personal goal. They expected to build a home that would provide them with security and fulfillment and shield them from the harsh realities of public life in the cold war era. Those realities included not only the existence of atomic bombs, but the massive impersonal organizations in which most men worked, institutional roadblocks to women with career ambitions, and hostility toward anyone whose private life did not conform to the heterosexual family pattern. But family life was more than simply "a shelter and haven from the stresses of the world," as one postwar wife put it.[2] In its idealized form, the home would contain sexual enjoyment, material comfort, well-adjusted children, and evidence of personal success for husbands and wives who performed well their clearly defined roles.

These weighty desires were a great deal to ask from the nuclear family, since private life was ultimately insufficient to solve social problems. But after investing so much in the family, how did these women and men respond when the domestic life they had built did not meet their original hopes? Compromise, accommodation, and lowered expectations were solutions for many disappointed people who still clung to the ideal of domestic containment. These women and men often focused on the rewards of marriage and minimized the sacrifices. As they struggled to achieve a successful family life, many redefined the meaning of "success" along the way.

For Carol Sears, domestic harmony was achieved through accommodation. Her marital happiness depended on her ability to handle her husband "very nicely" and to keep him smiling. That effort required sacrificing "some of my friends and [not] seeing my relatives as often as I liked. Not that my husband minded my seeing them as long as he was not included. I felt he was bored or embarrassed being with them. . . . I find I now depend on him entirely for fun, excitement and diversion. He prefers young people, I really feel best with people my own age and older. But I have grown away or shy away from people and never invite them in for an evening as he will be bored with them or just not like them." Carol gave her marriage high ratings, only "once and a while" regretted it, and had "not seriously" considered divorce. Robert Sears wrote that he gave up "nothing of any importance" and gained "a sense of fulfillment and happiness" from his marriage.[3]

Overall, Robert and Carol Sears both considered their marriage to be a success. She found her "place in life"; he found "fulfillment and happiness." In the lives of couples like the Sears, we can see what it really meant to live according to the prevailing family norm. Nothing inhibited these relatively affluent white middle-class couples from achieving their domestic goals. They had enough resources and faced no racial or religious discrimination, and no major catastrophe disrupted their lives. If the good life rested in the postwar family ideal, it was theirs for the asking. But they had to be willing to pay the price.

Because the home was an arena of work for women and leisure for men, it fulfilled different needs for husbands and wives. The 1950s version of the "super-woman" was the wife and mother who could fulfill a wide range of occupational roles—early-childhood educator, counselor, cook, nurse, housekeeper, manager, and chauffeur—all within the home. She was likely to seek diversion from her demanding job through volunteer or community work or even through employment outside the home. These activities supplemented her central work as a homemaker and opened up new areas in which she could gain other kinds of satisfactions and rewards.

For men like Robert Sears, the home was the realm of freedom where they could forget the troubles at work that made them "crabby." Although the Kelly Longitudinal Study (KLS) did not include open-ended questions about occupational satisfaction, it did ask respondents to describe the nature of any emotional difficulties they experienced. Husbands mentioned difficulties on the job: too much pressure, tense relationships with employers or employees, efforts to achieve promotions or raises, boredom or ennui, and financial difficulties. Unlike their wives, few included problems with spouses or children. For men, work was often a source of stress, while the home was a source of relative solace. For women, the situation was often the reverse: Employment or community work alleviated some of the pressures of full-time homemaking.

Pressures and disappointments notwithstanding, postwar Americans expected to find life's satisfactions at home. They were determined to get married and *stay* married. As the marriage rate went up, the divorce rate went down. Sociologist Andrew Cherlin noted that postwar married couples were the only ones "in the last hundred years to show a substantial, sustained shortfall in their lifetime levels of divorce."[4] One might expect that the higher the hopes, the greater the possibility for disappointment and divorce. Yet these Americans brought their high hopes into marriage and stayed married to a remarkably high degree. It cannot be assumed that fewer divorces necessarily meant fewer unhappy marriages. Part of the explanation for the viability of these marriages undoubtedly lies in the power of the prevailing norm. Men and women alike believed in marriage; a majority thought that single individuals were "either sick or immoral, too selfish or too neurotic."[5] Many couples stayed together through sheer determination.

Upwardly mobile couples often gave up close ties to extended families that might have provided support networks. For some, husbands' jobs or changing economic circumstances prompted a geographic move; for others, alienation from relatives led to an increased reliance on the nuclear family. Kinship ties were often strained if they infringed on the autonomy of the nuclear family, as was the case for Carol Sears, who ended up depending entirely on her husband for "fun, excitement and diversion." Many young marrieds intentionally severed ties with their relatives; some entered marriage to free themselves from their parents. Patricia Rollins expressed it this way: "I liked my husband when we married, but I had no great depth of feeling. I liked him much better than anyone else I'd met. I probably would not have married as soon if mother and I were more companionable." Mary Halsted had the same experience: "My husband was persistent in wanting to marry me. My mother was strongly against it. I was in the midst of friction at home and his persistence won me over. I *liked* him when I married him. I'm sure he knew that." Even if the relationship was not quite ideal, marriage gave her "a new type of freedom—from my family and *their* type of obligations."[6]

The isolation of the nuclear family sometimes helped keep couples together. As Kay Johnson explained before her marriage, she anticipated problems because of "the possibility that he might not be as successful as he wants to be." Later, she complained about her husband's "feelings of insecurity" and "need to prove he is tougher than the next fellow." Yet she realized that "breaking away from our parents has kept us together at moments when we were mad enough to part company. We have always had to consider that no one else would shoulder our problems. We had to face them alone and we didn't have outside opinions to make us more confused."[7]

Women who relinquished ties to relatives or gave up job possibilities were more likely than men to intensify their commitment to marriage because they had given up other sources of income and emotional support. Surely, this is one reason why so many women who abandoned occupational aspirations considered homemaking a new career. If men had to put on a "gray flannel suit" to join the "lonely crowd" at work, that was part of their job. For a housewife, on the job at home, adapting to the needs of her husband and focusing her creative energies on the family also came with the territory. The job definition of a homemaker included complex psychological as well as physical tasks. Few women were fully prepared to take on these tasks, especially if they assumed—as many did—that old-fashioned ways were not appropriate for the modern family. Having turned away from inherited wisdom, those who felt ill equipped to perform the necessary tasks often turned to experts for help.

The KLS respondents were remarkably open to professional help. They eagerly read and consulted with psychiatrists, pediatricians, and experts in numerous other fields. The enormous popularity of the Kinsey reports and Dr. Spock's child care books indicated the near deification of postwar professionals. So pervasive was the therapeutic approach to life that respondents quoted, cited, and discussed experts in their anonymous questionnaires. This reliance on professionals is further evidence of people's reluctance to trust their own instincts or to attempt political solutions to institutional problems. Expertise offered a distinctly apolitical means of solving problems. The "well adjusted" adult or child adapted to normative expectations.

While black people in the South challenged the prevailing racial order by direct political action, most white Americans accepted the status quo and tried to change themselves to fit into it. Rather than challenging the circumstances that made life stressful or difficult, the therapeutic model called on individuals to cope with and adapt to existing realities. In that way, experts reinforced the political consensus by pointing to individual weaknesses, rather than to structural or institutional flaws, as the sources of problems.

Men and women in the KLS sample used psychology and the advice of professionals in significantly different ways. For men, psychology offered an *explanation* for their distress; they claimed that "anxieties" or "inferiority complexes" generally resulted from problems at work. Rather than calling for social change, they looked to the home as the prescription for relief, where a man could find comfort, solace, and a release from stress. Women, however, identified stress at home, or resentment against one's spouse or domestic situation, as pathological. Psychology provided a way to articulate the problem and find a solution. If women experienced stress, they should seek professional assistance to help them adapt. In other words, although psychology provided an explanation for men's woes and the home offered a cure, the home was often the source of women's stress and psychology offered the cure.

These uses of psychology are apparent in the case of Nora and Chester Grey. Chester was satisfied with their marriage and rated it high. He claimed that he sacrificed only "money and financial independence," but gained "a happy home, complete with a loving wife and four children." Before his wedding, he saw no reason why the marriage would not be a success. But Nora had some concerns. Her own dependency needs were evident when she wrote that she chose him because "he gives me a feeling of being protected from life and someone to depend on." She also noted, "My feelings are too easily hurt," a statement that could be interpreted to mean that he frequently hurt her feelings, but the phrasing she used indicated that she considered oversensitivity her problem. Nora's next remark, however, suggests that her fiancé had some responsibility for her hurt feelings: "He sometimes gives me the idea that statements which I make have no merit and what he says is right." Part of the problem was that she tended to agree with his assessment of her abilities: "He denies this feeling and it may be due to my feeling of having inferior intelligence."

Years later, Nora reflected on the sacrifices she made for her marriage: "I always hoped to be just what I am—a wife and a mother. I gave up my office work which I enjoyed because of the contacts with other people. I have little time to see people during the day and at night I am tired enough usually to be content reading or watching T.V. I have desired to learn square dancing and to play cards occasionally with my husband, but he does not agree and I have become resigned. If I cared enough, I could do them alone but would enjoy activities more if we 'played' together." Nora's is a tale of adaptation: psychological adjustment to Chester's dominance, the sacrifice of her job, and acquiescence to his lack of interest in shared leisure pursuits. Yet Nora Grey also reaped what she felt were adequate rewards for her efforts: "A nice home I can run the way I want to. A husband to be a lifetime companion and 'protector.' A fine group of children who keep life from being monotonous. The self-confidence that comes from the knowledge that my husband loves me more than anyone else in the world."

Those benefits must have been worth a lot to her, for at the end of the questionnaire where she could add "anything else" she wished to say, Nora wrote a story of extreme hardship and intense bitterness:

Much of our trouble has centered around my husband's unwillingness to do work around the house, which he says is my sole responsibility. . . . By nature, I can't stand things in disrepair, so I have become a jack-of-all-trades. This was not too bad until I had the third baby within five years. My husband slept in a different room so as not to be disturbed by her night crying which she did for 5 months. I became so exhausted that I got very little sleep, even when she did, and I had to be up early with the other two little ones.

With the children's care, housework, repairs, leaf raking, snow shoveling, some lawn mowing and making all our clothing (so we could save every penny we could toward a house) I became physically and nervously exhausted. My husband refused to get up with the children or let me stay in bed even one morning. . . . He said, "You're not human and don't need sleep." . . . With the present baby he is extremely different and has slept in her room and cared for her nights whenever I needed rest. At the time I had the three small ones, he was entirely unappreciative of all I did and said, "If it takes you more than 2 hours a day to do your work, it's only the result of poor planning." He had this attitude during all our married life until the last two or three years and made me very unhappy, nervous and irritable. I lost my desire for sexual relations with him and had to feign it, but now that he has developed more understanding of my needs and an appreciation of my efforts, my interest is just beginning to return.

With all this misery, Nora wanted a psychiatrist to help her cope with her situation and make her feel better. But even her desire for professional assistance was out of reach:

I believe I had a nervous breakdown but I knew psychiatric help would be expensive and my husband said, "Your trouble is all in your head and you don't have to feel this way if you don't want to." With the children older, my work lessened and I returned to normal. Also he is gradually assuming more responsibility about repairs. I don't much mind doing what he fails to because I enjoy that kind of work and have more time for it. . . . For the above reasons we never had another baby until a year ago when I felt I could handle it. Now I feel that at 40 we are too old to take the responsibility of more.

Chester's responses to the questionnaire contained none of the evidence of the domestic strain and distress Nora described, but they revealed that his job was a major source of misery for him. In the question concerning emotional health, he noted, "Extreme depression, anxiety and insomnia caused by job. Solved by changing job." Nora, however, was unable to change her job. At the end of her questionnaire, she minimized her suffering and articulated her commitment to her marriage. Reflecting on the survey itself, she wrote, "I feel participation may have helped because it makes me realize that it is quite normal that married life is not all a 'bed of roses.' You list many troubles which we have never had and the little we have had are mostly over." In a remarkable series of superlative responses, Nora rated her marriage highly successful, "never" considered divorce, would "definitely" marry the same person again, "never" regretted her marriage, and considered it "decidedly more happy than the average."[8]

From the evidence, it would seem that Nora Grey was a martyr and Chester Grey was a monster. But it would be wrong to assume that Nora was simply the victim of a cruel husband. Nora clearly thought it was important to maintain a conspiracy of silence. Chester had severe troubles at work; he could not have known how much Nora suffered at home, and she may well have not wanted him to know. When things broke, she fixed them. When the baby cried, she got up. When she lost her sexual feeling for Chester, she "feigned it." Obviously, such deliberate deception was intended to keep him from knowing how she felt. For someone who "always hoped to be just what I am—a wife and mother," making demands or confronting her husband with her unhappiness carried high risks. So she hid her rage, until Chester finally began to help out. Maybe his new job relieved the pressure on him and enabled him to be more involved at home.

The questionnaires do not reveal why Chester changed. Whatever the reason, he cannot entirely be blamed for the situation. After all, Nora claimed that the rewards were worth the sacrifices: "A nice home I can run the way I want to," which clearly offered some autonomy; "a husband to be a lifetime companion and 'protector,'" providing security; "a fine group of children who keep life from being monotonous"; and pride in having a husband who "loves me more than anyone else in the world." For those rewards, Nora was willing to adapt to her circumstances, hide her true feelings from her husband, and tolerate a great deal of misery.

Psychological adaptation played an even greater role in the marriage of Clara and Harold Jones than it did for the Greys. Overall, Clara Jones, like Nora Grey, was satisfied with her marriage, and for many of the same reasons. She wrote that she gained "three intelligent and interesting children, close companionship based on mutual interests with my husband," and "a home which is a shelter and haven from the stresses of the world."

But Clara Jones also had her share of difficulties. "My husband's long working hours—even on Saturdays and Sundays—laid a great burden on me when the children were younger, and the low salary a minister receives prevented any paid help. Now that they are getting into outside activities, the pressure and tempo of life are quite hectic, which we try to surmount by more sleep or cutting down on our activities and by urging them to be selective of the possible choices of activity." These were real difficulties rooted in her daily routine, but she believed that her trouble was psychological. Using psychiatric terminology, she explained, "My overanxiety has made some problems seem bigger than they were . . . anxiety and guilt from overly severe and strict treatment in childhood, according to the psychiatrist who is now helping me." Clara may well have had a difficult childhood, but she had real problems in the present as well. From the beginning, she resisted the subordination her husband expected of her. She recognized this tendency, even before her marriage, but she translated it into *her* problem: "Sometimes I notice I want to dominate and direct him, which is not good."

Both Clara and Harold Jones turned to psychiatric aid for Clara's difficulties, assuming that the only way to ease her burdens was for her to change her attitude. It never occurred to Harold, Clara, or the psychiatrist, for that matter, that Harold might also change. Harold wrote, "Apparently a lack of emotional responsiveness and warmth in my personality irritated my wife in our early years together, as did the very humble circumstances of our home and job. This was complicated by her guilt feelings, anxiety and frustration about sex, homemaking, and child-rearing." Here, using an abundance of psychological jargon, he recognized that his own coldness contributed to his wife's distress. But his solution was not for him to warm up, but for his wife to get help so she could better accept him the way he was. "It took a crisis in which she suffered important psychosomatic reactions," he commented, "to bring us to the place where she was ready to accept psychiatric help." For his part, he expressed satisfaction with the marriage, saying he sacrificed "nothing really" and gained "children" and "a degree of intimacy beyond expectation."[9]

The popularization of psychology gave women and men a vocabulary with which to tame and manage their frustrations. Many of life's traumas could be categorized in psychological terms and, to some extent, then explained away. Jane Willis was another wife who dismissed her difficulties using the psychological terminology of the day: "I regard my emotional disturbances as quite ordinary—concern over a particularly difficult phase one of the children is passing through." She rated her marriage in all the superlative categories. Life might have been different if she had chosen an alternative path, but she made a rational decision based on realistic choices: "Possibly I might have been a successful 'career woman.' I had only worked a short time after college before marriage and gave up this job upon marriage because of geographical distance from my husband's place of work. A position with a future in the same city as my husband's work was offered me shortly after marriage. My husband preferred that I not work and I offered no objection to his position. We planned to start our family a year hence and did not feel it would be fair to take a job with a 'future' if I would have to quit in a year."

Jane Willis's willingness to give up her career no doubt involved more than her husband's wishes. She knew that beginning a career and a family at the same

time would have been fraught with difficulty: "Also there was no financial reason for me to work; my husband had a good job and we could live comfortably
without being extravagant." In the long run, Jane was not sorry: "I have never
regretted 'giving up' this doubtful 'successful career.'" In return for her sacrifice,
marriage brought her "a wonderfully balanced life—the emotional equilibrium
that comes from loving and being loved, the challenge and satisfactions of
bringing up four children, and a little time to spare for the outside stimulation of
participating in the governmental problems of our community." Jane Willis was
not willing to make the choice between children and a career—a choice women
of her generation were often forced to make. So she carved out an alternative
career based on "the challenge and satisfactions of bringing up four children"
and, like many homemakers of her generation, found fulfilling ways to contribute to the community through volunteer work.

Donald Willis also rated his marriage in all the superlative categories, but he
articulated more complaints. He began with his problems at work: "For the past
two or three years, I have had difficulty relaxing because of the constant pressure
and frustration at work." In addition, "I gave up all of my spare time and money
for my family." In return for these sacrifices, he expected his wife to be at home
for him and complained that she was "too easily involved in community affairs."
He concluded, "Our marriage could be even happier were it not for the physical
and mental strain of (a) my work and home activities and (b) my wife's community work and home activities. We are both always near exhaustion."[10]

Overall, these marriages met at least some of the needs of their participants,
considering there were few alternative routes to a fulfilling life at that time. For
women in particular, material considerations made it nearly impossible to abandon their marriages. Marriage was their meal ticket; it was also the best way for
them to gain social respect, status, and a sense of belonging. With so much at
stake, it is no wonder that these women hid their discontent, rarely made
demands on their husbands, and defined their marriages as successful.

More than 80 percent of both the husbands and the wives in the sample
rated their marriages as "above average," and nearly two out of three rated them
"extraordinarily happy" or "decidedly happier than average." Yet, in spite of
these high ratings, the women especially experienced a great deal of discontent.
In general, the men expressed more contentment with their marriages than did
their wives. They were more likely to complain about difficulties at work and
appreciate the comforts of home. Indeed, their wives took pride in making those
homes pleasant so the men would feel that their sacrifices at work were worthwhile. In this effort, they made significant sacrifices of their own.

Women were twice as likely as men to report that they were dissatisfied or regretted their marriage. Nearly half the women, but only a third of the men, said they had considered divorce. In response to the question "If you had your life to live over, would you marry the same person?" about half the men and women said "definitely." Yet nearly twice as many women as men said they would definitely *not* marry the same person. These findings are consistent with other studies that have demonstrated that in general, men are more happily married than women. Researchers who interviewed thousands of Americans in the mid-fifties concluded, "Women were always more negative about marriage than men were."[11]

There are several reasons for this discrepancy in satisfaction. For housewives, the home was the workplace; for men, it was the arena for leisure and freedom away from the job. A comparison of the "job satisfaction" of men and women reveals some interesting findings. Although men resented the alienation and subordination of their jobs, these postdepression security-minded breadwinners were reluctant to quit a steady job to risk finding an even more oppressive one or, worse yet, no job at all. Male blue-collar workers surveyed at the time complained about work and said that if they could start over, they would not take the same job. But when asked if they were satisfied, most claimed that they were. They would make the best of their imperfect employment and look for freedom and community elsewhere—in leisure pursuits, through the popular culture, and especially at home.[12]

When the middle-class homemakers in the KLS were asked about *their* job satisfaction (that is, their satisfaction with marriage), most said they were satisfied. But asked whether they would marry the same person if they had it to do over again, many said they might not. Like the blue-collar men surveyed, they were determined to make the best of the situation and reluctant to risk abandoning what they had for the slim possibility of finding something better. Unlike the men, however, they were unable to find an antidote in the home to their dissatisfactions in the workplace, since the home was all they had. Although many volunteered their time in communities or took jobs when their children were in school, their homemaking responsibilities did not diminish accordingly, and their primary responsibilities remained focused on their family's needs. This situation led to a number of disparities between men's and women's evaluations of their marriage.

The case of Joe and Margaret Bensen shows how widely divergent two partners' perceptions of the same "successful" marriage might be. Joe rated the marriage in all the superlative categories and had no complaints. His wife met all the expectations he noted when they were originally engaged: her wit, optimism, skill in the "culinary arts," and her potential to be "a good manager in the home." As he explained after more than a decade of marriage, "The more I see and know about other men and their wives and their attitudes toward each other, the better I like my marriage." All he gave up was "the empty, aimless, lonely life of a bachelor. I cannot think of anything I really wanted to do or have that has been sacrificed because of marriage." He gained "the love, care, and attention of a wonderful woman. The love, affection, and respect of 4 great children who will be a credit and comfort to me if I live to be an old man."

Joe Bensen claimed that his family would be a "credit" to him; his delight in their "attention" and "respect" indicates that they, almost like personal possessions, would serve his needs and reflect his success. Explaining the reason for his happy marriage, he wrote that his wife rarely crossed his will or resisted his demands:

> We have domestic tranquility because we don't argue; we almost always have same ideas, attitudes and feelings. My wife can get me to do most anything because of the nice way she goes about it. She makes a genuine effort to please me in many little ways, so it is only fair for me to try to please her in a few big things. Neither of us is selfish, stubborn, domineering or dishonest with the other. These are traits often found in one spouse or the other under the cloak of "strong character." Some people seem to think it is a sign of weakness or a wound in their pride to give in or try to go along with their spouses' reasonable demands without a fight.

The key to the Bensens' apparent domestic tranquillity was the lack of conflict in their marriage. Joe Bensen evaluated the marriage in terms of the personal services and attention his wife lavished on him. He described her skill in meeting his personal needs and her gentle power of persuasion. The process of filling out the questionnaire increased his self-awareness: It "stimulated thought about my true role as a husband and focused attention on some of the more important aspects. In other words it helped me 'take stock' of myself like a mirror. It is so easy to take too much for granted." Nevertheless, as his wife's testimony indicates, what he saw in the mirror was what he wanted to see and what she allowed him to see.

Margaret Bensen's responses to the questionnaire seem to describe a different marriage. Like her husband, Margaret claimed to be quite satisfied with their relationship. But her comments were hardly as enthusiastic as his. She began, "My husband is a real saint and, compared to other husbands, a perfect mate. I respect him and really love him, but I'm the insecure kind of a female who needs a close male companion to make life worthwhile." After this preface, in which she blamed her "insecurity" for her dissatisfaction, she continued:

> My husband expends his energies on carpentry hobbies or such and never seems to need me more than to have a hot meal ready and to have his clothes in good repair. . . . He likes to have me within calling distance, but never seems to need the closeness I require. . . . There have been several other men thrown into my life who have been so attractive that I've found them hard to resist. My husband never seemed to object to my interest in others, although I don't believe he knows to what extent I've become involved. I don't like the situation but I can't get out of the whirlpool.
>
> Had my husband been slightly more demonstrative once in a while, said "I love you" and kissed me at times other than just when he wanted sexual intercourse, I believe our marriage would have been ideal for me.

Margaret continued by accepting the responsibility for her husband's aloofness. "I don't blame *him*. I never feel any discrepancy in our marriage is too much his fault. Maybe I wasn't what *he* desired." Yet, according to the responses on his questionnaire, she was exactly what he desired. He wanted support and attention, and she provided it. She did not let him know that he was not meeting her needs and that she was attracted to other men as a result. Her comments indicate that their marriage was fraught with tensions: "I've just had a sterilization operation, so now I'll not be reluctant to take care of his physical needs at any time and that should bring us closer. Since I had a 'surprise' baby 2 years ago, I've been frightened of becoming pregnant again and have not been too cooperative at times, although his physical needs are few."

Margaret also resented the way in which Joe claimed her and the family as a "credit" to him: "[He] tries to play 'the big wheel,' impressing people with his unusual children, his home, and his town activities. I always cringe because people get bored and annoyed with his bragging when actually we have little about which to brag. It bothers me to see that he has to build himself up in that way." Yet she contributed to his self-deception by providing the support and encouragement he seemed so desperately to need from her: "I'm always building him up in any way I can, so I hope it isn't my fault."

Both Joe and Margaret Bensen defined marital success largely in terms of their possessions. For Joe, his wife and children counted among the possessions he displayed as marks of his achievement. For Margaret, the home and its furnishings were an important measure of success, and she expressed some discontent over their inability to match the standard of living of their peers: "Our contemporaries seem to have more of the material things and live better but then we're just starting a new business and we have 4 children in an expensive community, so I don't feel we're in too bad a condition, although I yearn for a more adequate house and not to have money worries." There were also tensions over the children, but Margaret again backed away from placing too much blame on Joe: "My husband has never taken the responsibility of the children and has waited for my direction. . . . It would have been more ideal if he had taken over occasionally."

Despite all her complaints—her discontent with his boasting, their money problems, her unfulfilled consumer desires, their sexual tensions, and her disappointment over his lack of affection and help with the children—Margaret claimed to be satisfied with the marriage. In the end, her assessment of the marriage was actually not that different from his: "We have had a good marriage, 4 wonderful children, and complete peace, which is essential to me. . . . I think I'm very lucky to have such a fine husband and probably don't deserve him in many ways." Margaret rated her marriage highly, said that it brought her "children, a normal home life, happiness and companionship," and claimed that she "can't think of anything important" that she sacrificed.[13]

Many subtle clues reveal Margaret Bensen's ambivalence about her marriage, as well as the enormous stake she had not only in *making* it successful but in *seeing* it as successful. Although she complained about her husband's failings, she insisted that she was happily married to "a real saint" and "a perfect mate." She was inclined to blame herself for any disappointments she felt. Submerging her anger at him for his lack of demonstrative affection, she labeled herself "insecure." She even faulted herself for providing him with praise and support that encouraged his boasting. By taking a measure of blame herself, she could point to her own character flaws, rather than to disappointments with her spouse or their marriage, as the source of her discontent.

Another case exhibited similarly discordant assessments. Peter Wells was quite satisfied with his marriage. His only complaints were his wife's leniency with the children and her "feeling that I should do more about the house." His wife Norma had quite a bit more to say about their relationship, even before their marriage: "We are both very independent and possibly I may not always be willing to bow to his wishes and ideas." Later, she described her marriage as "rather matter-of-fact." She complained that Peter was "too dictatorial" with their two adopted children and "disliked having his routine disturbed by the children. . . . Most of their activities were left up to me—both at home and outside. I felt he should take more time with them. Dinner was a constant source of annoyance. He wanted silence so he could listen to the news. Of late, these relations have improved since the children are older and he is taking more interest in their activities and doing more things with them."

Norma claimed that her marriage, although imperfect, provided "a stable, comfortable life. . . . I could always depend on my husband and, though I wouldn't say it has been exciting, our marriage has been pretty steady and generally pleasant. It has kept me economically comfortable and secure—given me a home and family to care for and generally pleasant surroundings. I have enjoyed being a part of the faculty (wife) at various universities and the social status has been pleasant." It is clear that the status, security, and affluence she enjoyed would not, in her estimation, have been available to her as a single or divorced woman.

Almost as an afterthought, Norma added a statement at the end of her questionnaire that expressed deep resentment against the subordinate role her husband expected from her:

One particular source of friction: My husband is a firm believer in "woman's place is in the home"—so it is, to a degree—but I have always felt the need for outside activities and interest in community affairs because I felt mentally stagnated by not taking part in outside programs and because I feel morally obligated to take part, in view of my education and some capabilities. He takes no interest in my interests and belittles most women's groups—and women in general (males are definitely superior beings). Whatever I have done has had to be at no inconvenience to him—and often with a scornful attitude on his part. It's not good to have to get your buildup outside your house.

I get the impression that what he wants is just a good housekeeper to keep everything comfortable at home and peaceful. And he doesn't want to be disturbed by conversation. [Although we are] within speaking distance 50 or 60 hours a week, usually there is a book, newspaper or radio between us. Actually we think a lot alike on many subjects but we're really not very companionable about it—at least we don't discuss things much between ourselves.

The other thing that makes our marriage less than ideal is my husband's lack of enthusiasm. He's a pessimist and I'm an optimist, and oh, how I've longed for a little "joie de vivre" on his part. So many things that to most people are fun are just too much trouble for him. He'd rather sit. His highest expression of enthusiasm is "uh huh, very nice,"—and that's that.

Norma Wells's final remarks demonstrate that in spite of her submerged feminist impulses and deep discontent, she had a great personal investment in the marriage and was committed to making the best of it. She wrote, "I have enjoyed considering the questions in this study. It gives me a line on what is good in our marriage and has given me ideas for possible improvements. It's also given me a chance to write down my pet peeves. Inadequate as it seems in some respects, it will last us 'till death us do part' and we'll live on an even keel."[14]

Susan Berk was another wife with an unswerving commitment to a less-than-ideal marriage. Susan's husband, Jeremy, was very satisfied with his marriage. He wrote that he gained "the companionship . . . of a wonderful girl" and sacrificed "nothing really important. Would merely have had money to spend for automobiles and the like." In the questionnaire he filled out before their wedding, Jeremy noted that "there have been times when she has been most undecided—the recurrence of such a 'mood' may bring trouble." Yet he did not mention any similar concern after they were married. Susan revealed the depth and persistence of that "mood." Like her husband, she noted before their marriage "temperamental difference, my own moodiness and instability," but she also mentioned as a potential problem "the lack of understanding of this in my fiancé."

Years later, although Susan claimed to be generally satisfied with the marriage, she wrote that she gave up a "career in the fine arts." She also said she would not marry the same person if she had to do it over again. As she explained at the end of her questionnaire:

> I realize that there are many inconsistencies and apparent contradictions in my answers to many of the questions in this section. This is due to the fact that I have been deeply in love with another man since the third year of my marriage. . . . I love [my husband] devotedly and deeply, but as a sort of combination of child and friend. My love affair I regard as having added to the happiness of my marriage, rather than decreasing it, as it has made me such a happy person. The other man and I see each other no more than once a year, that is, since we lived in the same place for a year at the beginning. However we're completely congenial, and just to know he's there makes me happy.

Divorce was out of the question. She concluded by stating, without explaining, her commitment to her marriage: "Although I'd marry him [the other man] if I were not married, I'll never leave my husband, as I'm sure my re-marriage couldn't be happy under such circumstances."[15]

All the women in the cases just described felt a deep ambivalence toward their husbands. They all resented their husbands' unquestioned authority in the home, wished for more attention to their own needs, and chafed against the subordination that was expected of them. Yet they also protested that they loved their husbands, were satisfied with their marriages, and blamed themselves frequently for their discontent. Joan Milford was another such wife. She wrote, "I think we'd both like our lives to be a little fuller, . . . mentally, physically, civically, socially, but we don't have the strength. We'd like more money, so we wouldn't have to do so much ourselves. I do all my own work and have all the ideas about almost everything from home decorating to picking out my husband's ties and socks each day—at his request!"

After her sudden shift from the plural *we* to the singular *I*, her complaints became more pointed and directed at her husband: "I work awfully hard. It's especially hard with a big house and a 5 year old and a 16 month old. My husband generally is a very selfish person. He really gives me a pain in the neck at times, but at that point, somehow he senses my feelings and shoos me out and takes over and I just melt like putty in his hands." Joan alternated between sharp criticism and expressions of affection. Yet the tone of despair prevailed. She noted that her husband sometimes realized how hard she worked and helped her out, but that if it was inconvenient to him, he would not: "He lets me down all the time in everything, but I've gotten hardened now. He's a real party boy and loves a good time, but I get the brunt of the work. However, he's quite a success in his work and is uncomplaining and we are the envy of many of our friends." In this last remark, she pointed to her husband's success, financial security, and the *appearance* of a happy and stable marriage as important bonuses that compensated for other, less pleasing, aspects of their relationship. She concluded with self-reproach and ambivalence: "I always end up in the wrong, being the heel and martyr, but I love him in spite of it so what can I do!"[16]

Men were much more reticent in describing their feelings. One reason, no doubt, was that the KLS asked few questions about the primary sources of their discontent: work. Another reason was the stoicism and lack of emotional display expected of "manly" men. Often the enormity of men's problems was visible only through their wives' comments. Linda Hilburn was one wife who pointed to her husband's difficulties as the primary source of her own. Although she was "generally satisfied" with her marriage and felt that she sacrificed "nothing," her statements indicate that both she and her husband experienced a great deal of discontent and frustration. Referring to her spouse through their coded number, she wrote, "Mr. 90 needs me full time, but that's not possible for the kids need me too. He realizes that but I am torn often between them, since he is away so much." She went on to say, "Mr. 90 has, at times, little control over his temper. He also has an inferiority complex, based primarily on his size (5'4"), and these two states of mind have not been improved by his health (two serious coronaries and one attack of angina since 1947). At times, the result is close to panic at not being able (in his opinion) to give the kids all he would like (private schooling, etc.). His health has made additional insurance impossible." With what must have been a stressful work life involving a great deal of travel and his severe emotional and physical difficulties, it is no wonder that Linda concluded, "The kids and I are far happier with our lot than is Mr. 90."

Clearly, Linda Hilburn recognized the pressures her husband felt as he tried to be a good provider, with his temper, "inferiority complex," and poor health. But the impact of his needs on her life was profound: "It is very important to Mr. 90 that he be 'head' of the house and that he control the finances; because it means so much to him, it's all right with me. With his heart condition, I should be more familiar with our family finances, but to me, his health is dependent on his feeling important, so I try to live 'one day at a time.' It's not always easy. . . . Underlying any misunderstandings is his temper. He realized that but not until too late. His last attack (angina) was definitely the result of temper over something not connected with our marriage (in fact something nonexistent); he said so when in the hospital five days."

Linda adapted to this tense situation by trying to protect her husband, stifling her resentments, and focusing on the children: "I often keep problems to myself if I think he will 'blow his top' or 'feel inferior.' Since Mr. 90 travels and is usually away 2–3 nites a week, I can do this!" Apparently, she did it very well. She rated her marriage as "decidedly more happy than the average," claiming that it brought her "a home, companionship, children and, if they are happy and well adjusted—able to care for themselves and their families—complete satisfaction. The children keep us so busy now, we have little time for much else."

Linda's "complete satisfaction" depended on how the children turned out in the end. For her, the satisfaction of a job well done, rather than day-to-day contentment, was the ultimate measure of marital success. In the end, she came back to a common theme: "I still say no one can explain 'Love' and one who hasn't loved hasn't lived! We have and will for a long time, I hope, in spite of differences."

Ralph Hilburn recognized that a nervous breakdown led to his heart attack. But compared to his wife's responses, his questionnaire was not self-reflective.

Noting that all he gave up when he married was "other girls," he said he gained "position, home, children and general well-being." He did not discuss his work and made no complaints about his home life, except to say that his wife "lacks interest in dress around the house" and "weeps easily."[17]

The cases described in this chapter form a pattern: Women expressed more dissatisfaction than their husbands but were more willing to make sacrifices for the sake of their relationships and eager to define their marriages as workable and successful, even if imperfect. The men gave up things they considered trivial, such as "other girls," more "money to spend," or "so-called personal freedom." In return, they gained "love and devotion," "position," and a family that would be a "credit" to them. Had the survey asked more questions about work, it might have sparked more expressions of discontent from the men, who no doubt experienced more of their stresses and strains in the workplace. In addition, the women clearly thought it was part of their job to keep men happy at home because their material well-being depended on it. Thus, they were as reluctant to risk "annoying the boss" at home as their husbands were on the job.

Women had to make different kinds of choices than did men. They gave up careers in medicine and the fine arts and activities they enjoyed, such as music and sports. In almost every case, they complained about the burdens of their household tasks, particularly their husbands' lack of help with the children. They also complained of their husbands' selfishness, demands on them, and need to be the boss. Yet, in all these cases, the wives not only put up with these problems but claimed to be satisfied with their marriages. Why? What did they gain? Here women's responses were even more concrete than their husbands'. For these women, life was "economically comfortable and secure"; marriage provided "complete peace," a "stable, comfortable life," "status," and "stability, children, a nice home," which made them the "envy" of many of their friends.

To achieve this secure, stable, and materially comfortable life, women had to adapt. The adaptation took two forms: adapting to their husbands' needs and adapting their own goals and aspirations to fit the marriages they had created. Both husbands and wives recognized that marriage required more adjustments for women than for men. When asked specifically how much they had to change their "early ideas, habits, and expectations" in regard to relations with relatives, choice of friends, recreation and social activities, and running the household, women indicated much more adjustment than did men, and the men agreed. After making so many adjustments, women may have felt some measure of accomplishment or, at the least, a sense of personal investment in the relationship.[18]

What were the alternatives for women who had given up outside-the-home career possibilities and worked to build a family life that would provide them with children, security, and comfort? Most seemed to agree that a less-than-ideal marriage was much better than no marriage at all, and that marriage itself offered benefits that compensated for the shortcomings of their husbands. For women who planned to be career homemakers, a personal investment in marriage helped them achieve their goals. For example, when asked if "being married" helped them attain their goals, more than three-fourths of the men and women responded affirmatively. Women were more likely to have already achieved their goals, since for many, marriage and motherhood were their goals. Their husbands, most at mid-career, were still aspiring to rise in their jobs. Yet they recognized the important role marriage played in their efforts. When asked if their *partner* helped or hindered the attainment of their goal, however, men were more likely than women to say that their partners helped. Nearly twice as many women as men said that their spouses actually hindered them.[19]

Ratings of emotional health also reflected these differences. Women were less likely than men to rate their emotional health as "excellent"; 11 percent said they had "a great deal" of emotional disturbance, compared to only 3 percent of the men.[20] Nevertheless, marriage remained a high priority in their lives. Although many more women than men regretted their marriage and considered divorce, they were not likely to give up on marriage altogether. When the full sample is considered, including those who were divorced, twelve men said they would "not marry at all" if they had their life to live over, compared to only two women.[21] Clearly, marriage remained an important goal for women, even if their particular spouses turned out to be disappointments.

So powerful were the imperatives to achieve a successful family that even when marital happiness was obviously lacking, some individuals were not even willing to admit the fact to themselves, much less to venture into the realm of social deviance through such a drastic measure as divorce. These were years when countless articles in the popular press warned of the evils of divorce. Those whose marriages ended in divorce were deemed "selfish," "irresponsible," and "immature." One psychiatrist equated divorce with psychological maladjustment. He described it as a "neurotic solution adopted chiefly by neurotic persons" resulting from "the neurosis which brought the couple together in the first place." Describing a "typical" divorcée, he continued, "She is unhappy, struggling, neurotic, misunderstood and maligned by herself and her environment. Even her frequent promiscuity is a neurotic symptom."[22] With such prevalent assumptions, few would want to be tarnished by the taint of divorce. Worst of all, many experts argued that divorce placed children at risk of emotional trauma and maladjustment. A psychology professor at Hunter College, writing in *Parents Magazine,* explained "Why Boys and Girls Go Wrong or Right." He noted that the "delinquent" child comes from a family where "the parents don't get along and that his home has been or will be broken by separation, desertion or divorce." These parents were also condemned for their inability to fulfill their roles as breadwinners and homemakers: "His mother neglects herself, her apartment and Johnny. . . . His father is likely to be shiftless and often on relief."[23] Along with social ostracism and character defamation, divorce might mean financial disaster for women. These were risks many women were determined to avoid.

The determination to stay together at all costs is one of the most striking characteristics of the men and women in the KLS. The idea of a "working marriage" was one that often included constant day-to-day misery for one or both partners. The case of Maria and Norman Kimball, which opened Chapter 5, demonstrates this attitude at its most extreme. The Kimballs had troubles from the beginning: Norman never fully trusted Maria after their premarital intercourse. The relationship went from bad to worse, as he justified his extramarital affairs by convincing himself, inaccurately, that his wife was doing the same. But they had other problems as well.

Before their marriage, Maria articulated some of the difficulties facing postdepression young adults: "I have been raised in a background of extreme financial instability—charge accounts, long overdue bills, social ostentation—and can't live that way. He offers a prospect of honesty and financial management that I need. We are amazingly congenial, and I am in love with him although I have been skeptical of such a thing for years (since my broken engagement). I have complete faith in the continuation of that romantic relationship." Nevertheless, she was aware of some potential problems: "I am out of school, self-supporting and successful on my job (social service work with delinquent minors); he has one and a half years of college and then his prospect is very hazy. It is doubtful if I can get a good job nearer, and separated married life is practically out of the question." Ultimately, she gave up her job, but financial pressures continued to plague them, particularly her husband, who struggled to provide for them adequately. Although his responses revealed none of his distress, Maria described him as "somewhat withdrawn; he makes no close friends. Has periodic depression and restlessness. Constant anxiety around financial security."

By the mid-1950s, Maria had lost her "complete faith in the continuation of that romantic relationship." When asked what she sacrificed because of her marriage, she replied, "The hope of being loved—the security of living with some-one I was sure was fond of me. Nothing else, really, unless one could loosely blame my marriage for the loss of my close relationship with my father, which did not stand up under his jealousy of my husband." When Maria listed her rewards, however, she articulated the compensations she gained from the mar-riage: "The selfish satisfaction of physical nearness to someone whose nearness alone provides a thrill and a pleasure, two lovely children, an economic position stable enough so I can work at an ill-paid job I enjoy and have leisure time for friends I care about."

Like others in the survey, Maria Kimball worked at an "ill-paid job" she enjoyed once the children were in school. For her, work was an arena of free-dom, as the home was for many of the men. But it was her marriage to a success-ful provider that enabled her to hold this job without facing financial hardship. She continued by pointing to the benefits of having a marriage that *appeared* to be successful: "The purely female pleasure of having a husband whose behavior is never an embarrassment, who never lets one down in public, never vents malicious humor, and whose ideas and attitudes rarely jar one's own beliefs. In outside contacts, we work like a well-oiled team. It may be wryly amusing at times, but there's some satisfaction in having acquaintances envy one's apparent compatibility."

Maria went on to enumerate her conflicts with her husband:

> My rigidity frustrates him. Basically a salesman, he will continue to batter at my tastes and prejudices and suffers from a sense of personal failure when they do not change. He assembles reasons for a decision and parades them like an army, sin-cerely believing in his logical and rational mode of thought. To me this is so much rationalization and is unconvincing and wearisome. I think intuitively, and naturally he concludes I do not *think* at all. Maybe he's right, but when forced to give reasons for my preferences, I get a moral kickback because to me any reasons I dream up to support my positions are imaginative lying.

Although Maria resisted her husband's efforts to bend her opinions to con-form to his own, it is clear she had begun to distrust her own strong feelings. Yet she continued, "I like to do things his way to please him, but I am incapable of taking the last necessary step of having his way become my way. For my satisfac-tion, I need him to feel pleasure in getting his way. He can't because the sense of obligation ruins it for him. So we're working it out by avoiding discussion. If we make no plans together, we have no arguments."

Using explicit cold war terminology, she continued:

Each retreats from any sphere of influence in which the other develops an interest. For instance, I now work outside the home and hire a houseworker. This has
eliminated the expression of divergent opinion over how the house is run. He
leaves the children to me. I don't suppose either of us is too satisfied with this
noncooperative impasse, but it works. In fact, it works very well. So long as we
maintain a state of breakdown in communication, we get along fine. Crazy, isn't
it? Yet these last few years I've come to believe that however irrational a human
relationship may be, if it *works*, it's valid.

At the end of the questionnaire, Maria reflected on their difficulties:

It seems to me that the key to what marital discord has dogged us lies simply in
the basic inability of each of us to accept the other's limitations. To me, warm-
hearted and expressive, my husband's stiff reticence is a sort of New Englander
pose through which he cuts himself off from pleasing relationships, and I cannot
grasp that an only child's lack of training in sharing could be a trait that could not
be unlearned. He gives me no approval or affection and very rare support. Sex,
which is completely without affection, gives me no lasting satisfaction, and it is
the only kind I get. Our marriage works very well, yet I am frequently dreadfully
lonely.

For Maria Kimball, the security and outward workings of the "well-oiled team"
compensated for her intense personal sadness.

Norman Kimball was not so explicit in his responses, but he, too, was less
than satisfied with the union. Although he liked his wife's "sexual ability, sense
of humor, and intelligence," he disliked her "possessiveness and disregard for
success and economics." He felt that her problem was "self-pity and failure to
accept unpleasant reality." Once again, he believed that his wife's lack of acceptance, rather than the "unpleasant reality," was the source of the problem. This
couple managed with their "working marriage" intact for more than three
decades. Finally, when their children were grown, the sixties had come and
gone, and divorce had become more acceptable, the Kimballs divorced in the
1970s.[24]

These cases represent the essence of domestic containment. The home
contained not only sex, consumer goods, children, and intimacy, but enormous discontent, especially for women. For many, there was no place else for

this discontent to go, so it remained contained in the home. Women learned to adjust and adapt, working hard at their job of building successful families that would bring them a sense of accomplishment. They poured themselves into it and were unlikely to abandon it. Men, too, worked hard for their marriage. They put up with stress at work and struggled to earn enough income to provide "the good life." For these white middle-class couples, viable alternatives to domestic containment were out of reach. The cold war consensus and the pervasive atmosphere of anticommunism made personal experimentation, as well as political resistance, risky endeavors with dim prospects for significant positive results. So they made the choices they believed they had to make. Most thought that the gains were worth the sacrifices. With depression and war behind them, and with political and economic institutions fostering the upward mobility of men, the domesticity of women, and suburban homeownership, they were homeward bound. But as the years went by, they also found themselves bound to the home. This ambiguous legacy of domestic containment was not lost on their children. When the baby-boom children came of age, they would have different priorities and make different choices.

CHAPTER NINE

THE END OF CONTAINMENT: THE BABY BOOM COMES OF AGE

The thought of spending two weeks with two children in a close dark hole [family bomb shelter] was too horrible to think of and we knew we had to do something. Now that we women have started we will no longer be content to be dull uninformed housewives.

—PARTICIPANT AT A MEETING OF
WOMEN STRIKE FOR PEACE, 1963[1]

THE POLITICS of the cold war and the ideology and public policies that it spawned were crucial in shaping postwar family life and gender roles. As Americans emerged from years of depression and war, they yearned for an abundant life freed from hardship. Yet they also worried about the very developments that promised to free them from the constraints of the past: consumerism, women's emancipation, and technological advances. Contained within the home, these liberating but also potentially dangerous trends might be tamed, where they could contribute to happiness. In private life as well as in foreign policy, containment seemed to offer the key to security.

With security as the common thread, the cold war ideology and the domestic revival reinforced each other. The powerful political consensus that supported cold war policies abroad and anticommunism at home fueled conformity to the suburban family ideal. In turn, the domestic ideology encouraged private solutions to social problems and further weakened the potential for political challenges to the cold war consensus. Black Americans were willing to take huge risks and make massive sacrifices to fight against racial injustice, and to hold the nation's leaders accountable. For white Americans personal adaptation, rather than political resistance, characterized the era. But postwar domesticity never fully delivered on its promises. The baby-boom children who grew up in suburban homes abandoned the containment ethos when they came of age. As young adults in the 1960s and 1970s, they challenged both the imperatives of the cold war and the domestic ideology that came with it. At the same time, they forged new paths to pursue the unfulfilled dreams of their parents.

When many baby boomers were still infants, however, domestic containment began to crumble under its own weight. Gradually, in the early 1960s, an increasing number of white middle-class Americans began to question the private therapeutic approach to solving social problems. Among the first to criticize the status quo were postwar parents themselves. In 1963, Betty Friedan published her exposé of domesticity, *The Feminine Mystique*. Friedan had been a political activist and journalist prior to relinquishing her career for marriage. As a well-educated white woman, she spoke for thousands like herself whose dreams and desires withered under the weight of domesticity. She did not speak for black women who felt liberated rather than trapped in the role of homemaker, who had made the transition "from Mammy to Mom." Nor did she speak for countless white working-class wives who at long last could reap the fruits of prosperity and give up their menial jobs in the paid labor force. But she did give a name to the "problem that has no name" for career homemakers. A postwar wife and mother herself, Friedan spoke directly to women like those in the Kelly Longitudinal Study, who had lived according to the domestic containment ideology. She urged them to break away from their domestic confines, go back to school, pursue careers, and revive the vision of female independence that had been alive before World War II. *The Feminine Mystique* became an immediate best seller and created a national sensation. The book enabled discontented white middle-class homemakers across the country to find their voices. It was as if someone was finally willing to say that the emperor had no clothes; soon a chorus joined in support. Hundreds of readers wrote to Friedan, telling their stories. These personal testimonies reveal the stated and unstated messages that this generation of parents gave their children.[2]

The letters to Friedan reveal widespread disenchantment among women who had struggled to conform to the prevailing familial norm. Some of the writers were children of activist parents who had fought for equal rights in the early part of the century. Nearly all expressed the hope that their children would avoid the domestic trap in which they found themselves. One spoke harshly of herself and her peers, who embraced domestic containment:

> My life spans the two eras—the ebb tide of feminism and the rise of the "mystique." My parents were products of the early twentieth century Liberalism and believed firmly that everyone—poor, Negroes, and women too—had a right to have a "rendezvous with Destiny." . . . My feeling of betrayal is not directed against society so much as at the women who beat the drums for the "passionate journey" into darkness. . . . My undiluted wrath is expended on those of us who were educated, and therefore privileged, who put on our black organza nightgowns and went willingly, joyfully, without so much as a backward look at the hard-won freedoms handed down to us by the feminists (men and women). The men, in my experience, were the interested by-standers, bewildered, amused, and maybe a bit joyful at having two mommies at home—one for the children and one for themselves.

She ended with a note that was echoed by many others: "My children grew up in the mystique jungle but somehow escaped it."[3]

Another letter writer described herself as

> the mother of five and the wife of a successful partner in an investment banking firm. In seeking that something "more" out of life, I have tried large doses of everything from alcohol to religion, from a frenzy of sports activities to PTA . . . to every phase of church work. . . . Each served its purpose at the time, but I suddenly realized that none had any real future. Our children are all in school except for the baby. . . . However, I felt that if I waited until she's in school I'll be too close to forty to learn any new tricks. I've seen too many women say they would "do something" when the last child went to school. The something has usually been bridge, bowling or drinking.[4]

A Mount Holyoke graduate who joined the "stampede back to the nest" described her path into domesticity: "I entered graduate school at Yale, met a man, left school, and married in 1951. I have since then moved thirteen times, lived in eight states, had four miscarriages and produced two children." But she also struggled at home and alone to become a painter. So "finally, when I fill out the income tax now, it is occupation: Painter, not housewife." For this woman, the key was in her background: "My one advantage over the rest of my genera-tion is, I suppose, the fact that I was raised in a family of feminists. . . . I still tend, belatedly and belligerently, to champion women's rights. The cloying and sentimental public effort of the last decade to raise the prestige of the home and represent it as demanding all that we have to give has more than once precipi-tated me into incoherent outrage." Nevertheless, it had also precipitated her out of graduate school and into domesticity.[5]

Many of these educated women responded to Friedan's book by calling for a revival of political activism and lashing out at experts who promoted domestic-ity. Psychologists who endorsed the containment ideal were the targets of much of this wrath. In a six-page letter, a graduate of Cornell University with a mas-ter's degree—married to a physician and mother of two—complained, "Since scientific findings reveal the strong effect of the child's environment upon the child, the poor mother has been made to replace God in her omnipotence. It is the terror of this misinterpreted omnipotence that in many cases is keeping women home. I still remember the tear-stained face of a brilliant young woman economist who had earned a Ph.D. in her field when she had to give up a newly discovered exciting job because her pediatrician convinced her that her six- and three-year-old children would become social menaces without her presence 24 hours a day." She then quoted a school official who "politely drawled, 'Show me a delinquent child and I'll show you a working mother.'"[6] A Vasser graduate also questioned the wisdom of experts. She wrote of going to an alumnae counselor who told her, "Go back to your kitchen and stay there and make jam!" Drawing on the language of the 1950s, she recalled, "I was a sissy—I paid attention to her! . . . I wonder how many other frustrated housewives have been similarly dis-couraged . . . by such lamentable suggestions?"[7]

One of the most powerful indictments of the therapeutic model came from a resident in a mental institution. She explained that she never married because, as a college sophomore, she "became interested in a great variety of things more important than electric waxers." Still, she felt she was affected by the domestic ideology in her

> decision not to take fourth-year high school math for fear of being called a brain, and in a more important failure to ever make a real and substantial career choice. During college, I came close to marrying for security's sake, but at the last minute I called the wedding off; the world seemed so much bigger than split-level houses and I thought I had better start off to see it, which I did. . . . But when I began to think about marriage again at the ripe old age of 25, I found it was already too

late: most of my contemporaries were already on the 3rd child and too busy mowing lawns and buying things to be much interested in existentialism or the political situation in Algeria.

Next she went to Europe, where she had a series of love affairs with European men who were "much less fazed by my 'aggressive and competitive' personality than most of the American M.D.s and Ph.D.s that I had known." Finally, she returned home "to make the fatal mistake of embarking on psychoanalysis which . . . had the effect of landing me in my present residence: inside a mental hospital." She claimed that her "crackup" was due, in part, to her belief that "it was immoral not to be interested in matters such as poverty and the bomb." She believed that she had "wasted a life throwing tin spears at other people's electric dishwashers." At the end of her letter, she proposed some practical solutions to the problems that plagued her peers: later marriage, more sexual experimentation, divorce "as a reflection of the fact that some individuals do change over time" rather than "a sign of hopeless neuroticism or failure to adjust to one's sex role." She argued that "love and security are simply not the same thing. Security can come from many kinds of social relationships . . . among which marriage is only one, from continued contact with one's primary kin, from friendships, or from socially meaningful work." This nonconformist closed with a telling remark: "The price of deviating for me turned out to be an awfully high one but, nevertheless, the aim was real only because the bomb really does exist and hangs over the suburbs."[8]

Other readers noticed other menaces hanging over the suburbs. One suburban housewife described ten of her neighbors whose problems ranged from hysteria to alcoholism. She wrote that "the only normal, happy one" was "a brilliant 46 year old teacher. . . . Her teenage daughter is a beautiful girl, a Merit scholarship finalist, who wants to be a mother!" As for herself, she claimed to be "a compulsive eater, have fits of extreme depression, once seriously considered suicide. I have an I.Q. in the 145–150 range." While an honors student in college, "I 'caught' a husband at 19, married him on my twentieth birthday, quit school pregnant, and now have six children! I am the typical stay-at-home, domineering mother and wife. I love my children yet I hate them, have actually wished them dead."[9]

Not all the letters were so harsh, yet most agreed with Friedan that women suffered more than men from the effects of domesticity. Nevertheless, many readers thought that Friedan had slighted the oppressive nature of male gender roles. One wrote, "When I think of some of the problems the men students faced, I realize that they too suffer enormous stress and confusion. Don't both images have to be changed before woman's situation truly improves?" Echoing similar sentiments, a writer from Far Rockaway, New York, recognized the connection between boredom at work and frustration at home: "What is wrong with the women trapped in the Feminine Mystique is what's wrong with men trapped in the Rat Race. . . . Isn't it true, that one of the problems, the biggest really, of our present day society is that there isn't enough meaningful creative work for *anyone* these days? Isn't that one of the reasons fathers are taking their parental role with the seriousness of a career?" Another chimed in, "I would very much like to see a book for the sons which does for them what yours does for the daughters." Added a 1951 college graduate who married in her senior year and ended up divorced with two children after six years, "How about the poor 'Male Mystique'? Seriously, they too have problems—'real men' so seldom match the popularly accepted image." An assistant professor of home economics argued, "The 'anomie' that you describe is not restricted to middle-class college-trained women. It is shared by middle-class men and women, but because the men are more absorbed in business and professions, they are less likely to find their way to the psychiatrist's couch."[10]

Friedan's book sparked readers to comment on the connection not only between women's and men's fate, but between domesticity and cold war politics. One woman believed that political activism was the only way to bring women out of "their cozy cocoons in America," but she also perceived that challenges to women's roles would be seen as un-American. Women would need to "make determined efforts to free themselves," she noted, "and they may expect hostility from conservative elements politically as well as from their fellow timid sisters and timid men. I am not advocating that women become Communist sympathizers, but I am expecting that progressive women will be so labeled."[11] One reader framed her response in a larger political context: "I should say that roots of *both* the Feminine Mystique *and* the tiresomeness of so many children could be traced to larger things like the cold war and the Bomb, and all the implications of same."[12]

The common thread that linked those who responded to Friedan's book was their hope for their children. These postwar parents wanted to leave a different legacy to their children than the one provided by the model of their own lives. One wrote, "I want [my daughter] to grow up in a society where she will have a comfortable and important place." Another urged mothers "to help their daughters to avoid the traps into which they have already fallen." A housewife who was driven "very close to severe emotional illness" saved her sanity by going into business, but she had a "guilty feeling" for five years. She was one of many "parents who want to avoid these problems in their children. . . . It would be a crime to let another generation go as mine has; they would never know anything else! . . . I hope one day, when my daughter is older . . . perhaps she will understand enough that she will avoid becoming a miserable housewife!" One reader who described herself as "a drop-out from Oberlin College after two years to marry in 1947 . . . a victim of the Feminine Mystique . . . the mother of five" hoped that her daughter would avoid the "servile feeling" she experienced. "How can we help our daughters to avoid making the mistake of following the crowd into early marriage?"[13]

Many of the daughters of these women got the message. Some of the early baby-boom children were already coming of age when Friedan's book appeared. They responded in ways that differed from those of the older readers. One young woman, reared during the era of domestic containment, resented the fact that her mother had not been a full-time homemaker. While her friends' mothers were home waiting for them after school with milk and cookies, her mother was completing her education. She decided that she would never deprive her own children that way. She was about to graduate from college when she suddenly began to question her goals. She confessed to Friedan that she had been desperate about marriage. "And, of course, my marriage would be ideal," she wrote. "Unlike my mother, who is back at school finishing her degree, I would be the *ideal* wife—unaggressive and feminine, subordinate—you know, a kind of nice ball of fluff for a rock of a man."

Gradually she came to a new realization: "These occasional thoughts, my love for my roommate entering medical school next fall, my confusion over Mom's 'home abandonment,' and my love for both books and children caused a kind of pervading uncertainty about my future that I could not shake. In the last few months, I found it hard to be patient, sympathetic, cheerful—hard to be anything but either grasping or weeping." Expressing remarkable insight into the sexual containment ethos, she continued, "And to top it off, my boyfriend and I nearly went too far (as they say) supported by *my* anxious feelings that he was all there was to hang on to, and the only future. I began to wonder, in light of my behavior, what was the matter with me anyway." She finally decided to go to graduate school, with the goal of teaching college English or editing children's books.[14]

This college student shifted gears in time to avoid full-time domesticity, but others were well along the path before they discovered that it did not lead to paradise. A twenty-six-year-old mother of two sent Friedan the saga of her life:

For the last few years, I have been on the "old housekeeping merry-go-round." . . . I cleaned and I cleaned . . . and then I cleaned some more! All day—every day. My mother had returned to teaching school when I was twelve, and I had resented it, and consequently vowed that when I married and had children I would make it my vocation. I was quite convinced that I was very happy with my role in life as we had our own home and my husband is a good husband and father and a very sufficient provider. However, one night last November, all Hell broke loose in my psyche. I was sitting calmly reading when I became overwhelmed with waves of anxiety. I couldn't imagine what was happening. . . . I visited my family doctor. He put me on tranquilizers and diagnosed it as a mild state of anxiety. However there was no explanation.

She went on to relate her happy childhood, her college education, her plans to marry, and her job as a secretary that ended after eleven months when her first child was born. "I see now. . . . I chose security over everything else." Finally, she went to see a psychiatrist. Like many other professionals at the time, he prescribed drugs to improve her mental state so she could better adapt to her situation. Rather than encourage her to alter the conditions that caused her emotional problems, the psychiatrist changed her tranquilizers. Four days later, she asked to go to the hospital and spent eleven days in a psychiatric ward.

Ultimately, it was not the medical experts but a friend who suggested what was causing "the nervousness and crying spells and sleeplessness" that had become "unbearable." Her friend "volunteered that the trouble was with my marriage." She and her husband began to see a marriage counselor who was a psychologist. She told him, "I felt I had something more to offer the world and wanted to do something about it." He suggested that she go back to school, which she did: "I now have a goal and no longer feel like a vegetable!" She discovered that the problem was not with her marriage; it was with her circumscribed life. But through it all, with the exception of the marriage counselor she consulted, the experts were decidedly unhelpful.[15]

Many of the women who wrote to Friedan were those with the resources to respond to her call for self-realization through education and careers. They were affluent. If they were married, their husbands' incomes allowed them to develop outside interests for self-fulfillment. But there were others who found Friedan's message troubling. It was fine to have ambitions, but it was another matter to work out of necessity, face a sex-segregated job market, and do double duty at home as well.

One woman expressed her irritation at "the false emphasis that is placed on the entire matter of women fulfilling themselves through a career. The vast majority of working women don't have careers. We have jobs, just like men. We work for money to buy things that our families need. If we're lucky, we like our jobs, and find some satisfaction in doing them well, but it is hard to hold a commercial job, raise a family and keep a house." Speaking for many of her peers, she continued:

> Most of us would be delighted to chuck the wage earning back in our husbands' laps and devote ourselves exclusively to homemaking and community projects. We worry about the children while we're at work. We don't really like to throw the last load of clothes in the washer at 11:30 p.m., and set the alarm for 6:00 so we can iron a blouse for a school age daughter, fix breakfast and school lunches all at the same time, do as much housework as possible before bolting for the office, and face the rest of it, and the grocery shopping and preparing dinner when we get home. This isn't our idea of fulfillment. It doesn't make us more interesting people or more stimulating companions for our husbands. It just makes us very, very tired.

Describing the realities that prompted her to seek employment, this woman explained why employed wives were often "pretty good sports." She wrote, "Our husbands feel bad enough about not being able to handle the whole job without our financial help. Do you think we're going to say right out, 'My Joe just can't put five kids through college, and then Sue needed braces last year, and Johnny will need them, too, and the washer had to be replaced, and Ann was ashamed to bring friends home because the living room furniture was such a mess, so I went to work.'"[16]

Another employed wife was not such a good sport. "Believe me," she wrote, "a modern woman of today would have to be *four* women to be everything that is expected of her." This thirty-seven-year-old mother of three had two years of college. She had held jobs on and off since her marriage:

> My husband wants me to work not for the satisfaction I might get out of working, but for the extra money *he* will have for himself. . . . *But,* how about the extra burden it would put on me? I would go out to work if possible, but I cannot do that and come home to a house full of screaming kids, dishes piled in the sink, and mountains of laundry to do. It is no fun to come home and see the sweet, dear, lazy bum asleep on the couch after being on my feet all day. He still likes his home-made pies, cakes, and appetizing meals.

She continued with a history of her work roles:

I have worked in stores; the post-office; given dinners for a pot and pan outfit; minded children; and sold things door-to-door. At present, I take in sewing and ironing. . . . If I work, then my housework suffers and I get told about that. I would like nothing better than to just do my own work, have some time to myself once in a while so I could just go down-town once in [a]while without having someone else's work staring at me. I get very tired of reading about women working outside the home. . . . I cannot divide myself into more than one person. . . . I have plenty to occupy my time and I happen to enjoy being a house-wife.

This woman's bitterness against the demands of double duty was directed largely toward her husband. Her anger was intense:

My husband . . . thinks it's great for women to work, but until men get some of their Victorian ideas out of their heads then I am staying home. Unless he would be willing to help with the housework then I cannot go to work. He thinks he would lose some of his masculinity if anyone saw him hanging out the wash, or washing dishes. And if he *had* to give up any of his fishing or hunting or running around visiting his buddies to keep an eye on the kids, well, I'm not killing myself for the almighty dollar.[17]

As these letters indicate, domestic containment was not going to die a quick or natural death. Yet it was clearly doomed from its own internal contradictions. Betty Friedan spoke for a generation whose children would later be credited with initiating a decade of political and social upheaval, but many of their parents had paved the way. Even those who thought that it was too late to change their own ways and routines knew it was not too late for their children. They encouraged their children—implicitly if not explicitly—to follow new paths. Frustrated women and exhausted men provided ambiguous role models for children hoping to avoid the discontent of their mothers and the pressure and ill health the stresses of the workplace had inflicted on their fathers.

Still, change came slowly. In the early 1960s, it was not immediately obvious that a unique historical era was coming to an end. Signs that the postwar consensus was beginning to crack were hardly more visible than they had been in the fifties: a few voices of dissent from the intelligentsia, the growing popularity of counterculture heroes such as Elvis Presley and James Dean, and the spread of the civil rights movement from black activists in the South to northern whites.

Oral contraceptives first became available in 1960, but they did not immediately bring about a change in behavior, even though years later, many would credit (or blame) "The Pill" for the "sexual revolution." Most cultural signs still pointed toward the cold war consensus at home and abroad. The ideology of domesticity was still alive and well.

Although John F. Kennedy's election to the presidency in 1960 signaled the rise to power of a new, younger generation, Kennedy himself did little immediately to challenge the status quo after his close victory over Eisenhower's vice president, Richard M. Nixon. Aside from his youthful appearance and Irish Catholic background, Kennedy represented cold war militance and masculine authority that was in tune with the American establishment. With his stylish wife at his side and his two small children, he seemed to embody the virtues of the American domestic ideal par excellence: the tough cold warrior who was also a warm family man.

Nevertheless, Kennedy's style and rhetoric, emphasizing vigor and the promise of change, encouraged Americans to embrace political activism and risk. Kennedy's famous inaugural challenge, "Ask not what your country can do for you; ask what you can do for your country," invited individual political engagement and implied that each person could make a difference in creating a better society. Shortly after Kennedy's election, the frustrations and resentments that had been expressed in the fifties not only publicly by black civil rights activists, artists, intellectuals, and the "beats," but privately by many members of the white middle class, began to surface.

On November 1, 1961, fifty thousand American housewives walked out of their homes and jobs in a massive protest, "Women Strike for Peace." These activists were among the first postwar middle-class whites to organize against the social and political status quo. Several of the leaders of the strike were part of a small group of feminists who had worked on behalf of women's rights throughout the forties and the fifties. According to *Newsweek*, the strikers "were perfectly ordinary looking women. . . . They looked like the women you would see driving ranch wagons, or shopping at the village market, or attending PTA meetings. . . . Many [were] wheeling baby buggies or strollers." Within a year their numbers grew to several hundred thousand.[18]

Anticommunists worried that Women Strike for Peace signaled that "the pro-Reds have moved in on our mothers and are using them for their own purposes," and the Federal Bureau of Investigation kept the group under surveillance from its inception in 1961. The following year, the leaders of Women Strike for Peace were called before the House Un-American Activities

Committee. Under questioning, these women spoke as mothers, claiming that saving American children from nuclear extinction was the essence of "Americanism," thereby turning the ideology of domesticity against the assumptions of the cold war. These women carried the banner of motherhood into politics, much as had their reformist sisters in the previous century. But their ability to attack the cold war with domesticity as their tool and make a mockery of the congressional hearings indicates that the familial cold war consensus was beginning to lose its grip.[19]

Increasing political pressure resulted in several important new public policies that challenged the status quo. In 1961, President Kennedy established the President's Commission on the Status of Women, chaired appropriately by an activist from the 1930s, Eleanor Roosevelt. Within the next three years, Congress passed the Equal Pay Act and Title VII of the Civil Rights Act (which prohibited discrimination on the basis of sex, as well as race, color, religion, and national origin), and the United States and the Soviet Union signed the first treaty banning the atmospheric testing of nuclear weapons.

While these policies were taking shape, Students for a Democratic Society (SDS), inspired largely by the civil rights movement, gained thousands of members in chapters across the country. Out of the student movement came the antiwar movement and the new feminism. By the late 1960s, hundreds of thousands of young activists mobilized against the gender assumptions as well as the cold war policies that had prevailed since World War II.[20]

The simultaneous attack on domestic containment and the cold war ideology also found expression in the popular culture. Within a few months of the publication of *The Feminine Mystique* came Stanley Kubrick's film *Dr. Strangelove: Or, How I Learned to Stop Worrying and Love the Bomb*, a biting satire that equated the madness of the cold war with Americans' unresolved sexual neuroses. Such attacks against the sanctity of the postwar domestic ideology and the politics of the cold war would have been risky endeavors ten years earlier. The film probably would have been suppressed and its creators called before the House Un-American Activities Committee. By the early 1960s, however, although the cold war was still in full force, and some viewers found the film offensive and un-American, critics as well as audiences were, for the most part, wildly enthusiastic.[21]

By the end of the decade, the new feminist movement had pushed beyond Betty Friedan's call for self-realization into a full-fledged assault on sexism in all its forms, organized by younger women who emerged from their activism in the civil rights movement and the New Left with newly discovered skills and strengths. The new feminists demanded access to professional occupations and skilled jobs, protested low wages, and worked for pay equity. They formed consciousness-raising groups all over the country, challenged the gender division of labor in the home, demanded reproductive rights, and railed against the sexual double standard. In a 1970 survey of women entering an open-admission, tuition-free public university, most saw their future role as "married career woman with children"—a vast change from the 1950s, when most women of all classes saw their future career as homemaker. (By the 1980s, college women would be as career-oriented as college men.) Young middle-class men also began to rebel. They reacted against the rigidity of male gender expectations by growing their hair long, rejecting the "grey flannel suit" for flowered shirts and beads, and resisting the draft that would force them to fight in Vietnam on behalf of cold war principles they did not endorse.[22] As domestic containment began to crumble at home, the antiwar movement gave rise to the first large-scale rejection of the containment policy abroad.

As these political movements gained momentum, public opinion remained resistant to change. Polls taken during the years that gave rise to widespread criticism of the status quo indicate that mainstream Americans continued to uphold the political consensus forged during the forties and fifties. In 1960, the majority of those polled were willing to pay higher taxes to keep the United States ahead in the arms race, and they favored public funding for bomb shelters. Although atmospheric testing was banned in 1963 after a flurry of protest, testing continued underground, with little public resistance. Throughout most of the decade, the cold war continued to top the list of people's concerns.[23]

Conservative attitudes toward sex and gender also prevailed. In 1965, 80 percent of those polled believed that schools should prohibit boys from wearing their hair long. A 1966 poll to determine the "ideal" family size yielded results that matched surveys taken in 1945 and 1957: The most common response was four or more children, given by 35 percent of those polled. It was not until 1971 that the figure dropped markedly, to 23 percent. In 1968, three out of four of those polled believed the nation's morals were getting worse, and as late as 1969, more than two-thirds believed that premarital sex was wrong.[24]

Nevertheless, behavior was changing. The year 1960 signified a demographic watershed. The age at marriage began to rise after decades of decline. The birthrate began to dwindle as the first baby boomers reached childbearing age; within a decade, it was at an all-time low and still plummeting. The marriage rate also declined, as more people remained single or lived together as couples, families, and households without marriage. The divorce rate, after more than a decade of stability, began to rise gradually in the early 1960s and then dramatically by the end of the decade, skyrocketing to unprecedented heights in the early 1970s.[25]

Critics of the youths of the 1960s complained that the family-centered ethic of "togetherness" gave way to the hedonistic celebration of "doing your own thing." But the moral distance between the baby boomers and their parents is a matter of some debate. The baby boomers continued to pursue the quest for meaning through intimacy that had been at the heart of the containment ethos, but they gave up on containment. Many abandoned the old containers: the traditional family, home-centered consumerism, marriage-centered sex, and cold war–centered politics. The youth culture, as well as the booming economy, encouraged them to be risk takers in ways that their security-oriented parents found unthinkable.

Spending became less home-centered. Although some observers labeled the rebellious middle-class youths "antimaterialist," the younger generation did not give up on consumerism. They simply took it outside the home. Expenditures for housing and household operations, which had increased in the postwar years, leveled off in the 1960s, while recreational expenditures, which had been stable in the 1950s, accelerated in the 1960s. Spending was hardly out of fashion, but consumers used their purchasing power for more individualistic, less familial, purposes.[26]

Sexual containment also lost its power as a behavioral code, as intercourse outside marriage became the rule. Those who disapproved of premarital sex dropped from 68 percent in 1969 to 48 percent by 1973. The birth control pill undoubtedly made it easier and safer to have sexual intercourse without being married. Its availability was not the impetus for initiating those relationships, however, since most unmarried women did not use the Pill (or any form of birth control, for that matter) during their first intercourse experience. Time-honored sexual attitudes lingered long after behavior changed; as late as the 1970s, the majority of unmarried college students who had already engaged in sexual intercourse disapproved of premarital sex. In effect, they disapproved of their own behavior.[27] Although sexual containment may have disappeared, guilt and regret did not. Baby boomers did not abandon the quest for intimacy and sexual fulfillment; they simply abandoned the marital imperative.

Along with sex, living together no longer depended on marriage. In the late 1960s, the *New York Times* claimed that "cohabitation" (unmarried couples living together) was limited to a "tiny minority" within "the dissident youth subculture—the intellectual, politically liberal to radical, from middle- and

upper-middle-class backgrounds, anti-materialistic and anti-Establishment."
The phenomenon became much more commonplace in the 1970s. During that
decade, the number of unmarried couples who were living together tripled;
among those aged twenty-five and under with no children, it increased eight-
fold. Although living together usually represented a postponement rather than a
rejection of marriage, it changed the pattern of dating and mating that had characterized earlier decades. The marital-heterosexual imperative was further
eroded by the increasing visibility and political activism of gay men and lesbians, who challenged prevailing definitions of sexual "normality" and called for
the right of free choice in matters of sexual preference and behavior.[28]

Marriage became much less "normative" than it had been (see Table 4). In
the late 1970s, only 62 percent of all households included a married couple and
only one-third contained two parents and children under age eighteen; 22 percent of all households consisted of people living alone. Compared to their parents, baby boomers were less inclined to scale down their expectations to sustain
unsatisfying unions. As divorce became more common, the stigma surrounding
it began to lift. Divorce did not mean a rejection of marriage, however; four out
of every five divorced persons remarried, half within three years. Divorced individuals at every age, in fact, were more likely to marry than those who had never
married.[29]

Marriage remained a popular institution, but it began to look different. As
the birthrate declined, voluntary childlessness was on the rise. Women had their
children later and held jobs outside the home to a greater extent than their
mothers had, even when their children were small. In the early 1980s, half the
married women with school-aged children held jobs, along with one-third of
those with children under age six. A solid majority of wives aged twenty to
twenty-four were employed, compared to only 26 percent in 1950. The vast
number of married women in the paid labor force called into question the
assumption that they should be responsible for all household chores when they,
like their husbands, came home after a hard day at work. According to polls
taken in the late 1970s, a majority of young single men, as well as women,
believed that when they married, both spouses would be employed and would
share child care and housework equally. Nevertheless, domestic gender roles
remained resistant to change. The evidence suggests that although men began
to "help out" more with domestic chores, women still suffered from double duty
and remained responsible for the lion's share of child care and housework.[30]

In spite of all the challenges to the status quo, institutions were slow to
change. As the baby boomers matured, many found that their aspirations had

moved far beyond their opportunities. Young women still faced enormous difficulties if they hoped to combine a career with marriage. Problems surrounding child care, parental leaves, and the burdens of housework continued to plague employed mothers. Because of these persistent obstacles, female college students had high levels of anxiety and ambivalence toward the future. Political activism had done a great deal to improve opportunities for women and minorities, but only the very tip of the institutional iceberg had begun to melt. Sex segregation still prevailed in the workforce. Although more women entered male-dominated professions, most working women still faced what their mothers had tried to avoid: overwork, inadequate pay, and extra burdens at home.[31]

Women who took the risk of divorce may have escaped oppressive or even brutal marriages, but they also encountered what their security-oriented mothers had feared: poverty, loneliness, difficulties in caring for their children, and the exhausting life of a single parent. Divorced women often experienced an immediate and sharp decline in their standard of living. Since they usually gained custody of children and received less-than-adequate child support, the meagerness of their incomes made their lives even more difficult. Divorced women and their children were much more likely than men to fall into poverty; men generally experienced a higher standard of living after divorce.[32] Even the legal triumphs that were hailed as harbingers of a more humane future often backfired, such as the no-fault divorce statutes. Because these new laws treated men and women "equally," they ignored the inequalities that marriage created and the lower earning power that left women with even more disadvantages after the dissolution of their marriages.[33]

Married or divorced, professional as well as nonprofessional wage-earning women continued to face inequalities at work and at home. Nevertheless, political activism opened up new opportunities for women to achieve autonomy that had been unavailable to their mothers. Women of the fifties, constrained by tremendous cultural and economic pressures to conform to domestic containment, gave up their independence and personal ambitions. Once they made the choice to embrace domesticity, they did their best to thrive within it and claimed that their sacrifices were ultimately worthwhile. Many of their daughters abandoned security and material comfort to follow a more autonomous path that brought them face to face with economic hardship and pervasive discrimination. Yet, like their mothers, many would say that the struggles were worth it. Their mothers paid a price for security and dependence; the daughters paid a price for autonomy and independence. In both cases, the lack of equal opportunity for women limited their options. Yet there is no question that the daughters

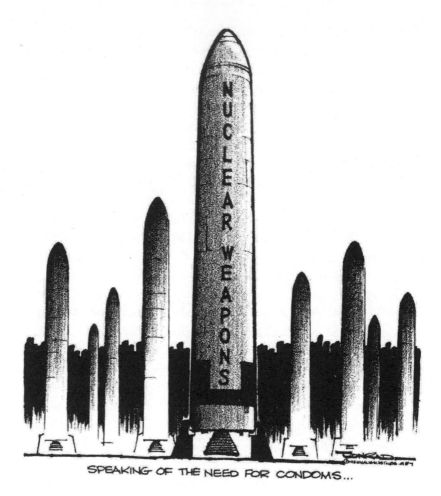

SPEAKING OF THE NEED FOR CONDOMS...

FIGURE 16   In 1987, at the height of raging controversies over arms control as well as sexual control, Paul Conrad of the *Los Angeles Times* commented upon the connection. *(Tribune Media Services, Inc. All rights reserved. Printed with permission.)*

had more opportunities than their mothers as a result of the hard-won political achievements of the feminist movement: They were no longer bound to the home.

Political goals were only partially achieved, however. Even before the end of the 1960s, the "silent majority" rose up against the noisy, youthful minority. In 1968, the quintessential fifties politician, Richard Nixon, was back in the White House, this time as president. The ideology of the cold war, although dealt a serious blow by the disastrous war in Vietnam, remained a powerful force in national politics—and it continued to be tied to the ideology of domesticity. Those who claimed that South Vietnam fell as a result of softness against communism also blamed feminism for what they perceived as the destruction of the family.

It is no accident that in the wake of feminism, the sexual revolution, and the peace movement of the 1960s, the New Right emerged in the 1970s and 1980s as a powerful political force with the dual aims of reviving the cold war and reasserting the ideology of domesticity. It should not be surprising that the most vigorous opponent of the feminist movement, Phyllis Schlafly, began her career as an avid cold warrior.[34] Proponents of the New Right gained strength by calling for militance in foreign policy, opposing the Equal Rights Amendment, and condemning student radicalism, the counterculture, feminism, and the sexual revolution. They went on to triumph in 1980, with the election of Ronald Reagan to the presidency.

Reagan, like Nixon, received his political groundings in the late 1940s and 1950s as an anticommunist crusader in California. Appropriately, his media image was that of the family man par excellence, as he promoted home-centered consumerism as host of the General Electric Theater from 1954 to 1962. The all-electric home that Reagan advertised (and also inhabited) was virtually identical to the "model home" Nixon praised in Moscow in 1959. In the 1960s, Reagan carried his image into California politics, where he promised to crack down on student protestors. With Reagan in the White House in the 1980s, the rhetoric of containment returned, with its support for cold war militance and calls for a strengthened "traditional" family.[35]

Although the cold war and the call for domesticity became fashionable once again, consensus no longer prevailed in the 1980s as it did in the years after World War II. The family landed squarely in the center of hotly contested politics. Insightful observers noted the continuing intersection of sexual and political ideology (see Figure 16). The New Right advocates of militance abroad also called for abolishing the feminist gains of the sixties and seventies, such as affirmative action and legalized abortion, while supporting "Star Wars" research and renewed civil defense strategies for a "winnable nuclear war."[36] Those who favored arms control also called for equal opportunities for women. The political divide continued to separate cold warriors from those in favor of equality between the sexes. Meanwhile, personal lifestyles began to reflect a much wider range than they did in the 1940s and 1950s, when nearly everyone conformed to a pattern of early marriage and several children. With domestic containment virtually dismantled, no consensus prevailed in the familial realm.

It is clear that in the later years of the cold war, the domestic ideology and cold war militance rose and fell together. Immediately after World War II, stable family life seemed necessary for national security, civil defense, and the struggle for supremacy over the Soviet Union. For a generation of young adults who grew up amid depression and war, domestic containment was a logical response to specific historical circumstances. It allowed them to pursue, in the midst of a tense and precarious world situation, the quest for a sexually fulfilling, consumer-oriented personal life that was free from hardship. But the circumstances were different for their children, who broke the consensus surrounding the cold war and domestic containment. Cold war tensions gave way to culture wars. By the time the cold war officially ended, Americans had become preoccupied with personal concerns. It would take another explosion, on September 11, 2001, to shake the nation's sense of security to its core.

ECHOES OF THE COLD WAR:
THE AFTERMATH OF
SEPTEMBER 11, 2001

Fly and enjoy America's great destination spots. . . . Get down
to Disney World in Florida. Take your families and enjoy life
the way we want it to be enjoyed.

—PRESIDENT GEORGE W. BUSH, SEPTEMBER 27, 2001[1]

THE TERRORIST attacks on September 11, 2001, jolted Americans out of
their domestic preoccupations as a stunned nation came together in shock
and grief. Lacking a vocabulary as well as any historical precedents to place the
event in a familiar and manageable context, the nation's leaders, pundits, and
large numbers of citizens struggled to find something familiar to draw out of historical memory. Almost immediately, they found reference points in World War
II and the cold war.[2]

President George W. Bush quickly declared a "war on terror." But unlike
World War II, when Franklin D. Roosevelt called upon Americans to sacrifice
comforts and commodities, Bush called for a celebration of the American way
of life, much as Richard Nixon had done at the "kitchen debate" in 1959.
Although the president launched a hot war in response to the attacks, the cold

war served as a model for the home front in the "war on terror." Telling his fellow citizens to "take your families and enjoy life the way we want it to be enjoyed," Bush, like Nixon, identified consumerism as the stealth weapon that would triumph over the enemy. Rather than addressing American foreign policies that might have fueled resentment abroad, in classic cold war terms the president declared, "They hate our freedoms."[3]

During World War II the government drafted men to fight, rationed food and other goods, converted consumer industries into war industries, and asked citizens to support the war effort by buying war bonds, planting "victory gardens," and conserving everything useful. During the "war on terrorism," the government called up its volunteer army but did not draft anyone. It gave back tax dollars for people to spend, rather than asking citizens to invest or save. Government policies went counter to all efforts to conserve resources of any kind. President Bush opposed efforts to promote energy efficiency for cars or industries and did nothing to minimize the nation's dependence on oil from the Middle East.[4] These policies were not wartime policies, but they did echo the emphasis on consumer freedom and the "American way of life" that was central to cold war propaganda.[5]

As the president invoked the ideological battles of the cold war, journalists and citizens revived the apocalyptic nightmares of the atomic age, with visions of civilians going about their daily business snuffed out in an instant. Within hours of the attack, the site of the destroyed World Trade Center became "ground zero"—a term long associated with nuclear targets. News reports published on September 12 suggest how quickly cold war terms reappeared in the national vocabulary. The *Baltimore Sun* quoted Neil Hare, a lawyer for the U.S. Chamber of Commerce who worked near the White House: "I think we're at war. . . . I'm running. This is probably ground zero, and I don't want to be anywhere near here." The *Boston Herald* described the site of the World Trade Center as "ground zero of the worst terrorist attack in American history." The *Boston Globe* noted that people in Washington, D.C., "live with the nightmare that their city is ground zero for a major terrorist attack." As Americans struggled to make sense of what happened, they reacted with familiar cold war sensibilities.[6]

The immediate response in the press reflected this effort to meet the unfamiliar with the familiar, marking the event as both unprecedented and precedented. In a typical news report published on September 12, Rosie DiManno wrote in the *Toronto Star:*

The heart of the American empire was Ground Zero. . . . Now U.S. fighter jets buzz overhead in a surreal tableau of war. . . . This is terrorism in the 21st century;

faceless, pointless, fanatical and cowardly. . . . If the mightiest nation in the world was caught unawares, so piteously vulnerable to the whims of madmen, then there is no hope and sanity is doomed. . . . The world will never be the same again. . . . All that steel and concrete convulsing, shuddering, reduced in seconds to a mountain of debris and a mushrooming cloud of smoke and dust. . . . Defense officials were herded into secured bunkers deep inside the earth. . . . How could this happen? Who is doing this to us? . . . For Americans, the infliction of terror and bloodshed was the worst single incident calamity since Pearl Harbor. That was an act of war, drawing the U.S. into a global conflict. But at least they knew their enemy then, how to retaliate, how to avenge their losses, and how to affirm their power. But what is this, whose outrageous crime, who to punish? . . . The flexing of U.S. military might is what [Americans] crave, the annihilation of those who perpetrated this grotesquerie. And who can blame them for wanting blood? But vengeance and retribution will not give back to America, to the entire world, any sense of safety, of invincibility. There is no place safe from the bedlam of madness and mania.[7]

Writing on the day of the attacks for publication the next morning, this journalist lamented that the "mightiest nation in the world" was "piteously vulnerable." She drew on historical memories to make sense of what happened: ground zero, the "tableau of war," the "mushrooming cloud of smoke and dust," and the memory of Pearl Harbor. She also asserted that Americans craved "blood" and "revenge" and the "flexing of U.S. military might." But when this article went to press to appear on September 12, there were no polls to substantiate those assertions. The nation's leaders and the press nevertheless quickly adopted the same assumptions, and soon the people accepted them, too.

This response went far beyond symbols, language, and vocabulary. Plans drawn up in an earlier era as preparedness for a very different sort of attack immediately went into effect. Taking cues from cold war emergency procedures, the president remained mostly airborne and flitted from one small city to another, drawing widespread criticism for his apparent flight in the face of danger. The defense establishment retreated to "secured bunkers deep inside the earth," fallout shelters constructed during the early years of the cold war.

Although the criminals responsible for the attacks represented no country, the president declared war and quickly deployed troops. As has been true of all wars waged by the United States since World War II, Congress did not declare this war. But few politicians or commentators questioned the president's unofficial declaration of war. Three days after the attack, Congress overwhelmingly passed a resolution authorizing the president to use "all necessary and appropriate force" against the terrorists and the nations that sponsored or protected them.[8]

Declaring war had a number of immediate consequences. It elevated a criminal network guilty of mass murder to the level of a legitimate enemy, and it recognized the authority of this network's leaders. It provided an opportunity for those who opposed American policies to join armies to fight against the United States, making them soldiers for a cause rather than accomplices in a crime. U.S. officials immediately identified Osama bin Laden as the mastermind behind the plot and declared war on his Al Qaeda network as well as any government that tolerated terrorists within its borders. President Bush then declared, in classic cold war terms, that those who were not "with us" were "against us"—both at home and abroad.[9]

Internationally, this declaration had important consequences, forcing nations to be either our allies or our enemies. Within the United States, a declaration of war allowed the government to compromise and constrict the normal workings of a democratic society in the name of national security. As they had during the cold war when the communist threat seemed to imperil the nation, most citizens willingly complied and rallied around their leaders. Trust in the federal government reached levels not seen in nearly half a century. Since 1958, the Gallup poll had asked Americans, "How much of the time do you think you can trust government in Washington to do what is right?" The percentage of those who answered "most of the time" peaked in 1963 at 75 percent, fell to 25 percent in 1979, and hit its lowest point in 1994 at about 18 percent. The percentage climbed after that, reaching above 40 percent in July 2000, and then leapt to 60 percent a month after September 11, 2001—the highest point in more than thirty years. "Not since the cold war has the government had such an important mission," said Carroll Doherty, a political analyst at the Pew Research Center for the People and the Press. "So this trust is not so much a reflection of what government has done, but a hope for what government can accomplish."[10]

Scholars of the last half of the twentieth century, including Michael Sherry and Andrew Bacevich, noted that militarism had shaped American life since World War II. Virtually every national crisis, from the War on Poverty to the War on Drugs, brought forth a new war metaphor, if not a new war. During the cold war, the apparatus of wartime became a permanent feature of American life. Sherry wrote:

National security assumed permanent and paramount importance in American life, so that much of the nation's treasure was devoted to it, its armed forces spread over much of the globe, and its science and industry were profoundly reoriented. . . . War defined much of the American imagination . . . to the point that Americans routinely declared "war" on all sorts of things that did not involve physical combat at all. Thus, militarization reshaped every realm of American life—politics and foreign policy, economics and technology, culture and social relations—making America a profoundly different nation. To varying degrees, almost all groups were invested in it and attracted to it—rich and poor, whites and nonwhites, conservatives and liberals (the last more so than is usually recognized today). Certainly, all were changed by it.[11]

Sherry's insights help explain why, in a situation so unpredictable, the national response was remarkably predictable, on the part of leaders as well as citizens. When the president declared "war on terrorism" immediately after the September 11 attacks, he announced that this would be a "new" type of war. But the war he initiated was not really a new type of war. It was modeled on older wars—not on World War II, but on the various military actions of the cold war. It was the cold war that echoed most loudly across the post-9/11 landscape. The terrorists seemed to have brought into reality national nightmares that dated back more than half a century. The villains seemed to personify the characteristics of the communist threat: foreigners who were part of an international conspiracy who infiltrated the nation, studied our technology, and used our own power against us. They blended into society, plotting against us while enjoying the good life they professed to disdain. They turned our own proud monuments of postwar technological and consumer triumph, commercial airliners and towering skyscrapers, into the means of our destruction. Like suspected communist spies, they represented the enemy within, loyal to a foreign foe. The worst cold war fears seemed to have become a reality, more than a decade after the end of the cold war. The Bush administration responded in cold war fashion: increasing the defense budget by $48 billion (a sum larger than the entire defense budget of any other nation) and developing new nuclear weapons, according to a secret Pentagon report. The president also insisted upon continued funding for the "Star Wars" missile shield, an idea dating back to the Reagan era, which would be useless as a defense against terrorist attacks.[12]

In its domestic ramifications, the waging of the war against terrorism resembled the waging of the cold war. Just as the red and lavender scares of the 1950s had targeted citizens whose political views or personal identities raised questions about their loyalty or patriotism, post-9/11 antiterror strategies targeted people of Middle Eastern descent as well as anyone who expressed criticism of the nation's leaders. Government policies resulted in rounding up people of Arab descent for questioning and incarceration without charging them with any crime. After September 11, the Justice Department detained more than nine hundred people in connection with the attacks. On November 9, 2001, the State Department announced it would subject male visa applicants aged sixteen to forty-five, from twenty-six nations in the Middle East, South Asia, Southeast Asia, and Africa, to special scrutiny. Students were particular targets of investigation. In the first two months after September 11, federal investigators questioned students from Middle Eastern countries at more than two hundred college campuses. The students were asked about the subjects they were studying, their academic achievement, where they lived, and their opinions of Osama bin Laden. College administrators said that this type of investigation on campuses had not been seen since the cold war. Yet, in nearly every case, just as they had participated in the anticommunist purges of the 1950s, the colleges cooperated with the post-9/11 investigations.[13]

As in the early years of the cold war, in the wake of September 11 government officials asserted the need to stifle public debate and suppress the expression of political dissent. Six weeks after the attacks, political scientist Lawrence Jacobs noted, "There's a real conformitarian spirit in America right now. . . . It's flipped gradually into an expectation that you won't raise critical issues, that you'll fall into line. It's the new 1950s."[14] Democrats and Republicans closed ranks and few if any dared to question the president or the administration. Republicans were quick to brand anyone who criticized the administration as "giving aid and comfort to our enemies." When Democratic Senator Tom Daschle opposed drilling in the Arctic National Wildlife Refuge, the Family Research Council compared Daschle to Saddam Hussein. When Daschle raised questions about the "war on terror," Republican Senator Trent Lott scolded, "How dare Senator Daschle criticize President Bush while we are fighting our war on terrorism?"[15] Journalists, academics, and even entertainers faced censure for criticizing the nation's leaders. Tom Guttig of the *Texas City Sun* and Dan Guthrie of the *Grants Pass Daily Courier* (Oregon) were fired for suggesting that President Bush should have returned immediately to the White House after the September 11 attacks, rather than dart furtively around the country. Several television stations suspended ABC's news satire program *Politically Incorrect* when comedian Bill Maher questioned Bush's characterization of the terrorists as "cowards." Maher was forced to make a public apology for saying, "We have been the cowards, lobbing cruise missiles from 2,000 miles away. That's cowardly. Staying in the airplane when it hits the building, say what you want about it, it's not cowardly." The *Washington Post* noted that the networks had caved in to pressure when White House spokesman Ari Fleisher denounced Maher, saying that Americans "need to watch what they say."[16]

Academic freedom also came under siege in a revival of disturbing memories of the McCarthy era. On November 11, 2001, the American Council of Trustees and Alumni, founded in 1995 by former National Endowment for the Humanities chair Lynn Cheney and Senator Joseph Lieberman, released a report that included a list of names of academics who had made public statements that questioned aspects of the war on terrorism. Evoking McCarthyite tactics, the report stated that college and university faculty "have been the weak link in America's response to the attack" and urged alumni to express their displeasure to university administrators. On December 6, 2001, Attorney General John Ashcroft told the Senate Judiciary Committee that those who criticized the post-9/11 curtailment of civil liberties "aid terrorists . . . erode our national unity and diminish our resolve."[17]

The war against terrorism, like the struggle against communism, defined the enemy as a worldwide conspiracy, with cells operating in many countries around the world and with operatives infiltrating the United States as well. The Bush administration borrowed language and policies from the cold war era. The term *Axis of Evil* fused the World War II memory of the Axis powers to Ronald Reagan's cold war description of the Soviet Union as the "Evil Empire." The establishment of the Office of Homeland Security echoed the civil defense bureaucracy that had been set up during the cold war to bolster morale and develop visible security measures that offered the illusion of safety.

Creating a sense of security after the attacks of September 11 was virtually impossible, just as it was impossible to reassure a frightened nation about the danger of a nuclear attack after the world had witnessed the effects of an atomic bomb. In the early years of the cold war, civil defense measures such as teaching housewives how to stock a fallout shelter, or training children to "duck and cover" in their school classrooms, offered the illusion that survival was possible in the event of a nuclear attack.[18] Similar efforts to reassure a nervous public emerged in the wake of September 11. The most obvious of those were the attempts to achieve airport security. Most Americans and foreign visitors patiently accepted the long waits in security lines at airports, the frequent checking of documents, the intrusions into their privacy as a result of random baggage checks, and the affronts to their bodies in routine pat-down searches. But just as the civil defense campaigns did nothing to minimize the danger of death from an atomic attack in the midst of an escalating arms race, these highly visible but feeble efforts at airport security offered the illusion of safety but little real protection.[19]

Patience at airports was only one of many ways that citizens expressed their acquiescence with the "war on terror." As in the early years of the cold war, Americans joined ranks to rally around the flag, quite literally. Reflecting the fusion of nationalism and consumerism, patriotic symbols proliferated instantly after the attack. Flag waving became ubiquitous around the country and sparked a new market for patriotic consumer goods. Flags appeared on houses and in public spaces, on lapels, bags, bumper stickers, and billboards. Foreign journalists noted this patriotic spending frenzy. On September 29, 2001, the London *Guardian* described the scene at the Mall of America in Bloomington, Minnesota:

> You are never far from a flag in the Mall of America. All four miles of walkway are bedecked with red, white and blue banners, hammering home the warlike mantra "United We Stand." The country's biggest indoor shopping centre, on the outskirts of Minneapolis, reflects the patriotic fervour now in evidence across the stunned US. . . . Patriotism seems to go hand-in-hand with shopping. A choice of how to spend money is one of the great "freedoms" cited by many in the mall as American characteristics. "I'm proud of our freedoms—perhaps we've even got too many—that's why all this has been allowed to happen," says Elizabeth Smith, 69, from Seattle. "We have so much more freedom here than in other countries." Mike Wilson, a factory electrician from Muncie, Indiana, echoes: "If you're proud of your country, you need to show it all the time."[20]

Topps, the bubble gum company that invented baseball trading cards in the 1950s, quickly produced and marketed "Enduring Freedom" card packets immediately after September 11. The cards, which came in several different sets, included a "God Bless America" sticker picturing the American flag, along with cards commemorating the war on terror, designed to educate and inspire support for the campaign. One card pictured "Army Paratroopers Boarding an Aircraft" and quoted Bush on the back: "This war will not be like the war against Iraq a decade ago, with a decisive liberation of territory and a swift conclusion." Another card pictured Bush with Federal Emergency Management Agency director Joe M. Allbaugh and quoted Allbaugh praising all the federal, state, and local agencies for their cooperation and professionalism. Other cards contained images and descriptions of warships and fighter planes.[21] Consumer items such as these provided effective propaganda to build support for the war on terror.

Flags flew across the land at the same time that lawmakers debated and enacted legislation that included some of the most serious threats to civil liberties since the draconian measures of the McCarthy era. Less than two months after September 11, Congress passed the USA Patriot Act, authorizing new powers for law enforcement agencies. The bill granted federal agents access to e-mails and voice mails of suspected terrorists and allowed the prosecution of hundreds of people detained after 9/11 for immigration violations. The law expanded the authority of the federal government to conduct electronic surveillance and wire-taps, to screen computers, and to access private records. It permitted the deten-tion of immigrants suspected of supporting terrorism for as long as a week without charging them with a crime or immigration violations. American Civil Liberties Union lawyers expressed concern that the law would harm civil liber-ties and give the federal government "unchecked powers." But there was little public outcry. By strategically naming the bill the Patriot Act, political leaders symbolically wrapped themselves in the flag.[22]

In addition to national legislation, across the country state legislatures debated measures that would require citizens to express their patriotism, reminis-cent of the loyalty oaths of the early cold war. In Minnesota, for example, legis-lators passed by a huge margin a bill that required schoolchildren to recite the Pledge of Allegiance. Students and teachers were allowed to opt out, but they would then be singled out as dissenters. An editorial in the local paper asked, "Should government *mandate* demonstrations of patriotism? Or is love of coun-try something that occurs when government serves people well and protects the freedom to disagree?" With this bill, Minnesota became the twenty-sixth state to require the Pledge of Allegiance.[23]

Along with the invigorated stature of public officials, security concerns cre-ated heroes among firefighters and law enforcement officers, who suddenly achieved a newly exalted stature. The New York City police, who had recently faced severe public condemnation for acts of brutality against racial minorities, rose above criticism as quickly as smoke rose above the Twin Towers. The nation's police and security forces suddenly gained a panache not equaled since the heyday of the FBI G-man during the early years of the cold war. Even after the revelations of serious problems of communication, discipline, and turf wars within and between the police and fire departments that had led to catastrophic results on September 11, the stature of these agencies and their members did not diminish.[24]

The elevation of male heroism reflected a widespread invocation of tradi-tional gender roles. In the twenty-first century it was impossible to revive the male breadwinner and the female homemaker; the feminist movement as well as harsh economic realities made that household form a rarity. But the crisis brought forth images of strong, competent men rescuing and protecting weak, vulnerable women. The presence of women in all areas of public life, as well as on foreign battlefields, may have fueled the apparent need to showcase male valor. As feminist critic Susan Faludi demonstrated in *The Terror Dream*, government and military leaders as well as the national media went to great lengths to promote visions of strong men and weak women. Female commentators suddenly disappeared from the pages of newspapers. Fiction captured headlines, such as the invented story of the rescue of Private Jessica Lynch. For weeks the media carried stories of heroic American military men storming an Iraqi hospital to save Private Lynch from her brutal captors. When she was able to face the press herself, an irate Private Lynch told what had actually happened: Concerned Iraqis had taken her to the hospital, where Iraqi medical professionals treated her with care and respect. She had never been captured or detained against her will and had never been in need of rescue by American male "heroes."[25]

Men in uniform—and they were almost all men—gained public reverence, while women faded into the background. Although many of the law enforcement officers were women, along with powerful women leaders, the names in the headlines were all of powerful men, from the terrorists to the heroes: the hijackers, George W. Bush, Dick Cheney, Osama bin Laden, Tony Blair. As in the cold war, the time had arrived for an image of reinvigorated manhood. Powerful men appeared as the major players on both sides of the "good" and "evil" equation, while women and children seemed vulnerable, in need of protection, whether it was the widows of 9/11 firefighters or the women of Afghanistan. Of course, these women and children did need support, as did countless men. But the framing of the media images, focusing on heroic men and dependent women, reinforced gender constructions that dated back half a century.

Meanwhile, Bush and the Office of Homeland Security urged citizens to become "citizen-sentinels" and create a "national neighborhood watch" to become vigilant in spotting terrorist threats. Using the language of the cold war era, when "communist infiltration" was the prevailing fear, the government called for "improved domestic preparedness," as the *Christian Science Monitor* noted, in order "to let people know what it really means to be prepared—to be vigilant [so that] Americans can better provide for their common defense."[26] In July 2002, the Bush administration called for the establishment of the Terrorism Information and Prevention System, which would recruit volunteers among delivery people, utility workers, and others to snoop on their fellow citizens when their jobs required them to enter people's homes. The plan evoked visions of the excesses of the cold war anticommunist crusade when "naming names" of possible subversives was a sign of patriotism, and schoolchildren viewed propaganda films in which patriotic youngsters turned their parents in to authorities.

Whether or not they considered themselves "citizen sentinels," most Americans followed their leaders uncritically and turned to personal life for solace. This response also echoes the behavior of Americans in the early years of the cold war, when men and women sought security within the intimate realm of marriage and the family. "Many people are looking around after these events and feeling like they want to get closer to the people they care about," noted the Montreal *Gazette*. As one single woman noted, "Somehow, people want to connect." Many New Yorkers interviewed after the attacks expressed their immediate desire to get close to another person on an intimate level. Newspapers reported "quickly kindled romances and rampant post-disaster intimacy." In Denver, requests for marriage licenses went up 10 to 15 percent after September 11. The proprietor at the Chapel of Love in the Mall of America in Bloomington, Minnesota, noted that while most of the mall's shops went begging for customers, her business boomed. Couples rushed to the chapel to get married in a hurry. Some observers predicted that there might be a baby boom nine months after September 11 (although this prediction turned out to be false).[27]

Articles in the *New York Times*, the *Los Angeles Times*, and elsewhere noted the sudden outpouring of neighborliness and kindness among strangers and within communities. Spontaneous acts of generosity, a spirit of voluntarism and charity, and a coming together in the face of tragedy permeated the country. People reached out to their family members across the country and the world, contacted friends and kinfolk, offered assistance to people they hardly knew, and donated generously to charities to help the families of victims. Political scientist Robert Putnam, author of *Bowling Alone*, in which he documented a drastic decline in community and civic life in recent decades, conducted a survey after 9/11. He concluded that in response to the tragedy, "Almost instantly, we rediscovered our friends, our neighbors, our public institutions, and our shared fate."[28] This outpouring of community spirit saturated the media, the press, and the airwaves, garnering so much attention that it seemed to suggest that Americans normally behaved with selfishness and hostility toward one another. The phenomenon prompted the political satire magazine *The Onion* to quip, "Hugging Up 76,000 Percent . . . Rest of Country Temporarily Feels Deep Affection for New York," and to publish mock interviews with New Yorkers who couldn't wait for life to return to normal so they could be mean and selfish again.[29]

Despite the media fanfare, the quest for security was not all loving and sharing. The message of preparedness in the early years of the cold war had urged
American citizens to protect themselves. Civil defense guidelines for atomic age
safety focused on private efforts such as home bomb shelters, civil defense training, and surveillance of one's neighbors. After September 11, Americans revived
the notion of do-it-yourself defense and sprang into action to protect themselves—this time with weapons of their own. In the first six months after the terrorist attacks, the FBI conducted 455,000 more background checks for gun
purchases than in the same period during the previous year. The FBI also handled
130,000 more applications to carry concealed weapons. Gun ownership also
spread to new groups. Although the media portrayed women as needing men to
protect them, many women chose to protect themselves. For the first time, the
Second Amendment Sisters, a national women's progun group, formed a chapter
on a college campus. About fifty women at Mount Holyoke joined the new chapter. One new member boasted, "One of my guy friends said, 'You're a chick with a
gun—I'm scared.'" Women's gun organizations proliferated, such as Mother's
Arms and Armed Females of America. Drawing a rather illogical connection to
September 11, the Web site for Armed Females of America asserted, "Those who
push for 'gun control' are of the same mindset as Palestinian suicide-bombers and
the Taliban who kidnap women for rape and sex-slave trade. Both don't like the
possibility of armed citizens, in these cases, especially armed WOMEN."[30]

"Chicks with guns" may not be the most reassuring image in the wake of
September 11. But we should remember that in the early years of the cold war,
homemakers who stocked makeshift fallout shelters in their basements also
served as visible icons of women doing their part to protect themselves and their
families from danger. These and similar strategies did little to minimize danger.
Trumpeting consumerism, fawning over law enforcement officials, demanding
displays of patriotism, retreating into the private world of family and sex, and
creating the illusion of safety through visible but largely useless performances of
security did not bring about the end of the cold war and are not likely to hasten
the end to this crisis either. The domestic consensus supporting the cold war
finally broke when the nation became embroiled in a tragic and unwinnable
war. But it took the loss of many thousands of lives—and many more years—
before the cold war finally ended. The United States may have "won" the cold
war, but it lost quite a bit in the process. Hopefully, the toll on the nation of the
"war on terror" will not be so severe.

APPENDICES

THE FOLLOWING DOCUMENTS are from the Kelly Longitudinal Study (KLS) in their original form. Appendix I includes tables that provide some statistical data on the respondents. The tables are drawn from printouts of the original data collection coded and entered by E. Lowell Kelly and his research team. I have not altered the categories or the labels in any way. These tables, therefore, serve as documentation not only of the sample of respondents, but also of the social science methodology used in Kelly's data base, which was gathered from the late 1930s through the mid-1950s. Appendix II is a sample of one of the questionnaires that was completed by the respondents. It enables the reader to see how questions were asked, and how responses were coded. The coded responses were entered into machine-readable data; the open-ended questions were placed in the archives in their original form. (Questionnaires for husbands and wives were essentially the same, except for references to gender. The sample form included here was filled out by men; those sent to women used the words "your husband" instead of "your wife," etc.)

The KLS collection is a valuable resource for scholars, but it is extremely clumsy to use. Computer technology was in its infancy when the project was coded and entered into machine-readable form. As a result, tables are printed with no labels, and the titles as well as the variables must be decoded from the original codebook. In order to provide some guidance for scholars who may wish to use the data, I have provided deck and column numbers, as well as questions and variables, in the notes where appropriate. All parts of the original study, including the codebook, questionnaires, and machine-readable data, are available at the Henry Murray Research Center, Radcliffe College, Cambridge, Massachusetts.

As indicated in the notes, I have made slight changes in the quotes from the KLS in order to correct for minor grammatical, punctuation, and spelling errors. In addition, since the individuals in the KLS were identified only by number, the names used in the text are my invention.

A follow-up study of the KLS is in progress. I am grateful to James Conley for sharing with me data gathered in 1980 on the original KLS respondents.

APPENDIX I

Education Level

Level	No. of Men	%	No. of Women	%
More than 4 yrs of College	84	28.4	40	13
Four yrs of College	88	29.7	67	21.7
Some College	50	16.8	73	23.6
H.S. plus, but not College	21	7.0	33	10.7
Some H.S. plus some other	11	3.7	9	3.0
High School only	28	9.4	63	20.4
Some H.S.	12	4.0	23	7.4
Grade School only	1	.003	1	.003
TOTAL:	295	100%	298	100%

SOURCE: Deck 10, column 26, KLS.

Average Yearly Income of Family Over the Last Three Years (1952–1955)

Amount Per Year	Percentage of Respondents
$1,000–2,000	0.74
2,000–3,000	2.23
3,000–4,000	4.21
4,000–5,000	11.39
5,000–7,500	29.21
7,500–10,000	22.77
10,000–15,000	16.34
over 15,000	13.12
	100.00%

SOURCE: Deck 43, column 61, KLS. Amounts given are in 1955 dollars.

Status of Husbands'
Employment at Time of Marriage

	Percentage of Husbands
Unemployed	2.72
90 up	1.37
85–90	3.08
80–84	8.56
75–79	11.30
70–74	14.04
65–69	16.44
60–64	20.21
59	5.82
Student	16.44

SOURCE: Deck 9, column 48, KLS. Categories estimated in comparison with National Opinion Research Center, according to original KLS codebook.

Status of Wives' Employment
at Time of Marriage

	Percentage of Wives
Unemployed	14.48
Professional	21.89
Skilled	26.26
Unskilled	21.89
Student	15.49

SOURCE: Deck 9, column 48, KLS.

Years During Marriage that Wife Worked for Pay

	Percentage of Wives
Never	48.60
1st three years only	10.75
Middle Period Only	3.74
Last 3 Years	11.68
1st & Middle Period	7.94
1st & Last 3 Years	5.14
Middle & Last 3 Years	5.14
All 3 Year Periods	7.94

SOURCE: Deck 45, column 29, KLS.

"Racial Stock" of Husbands and Wives

	Husbands	Wives
American	10.75%	10.80%
English	27.88	26.62
Irish	4.24	6.02
German	8.98	6.57
Scotch	3.16	3.71
French	2.27	1.94
Scandinavian	2.82	3.89
Russian and Mid-European	1.94	2.13
Jewish	16.58	16.85
Combination	21.37	21.29

N = 287 fathers of respondents, 280 mothers of respondents, for husbands; 286 fathers of respondents, 278 mothers of respondents, for wives.
SOURCE: Deck 10, columns 10 and 11, KLS. Terms used in the table title and in the listed categories are Kelly's original terms. I have added quotation marks to suggest that "Racial Stock" is not the appropriate term to use for the various categories listed.

Kelly Longitudinal Study

RESEARCH ON PERSONALITY AND MARRIAGE
Summary Report of Present Marital Status
November 1, 1954

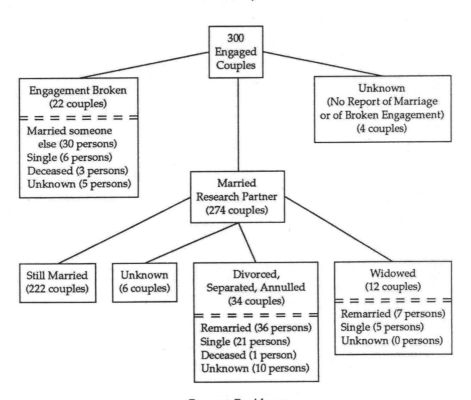

Present Residence
With respect to geography, the group is now more widely spread than when last reported. The largest group (over half of those located) are still living in Connecticut, while the states of Illinois, Maryland, Massachusetts, New Jersey, New York, and Pennsylvania are each home to at least 10 participants. At least one participant is living in each of 31 states and 4 foreign countries.

APPENDIX II

Husband's form   Reported by _____

Report on Marriage to Research Partner

Our goal in preparing this "Report on Marriage to Research Partner" was to collect enough information about each marriage to describe the marriage as fully as we had evaluated the personalities of the two participants at the time of engagement. We considered a great many more questions than are now included. Gradually we cut the form down until it contained only such questions as seem essential to provide a full description of a marriage relationship.

Unfortunately there seems to be no short, yet adequate, way of describing the complex human relationship of marriage. If we were studying boxes, we would need to measure only three dimensions—length, width, and height. As yet, we do not know enough about the essential "dimensions" of marriage to permit such a simple approach. Literally hundreds of writers have written on the subject, but there is surprisingly little agreement among them.

As far as possible, we have tried to make your task easier by providing alternate answers for the questions. In each case you are asked to check the answer which most nearly fits you and your marriage. Obviously, however, we could not include all possible answers to each question. If you feel that none of the answers provided for a question really describes your own situation, please check the alternative which most nearly fits and then write in such additional words or sentences as may be needed to give an accurate report.

Most of the questions are to be answered in terms of the present time; by present we mean the last few years of your marriage. A few of the questions call for separate answers for each of the three periods of your marriage: the first three years, the middle period and the last three years. Don't worry about exact dates—just think of these as guides to the earliest, middle and latest periods of your marriage.

I am sure that you understand the importance of accurate answers to all of the questions. Like all of us mortals, you may at times find yourself tempted to check a more flattering response than is actually justified. In such instances, I hope you will remember that the purpose of this research is to discover more facts about marriage—not to pry into your private life. Your honest answers to these questions, along with those of other participants, will provide facts to replace some of the folklore and false beliefs about personal relationships in marriage.

I hope you will answer all of the questions. However, if for any reason you should decide not to answer a question, please indicate your decision by writing "Omit" through the answer space; thus I will know that your failure to answer was *intentional* rather than *accidental*.

In spite of the length of this form, I think you will find filling it out an interesting experience.

PART A. EVENTS AND CHARACTERISTICS OF YOUR MARRIED LIFE

A I. *Marriage Ceremony*

1. Where were you married?
   ___ In a church or chapel
   ___ In the home of a relative or friend
   ___ Somewhere else (write in) _____

2. Who conducted the ceremony?
   ___ Minister, priest or rabbi
   ___ Justice of the peace, or other civil official
   ___ Other (write in) _____

A II. *Relationships with Other People*

1. How would you describe the relationship between you and each of the following people during your marriage? (Place one check in each column.)

	You and your mother	You and your father	You and your wife's mother	You and your wife's father
Completely warm, understanding, and close	___	___	___	___
Generally friendly and understanding	___	___	___	___
Get along O.K.	___	___	___	___
Slight or occasional tension or strain	___	___	___	___
Tense, strained, and full of conflict	___	___	___	___
Parent deceased before marriage	___	___	___	___

2. Among your relatives (parents, brothers, sisters, grandparents, aunts, etc.), you probably feel closer to some than to others. Think of the relative to whom you feel closest. (Do not include your wife or your children.) What relationship is this person to you? _____

3. Regardless of how much you and this relative agree or disagree about things:

   (a) How well do you feel this relative understands your ideas and feelings?
   ___ Completely
   ___ To a great extent
   ___ To some extent
   ___ Only slightly
   ___ Not at all

   (b) How well do you feel you understand this relative's ideas and feelings?
   ___ Completely
   ___ To a great extent
   ___ To some extent
   ___ Only slightly
   ___ Not at all

4. In the same way, you probably feel closer to some of your friends than to others. Think of the friend to whom you feel closest.
   Is this friend a man or a woman? ___ Man ___ Woman

5. Regardless of how much you and this friend agree or disagree about things:

   (a) How well do you feel this friend understands your ideas and feelings?
   ___ Completely
   ___ To a great extent
   ___ To some extent
   ___ Only slightly
   ___ Not at all

   (b) How well do you feel you understand this friend's ideas and feelings?
   ___ Completely
   ___ To a great extent
   ___ To some extent
   ___ Only slightly
   ___ Not at all

6. How important is this friendship to your happiness?
   ___ Extremely important
   ___ Quite important
   ___ Somewhat important
   ___ Not too important
   ___ Not at all important

7. How close is your wife to this friend?
   ___ Closer than I am
   ___ As close as I am
   ___ Not quite as close as I am
   ___ Much less close than I am
   ___ Wife has never met this friend

8. When you have problems in your personal life or in your marriage, how freely do you discuss these problems with your closest relative and with your closest friend? (Place one check in each column.)

	With closest relative	With closest friend
With complete frankness	___	___
With considerable frankness	___	___
With some reserve	___	___
With considerable reserve	___	___
Do not discuss such problems with this person	___	___

A III. *Running the Household*

1. How much of the *housework* (cooking, shopping, ironing, cleaning, physical care of the children, etc.) is usually done by each of the following people? (Place one check in each column.)

	You	Your wife	Children	Hired help	Other
A very great deal	___	___	___	___	___
Much	___	___	___	___	___
Some	___	___	___	___	___
A little	___	___	___	___	___
None	___	___	___	___	___

2. How much of the *physical maintenance of the house and yard* (care of lawn and garden, minor repairs, painting, etc.) is usually done by each of the following people? (Place one check in each column.)

	You	Your wife	Children	Hired help	Other
A very great deal	___	___	___	___	___
Much	___	___	___	___	___
Some	___	___	___	___	___
A little	___	___	___	___	___
None	___	___	___	___	___

A IV. *Recreation and Social Activities*

1. About how often do you attend meetings or other activities of groups or organizations? Include both social and community service activities of groups such as lodges, bridge clubs, sports clubs, civic organizations and church groups. (Place one check in each column.)

	Without your wife	With your wife
Never	___	___
Less than once a month	___	___
Once a month	___	___
Several times a month	___	___
Several times a week	___	___
Over five times a week	___	___

2. About how often do you get together informally with other people for social reasons? Include such activities as parties, picnics, card games and social visits. Do *not* include activities which you included in the previous question. (Place one check in each column.)

	Without your wife	With your wife
Never	___	___
Less than once a month	___	___
Once a month	___	___
Several times a month	___	___
Several times a week	___	___
Over five times a week	___	___

3. How many different people do you know with whom you get together informally for social reasons? Include such activities as parties, picnics, card games and social visits.

Just one or two ___
A small number ___
Quite a few ___
A great many ___

4. About how often do you and your wife get together for social or recreational activities *without* your children or anyone else? Include such activities as going to movies, going out to dinner, and an evening of recreation at home together. (Place one check in each column.)

	At home	Away from home
Never	___	___
Less than once a month	___	___
Once a month	___	___
Several times a month	___	___
Several times a week	___	___
Over five times a week	___	___

A V. *Earning and Spending the Family Income*

1. Where have you lived during the last three years? (Check as many as apply.)

___ A large city (pop. over 100,000)
___ A suburb of a large city
___ A small city (pop. 10,000 to 100,000)
___ A town (pop. under 10,000)
___ On a farm
___ In the country, but not on a farm

2. In what types of dwellings have you lived during the last three years? (Check as many as apply.)

___ Apartment
___ Rented house
___ Your own home
___ Other (write in) _____

3. About how much do you spend *per year* on housing? (Include rent or payments on a home, maintenance, utilities, property taxes, and insurance.) _____ dollars.

4. If you own or are buying your home, how much would you estimate you could sell it for at the present time? _____ dollars.

5. Describe the cars which your family owns at present.

Make of car	Year of car	Did you buy it new or used? (circle one)
_____	_____	new used
_____	_____	new used
_____	_____	new used

6. Which of the following best describes your family's use of installment buying?

____ Never buy anything on installments
____ Buy very few things on installments
____ Buy some things on installments
____ Buy most things on installments
____ Buy practically everything on installments

7. At present, what is the approximate total of your family debts which will fall due in the next two years? (Do not include mortgage payments.) _____ dollars.

8. What would you estimate was the average yearly income of your family over the last three years? Do not consider any years in which your income was unusually high or low. (Include the earnings of both husband and wife. Include all income, whether from wages or other sources.)

____ less than $1000
____ $1000 to $2000
____ $2000 to $3000
____ $3000 to $4000
____ $4000 to $5000
____ $5000 to $7500
____ $7500 to $10,000
____ $10,000 to $15,000
____ over $15,000

9. Although few families have a large enough income to buy everything they would like, the income of most American families is considerably more than is necessary to provide the bare necessities of living: shelter, food, clothes, and medical expenses. In other words, most families have some money left over for purchasing things or services they *want*. (For example, a better house than needed for shelter, better food than needed for health, a good car, good clothes, books, recreation, children's education, etc.)

Looking back over the last few years, how much money would you say your family had available to spend in a typical year for things over and above bare necessities?

____ None
____ Under $250
____ $250 to $500
____ $500 to $1000
____ $1000 to $2000
____ $2000 to $3000
____ $3000 to $4000
____ $4000 to $5000
____ $5000 to $7500
____ $7500 to $10,000
____ Over $10,000

10. Whatever the amount of money you have had available for things other than bare necessities, which of the following factors do you feel were most important in determining the way this money was spent? Place a "1" before the factor which you feel has had the most weight in your decisions, a "2" before the factor which has had the next most weight, and so on to "5" for the factor which has had the least weight. Be sure to write one number in every blank.

____ Providing future financial security for the family (for example: savings, insurance)
____ Increasing the enjoyment of day-to-day living of members of the family
____ Living in a way appropriate to your position in the community
____ Providing special opportunities for your children (for example: education, travel, music)
____ Assisting people outside the immediate family (for example: relatives, friends, church, charity)

11. How would you say your present standard of living compares with that of each of the following?

	Much below	A little below	About the same	A little above	Much above
Your neighbors	____	____	____	____	____
Your parents	____	____	____	____	____
Your parents-in-law	____	____	____	____	____
Your best friend	____	____	____	____	____
The people with whom you work	____	____	____	____	____

Which you would like
to have ___

12. One way to estimate your family's general financial status would be to consider the probable value of the estate if both you and your wife were to die within the next year and someone else were to settle the estate. If this were to happen, would you expect that:

___ Debts would amount to a great deal more than assets (By assets is meant the total amount which could be obtained from your bank account, savings, life insurance, sale of property, furniture, stocks, bonds, etc.)

___ Debts would amount to somewhat more than assets

___ Debts would just about equal assets

___ Assets would amount to somewhat more than debts

___ Assets would amount to a great deal more than debts

A VI. *Religion*

1. To what extent would you say the various members of your family generally take part in church and religious activities outside the home? (Place one check in each column.)

	You	Your wife	Your children
Not at all			
A little			
To some extent			
A great deal			
To a very great extent			

2. To what extent is religion included in the home activities of your family? (Consider such activities as discussion of religious matters, reading the Bible or other religious materials, family prayers, grace at meals, family worship services, etc.)

___ Not at all
___ A little
___ To some extent
___ A great deal
___ To a very great extent

A VII. *Sexual Relations*

1. How adequate do you feel your preparation for sexual relations was *at the time of your marriage?*

	Yours	Your wife's
Entirely adequate		
Reasonably adequate		
Somewhat inadequate		
Completely inadequate		

2. How would you describe your anticipations at the time of your marriage with regard to sexual relations?

	Yours	Your wife's
Extremely pleasant		
Mildly pleasant		
Neutral		
Mildly unpleasant		
Extremely unpleasant		

3. Would you say that your marriage was affected in any way by your sexual experiences before marriage or by the lack of them? Please consider both favorable and unfavorable effects.

4. Which of the following best describes the feelings of you and your wife about sexual relations with each other *during the last three years?*

	Yours	Your wife's
Great enjoyment		
Mild pleasure		
Indifference		
Mild displeasure		
Disgust and aversion		

5. On the average, about how many times a month did you and your wife have sexual intercourse with each other during the following periods of your marriage?

During the first three years, about ___ times a month

During the middle period, about ___ times a month

During the last three years, about ___ times a month

6. On the average, about how many times a month would you have *preferred* to have sexual intercourse *during the last three years?*
   About ____ times a month

7. On the average, about how many times a month do you think *your wife* would have preferred to have sexual intercourse *during the last three years?*
   About ____ times a month

8. During the last three years, about how often have you become impotent (unable to sustain an erection) with your wife?
   ____ Always
   ____ Almost always
   ____ Usually
   ____ Sometimes
   ____ Once in a while
   ____ Never

9. How considerate do you feel your wife is of your feelings about sexual relations?
   ____ Extremely considerate
   ____ Quite considerate
   ____ Somewhat considerate
   ____ Not too considerate
   ____ Not at all considerate

A   VIII.   *Children and Their Upbringing*

Note: Even if you have no children, answer questions 1, 2, 3, 4 and 5.

1. Are you hoping or intending to have any more children than you now have?
   ____ No
   ____ Yes
   If yes:
   How many more children? ____
   How many boys? ____
   How many girls? ____

2. At the time of your marriage, how large a family did you want? (Write in the number of children.)
   ____ children
   How many boys? ____
   How many girls? ____
   Were you and your wife in agreement on this?
   ____ Yes
   ____ No

3. If you could have had your choice, how large a family would you have had during your marriage? (Write in the number of children.)
   ____ children
   How many boys? ____
   How many girls? ____

4. Below are three statements reflecting different attitudes about how parents should bring up their children. Place an "M" by the item which you feel is *most important* for parents to do. Place an "L" by the item which you feel is *least important* for parents to do. Even if you feel that all of these are important, try to decide which you feel are most and least important.
   ____ Parents should teach the child what is right
   ____ Parents should give the child freedom to express himself
   ____ Parents should guide the child in learning to get along in the world

5. If your own wishes concerning the size or planning of your family changed during your marriage, what do you feel were the reasons for these changes?

☐ If you have no children, check here and omit questions 6, 7, 8 and 9.

6. How much weight would you say the ideas and feelings of the children are given in making plans and policies in your family?
   ____ None
   ____ A little
   ____ Some
   ____ Much
   ____ A very great deal

7. About how often do you get together with one or more of your children for fun or recreation? Include such activities as picnics, reading together, playing games, and working on hobbies together. (Place one check in each column.)

	At home	Away from home
Never	____	____
Less than once a month	____	____
Once a month	____	____
Several times a month	____	____
Several times a week	____	____
Over five times a week	____	____

8. About how often do *all* members of your family engage in some kind of recreation together? Include such activities as picnics, playing games, and working on hobbies at home. (Place one check in each column.)

	At home	Away from home
Never		
Less than once a month		
Once a month		
Several times a month		
Several times a week		
Over five times a week		

9. What would you say are the major problems that have developed in bringing up your children?

A IX. *Past Events*

1. Have you and your wife lived apart at any time during your marriage?
___ No
___ Yes
   If yes:

During what year(s)?	For how long?	Reason for living apart

2. Following is a list of events and circumstances which may or may not have occurred during your marriage. If an event did occur, it may have occurred during the first three years, the middle period, or the last three years of your marriage—or in more than one of these periods. For each event, place a check (√) under each period of your marriage in which the event occurred. You may have three, two, one or no checks before each item.

First 3 yrs.	Middle period	Last 3 yrs.	
			Living with relatives in their home
			Relatives living in your home
			Death of someone very close and dear to you
			Your own ill health or injury
			Ill health or injury of your wife
			Your own emotional illness
			Emotional illness of your wife
			Emotional illness of a close relative
			Your own excessive use of alcohol
			Excessive use of alcohol by your wife
			You were employed, but work not regular
			You lost your job
			You were unemployed for several months
			You changed your job once or twice
			You changed your job several times
			Your job required considerable traveling
			Your job required unusual working hours
			You disliked your job
			Wife worked for pay
			Family moved from one community to another once or twice
			Family moved from one community to another several times
			You were in military service
			Inadequate living conditions
			Serious difficulty in making ends meet financially
			Heavily in debt
			Received financial aid from relatives or friends
			Received financial aid from social or governmental agencies
			Gave financial support to relatives or friends
			Unplanned pregnancy
			Miscarriage or stillbirth
			Intentional termination of pregnancy
			Continued unsuccessful efforts for wife to become pregnant
			Informed by doctor that wife's pregnancy was unlikely or impossible
			Wife's menopause (change of life)
			You had love affair with someone other than your wife
			Wife had love affair with someone other than you

_____ You had sexual relations with someone other than your wife

_____ Wife had sexual relations with someone other than you

Now go back and circle those check marks indicating events or circumstances which you feel were of such a serious nature as to lessen the happiness of your marriage from the time of their occurrence until the present time.

PART B. YOU, YOUR WIFE, AND YOUR MARRIAGE

B 1. *The Parts You and Your Wife Play*

In some ways life is like a play. You each take a turn at playing a number of different parts. At various times you are a breadwinner, handyman, host, participant in community affairs, friend and companion to your wife, lover and sexual partner to your wife, and father. You have probably found that you are naturally better cast for some of these parts than you are for others. Some men may play the parts of father and handyman best. Others may be best fitted for breadwinner, host, and participant in community affairs. And still others may be best as friends to their wives.

Note: If you have no children, omit the questions about "mother" and "father" in this section.

1. How well do you think *you* play each of the following parts?

	Extremely well	Generally well	Fairly well	Not too well	Not at all well
Breadwinner					
Handyman					
Host					
Participant in community affairs					
Friend and companion to wife					
Lover and sexual partner to wife					
Father					

2. How well do you think *your wife* plays each of the following parts?

	Extremely well	Generally well	Fairly well	Not too well	Not at all well
Housekeeper					
Cook					
Hostess					
Participant in community affairs					
Friend and companion to you					
Lover and sexual partner to you					
Mother					

3. How important is it to you that *you* should play each of the following parts well?

	Extremely important	Quite important	Somewhat important	Not too important	Not at all important
Breadwinner					
Handyman					
Host					
Participant in community affairs					
Friend and companion to wife					
Lover and sexual partner to wife					
Father					

4. How important is it to you that *your wife* should play each of the following parts well?

	Extremely important	Quite important	Somewhat important	Not too important	Not at all important
Housekeeper					
Cook					
Hostess					
Participant in community affairs					
Friend and companion to you					
Lover and sexual partner to you					
Mother					

B II. *Your Views on What Is Important*

Circle the number which best indicates how important each of the following is to you.

1 = extremely important
2 = quite important
3 = somewhat important
4 = not too important
5 = not at all important

How important is it to you that:

1 2 3 4 5 You be active in many clubs and organizations?
1 2 3 4 5 You have some extremely close and intimate friends?
1 2 3 4 5 You take part in many social activities with other people?
1 2 3 4 5 You attend church and take part in religious activities?
1 2 3 4 5 You maintain close and harmonious relationships with your relatives?
1 2 3 4 5 You make good use of every minute of your time?
1 2 3 4 5 Your life be full of change and variety?
1 2 3 4 5 Your attitudes, values and standards be similar to those of your wife?
1 2 3 4 5 Your attitudes, values and standards be similar to those of your parents?
1 2 3 4 5 Your attitudes, values and standards be similar to those of your wife's parents?
1 2 3 4 5 Your attitudes, values and standards be similar to those of your friends?
1 2 3 4 5 You have some free time to spend on doing just what you feel like doing?
1 2 3 4 5 You get money and material wealth out of life?
1 2 3 4 5 Your life be free from sudden changes and unexpected events?
1 2 3 4 5 Most of the people you know approve of the things you do?
1 2 3 4 5 You keep your emotions under control at all times?
1 2 3 4 5 The things you do be planned and scheduled in advance?
1 2 3 4 5 You "get ahead" on your job?
1 2 3 4 5 Your wife find an outlet for her interests and energies in paid employment?
1 2 3 4 5 Your home be clean and in order at all times?
1 2 3 4 5 You and your wife both share in the housework (indoors and out) which is necessary to maintain your home and family?
1 2 3 4 5 Your wife devote the major part of her interests and energies to her home and family?

1 2 3 4 5 Your home be a place where family members and their friends can relax and enjoy themselves at all times?
1 2 3 4 5 You and your wife take part in many recreational activities together?
1 2 3 4 5 Your life make a contribution to the betterment of your community, nation or society?
1 2 3 4 5 You pay cash in full for all your purchases?
1 2 3 4 5 You have children in your family?

How important is it to you that:

1 2 3 4 5 You own material things (such as a home, car, furniture, clothes, etc.) which compare in value with those of your neighbors, your friends, and the people you work with?
1 2 3 4 5 You have sexual intercourse every time you desire it?
1 2 3 4 5 Your sexual relations be closely bound up with love and affection?
1 2 3 4 5 You have sexual intercourse every time your wife desires it?
1 2 3 4 5 You find pleasure in your sexual relations with your wife?
1 2 3 4 5 You have sexual intercourse with your wife every time you desire it?

Note: If you have no children, omit the following items:

How important is it to you that:

1 2 3 4 5 Your children grow up to hold religious beliefs similar to yours?
1 2 3 4 5 Your children be good and well-behaved at all times?
1 2 3 4 5 Your children grow up in a home atmosphere in which their ideas and feelings are considered and talked over in making family decisions?
1 2 3 4 5 You, your wife, and your children take part in many recreational activities together?
1 2 3 4 5 Your children receive a college education?
1 2 3 4 5 Your children grow up to hold attitudes, values and standards similar to yours?
1 2 3 4 5 Your children marry chiefly for love?
1 2 3 4 5 Your children marry persons of at least equal social standing?

B III. *Your Wife*

1. I regard my wife's physical health *at the present time* as:

____ Excellent
____ Good
____ Fair

_____ Poor
_____ Very poor

2. On the whole, I consider my wife's physical health *during the last 20 years* to have been:
   _____ Excellent
   _____ Good
   _____ Fair
   _____ Poor
   _____ Very poor

3. On the whole, I consider the general state of my wife's *emotional health* during the last 20 years to have been:
   _____ Excellent
   _____ Good
   _____ Fair
   _____ Poor
   _____ Very poor

4. Has your wife had any tendency toward emotional disturbances, nervousness, worry, special anxiety, or nervous breakdown?
   _____ A great deal
   _____ Some
   _____ A little
   _____ None whatsoever

   If any, indicate the nature of such emotional problems.

5. I regard the general state of my wife's emotional health *at the present time* as:
   _____ Excellent
   _____ Good
   _____ Fair
   _____ Poor
   _____ Very poor

6. Does your wife drink alcoholic beverages?
   _____ Not at all
   _____ A little
   _____ A fair amount
   _____ A considerable amount
   _____ A great deal

If your wife drinks at all, has her drinking ever been a problem for her or you?
   _____ A serious problem
   _____ Somewhat of a problem
   _____ No problem at all

   Indicate the nature of any such problem.
   _____
   _____

7. How closely would you say your wife resembles each of the following people in *physical characteristics?*

	Not at all	Somewhat	Closely
Your mother	_____	_____	_____
Your sister	_____	_____	_____
A former girl friend	_____	_____	_____

8. How closely would you say the *personality* of your wife resembles the personality of each of the following people?

	Not at all	Somewhat	Closely
Your father	_____	_____	_____
Your mother	_____	_____	_____
Your sister	_____	_____	_____
Your brother	_____	_____	_____
A former girl friend	_____	_____	_____

9. On the whole, do you feel *your wife* has helped or hindered you in attaining the goals which are really important to you in life?
   _____ Helped much more than hindered
   _____ Helped a little more than hindered
   _____ Helped and hindered about equally
   _____ Hindered a little more than helped
   _____ Hindered much more than helped

10. What three traits or characteristics do you admire most in your wife?
    1. _____ 2. _____ 3. _____

11. What three traits or characteristics do you wish most your wife did not have?
    1. _____ 2. _____ 3. _____

B IV. *How You Get Along*

Note: In this section, if you have no children, omit the items about "bringing up children".

1. When you have problems in your personal life or in your marriage, how freely do you discuss these problems with your wife?

    ___ With complete frankness
    ___ With considerable frankness
    ___ With some reserve
    ___ With considerable reserve
    ___ Do not discuss such problems with my wife

2. How much would you say *you* had to change your own early ideas, habits, and expectations to arrive at the way your family now does things in each of the following areas?

	A great deal	To some extent	Hardly at all
Relationships with relatives	___	___	___
Choice of friends	___	___	___
Recreation and social activities	___	___	___
Earning family income	___	___	___
Spending family income	___	___	___
Running the household	___	___	___
Religion	___	___	___
Sexual relations	___	___	___
Size of family	___	___	___
Bringing up children	___	___	___

3. How much would you say *your wife* had to change her early ideas, habits, and expectations to arrive at the way your family now does things in each of the following areas?

	A great deal	To some extent	Hardly at all
Relationships with relatives	___	___	___
Choice of friends	___	___	___
Recreation and social activities	___	___	___
Earning family income	___	___	___
Spending family income	___	___	___
Running the household	___	___	___
Religion	___	___	___
Sexual relations	___	___	___
Size of family	___	___	___
Bringing up children	___	___	___

4. How different would you say your ideas and feelings in each of the following areas are from those of your wife *at the present time?*

	Very different	Quite different	Somewhat different	Slightly different	No difference
Relationships with relatives	___	___	___	___	___
Choice of friends	___	___	___	___	___
Recreation and social activities	___	___	___	___	___
Earning family income	___	___	___	___	___
Spending family income	___	___	___	___	___
Running the household	___	___	___	___	___
Religion	___	___	___	___	___
Sexual relations	___	___	___	___	___
Size of family	___	___	___	___	___
Bringing up children	___	___	___	___	___

Some of the differences which you indicated in this question may not disturb you at all, while others may bother you a good deal. *Now go back and circle the check marks for any differences which you feel have resulted in your marriage being less happy than it might have been.*

☐ Check here if you feel that *none* of the differences you indicated have resulted in your marriage being less happy than it might have been.

5. Regardless of how much you and your wife agree or disagree about things:

    (a) How well do you feel your wife understands your ideas and feelings?

    ___ Completely
    ___ To a great extent
    ___ To some extent
    ___ Only slightly
    ___ Not at all

    (b) How well do you feel you understand your wife's ideas and feelings?

    ___ Completely
    ___ To a great extent
    ___ To some extent
    ___ Only slightly
    ___ Not at all

6. Of the hours you are awake during the week, about how many would you estimate you spend within speaking distance of your wife?

   About _____ hours a week.

7. In general, who has more influence in determining the way your family does things in each of the following areas?

	Husband much more than wife	Husband somewhat more than wife	Husband and wife about same	Wife somewhat more than husband	Wife much more than husband
Relationships with relatives	_____	_____	_____	_____	_____
Choice of friends	_____	_____	_____	_____	_____
Recreation and social activities	_____	_____	_____	_____	_____
Earning family income	_____	_____	_____	_____	_____
Spending family income	_____	_____	_____	_____	_____
Running the household	_____	_____	_____	_____	_____
Religion	_____	_____	_____	_____	_____
Sexual relations	_____	_____	_____	_____	_____
Size of family	_____	_____	_____	_____	_____
Bringing up children	_____	_____	_____	_____	_____

You may be satisfied with the way influence is divided between you and your wife in some of the areas above, and not satisfied with the way it is divided in others. For each area in which you are *not* satisfied, go back and write a "P" under the heading which shows the division of influence that you would prefer in that area.

☐ Check here if you are satisfied with the present division of influence in *all* of the areas above.

8. When you and your wife have serious disagreements, what usually happens?

   _____ I give in

   _____ She gives in

   _____ Sometimes one gives in, sometimes the other

   _____ We both give in and reach a compromise

   _____ Neither of us gives in

   _____ We never have serious disagreements

9. When you and your wife have serious disagreements, how often do you feel satisfied with the way things are finally settled?

   _____ Almost always

   _____ Usually

   _____ Sometimes

   _____ Occasionally

   _____ Never

   _____ We never have serious disagreements

B V. *Looking Back Over Your Marriage*

1. All of us have ideas about what we expect from marriage and what marriage should be like ideally. In terms of the things which you expect from marriage, how satisfied would you say you are with your marriage?

   _____ Completely satisfied

   _____ Generally satisfied

   _____ Somewhat satisfied

   _____ Somewhat dissatisfied

   _____ Generally dissatisfied

   _____ Completely dissatisfied

2. If you had your life to live over, do you think you would:

   _____ Definitely marry the same person

   _____ Most likely marry the same person

   _____ Perhaps marry the same person

   _____ Not marry the same person

   _____ Not marry at all

3. Have you ever regretted your marriage?

   _____ Constantly

   _____ Frequently

   _____ Sometimes

   _____ Once in a while

   _____ Never

4. Have you ever considered divorce or separation from your wife?

   _____ Seriously

   _____ Somewhat seriously

   _____ Not seriously

   _____ Have never considered it

5. Did you ever consult with any professionally trained person regarding problems in your marriage?

    _____ No
    _____ Yes

    If yes:
    (Check as many as apply.)
    _____ With minister, priest or rabbi
    _____ With personal physician
    _____ With specialist (psychiatrist, psychologist, social worker, etc.)
    About _____ visits over a period of _____ months.

6. How would you say your present feelings of love for your wife compare with your feelings at the time of your marriage?

    _____ Much deeper than they were
    _____ A little deeper than they were
    _____ About the same
    _____ A little less than they were
    _____ Much less than they were

    Comments, if any: _____
    _____
    _____
    _____
    _____
    _____

7. Looking back over your life, what did you have to sacrifice or give up because of your marriage?

8. Looking back over your life, what has marriage brought you that you could not have gained without your marriage?

9. On the whole, do you feel that *being married* has helped or hindered you in attaining the goals which are really important to you in life?

    _____ Helped much more than hindered
    _____ Helped a little more than hindered
    _____ Helped and hindered about equally
    _____ Hindered a little more than helped
    _____ Hindered much more than helped

10. Considering everything, how happy has your marriage been?

    _____ Extraordinarily happy
    _____ Decidedly more happy than the average
    _____ Somewhat more happy than the average
    _____ About average
    _____ Somewhat less happy than the average
    _____ Decidedly less happy than the average
    _____ Extremely unhappy

11. The following chart is designed to help us get a picture of the "ups" and "downs" in your marriage. Some marriages have lots of these ups and downs, while others run along at a fairly even level. All kinds of stresses and strains, and various circumstances beyond your control, may have influenced the happiness of your marriage at various times. In the following chart, please place a check (✓) under the two-year period in which your marriage took place to indicate approximately how happy your marriage was at that time. Then place a check under each two-year period from then until the present time. We know you won't be able to remember exactly what every year was like. Just give us your best estimate. Please be careful that the periods you check correspond with the years during which you were married.

    Make one check *for each period during which you were married.*

| | 1935 | '37 | '39 | '41 | '43 | '45 | '47 | '49 | '51 | '53 |
	-36	-38	-40	-42	-44	-46	-48	-50	-52	-54
Extraordinarily happy										
Decidedly more happy than average										
Somewhat more happy than average										
About average										
Somewhat less happy than average										

Decidedly less
happy than
average | | | | | | |
Extremely
unhappy | | | | | | |

B VI. *Anything Else?*

1. Because marriages are as varied as the personalities of the people who make them, we may not have given you a chance to tell us about everything which is important to understand your particular marriage. If we have missed anything, won't you add it here? (Use additional sheets if necessary.)

2. This last question is one which we are certain will be asked by many of those who read the report of this research: "Did participation in this research have any influence, either positive or negative, on the lives and marriages of the participants?" While we can never be sure of the answer to this question, it would be most interesting to report the opinions of our participants. What is yours?

Notes

Introduction

1. "Their Sheltered Honeymoon," *Life*, 10 August 1959, pp. 51–52.

2. Ronald R. Rindfuss and James A. Sweet, *Postwar Fertility Trends and Differentials in the United States* (New York: Academic Press, 1977), p. 191. On the similarities and differences of the demographic patterns of whites and nonwhites, see Andrew Cherlin, *Marriage, Divorce, Remarriage* (Cambridge, Mass.: Harvard University Press, 1992). For distinctive patterns of black family life, see, for example, Herbert Gutman, *The Black Family in Slavery and Freedom, 1750–1925* (New York: Pantheon, 1976); Jacqueline Jones, *Labor of Love, Labor of Sorrow: Black Women, Work and the Family from Slavery to the Present* (New York: Basic Books, 1985); and Carol Stack, *All Our Kin* (New York: Harper & Row, 1974). On the exclusion of blacks from the suburbs, see Kenneth T. Jackson, *Crabgrass Frontier: The Suburbanization of the United States* (New York: Oxford University Press, 1985). For comparisons with European demographic patterns, see Hugh Carter and Paul C. Glick, *Marriage and Divorce: A Social and Economic Study* (Cambridge, Mass.: Harvard University Press, 1976), pp. 22–24, 31, 41.

3. In the historical literature, most references to the boom in family life after the war refer to the return to peace and prosperity. Investigations point to the legacy of the depression as well. For an excellent summary and critique of scholarly explanations of postwar demographic trends, seesee Cherlin, *Marriage, Divorce*, pp. 33–44.

4. Scholars have uncovered the contradictions inherent in the postwar culture, particularly the potential for radically altered gender relations that did not occur. For an insightful analysis, see Winifred Breines, "The 1950s: Gender and Some Social Science," *Sociological Inquiry* 56 (Winter 1986), pp. 69–92. The prescriptive literature at the time was filled with worries about postwar family life. See, for example, Judson T. Landis and Mary G. Landis, *Building a Successful Marriage* (New York: Prentice-Hall, 1948), and Reuben Hill and Howard Baker, eds., *Marriage and the Family* (Boston: D. C. Heath, 1942). These sources express widespread fears about the future of the family, particularly following the disruptions in gender roles brought about by the war.

5. Cherlin, *Marriage, Divorce*, pp. 1–5.

6. See, for example, the account of the study by the Battille Memorial Institute's Health and Population Research Center in Seattle, Washington, in Nadine Brozan, "What's New about Women Really Isn't," Minneapolis *Star and Tribune*, 1 September 1986, pp. 1C, 2C.

7. There were a few notable exceptions to the all-white suburbs, such as Shaker Heights, Ohio, a suburb outside Cleveland. The residents of Shaker Heights decided to create a racially integrated community, in part by keeping class constant and recruiting

prosperous and respectable black families into the neighborhood. The Shaker Heights experiment in racial integration is one of a small number of exceptions that prove the rule of postwar residential segregation. See Cynthia Mills Richter, "Integrating the Suburban Dream: Shaker Heights, Ohio," Ph.D. dissertation, University of Minnesota, 1999. For outstanding examinations of the connections between the cold war and the civil rights movement, see Thomas Borstelmann, *The Cold War and the Color Line: American Race Relations in the Global Arena* (Cambridge, Mass.: Harvard University Press, 2003); Mary Dudziak, *Cold War Civil Rights: Race and the Image of American Democracy* (Princeton, N.J.: Princeton University Press, 2002); Penny M. Von Eschen, *Satchmo Blows Up the World: Jazz Ambassadors Play the Cold War* (Cambridge, Mass.: Harvard University Press, 2006), and *Race against Empire: Black Americans and Anticolonialism, 1937–1957* (Ithaca, N.Y.: Cornell University Press, 1997).

8. See Eric Foner, *The Story of American Freedom* (New York: Norton, 1998). For public opinion poll data, see Gertrude J. Selznick and Stephen Steinberg, *The Tenacity of Prejudice: Anti-Semitism in Contemporary America* (New York: Harper & Row, 1969), p. 171.

9. On racial segregation and redlining in the postwar suburbs, see Kenneth Jackson, *Crabgrass Frontier: The Suburbanization of the United States* (New York: Oxford University Press, 1985); Thomas Sugrue, *The Origins of the Urban Crisis: Race and Inequality in Postwar Detroit* (Princeton, N.J.: Princeton University Press, 2005); and Robert O. Self, *American Babylon: Race and the Struggle for Postwar Oakland* (Princeton, N.J.: Princeton University Press, 2005).

10. For public opinion poll data, see Gertrude J. Selznick and Stephen Steinberg, *The Tenacity of Prejudice: Anti-Semitism in Contemporary America* (New York: Harper & Row, 1969), p. 171. Also included was the statement "Before Negroes are given rights they have to show that they deserve them." Fifty-eight percent of northerners and seventy-four percent of southerners agreed. Other poll data cited are from George H. Gallup, *The Gallup Poll: Public Opinion, 1935–1971*, vols. 1, 2 (New York: Random House, 1972), pp. 1465–1466, 1486–1487, 1572–1573.

11. Recently, scholarship on theories of race and race formation has flourished, with a number of important works that look particularly at the historical construction of whiteness and its impact on race privilege and race relations in the United States. See, for example David Roediger, *The Wages of Whiteness: Race and the Making of the American Working Class* (London: Verso, 1991) and *Working toward Whiteness: How America's Immigrants Became White* (New York: Perseus Books, 2006), as well as David Roediger, ed., *Toward the Abolition of Whiteness: Essays on Race, Politics, and Working Class History* (London: Verso, 1994). See also Noel Ignatiev, *How the Irish Became White* (Cambridge, Mass.: Harvard University Press, 1995); George Lipsitz, *The Possessive Investment in Whiteness: How White People Profit from Identity Politics* (Philadelphia: Temple University Press, 1998); Mathew Frye Jacobson, *Whiteness of a Different Color: European Immigrants and the Alchemy of Race* (Cambridge, Mass.: Harvard University Press, 1998); Ruth Frankenberg, *White Women, Race Matters: The Social Construction of Whiteness* (Minneapolis: University of Minnesota Press, 1993); Karen Brodkin, *How Jews Became*

White Folks and What That Says about Race in America (New Brunswick, N.J.: Rutgers University Press, 1998).

12. Scholarship on the cultural history of the cold war era has begun the process of integrating these approaches. See, for example, Paul Boyer, *By the Bomb's Early Light: American Thought and Culture at the Dawn of the Atomic Age* (New York: Pantheon, 1985); Martin Sherwin, *A World Destroyed: The Atomic Bomb and the Grand Alliance* (New York: Knopf, 1975); Godfrey Hodgson, *America in Our Time: From World War II to Nixon; What Happened and Why* (New York: Random House, 1976); Lisa McGirr, *Suburban Warriors: The Origins of the New American Right* (Princeton, N.J.: Princeton University Press, 2002); Christina Klein, *Cold War Orientalism: Asia in the Middlebrow Imagination, 1945–1961* (Berkeley: University of California Press, 2003); Stephen J. Whitfield, *The Culture of the Cold War* (Baltimore: Johns Hopkins University Press, 1996); Lawrence S. Wittner, *Cold War America: From Hiroshima to Watergate* (New York: Praeger, 1974); James Gilbert, *Another Chance: Postwar America, 1945–1985*, 2nd ed. (Chicago: Dorsey Press, 1986); Lary May, ed., *Recasting America: Culture and Politics in the Age of Cold War* (Chicago: University of Chicago Press, 1989); William Chafe, *The Unfinished Journey: America since World War II* (New York: Oxford University Press, 1986); and Leo P. Ribuffo, "Abusing the Fifties," *Worldview*, November 1973, pp. 143–147. For examinations of women in the 1950s, see Dennis Lee Frobish, "The Family and Ideology: Cultural Constraints on Women, 1940–1960," Ph.D. dissertation, University of North Carolina at Chapel Hill, 1983; Eugenia Kaledin, *Mothers and More: American Women in the 1950s* (Boston: Twayne, 1984); Leila J. Rupp and Verta Taylor, *Survival in the Doldrums: The American Women's Rights Movement, 1945 to the 1960s* (New York: Oxford University Press, 1987); and Joanne Meyerowitz, ed., *Not June Cleaver* (Philadelphia: Temple University Press, 1994). For opposing views on the postwar era, see, for example, Marty Jezer, *The Dark Ages: Life in the United States, 1945–1960* (Boston: South End Press, 1982), and William O'Neill, *American High: The Years of Confidence, 1945–1960* (New York: Free Press, 1986). For the specific connection between sex and politics, see John D'Emilio, *Sexual Politics, Sexual Communities: The Making of a Homosexual Minority in the United States, 1940–1970* (Chicago: University of Chicago Press, 1983). Recent studies of the family and demographic trends after World War II have offered valuable insights, as well as widely differing interpretations. For example, Richard Easterlin, in *Birth and Fortune: The Impact of Numbers on Personal Welfare* (New York: Basic Books, 1981), explains demographic swings in terms of the relative economic well-being of each generation, but he does not consider the unique historical circumstances that affected each in different ways. Glen Elder, Jr., in *Children of the Great Depression: Social Change in Life Experience* (Chicago: University of Chicago Press, 1974), focuses on the impact of the thirties by examining the long-term effects of the depression on the people who grew up in that era. But Elder slights the profound impact of the later historical developments that faced this cohort in early adulthood, specifically the changes in men's and women's lives brought about by the war and the cold war. Christopher Lasch, in *Haven in a Heartless World: The Family Besieged* (New York: Basic Books, 1977), portrays the modern family besieged by outside institutions that

strip it of its vital functions of educating and socializing children. But Lasch does not explore the motivations of family members themselves, who were active participants in the shift toward reliance on outside experts. Barbara Ehrenreich, in *The Hearts of Men* (Garden City, N.Y.: Doubleday, 1983), explores the revolt against the breadwinner ethic of the 1950s but leaves us wondering why so many postwar men embraced that role in the first place.

13. George H. Gallup, *The Gallup Poll: Public Opinion, 1935–1971*, vols. 1, 2 (New York: Random House, 1972), pp. 339, 501, 639–640, 853, 869, 873, 916, 929, 933–934, 950, 1213–1214, 1434.

14. Brett Harvey, *The Fifties: A Women's Oral History* (New York: HarperCollins, 1993), p. 175. See also Lillian Faderman, *Odd Girls and Twilight Lovers: A History of Lesbian Life in Twentieth-Century America* (New York: Columbia University Press, 1991); Robert D. Dean, *Imperial Brotherhood: Gender and the Making of Cold War Foreign Policy* (Boston: University of Massachusetts Press, 2003); David K. Johnson, *The Lavender Scare: The Cold War Persecution of Gays and Lesbians in the Federal Government* (Chicago: University of Chicago Press, 2006); and K. A. Cuordileone, *Manhood and American Political Culture in the Cold War* (New York: Routledge, 2005).

15. Feminist scholarship has done a great deal to break down the academic barriers between public and private life by demonstrating that the personal is political. The feminist scholarship that has influenced this work is too voluminous to list here. For a discussion of its impact on the writing of American history, see Elaine Tyler May, "Expanding the Past: Recent Scholarship on Women in Politics and Work," *Reviews in American History* 10 (December 1982), pp. 216–233. The following are a few pathbreaking historical studies that are particularly relevant to the relationship between gender, family, and politics: Linda Kerber, *Women of the Republic: Intellect and Ideology in Revolutionary America* (Chapel Hill: University of North Carolina Press, 1980); Nancy Cott, *The Bonds of Womanhood: "Women's Sphere" in New England, 1780–1835* (New Haven, Conn.: Yale University Press, 1977), and *The Grounding of Modern Feminism* (New Haven, Conn.: Yale University Press, 1987); Sara Evans, *Personal Politics: The Roots of Women's Liberation in the Civil Rights Movement and the New Left* (New York: Knopf, 1979); Estelle Freedman, *Their Sisters' Keepers: Women's Prison Reform in America, 1830–1930* (Ann Arbor: University of Michigan Press, 1980); Linda Gordon, *Woman's Body, Woman's Right: A Social History of Birth Control in America* (New York: Grossman, 1976); Mari Jo Buhle, *Women in American Socialism, 1870–1920* (Urbana: University of Illinois Press, 1981); Mary Ryan, *Cradle of the Middle Class: The Family in Oneida County, New York, 1790–1865* (New York: Cambridge University Press, 1981); and Susan Faludi, *Backlash: The Undeclared War against American Women* (New York: Three Rivers Press, 2006). Other studies that provide important insights into postwar America include Robert J. Lifton, *The Broken Connection: On Death and the Continuity of Life* (New York: Simon & Schuster, 1979), and Robert N. Bellah et al., *Habits of the Heart: Individualism and Commitment in American Life* (Berkeley: University of California Press, 1985). For studies of theoretical issues pertaining to the relationship between the state, the structure

of the economy, and the family in advanced capitalist systems, see Eli Zaretsky, *Capitalism, the Family, and Personal Life* (New York: Harper & Row, 1976); Jurgen Habermas, *Legitimation Crisis*, trans. Thomas McCarthy (Boston: Beacon Press, 1975); and Joel Kovel, "Rationalization and the Family," *Telos* 37 (Fall 1978), pp. 5–21.

16. This research used the *Kelly Longitudinal Study, 1935–1955* data set (made accessible in 1979, raw and machine-readable data files). These data were collected by E. L. Kelly and donated to the archive of the Henry A. Murray Research Center of Radcliffe College, Cambridge, Massachusetts (Producer and Distributor). This data set is hereafter referred to as the KLS, in the text and the notes. Two articles from the study were published: Charles F. Westoff, Elliot G. Meshler, and E. Lowell Kelly, "Preferences in Size of Family and Eventual Fertility Twenty Years After," *Journal of American Sociology* 62 (March 1957), pp. 491–497, and E. Lowell Kelly, "Constancy of the Adult Personality," *American Psychologist* 10 (1955), pp. 659–681. An earlier article, based on a different database, suggests the direction of Kelly's research in the early years of the study: Kelly, "Marital Compatibility as Related to Personality Traits of Husbands and Wives as Rated by Self and Spouse," *Journal of Social Psychology* 13 (1941), pp. 193–198. Kelly spent years gathering, organizing, coding, and entering into machine-readable form an enormous amount of information. He then became involved in other projects without publishing a major work summarizing the findings of his study. Quotes from the KLS in the text have been edited slightly to correct spelling and punctuation, and occasionally grammar, since responses were often written in haste. Also, all names used are fictitious.

17. Kelly's data are a social historian's dream, but they are also something of a nightmare. Kelly devised his questionnaires for his purposes, not mine. As one among a growing number of social scientists who were interested in the scientific determinants of marital compatibility, he hoped to identify long-term patterns of marital adjustment that could be used as predictors of successful marriage in the future. His assumptions were implicitly ahistorical, since his study was based on the premise that personality characteristics are as likely to surface in one generation as another, regardless of historical circumstances. Accordingly, he believed that marriage is an institution grounded in personality adjustment, not social or cultural change. My assumptions are the opposite.

The questions Kelly asked locate his study in its era, in spite of the survey's presumed timeless objectivity. Kelly assumed, for example, that distinct domestic gender roles were universally endorsed. Thus, he asked women to rate their adequacy as "cooks" and "homemakers" and men to rate themselves as "handymen" and "providers." In addition to these value judgments, the questionnaires focused exclusively on personal life. There were literally hundreds of questions concerning the respondents' sex lives, but—remarkably—not one item about their political views, not even party affiliation. Kelly and his data, then, were raw material for this study, for they provide evidence of certain assumptions prevalent at the time. It is nevertheless frustrating to draw on a collection of data so rich in some areas and so silent in others. The problem is unavoidable, since my intention is to break down the traditional disciplinary division between public and private lives—a division that provided the guiding assumptions for scholars such as Kelly.

18. See Elaine Tyler May, *Barren in the Promised Land: Childless Americans and the Pursuit of Happiness* (Cambridge, Mass.: Harvard University Press, 1997), especially Chapter 4, "The Baby Craze."

19. For a discussion of Kennan's articulation of the containment theory of foreign policy, see John Lewis Gaddis, *Strategies of Containment: A Critical Appraisal of Postwar American National Security Policy* (New York: Oxford University Press, 1982), pp. 302–304.

20. Some of the scholarship on the 1950s, including the power of the domestic ideal, the risks of deviating from it, the strains within it, and the efforts to resist it, includes Winifred Breines, *Young, White, and Miserable: Growing Up Female in the Fifties* (Boston: Beacon Press, 1992); William Chafe, *The Unfinished Journey: American since World War II*, 2nd ed. (New York: Oxford University Press, 1991); Andrew J. Cherlin, *Marriage, Divorce, Remarriage* (Cambridge, Mass.: Harvard University Press, 1992); Barbara Ehrenreich, *The Hearts of Men: American Dreams and the Flight from Commitment* (Garden City, N.Y.: Anchor Press/Doubleday, 1983); Betty G. Farrell, *Family: The Making of an Idea, an Institution, and a Controversy in American Culture* (Boulder, Colo.: Westview Press, 1999); Peter Filene, *Him/Her/Self: Gender Identities in Modern America*, 3rd ed. (Baltimore: Johns Hopkins University Press, 1998); William Graebner, *Coming of Age in Buffalo: Youth and Authority in the Postwar Era* (Philadelphia: Temple University Press, 1990); Susan Lynn, *Progressive Women in Conservative Times: Racial Justice, Peace, and Feminism, 1945 to the 1960s* (New Brunswick, N.J.: Rutgers University Press, 1992); Joanne Meyerowitz, "Beyond the Feminine Mystique: A Reassessment of Postwar Mass Culture, 1946–1958," *Journal of American History* 79, 4 (March 1993); Joanne Meyerowitz, ed., *Not June Cleaver: Women and Gender in Postwar America, 1945–1960* (Philadelphia: Temple University Press, 1994); Melody L. Miller et al., "Motherhood, Multiple Roles, and Maternal Well-Being: Women of the 1950s," *Gender and Society* 5, 4 (December 1991); Steven Mintz and Susan Kellogg, *Domestic Revolutions: A Social History of American Family Life* (New York: Free Press, 1988); Andrea L. Press, *Women Watching Television: Gender, Class, and Generation in the American Television Experience* (Philadelphia: University of Pennsylvania Press, 1991); Leila J. Rupp and Verta Taylor, *Survival in the Doldrums: The American Women's Rights Movement, 1945 to the 1960s* (New York: Oxford University Press, 1987); Arlene Skolnick, *Embattled Paradise: The American Family in the Age of Uncertainty* (New York: Basic Books, 1991); Rickie Solinger, *Wake Up Little Susie: Single Pregnancy and Race before* Roe v. Wade (New York: Routledge, 1992); Lynn Spigel, *Make Room for TV: Television and the Family Ideal in Postwar America* (Chicago: University of Chicago Press, 1992).

21. For a discussion of this therapeutic ethos, see Bellah et al., *Habits of the Heart*.

CHAPTER 1: CONTAINMENT AT HOME

1. Quotes from the debate between Vice President Richard Nixon and Soviet premier Nikita Khrushchev in Moscow are drawn from "The Two Worlds: A Day-Long Debate," *New York Times*, 25 July 1959, pp. 1, 3; "When Nixon Took On Khrushchev," a

report of the meeting, and the text of Nixon's address at the opening of the American National Exhibition in Moscow on 24 July 1959, printed in "Setting Russia Straight on Facts about the U.S.," *U.S. News and World Report,* 3 August 1959, pp. 36–39, 70–72; and "Encounter," *Newsweek,* 3 August 1959, pp. 15–19. For a discussion of the propaganda battles of the cold war, which includes an analysis of the "kitchen debate," see Walter L. Hixson, *Parting the Curtain: Propaganda, Culture, and the Cold War, 1945–1961* (New York: St. Martin's Press, 1997), especially pp. 176, 179–180.

2. "Setting Russia Straight," *U.S. News and World Report.*

3. Eric Johnston, *We're All in It* (New York: Dutton, 1948), pp. 60–61. See *also* Johnston, *America Unlimited* (Garden City, N.Y.: Doubleday, 1944), p. 234.

4. Susan Hartman, *The Home Front and Beyond: American Women in the 1940s* (Boston: Twayne, 1982), p. 165. U.S. Bureau of the Census, *Historical Statistics of the United States, Colonial Times to 1970,* part 1 (Washington, D.C.: U.S. Government Printing Office, 1975), pp. 49, 54, 55, 64; John Modell et al., "The Timing of Marriage in the Transition to Adulthood: Continuity and Change," in *Turning Points: Historical and Sociological Essays on the Family,* supplement to *American Journal of Sociology* 84 (1978), pp. 120–150; Paul C. Glick, "A Demographer Looks at American Families," *Journal of Marriage and the Family* 37 (February 1975), pp. 15–26; and Andrew Cherlin, *Marriage, Divorce, Remarriage* (Cambridge, Mass.: Harvard University Press, 1981), pp. 22–23.

5. No widely read examination of women's oppression in the 1950s appeared until Betty Friedan's *The Feminine Mystique* (New York: Dell, 1963). William H. Whyte, *The Organization Man* (New York: Simon & Schuster, 1956), p. 267, and David Riesman, *The Lonely Crowd: A Study of the Changing American Character* (New Haven, Conn.: Yale University Press, 1950). See also George Lipsitz, *Class and Culture in Cold War America: "A Rainbow at Midnight"* (South Hadley, Mass.: J. F. Bergin, 1982), pp. 7, 88–95; C. Wright Mills, *White Collar: The American Middle Classes* (New York: Oxford University Press, 1956).

6. The survey of housewives is reported in Lipsitz, *Class and Culture,* p. 94; attitudes of middle-class housewives are drawn from responses of wives to open-ended questions in the 1955 Kelly Longitudinal Study (KLS), Henry Murray Research Center, Radcliffe College, Cambridge, Mass. For a detailed description of the KLS, see the Introduction and Appendices to this volume.

7. See Martin Sherwin, *A World Destroyed: The Atom Bomb and the Grand Alliance* (New York: Knopf, 1975); John Lewis, *A Critical Appraisal of Postwar National Security Policy* (New York: Oxford University Press, 1982); Truman's belief about World War III is discussed in William Chafe, *The Unfinished Journey: America since World War II* (New York: Oxford University Press, 1986), pp. 248–251.

8. George H. Gallup, *The Gallup Poll: Public Opinion, 1935–1971,* vols. 1, 2 (New York: Random House, 1972), pp. 916, 869, 929, 950, 1434.

9. Paul Boyer, *By the Bomb's Early Light: American Thought and Culture at the Dawn of the Atomic Age* (New York: Pantheon, 1985). On the unrealistic nature of civil defense strategies, see the excellent documentary film by the Archives Project, *The Atomic Cafe,*

1982, Thorn Emi Video. Robert J. Lifton, *Broken Connections: On Death and the Continuity of Life* (New York: Simon & Schuster, 1979), p. 338. Data from the poll appear in Boyer, *By the Bomb's Early Light*, p. 335.

10. Conversation with Jewish writer Ruth F. Brin, 11 April 1987, Minneapolis, Minn.

11. Mildred Gilman, "Why They Can't Wait to Wed," *Parents Magazine*, November 1958, p. 46.

12. *Ebony* photo editorial, "Goodbye Mammy, Hello Mom," *Ebony*, March 1947, pp. 36–37.

13. Xiaolan Bao, "When Women Arrived: The Transformation of New York's Chinatown," in Joanne Meyerowitz, ed., *Not June Cleaver: Women and Gender in Postwar America, 1945–1960* (Philadelphia: Temple University Press, 1994), pp. 19–36. For a powerful comment on Japanese-American experiences in the wake of internment, see John Okada's novel *No-No Boy* (Seattle: University of Washington Press, 1980).

14. Judith Smith shows that this process began before 1940 and intensified after the war. See Judith Smith, *Family Connections: A History of Italian and Jewish Immigrant Lives in Providence, Rhode Island, 1900–1940* (Albany: State University of New York Press, 1985), pp. 107–123. Whyte, *The Organization Man*, p. 284. See also Kenneth Jackson, *Crabgrass Frontier: The Suburbanization of the United States* (New York: Oxford University Press, 1985).

15. Whyte, *The Organization Man*, pp. 268–270.

16. George Lipsitz, "The Meaning of Memory: Family, Class and Ethnicity in Early Network Television Programs," *Cultural Anthropology* 1 (November 1986), pp. 355–387; *Marty*, 1955, screenplay by Paddy Chayefsky.

17. For an excellent analysis of the television and film versions of *Marty*, see Judith E. Smith, "Ethnicity, Class and Sexuality: Popular Conceptions of Gender in *Marty*," paper presented at Gender: Literary and Cinematic Representations, Florida State University, 1986.

18. See, for example, Mathew Frye Jacobson, *Whiteness of a Different Color: European Immigrants and the Alchemy of Race* (Cambridge, Mass.: Harvard University Press, 1998); Ruth Frankenberg, *White Women, Race Matters: The Social Construction of Whiteness* (Minneapolis: University of Minnesota Press, 1993); Karen Brodkin, *How Jews Became White Folks and What That Says about Race in America* (New Brunswick, N.J.: Rutgers University Press, 1998).

19. Whyte, *The Organization Man*, pp. 287, 300, 380; William O'Neill, *American High: The Years of Confidence, 1945–1960* (New York: Free Press, 1986), pp. 212–215; Chafe, *Unfinished Journey*, pp. 120–121. For an excellent discussion of the role of the suburban synagogue in the community life of upwardly mobile, assimilating Jews, see Riv-Ellen Prell, *Recreating Judaism in America: An Anthropology of Contemporary Prayer* (Detroit: Wayne State University Press, 1988).

20. Of course, the cult of the professional or expert did not emerge suddenly after World War II, although it was institutionalized in new ways then, especially during the Eisenhower years. See, for example, Burton J. Bledstein, *The Culture of Professionalism:*

The Middle Class and the Development of Higher Education in America (New York: Norton, 1976); Terrence Ball, "The Politics of Social Science," in Lary May, ed., *Recasting America: Culture and Politics in the Age of Cold War* (Chicago: University of Chicago Press, 1989); Robert Griffith, "Dwight D. Eisenhower and the Corporate Commonwealth," *American Historical Review* 87 (February 1982), pp. 87–122; and Joseph Veroff et al., *Mental Health in America: Patterns of Help-Seeking from 1957 to 1976* (New York: Basic Books, 1981), pp. 8, 10, 226; Christopher Lasch, *Haven in a Heartless World: The Family Besieged* (New York: Basic Books, 1977). For the professionalization of motherhood through expertise, see Nancy Pottishman Weiss, "Mother, the Invention of Necessity: Dr. Benjamin Spock's *Baby and Child Care*," *American Quarterly* 29 (Winter 1977), pp. 519–546. On Peale, see Donald Meyer, *The Positive Thinkers: A Study of the American Quest for Health, Wealth, and Personal Power from Mary Baker Eddy to Norman Vincent Peale* (Garden City, N.Y.: Doubleday, 1965). Quote from *Look* magazine is from an undated, unpaginated clipping in the Social Welfare History Archives (SWHA), University of Minnesota.

21. Joseph Veroff et al., *The Inner American: A Self-Portrait from 1957 to 1976* (New York: Basic Books, 1981), p. 194.

22. Aggregate data from the KLS. For a detailed explanation of the KLS, see the Introduction to this volume.

23. For an interesting discussion of Spock's struggle to come to terms with an unsettling world, see William Graebner, "The Unstable World of Benjamin Spock: Social Engineering in a Democratic Culture, 1917–1950," *Journal of American History* 67 (December 1980), pp. 612–629. For a social scientist's criticism of social science at the time, see Robert S. Lynd, *Knowledge for What? The Place of Social Science in American Culture* (Princeton, N.J.: Princeton University Press, 1948). Perhaps the most eloquent expression of the expert's discomfort with the impact of scientific expertise is in J. Robert Oppenheimer, "Speech to the Association of Los Alamos Scientists," Los Alamos, 2 November 1945, reproduced in Alice Kimball Smith and Charles Weiner, *Robert Oppenheimer: Letters and Recollections* (Cambridge, Mass.: Harvard University Press, 1980), pp. 315–325. For an excellent discussion of the scientists' activism after the war, see Boyer, *By the Bomb's Early Light*. Margaret Mead, "Problems of the Atomic Age," *The Survey*, July 1949, p. 385.

24. On the decline of bachelor culture in the postwar years, see Howard P. Chudacoff, *The Age of the Bachelor: Creating an American Subculture* (Princeton, N.J.: Princeton University Press, 1999), especially Chapter 8. Quote is on p. 252.

25. Quotes are from responses to open-ended question #B.V.7., 1955 survey, KLS: "Looking back over your life, what did you have to sacrifice or give up because of your marriage?"

26. Responses to #B.V.7, 1955 survey, KLS.

27. Ibid.

28. Responses to open-ended question #B.V.8., 1955 survey, KLS: "Looking back over your life, what has marriage brought you that you could not have gained without your marriage?"

29. Ibid.

30. Case 158, KLS. All names are fictitious; the KLS respondents were identified in the survey only by number.

31. Case 290, KLS.

CHAPTER 2: DEPRESSION

1. Case 145, KLS.

2. Case 145, KLS.

3. Case 147, KLS.

4. Case 83, KLS.

5. Susan M. Hartmann, *The Home Front and Beyond: American Women in the 1940s* (Boston: Twayne, 1982), pp. 16–19, and Sherna Berger Gluck, *Rosie the Riveter Revisited: Women, the War, and Social Change* (Boston: Twayne Publishers, 1987), pp. 13–14.

6. William Chafe, *The Unfinished Journey: America since World War II* (New York: Oxford University Press, 1986), pp. 8–9; Jacqueline Jones, *Labor of Love, Labor of Sorrow: Black Women, Work, and the Family from Slavery to the Present* (New York: Basic Books, 1985), pp. 199, 209–210.

7. Paul Popenoe, as quoted in John Modell, "Institutional Consequences of Hard Times: Engagement in the 1930s," in Joan Aldous and David M. Klein, eds., *Social Stress and Family Development* (New York: Guilford Press, 1988).

8. U.S. Bureau of the Census, *Historical Statistics of the United States, Colonial Times to 1970*, part 1 (Washington, D.C.: U.S. Government Printing Office, 1975), pp. 20–21, and 64; Ruth Milkman, "Woman's Work and the Economic Crisis: Some Lessons from the Great Depression," *The Review of Radical Political Economics* 8 (Spring 1976), pp. 73–91, 95–97; Peter Filene, *Him/Her/Self: Sex Roles in Modern America*, 2nd ed. (Baltimore: Johns Hopkins University Press, 1986), p. 158.

9. Judith Smith, *Family Connections: A History of Italian and Jewish Immigrant Lives in Providence, Rhode Island, 1900–1940* (Albany: State University Press of New York, 1985), p. 115.

10. Robert S. Lynd and Helen Merrell Lynd, *Middletown in Transition* (New York: Harcourt Brace & World, 1937), p. 11; U.S. Bureau of the Census, *Historical Statistics of the United States*, part 1, p. 133.

11. Lary May, "Making the American Way: Modern Theaters, Audiences, and the Film Industry, 1929–1945," *Prospects: Journal of American Culture* 12 (1987), pp. 89–124.

12. "What Hollywood Is Thinking," *Photoplay* 52 (December 1938), pp. 17, 89.

13. On the twenties, see Lary May, *Screening Out the Past: The Birth of Mass Culture and the Motion Picture Industry, 1896–1929* (New York: Oxford University Press, 1980). On the portrayal of marriage in films in the twenties, see Elaine Tyler May, *Great*

Expectations: Marriage and Divorce in Post-Victorian America (Chicago: University of Chicago Press, 1980), Chapter 4.

14. Steven Lassonde, "A Survey of Major Themes in *Photoplay* Magazine, 1920–1960," unpublished paper, University of Minnesota, 1984.

15. David Seabury (psychologist), "Why Can't the Stars Stay Married?" *Photoplay* 51 (December 1937), p. 81.

16. Jane Hampton, "Lupe and Johnny Were Lovers," *Photoplay* 45 (June 1934), pp. 58, 100.

17. Jeanette MacDonald, "Up the Ladder with Jeanette," *Photoplay* 43 (December 1932), pp. 77, 102–103; Sara Hamilton, "The Stormy Heart of Margaret Sullivan," *Photoplay* 49 (June 1936), p. 99; Joan Crawford, "Fan Experiences with the Stars: Joan Crawford—My ideal," *Photoplay* 50 (December 1936), p. 16.

18. Hart Seymore, "Carole Lombard Tells: 'How I Live by a Man's Code,'" *Photoplay* 51 (June 1937), p. 12.

19. *Blonde Venus*, 1931, starring Marlene Dietrich, directed by Erich Von Sternberg.

20. *His Girl Friday*, 1940, directed by Howard Hawks, remake of *Front Page*, 1931, screenplay by Ben Hecht. In the 1931 version, the hero is a newspaperman, Hilde Johnson, whose boss will not let him marry and quit the paper.

21. David O. Selznick, producer, *Gone with the Wind*, 1939.

22. See Lois Scharf, *To Work and to Wed: Female Employment, Feminism, and the Great Depression* (Westport, Conn.: Greenwood Press, 1980), pp. 46, 111.

23. Winifred D. Wandersee, *Women's Work and Family Values, 1920–1940* (Cambridge, Mass.: Harvard University Press, 1981), and "The Economics of Middle-Income Family Life: Working Women during the Great Depression," *Journal of American History* 65 (June 1978), pp. 60–74; see also Susan Ware, *Beyond Suffrage: Women in the New Deal* (Cambridge, Mass.: Harvard University Press, 1981); Scharf, *To Work and To Wed*, Chapter 5; and Linda Gordon, *Pitied but Not Entitled: Single Mothers and the History of Welfare* (Cambridge, Mass.: Harvard University Press, 1994).

24. Filene, *Him/Her/Self*, pp. 155–157; Mirra Komarovsky, *The Unemployed Man and His Family* (New York: Dryden Press, 1940), pp. 23–47.

25. Roland Marchand, *Advertising the American Dream: Making Way for Modernity, 1920–1940* (Berkeley: University of California Press, 1985), pp. 324–333.

26. Elder, *Children of the Great Depression*, cites polls on pp. 50 and 202. See also Smith, *Family Connections*, pp. 80–81; Susan Ware, *Holding Their Own: American Women in the 1930s* (Boston: Twayne, 1982), pp. 27–29; and Hartmann, *The Home Front and Beyond*, pp. 16–19.

27. Ware, *Beyond Suffrage*; Scharf, *To Work and To Wed*, p. 86; and Frank Stricker, "Cookbooks and Law Books: The Hidden History of Career Women in Twentieth-Century America," *Journal of Social History* 10 (Fall 1976), pp. 1–19; Filene, *Him/Her/Self*, pp. 150–152, 159–160, quote is on p. 60.

28. Milkman, "Woman's Work," pp. 73–91, 95–97, and Ware, *Holding Their Own*, p. 6.

29. Elder, *Children of the Great Depression*, p. 77.

30. Letter to Betty Friedan, from Queens Village, New York, 23 October 1963, in Friedan Papers, Schlesinger Library Manuscript Collection, Radcliffe College, Cambridge, Mass.

31. Elder, *Children of the Great Depression*, p. 102, 110; Glen Elder, Jr., and S. Bennett, "Women's Work in the Family Economy," *Journal of Family History* 4 (Summer 1979), pp. 153–176.

32. On the youth culture of the twenties, see Lary May, *Screening Out the Past*. *Life* is quoted in Ware, *Holding Their Own*, p. 55, and Elder, *Children of the Great Depression*.

33. Computed from KLS items D10C31, "Approximate income during the next year"; D45C34, "Occurrence of serious difficulty in making ends meet financially"; D49C28, "Importance of you (your wife's) finding an outlet for your (her) interests and energies in paid employment"; D10C32, "Approximate savings at present time"; D10C33, "Approximate debts at present time"; and D9C49, "Plans for continuing present employment after marriage." Income computed from items D9C64 and D43C61, KLS. See also Appendix1.

34. Case 66, KLS.

35. Case 147, KLS.

36. Cases 16, 141, 93, KLS.

37. Computed from Table D10C31, "Approximate income during the next year," KLS.

38. Case 208, KLS.

39. Cases 49, 246, 74, 14, KLS.

40. Cited in Filene, *Him/Her/Self*, pp. 150, 160–161.

41. Elder, *Children of the Great Depression*, p. 233.

Chapter 3: War and Peace

1. Joseph Adelson, "Is Women's Lib a Passing Fad?" *New York Times Magazine*, 19 March 1972, p. 94.

2. Polls cited in Peter Filene, *Him/Her/Self: Sex Roles in Modern America*, 2d ed. (Baltimore: Johns Hopkins University Press, 1986), pp. 161–162.

3. Ibid., p. 163.

4. Susan Hartmann, *The Home Front and Beyond: American Women in the 1940s* (Boston: Twayne, 1982), pp. 7, 164.

5. Quoted in John Costello, *Virtue under Fire: How World War II Changed Our Social and Sexual Attitudes* (Boston: Little, Brown, 1985), p. 17.

6. Quoted in John Morton Blum, *V Was for Victory: Politics and American Culture during World War II* (New York: Harcourt Brace Jovanovich, 1976), p. 28.

7. Samuel Goldwyn, producer, *This Is the Army*, Warner Brothers, 1943, and Allan Berube, *Coming Out under Fire: The History of Gay Men and Women in World War II* (New York: Free Press, 1990), especially Chapter 3.

8. Hartmann, *The Home Front and Beyond,* pp. 190–193. See also Donald Robin Makosky, "The Portrayal of Women in Wide-Circulation Magazine Short Stories, 1905–1955," Ph.D. dissertation, University of Pennsylvania, 1966.

9. For discussions of film noir, see Hartmann, *The Home Front and Beyond,* pp. 201–202; George Lipsitz, *Class and Culture in Cold War America: "A Rainbow at Midnight"* (South Hadley, Mass.: J. F. Bergin, 1982), pp. 175–179; Alain Silver and Elizabeth Ward, eds., *Film Noir: An Encyclopedic Reference to the American Style* (Woodstock, N.Y.: Overlook Press, 1979); and E. Ann Kaplan, ed., *Women in Film Noir,* rev. ed. (London, England: British Film Institute, 1980).

10. Hartmann, *The Home Front and Beyond,* pp. 189–205; on *Niagara,* see Silver and Ward, *Film Noir,* pp. 199–200.

11. Adele Whiteby Fletcher, "Hollywood at Home: How Claudette Colbert Lives," *Photoplay* 54 (December 1940), pp. 24, 70.

12. Claudette Colbert, "What Should I Do?" *Photoplay* 25 (June 1944), p. 104.

13. Ann Sothern, "What Kind of Woman Will Your Man Come Home To?" *Photoplay* 25 (November 1944), pp. 85–86.

14. Ibid.

15. Bette Davis, "Is a Girl's Past Ever Her Own?" *Photoplay* 19 (October 1941), p. 74.

16. Anita Colby, "That Romantic Look," *Photoplay* 30 (December 1946), pp. 48, 128.

17. "Men's Women," *Photoplay* 31 (December 1943), pp. 63–64, 72–73; Wanda Hendrix, "Hero's Wife," *Photoplay* 36 (December 1949), pp. 30–31.

18. Jerry Asher, "We're the Ray-Gans," *Photoplay* 30 (December 1946), p. 120; Garry Wills, *Reagan's America: Innocents at Home* (Garden City, N.Y.: Doubleday, 1987); and Anne Edwards, *Early Reagan: The Rise to Power* (New York: William Morrow, 1987), pp. 375–447.

19. See William Chafe, *The American Woman: Her Changing Social, Economic, and Political Roles, 1920–1970* (New York: Oxford University Press, 1972), and Karen Anderson, *Wartime Women: Sex Roles, Family Relations, and the Status of Women during World War II* (Westport, Conn.: Greenwood Press, 1981).

20. Hartmann, *The Home Front and Beyond,* pp. ix, 4, 19.

21. William Chafe, *The Unfinished Journey: America since World War II* (New York: Oxford University Press, 1986), pp. 15–16. The British cared for three times as many children in day care centers as did Americans, despite their smaller population.

22. Anderson, *Wartime Women;* Hartmann, *The Home Front and Beyond,* pp. 19–21; and Ruth Milman, *Gender at Work: The Dynamics of Job Segregation during World War II* (Urbana: University of Illinois Press, 1987).

23. Hartmann, *The Home Front and Beyond,* Chapter 5; Chafe, *The Unfinished Journey,* p. 83; and Leila Rupp, *Mobilizing Women for War: German and American Propaganda, 1939–1945* (Princeton, N.J.: Princeton University Press, 1978), especially Chapters 4–6.

24. "Boy Meets Girl in Wartime," Pamphlet A496, 1943, American Social Hygiene Association Papers, Social Welfare History Archives, University of Minnesota (hereafter referred to as ASHA papers).

25. Reuben Hill and Howard Baker, eds., *Marriage and the Family* (Boston: D. C. Heath, 1940), pp. 587–588.

26. As quoted in Chafe, *The Unfinished Journey*, p. 29.

27. Allan M. Brandt, *No Magic Bullet: A Social History of Venereal Disease in the United States since 1880* (New York: Oxford University Press, 1985), Chapter 5; Beth Bailey and David Farber, *The First Strange Place: The Alchemy of Race and Sex in World War II Hawaii* (New York: Free Press, 1992).

28. As quoted in ibid., pp. 164–165.

29. Costello, *Virtue under Fire*; U.S. Bureau of the Census, *Historical Statistics of the United States, Colonial Times to 1970*, part 1 (Washington, D.C.: U.S. Government Printing Office, 1975), p. 49; and John D'Emilio, *Sexual Politics, Sexual Communities: The Making of a Homosexual Minority in the United States, 1940–1970* (Chicago: University of Chicago Press, 1983), Chapters 2, 3.

30. Hartmann, *The Home Front and Beyond*, pp. 31–33, and Herbert Burstein, *Women in War: A Complete Guide to Service in the Armed Forces and War Industries* (New York: Service Publication, 1943), pp. 1–3, 21–22.

31. Burstein, *Women in War*, p. 37; Hartmann, *The Home Front and Beyond*, pp. 38–41.

32. Hartmann, *The Home Front and Beyond*, pp. 38–39; Estelle B. Freedman and John D'Emilio, *Intimate Matters: A History of Sexuality in America* (New York: Harper & Row, 1988); and D'Emilio, *Sexual Politics, Sexual Communities*, pp. 23–39.

33. Burstein, *Women in War*, p. 100.

34. See Rupp, *Mobilizing Women for War*, Chapter 4, and Cherlin, *Marriage, Divorce, Remarriage*, pp. 10–11, 19–21.

35. Mary Beth Norton, *Liberty's Daughters: The Revolutionary Experience of American Women, 1775–1800* (Boston: Little, Brown, 1980), and Linda Kerber, *Women of the Republic: Intellect and Ideology in Revolutionary America* (Chapel Hill: University of North Carolina Press, 1980).

36. Helen Dallas, *How to Win on the Home Front*, Public Affairs Pamphlet No. 72 (New York: Public Affairs Committee, 1942), pp. 1–3. See also Blum, *V Was for Victory*, pp. 91–95.

37. Hartmann, *The Home Front and Beyond*, p. 22; "Parenting in Wartime," *Parents Magazine*, October 1944, p. 159; "Parents Can Win or Lose This War," *Parents Magazine*, January 1943, editorial page; and J. Edgar Hoover, "Mothers . . . Our Only Hope," *Woman's Home Companion*, January 1944, pp. 20–21, 69.

38. Philip Wylie, *Generation of Vipers* (New York: Rinehart, 1942).

39. Rachel Rubin, "Whose Apronstrings?" *American Home* 31 (May 1944), p. 28; Amram Scheinfeld, "Are American Moms a Menace?" *Ladies Home Journal*, November 1945, pp. 36, 38, 140; Edward A. Strecker, "What's Wrong with American Mothers?"

Saturday Evening Post, 24 October 1946, p. 14; and Wainwright Evans, "Are Good Mothers Unfaithful Wives?" *Better Homes and Gardens*, July 1941, pp. 23, 66, 67.

40. See Kyolo Hirano, *Mr. Smith Goes to Tokyo: Japanese Cinema under the American Occupation, 1945–1952* (Washington, D.C.: Smithsonian Institution Press, 1992).

41. Hartmann, *The Home Front and Beyond*, pp. 43, 66, 77, 91–94; Sherna Berger Gluck, *Rosie the Riveter Revisited: Women, the War, and Social Change* (Boston: Twayne, 1987), p. 21; Filene, *Him/Her/Self*, pp. 163–65; U.S. Bureau of the Census, *Historical Statistics of the United States*, part 1, p. 235; Rupp, *Mobilizing Women for War*, p. 175; and Chafe, *The Unfinished Journey*, p. 84.

42. For the historical continuity of women's employment to support their families' needs, see Winifred D. Wandersee, *Women's Work and Family Values, 1920–1940* (Cambridge, Mass.: Harvard University Press, 1981), and Chafe, *The Unfinished Journey*, pp. 84–85. Poll of employed wives is in Filene, *Him/Her/Self*, p. 167.

43. *Fortune* quote in Chafe, *The Unfinished Journey*, p. 29.

44. Blum, *V Was For Victory*, pp. 29, 333–335; William O'Neill, *American High: The Years of Confidence 1945–1960* (New York: Free Press, 1986), p. 9, and James Gilbert, *Another Chance: Postwar America, 1945–1985*, 2nd ed. (Chicago: Dorsey Press, 1986), p. 25.

45. O'Neill, *American High*, p. 10. On upward mobility, see Elder, *Children of the Great Depression*, pp. 163–175.

46. Diane Ravitch, *The Troubled Crusade: American Education, 1945–1980* (New York: Basic Books, 1983), p. 292; Hartmann, *The Home Front and Beyond*, pp. 101–110, 144.

47. Filene, *Him/Her/Self*, p. 165, and Hartmann, *The Home Front and Beyond*, p. 114.

48. Judson T. Landis and Mary G. Landis, *Building a Successful Marriage* (New York: Prentice-Hall, 1948), pp. 34 and 77, and "Subsidized Marriage . . . Pattern of the Future," *Ladies Home Journal*, December 1949, pp. 58, 193–196.

49. Joseph Veroff, Elizabeth Douvan, and Richard A. Kulka, *The Inner American: A Self-Portrait from 1957 to 1976* (New York: Basic Books, 1981), pp. 146–151.

50. Jean and Eugene Benge, *Win Your Man and Keep Him* (New York: Windsor Press, 1948), p. 10. Counselor quoted in Hartmann, *The Home Front and Beyond*, p. 169.

51. Letter to Betty Friedan from Pittsburgh, Penn., 24 August 1963, Friedan Papers, Manuscript Collection, Schlesinger Library, Radcliffe College, Cambridge, Mass.

52. Letter to Betty Friedan from Guilford, Conn., 24 March 1963, Friedan Papers.

53. Letter to Betty Friedan, 19 September 1964, pp. 2–4, Friedan Papers.

54. Hartmann, *Home Front and Beyond*, pp. 108–115, and Robert G. Foster and Pauline Park Wilson, *Women after College* (New York: Columbia University Press, 1942).

55. As quoted in Lipsitz, *Class and Culture*, p. 235.

56. Marguerite J. Fisher, "Educating Women for What?" *Independent Woman*, August 1950, pp. 231–232, 256.

57. Speaker from the National Organization for Women testifying at a 1973 hearing on the Women's Educational Equity Act, quoted in Diane Ravitch, *The Troubled Crusade: American Education, 1945–1980* (New York: Basic Books, 1983), p. 299.

58. See Appendix 1; see also ibid., p. 322.

59. Case 198, KLS.

60. The reader is reminded that the names of the KLS respondents are fictitious and that the KLS identified couples only by case number.

61. Case 277, KLS.

62. Case 264, KLS.

63. Case 273, KLS.

64. Case 116, KLS.

65. Case 188, KLS.

66. Filene, *Him/Her/Self*, p. 169.

67. See William H. Whyte, *Organization Man* (New York: Simon & Schuster, 1956); David Riesman, *The Lonely Crowd: A Study of the Changing American Character* (New Haven, Conn.: Yale University Press, 1950); Filene, *Him/Her/Self*, p. 169; and Estelle B. Freedman, "'Uncontrolled Desires': The Response to the Sexual Psychopath, 1920–1960," *Journal of American History* 74 (June 1987), pp. 83–106.

68. Survey cited in Filene, *Him/Her/Self*, pp. 174–175. The early manifestations of this emphasis on the provider role are explored in Elaine Tyler May, *Great Expectations: Marriage and Divorce in Post-Victorian America* (Chicago: University of Chicago Press, 1980), Chapter 9. For the postwar situation, see C. Wright Mills, *White Collar: The American Middle Classes* (New York: Oxford University Press, 1956); Reisman, *The Lonely Crowd*; Whyte, *Organization Man*; and Gilbert, *Another Chance*, p. 9.

69. Computed from KLS items D41C16, "How important that husband 'wear the pants' in the family?" D41C26, "How important that wife should have money of her own, or should earn her own living by paid employment and not be financially dependent on her husband?" D49C28, "Importance of you (your wife's) finding an outlet for your (her) interests and energies in paid employment?" D49C31, "Importance of your wife's (your) devoting the major part of her (your) interests and energies to her (your) home and family?" D41C62, "It is somehow unnatural to place women in positions of authority over men." (Rate level of agreement.)

70. *Economic Report of the President* (Washington, D.C.: U.S. Government Printing Office, 1987), p. 274, provides a table showing that the percentage of disposable personal income saved during 1933 was 3.6, up to 4.0 in 1940, and peaking at 25.1 in 1944. Since the end of the war, it has hovered between 5 and 9 percent, dipping to a new low in 1986 of 2.7. For an analysis of the recent decline in savings, which compares the United States to western European nations and Japan with much higher savings levels, see "The American Savings Slump—A Fluke or a Real Threat?" *U.S. News and World Report*, 25 November 1985, pp. 64–65, and "Should You Save or Spend?" *Changing Times*, March 1984, p. 10.

71. Dean Acheson, quoted in Daniel Yergin, *Shattered Peace: The Origins of the Cold War and the National Security State* (Boston: Houghton Mifflin, 1977), p. 5.

72. Case 299, KLS.

CHAPTER 4: EXPLOSIVE ISSUES

1. Dickie Thompson, "Thirteen Women (and Only One Man in Town)," recorded by Bill Haley and His Comets, released by Decca Records as Decca 29124, on 10 May 1954. Permission to reprint from Danby Music Co. The flip side of this single, "Rock around the Clock," was the seventh best-selling rock-and-roll record of the 1950s. Joel Whitburn, *Billboard Book of Top 40 Hits* (New York: Billboard Publications, 1985), p. 552. For other atomic age songs, see the documentary film *The Atomic Cafe*, by the Archives Project, 1982, Thorn Emi Video.

2. Charles Walter Clarke, "Social Hygiene and Civil Defense," *Journal of Social Hygiene* 37 (January 1951), pp. 3–7.

3. The draft, cover letter, and responses are in the file "Walter Clarke, V.D. in Atom Bombed Areas, 1950," Papers of the American Social Hygiene Association, Social Welfare History Archives, University of Minnesota, Minneapolis, Minn. (hereafter cited as ASHA papers).

4. For discussions of these fears in earlier times, see Ben Barker-Benfield, "Ann Hutchinson and the Puritan Attitude toward Women," *Feminist Studies* 1 (Fall 1972), pp. 65–96; Lyle Kohler, "The Case of the American Jezebels: Ann Hutchinson and Female Agitation during the Years of Antinomian Turmoil, 1636–1640," in Jean E. Friedman and William G. Shade, eds., *Our American Sisters,* 2nd ed. (Boston: Allyn & Bacon, 1976), pp. 52–75; and Linda Kerber, *Women of the Republic: Intellect and Ideology in Revolutionary America* (Chapel Hill: University of North Carolina Press, 1980). One of the most insightful discussions of how this symbolic process has operated in the past is Natalie Zemon Davis, "Women on Top," in Natalie Zemon Davis, *Society and Culture in Early Modern France* (Stanford, Calif.: Stanford University Press, 1965), pp. 124–151.

5. Gabrielson is quoted in John D'Emilio, *Sexual Politics, Sexual Communities: The Making of a Homosexual Minority in the United States, 1940–1970* (Chicago: University of Chicago Press, 1983), p. 41. On "sanctions against male deviance," see Barbara Ehrenreich, *The Hearts of Men* (Garden City, N.Y.: Doubleday, 1983), pp. 14–28, and Estelle B. Freedman, "'Uncontrolled Desires': The Response to the Sexual Psychopath, 1920–1960," *Journal of American History* 74 (June 1987), pp. 83–106.

6. The quote from the Senate report is in D'Emilio, *Sexual Politics, Sexual Communities,* pp. 42–43. See also Robert D. Dean, *Imperial Brotherhood: Gender and the Making of Cold War Foreign Policy* (Boston: University of Massachusetts Press, 2003); David K. Johnson, *The Lavender Scare: The Cold War Persecution of Gays and Lesbians in the Federal Government* (Chicago: University of Chicago Press, 2006); and K. A. Cuordileone, *Manhood and American Political Culture in the Cold War* (New York: Routledge, 2005).

7. See Johnson, *Lavendar Scare*, and Cuordileone, *Manhood*. The interview was with Lary May, who worked as a file clerk for the State Department in the Passport Office when he was a college student in Washington, D.C. He told this story on May 16, 1987.

8. Ibid., p. 49.

9. On the paranoia about sexual psychopaths, see Freedman, "'Uncontrolled Desires,'" and George Chauncey, Jr., "The National Panic over 'Sex Crimes' and the Construction of Cold War Sexual Ideology, 1947–1953," paper presented at the Annual Meeting of the Organization of American Historians, New York City, April 1986. The survey on attitudes toward punishment is from KLS D41C53, "Sex crimes, such as rape and attack on children, deserve more than mere imprisonment; such criminals ought to be publicly whipped or worse."

10. Myrl C. Boyle, "Which Are You First of All, Wife or Mother?" *Parents Magazine*, August 1955, pp. 35, 77–78. See *also* Dr. Herman N. Bundesen, "The Overprotective Mother," *Ladies Home Journal*, March 1950, pp. 243–244; Abraham Myerson, "Let's Quit Blaming Mom," *Science Digest* 29 (March 1951), pp. 10–15; and Elizabeth B. Hurlock (Ph.D., past president of the American Psychological Association's Division on the Teaching of Psychology), "Mothering Does Not Mean Smothering," *Today's Health* 33 (September 1955), pp. 60–61.

11. Philip Wylie, *Generation of Vipers* (New York: Farrar & Rinehart, 1942); Edward Strecker, *Their Mothers' Sons: The Psychiatrist Examines an American Problem* (Philadelphia: J. B. Lippincott, 1946); and Ferdinand Lundberg and Marynia F. Farnham, *Modern Woman: The Lost Sex* (New York: Harper & Bros., 1947).

12. These little-known works of Wylie are discussed in Michael Rogin, "Kiss Me Deadly: Communism, Motherhood, and Cold War Movies," in *Ronald Reagan: The Movie and Other Episodes in Political Demonology* (Berkeley: University of California Press, 1987), pp. 236–271.

13. On the association between communism and moral weakness, see Joseph McCarthy, "Speech at Wheeling, West Virginia," in William H. Chafe and Harvard Sitkoff, eds., *A History of Our Time: Readings on Postwar America*, 2nd ed. (New York: Oxford University Press, 1987), pp. 64–67, in which McCarthy called for a "moral uprising" to combat atheistic communists who were "enemies from within." On the FBI and J. Edgar Hoover, especially Hoover's belief that communism was "an evil and malignant way of life . . . that eventually will destroy the sanctity of the home. [Therefore] a quarantine is necessary to keep it from infecting the nation," see Richard Gid Powers, *Secrecy and Power: The Life of J. Edgar Hoover* (New York: Free Press, 1987), pp. 288–289.

14. Mickey Spillane, *One Lonely Night* (New York: Dutton, 1951), pp. 170–171. Themes of the dangers of women's sexuality, although without the connection to communists, can be found in Alfred Hitchcock's classic thriller *Psycho*, 1960, in which an adulterous woman, on the way to a meeting with her illicit lover, is murdered by a crazed psychopath with a mother obsession. In this film, both women have displaced their sexual impulses, to their own detriment and that of their sons and lovers. The

theme of villains stealing atomic secrets appears over and over again, sometimes in the most unlikely places, such as Walt Disney's playful fantasy film *The Shaggy Dog* (1959).

15. Quotes of Arthur M. Schlesinger, Jr., are from Schlesinger's *The Vital Center: The Politics of Freedom* (Cambridge, Mass.: Riverside Press, 1962), also quoted and analyzed in Garry Wills, *Nixon Agonistes* (Boston: Houghton Mifflin, 1970), pp. 573–575.

16. See Chauncey, "The National Panic over Sex Crimes," p. 38, in which are cited the testimonies of many gay men and lesbians who married because "the pressures to marry had to be experienced to be comprehended."

17. Reagan's defense of Hollywood was in the Dixon *Evening Telegraph*, 22 August 1950, as cited in Garry Wills, *Reagan's America: Innocents at Home* (Garden City, N.Y.: Doubleday, 1987), p. 144. The unnamed Hollywood executive is quoted in Lillian Ross, "Onward and Upward with the Arts," *New Yorker*, 21 February 1948, p. 47. On the rhetoric of virility and cold war politics, see Marc Fasteau, "Vietnam and the Cult of Toughness in Foreign Policy," in Elizabeth A. Pleck and Joseph H. Pleck, eds., *The American Man* (Englewood Cliffs, N.J.: Prentice-Hall, 1980), pp. 377–315.

18. Minutes of the Executive Committee meeting of 11 December 1950, Massachusetts Society for Social Health (MSSH); minutes of the MSSH Advisory Committee on Defense, 19 January 1951; List of Members of the Executive Committee, Advisory Committee on Defense Activities, 1951–1952; and memo to committee members from Nicholas J. Fiumara, M.D., chair and director of MSSH, 6 April 1951—all in MSSH papers, MC 203, Boxes 1 and 2, Schlesinger Library, Radcliffe College, Cambridge, Mass. (hereafter cited as Schlesinger Library).

19. Address by Dr. Lewis M. Terman, a Stanford University psychologist, to the International Council for Exceptional Children, discussed in Dorothy Thompson, "Race Suicide of the Intelligent," *Ladies Home Journal*, May 1949, p. 11.

20. Thompson, "Race Suicide," p. 11.

21. These prescriptions were examined in pamphlets and articles contained in the ASHA papers, Boxes 93, 94, 95.

22. Alfred C. Kinsey et al., *Sexual Behavior in the Human Male* (Philadelphia: W. B. Saunders, 1948), and Alfred C. Kinsey et al., *Sexual Behavior in the Human Female* (Philadelphia: W. B. Saunders, 1953). Kinsey's findings are discussed more fully in Chapter 5.

23. See D'Emilio, *Sexual Politics, Sexual Communities*, p. 36, and Regina Markell Morantz, "The Scientist as Sex Crusader: Alfred C. Kinsey and American Culture," *American Quarterly* 29 (1977), pp. 563–589.

24. Mary Steichen Calderone papers, Box 1, File 1, Schlesinger Library.

25. I am grateful for the research assistance of Erin Egan, who compiled a qualitative as well as quantitative survey of the *Periodic Guide* entries from 1940 to 1980. One poll taken by the *Ladies Home Journal* asked teenage boys about dating and sex. Most boys polled said they expected girls to set the limits. See "Sex Freedom and Morals in the United States," *Ladies Home Journal*, June 1949, pp. 48, 89. See also Esther Emerson Sweeney, "Dates and Dating," New York ASHA, 1958, and "Behavior in Courtship,"

undated, unpaginated clipping from *Look,* both in ASHA Box 94; John Modell, "Dating Becomes the Way of American Youth," in Leslie Page Moch and Gary D. Stark, eds., *Essays on the Family and Historical Change* (Arlington: Texas A & M University Press, 1983), pp. 91–126; and Ellen Rothman, *Hands and Hearts: A History of Courtship in America* (New York: Basic Books, 1984), pp. 285–311.

26. William F. Snow, "Marriage and Parenthood," p. 6, Pamphlet A542, 1949, ASHA.

27. On the ideal marriage age for women and men, see John Modell, "Normative Aspects of American Marriage Timing since World War II," *Journal of Family History* 5 (Summer 1980), pp. 210–234; Jean and Eugene Benge, *Win Your Man and Keep Him* (Chicago: Windsor Press, 1948), p. 24; and "Health for Girls," Pamphlet A604, 1952, ASHA.

28. Carl C. Zimmerman and Lucius F. Cervantes, *Successful American Families* (New York: Pageant Press, 1960), p. 12, and Kerber, *Women of the Republic.*

29. Quoted in Paul Boyer, *By the Bomb's Early Light: American Thought and Culture at the Dawn of the Atomic Age* (New York: Pantheon, 1985), p. 323.

30. See Howard papers, A-64, and Fuller papers, F-96, both in the Schlesinger Library.

31. Jean Wood Fuller, "Los Angeles Woman in Trench at A-Blast," *Los Angeles Times,* 6 May 1955, Part 1, p. 2, Fuller Papers, F-96, Schlesinger Library.

32. Jean Wood Fuller, "Wisdom Is Defense," address before the state meeting of Women in Civil Defense, Richmond Hotel, Augusta, Ga., 10 November 1954, pp. 2, 4, 6–8. The same messages were contained in speeches in St. Petersburg, Fla., 11 November 1954, and Nashville, Tenn., 2 February 1954, in Fuller papers, F-96, Schlesinger Library. Criticism of the American Association of University Women is in Jean Wood Fuller: "Organizing Women: Careers in Volunteer Projects and Government Administration," an oral history conducted in 1976, by Miriam Stein, Regional Oral History Office, University of California, Berkeley, 1977, p. 218, Schlesinger Library. Many women and women's groups were for peace and advocated disarmament rather than civil defense. They, too, appealed to women's domesticity. See, for example, Dorothy Thompson, "We Live in the Atomic Age," *Ladies Home Journal,* February 1946, pp. 24–25, and Bruce Gould, "Last Trump," *Ladies Home Journal,* January 1946, p. 6, which claims that women can save the world by love. On taming fears, see Boyer, *By the Bomb's Early Light,* and Robert J. Lifton, *Broken Connections: On Death and the Continuity of Life* (New York: Simon & Schuster, 1979).

33. Address to the Dade Civil Defense Council, Miami, Fla., 15 November 1954, pp. 2, 7, Fuller papers, F-96, Schlesinger Library.

34. *By, for and about Women in Civil Defense: Grandma's Pantry Belongs in Your Kitchen* (Washington, D.C.: U.S. Government Printing Office, May 1958). Grandma's Pantry and the other civil defense crusades for women are discussed in Fuller oral history, pp. 189–191, 203–204B, Schlesinger Library.

35. Fuller oral history, pp. 203–204B, Schlesinger Library.

36. Boyer, *By the Bomb's Early Light*, p. 311.

37. The author is a veteran of many such "drop drills" in the 1950s. For the publicity surrounding the "duck and cover" campaigns, as well as the family imagery, see the documentary film *The Atomic Cafe*. See also JoAnne Brown, "'A' Is for 'Atom'; 'B' Is for 'Bomb': Civil Defense in American Public Education, 1948–1963," *Journal of American History* 75 (June 1988), pp. 68–90. In *The Broken Connection*, p. 337, Lifton discusses the concept of "nuclear numbing," or "the domestication of the ultimate," by which he means the reduction of the incomprehensible to familiar, less threatening terms. He also discusses the importance of symbols in terms of the unknown. Boyer also provides an in-depth examination of postwar efforts to "domesticate" or minimize fears of atomic power in *By the Bomb's Early Light*.

38. "What Kind of Shelters?" *Architectural Record*, January 1951, p. 15.

39. Quote from RAND psychologist is in Boyer, *By the Bomb's Early Light*, p. 331.

40. "Wonderful to Play In," *Time*, 5 February 1951, p. 12; "Atomic Cave," *Time*, 11 September 1950, p. 51.

41. Charles Grutzner, "City Folks' Fear of Bombs Aids Boom in Rural Realty," *New York Times*, 27 August 1950, p. 1:2. See also "A Cure for Atom Jitters," *New York Times*, 5 July 1950, p. 33:3.

42. "Their Sheltered Honeymoon," *Life*, 10 August 1959, pp. 51–52.

43. Clifford Edward Clark, Jr., "How to Plan a Family," *The American Family Home, 1800–1960* (Chapel Hill: University of North Carolina Press, 1986), pp. 212–213.

44. Zimmerman and Cervantes, *Successful American Families*, p. 13.

45. Defense Civil Preparedness Agency, *Your Chance to Live* (San Francisco, Calif.: Far West Laboratory for Educational Research and Development, 1972), pp. 79, 82.

46. As quoted in John Morton Blum, *V Was for Victory: Politics and American Culture during World War II* (New York: Harcourt Brace Jovanovich, 1976), p. 95.

47. On Rita Hayworth's photograph being attached to the bomb, see her obituary by Albin Krebs of the *New York Times*, reprinted in the Minneapolis *Star and Tribune*, 16 May 1987, pp. 1C, 2C. On the bikini, see Veronique Mistial, "Le Bikini a 40 ans," *Le Journal Français d'Amerique* 8 (4–31 July 1986).

48. See Boyer, *By the Bomb's Early Light*, Chapter 24.

49. See Hartmann, *The Home Front and Beyond: American Women in the 1940s* (Boston: Twayne, 1982), pp. 203–204, and Lois W. Banner, *American Beauty* (New York: Knopf, 1983), especially Chapter 13.

Chapter 5: Brinkmanship

1. Case 83, KLS.

2. Case 244, KLS.

3. See Alfred C. Kinsey et al., *Sexual Behavior in the Human Male* (Philadelphia: W. B. Saunders, 1948) and *Sexual Behavior in the Human Female* (Philadelphia: W. B. Saunders, 1953).

4. On the critics, see Robert R. Bell, *Premarital Sex in a Changing Society* (Englewood Cliffs, N.J.: Prentice-Hall, 1966), pp. 6–7. On the accusation that Kinsey was a communist, see Regina Markell Morantz, "The Scientist as Sex Crusader: Alfred C. Kinsey and American Culture," *American Quarterly* 29 (1977), pp. 563–589. The best of the sex surveys began to appear in the postwar years, although some important studies were done earlier. The work of Kinsey intensified sex research, which was taken up by sociologists, psychologists, and medical professionals. Kinsey set the tone with a quantitative and behavioral emphasis. See Ira Reiss, *Premarital Sexual Standards in America* (Glencoe, Ill.: Free Press, 1960).

5. For a review of the literature that illustrates its behavioral emphasis and its primary concern with premarital sexuality, see Catherine S. Chilman, *Adolescent Sexuality in a Changing American Society: Social and Psychological Perspectives* (Washington, D.C.: U.S. Public Health Service, January 1980). "Rates of premarital sex," as defined in the scholarly literature, often refer to statistics derived from childbirth within seven months of marriage, which represents only sexual encounters resulting in pregnancy followed by marriage, or to surveys that measure the frequency of intercourse among unmarried individuals. The designator *premarital* is a misnomer in the latter case, for it implies that the couple will marry in the future. Many people who engage in "premarital" sex, however, never marry. The term is appropriate for the KLS respondents, since they all did marry.

6. Estelle B. Freedman and John D'Emilio, *Intimate Matters: A History of Sexuality in America* (New York: Harper & Row, 1988), Chapters 11, 12.

7. Dorothy Baruch (Ph.D.), "Children Need Happily Married Parents," *Parents Magazine*, April 1940, p. 113, and Anna W. Wolf, "Will Your Child Have a Happy Marriage?" *Woman's Home Companion*, April 1948, pp. 132–133. See Chapter 4, this volume, for a discussion of links between "Momism," sexual frustration, and subversion.

8. Bell, *Premarital Sex in a Changing Society*, pp. 12, 57–58; Freedman and D'Emilio, *Intimate Matters*, Chapter 11.

9. For the trends in the marriage age, see Andrew Cherlin, *Marriage, Divorce, Remarriage* (Cambridge, Mass.: Harvard University Press, 1981), pp. 8–19.

10. Conservative professionals continued to declare that sex within marriage was "morally right" and sex outside marriage was "morally wrong." See Edward B. Lyman, "Let's Tell the Whole Story about Sex," lecture presented to a sex education class at the University of Pennsylvania, reprinted in the *Journal of Social Hygiene* 37 (1 January 1951), p. 9.

11. The "naturalness" of heterosexual marital intercourse perceived among postwar professionals is discussed in Linda Gordon, *Woman's Body, Woman's Right: A Social History of Birth Control in America* (New York: Penguin Books, 1977), Chapter 12.

12. James A. Peterson, *Education for Marriage* (New York: Scribner's, 1956), p. 5.

13. Roald Dahl, "Love," *Ladies Home Journal*, May 1947, p. 44.

14. Responses to questions in initial KLS survey, #1: "Tell why you chose this particular person for a life partner, and why you prefer (her) (him) to all others you have known." #2: "State reasons why you think your marriage will be a successful one."

15. Cases 229, 14, 296, 49, 18, 67, KLS.

16. Case 74, KLS.

17. John Modell, "Dating Becomes the Way of American Youth," in Leslie Page Moch and Gary D. Stark, eds., *Essays on the Family and Historical Change* (Arlington: Texas A & M University Press, 1983), p. 124. See also Ellen Rothman, *Hands and Hearts: A History of Courtship in America* (New York: Basic Books, 1984), pp. 285–311.

18. Ruth Imler, "The Late Dater," *Ladies Home Journal*, September 1955, p. 54.

19. Sarah Barish, as told to Herman Style, "How to Snare a Male," *Ladies Home Journal*, June 1950, pp. 56ff.; G. M. White, "How to Catch a Husband," *Ladies Home Journal*, May 1949, p. 31.

20. Gifford R. Adams (Ph.D., Pennsylvania State College, Department of Psychology), "Making Marriage Work: If You Don't Get Dates," *Ladies Home Journal*, July 1955, p. 26.

21. See Michael Gordon, "From an Unfortunate Necessity to a Cult of Mutual Orgasm: Sex in American Marital Education Literature, 1830–1940," in James M. Henslin and Edward Sagarin, eds., *The Sociology of Sex* (New York: Schocken Books, 1978), pp. 59–83.

22. Thirty-two percent of the men and twenty-seven percent of the women said they were "ill at ease" or "very shy and uncomfortable." Computed from KLS item D40C61, "Relationships with opposite sex until time of engagement."

23. The statistics pertaining to "casual" dates reflect different definitions of the relationships rather than actual differences; that is, women may have been more likely to define a relationship as serious if intercourse occurred. Computed from KLS items D40C70–D40C72.

24. Kinsey et al., *Sexual Behavior in the Human Male*, pp. 378–383.

25. Nora Johnson, "Sex and the College Girl," *Atlantic*, November 1959, pp. 57–58, as quoted in Rothman, *Hands and Hearts*, p. 304. KLS data computed from items D40C69, "Physical relations with research partner to end of engagement"; D40C70, "Physical relations with other persons for whom you felt considerable affection"; D40C72, "Greatest extent of physical relationship with anyone"; D40C71, "Physical relations with others (casual dates and acquaintances)."

26. Kinsey et al., *Sexual Behavior in the Human Female*, p. 79.

27. Robert Bell and Jay Chaskes, "Premarital Experience among Coeds, 1958 and 1968," *Journal of Marriage and the Family* 32 (February 1970), pp. 81–84.

28. KLS question D40C69, "Relations with research partner to end of engagement," and Modell, "Dating Becomes the Way of American Youth," pp. 124–125.

29. Case 165, KLS, and Kinsey et al., *Sexual Behavior in the Human Female*, p. 345.

30. Ira Reiss, "Sexual Codes in Teen-Age Culture," *Annales*, November 1961, p. 57.

31. Case 14, KLS, and Kinsey et al., *Sexual Behavior in the Human Female*, pp. 314–321.

32. Case 252, KLS.

33. Kinsey et al., *Sexual Behavior in the Human Male*, p. 364; Kinsey et al., *Sexual Behavior in the Human Female*, p. 344; and KLS items D40C69 and D41C36.

34. Case 93, KLS. Item D40C69 cross-tabulated with item D41C36.

35. Case 205, KLS.

36. Case 287, KLS.

37. Case 21, KLS.

38. Case 83, KLS.

39. Case 86, KLS.

40. Cases 38, 296, KLS.

41. Case 147, KLS.

42. Case 272, KLS.

43. Case 101, KLS.

44. Case 81, KLS.

45. Case 66, KLS.

46. In the KLS, most of the couples who had refrained from intercourse prior to marriage had experienced a great deal of physical intimacy. Among the group who felt most strongly that it was "essential" to refrain from intercourse prior to marriage, fully two-thirds said that they had experienced considerable physical intimacy before marriage; Item D40C69 and the same item cross-tabulated with D41C36, "Importance that husband and wife should *not* have had sex with each other before marriage."

47. Kinsey et al., *Sexual Behavior in the Human Female*, p. 243; Kinsey et al., *Sexual Behavior in the Human Male*, p. 407; Freedman and D'Emilio, *Intimate Matters*, Chapter 11; and Reiss, "Sexual Codes in Teenage Culture." For a discussion of the increase in petting during the decades when the rates of premarital intercourse remained stable, see Bell, *Premarital Sex in a Changing Society*, p. 58. Bell also noted that in the United States (more than in other countries), there was a "particularly strong contradiction between dominant moral values and sexual behavior."

48. Kinsey et al., *Sexual Behavior in the Human Female*, pp. 329–330.

49. Case 223, KLS.

50. Case 290, KLS.

51. Case 264, KLS.

52. Case 252, KLS.

53. Case 117, KLS.

54. Case 109, KLS.

55. Case 21, KLS.

56. Case 198, KLS.

57. Kinsey et al., *Sexual Behavior in the Human Female*, pp. 329–330.

58. Bell, *Premarital Sex in a Changing Society* p. 144.

59. Case 244, KLS.

60. Cases 258, 117, 242, 37, 101, KLS.

61. Case 297, KLS.

62. Case 271, KLS.

63. Case 118, KLS.

64. Cases 116, 289, KLS.

65. Computed from KLS item D49C39, "Importance of your sexual relations being closely bound up with love and affection". Women responded 52 percent "extremely important," 34 percent "quite important"; men responded 37 percent "extremely important," 46 percent "quite important." KLS item D41C34, "How important that husband and wife frequently express their love for each other in words?" Women responded 55 percent "essential," 45 percent "desirable"; men responded 41 percent "essential," 50 percent "desirable." KLS items D49C42, "Importance of having sexual intercourse with your spouse every time you desire it"; D49C40, "Importance of having sexual intercourse every time your spouse desires it"; D44C32, "Frequency of orgasm during sexual intercourse with spouse during last 3 years (men: frequency of impotence)"; D44C33, "Spouse's considerateness of feelings about sexual relations."

66. Gordon, *Woman's Body, Woman's Right*, Chapter 12, discusses the sex technique literature and marriage counseling during this period. See also Michael Gordon, "From an Unfortunate Necessity to a Cult of Mutual Orgasm."

67. Kinsey et al., *Sexual Behavior in the Human Male*, p. 236, and Kinsey et al., *Sexual Behavior in the Human Female*, p. 408. KLS items D44C13, "Anticipation at the time of marriage with regard to sexual relations"; D44C19, "Feelings about sexual relations with spouse during last 3 years"; D44C22, "Frequency of sexual intercourse with spouse per month."

68. Kinsey found a somewhat higher incidence of sex outside marriage, about 25 percent among college-educated men and 20 percent among women. See *Sexual Behavior in the Human Male*, p. 348, and *Sexual Behavior in the Human Female*, p. 417. KLS items D41C40, "Importance that husband be 100 percent faithful to wife"; D41C39, "Importance that wife be 100 percent faithful to husband"; D41C35, "Importance that the same standard of sexual morality should apply to both husband and wife"; D45C45, "Respondent had a love affair with someone other than spouse—times of occurrence"; D45C46, "Spouse had a love affair with someone other than respondent—times of occurrence"; D45C47 and D45C48, "Respondent (spouse) had sexual relations with someone other than spouse (respondent)—times of occurrence."

69. Cases 86 and 296, KLS.

Chapter 6: Baby Boom and Birth Control

1. Louisa Randall Church, "Parents: Architects of Peace," *American Home*, November 1946, pp. 18–19.

2. Case 230, KLS. The reader is once again reminded that any names attached to the KLS respondents in this chapter are the author's invention. Respondents to the KLS were identified only by case number.

3. Church, "Parents." See also Viviana A. Zelizer, *Pricing the Priceless Child: The Changing Social Value of Children* (New York: Basic Books, 1985), for an analysis of the shift from children as economically useful to economically useless but sentimentally priceless.

4. Andrew Cherlin, *Marriage, Divorce, Remarriage* (Cambridge, Mass.: Harvard University Press, 1976), pp. 19–21, and Denise Polit-O'Hara and Judith Berman, *Just the Right Size: A Guide to Family-Size Planning* (New York: Praeger, 1984), p. 5.

5. Ronald R. Rindfuss and James A. Sweet, *Postwar Fertility Trends and Differentials in the United States* (New York: Academic Press, 1977), p. 191.

6. Ira S. Steinberg, *The New Lost Generation: The Population Boom and Public Policy* (New York: St. Martin's Press, 1982), p. 3. The conformity to patterns is described in John Modell et al., "The Timing of Marriage in the Transition to Adulthood: Continuity and Change, 1860–1975," in John Demos and Sarane Spence Boocock, eds., *Turning Points: Historical and Sociological Essays on the Family*, supplement to the *American Journal of Sociology* 84 (1978), pp. 120–150.

7. Joseph Veroff et al., *Mental Health in America: Patterns of Help-Seeking from 1957 to 1976* (New York: Basic Books, 1981), pp. 6, 31; Veroff et al., *The Inner American: A Self-Portrait from 1957 to 1976* (New York: Basic Books, 1981), p. 200.

8. Robert O. Blood, Jr., and Donald M. Wolfe, *Husbands and Wives: The Dynamics of Married Living* (Glencoe, Ill.: Free Press, 1960), p. 117.

9. J. Edgar Hoover, "The Twin Enemies of Freedom: Crime and Communism," address before the Twenty-eighth Annual Convention of the National Council of Catholic Women, Chicago, Ill., 9 November 1956, in *Vital Speeches* 23 (1 December 1956), p. 104.

10. John D. Durand, "Married Women in the Labor Force," *American Journal of Sociology* 52 (November 1946), pp. 217–223.

11. "Books versus Babies," *Newsweek* 27 (14 January 1946), p. 79.

12. The quote is from a study of 1950 census figures reported in *U.S. News and World Report* 41 (14 September 1956), p. 8.

13. Susan Hartmann, *The Home Front and Beyond: American Women in the 1940s* (Boston: Twayne, 1982), p. 70.

14. N. Sanford, "Is College Education Wasted on Women?" *Ladies Home Journal* 74 (May 1957), pp. 78–79ff.

15. Dr. Eustace Chesser, *How to Make a Success of Your Marriage* (London: Bodley Head, 1952), pp. 33–34.

16. In *The Inner American*, p. 6, Veroff et al. discuss the importance of celebrities as role models during these years.

17. Kay Proctor, "Hollywood Birth Rate—Going Up!" *Photoplay* 54 (June 1940), p. 16; Cheryl Christina Crane, "Hollywood's Newest Pin-up Girl," *Photoplay* 29 (December

1943), pp. 32–33, 70; and Elsa Maxwell, "Hollywood Mothers: How Wise and Intelligent Parents Do They Make?" *Photoplay* 25 (June 1944), pp. 100–101. See also Joan Crawford, "Fan Experiences with the Stars: Joan Crawford—My Ideal," *Photoplay* 50 (December 1936), p. 16.

18. Carole Landis Wallace, "Should War Wives Have Babies?" *Photoplay* 29 (December 1943), pp. 54–55. See also Eleanor Harris, "Olivia de Havilland" (interview) *Photoplay* 25 (June 1944), pp. 39, 87.

19. Maureen O'Hara, "I'm Waiting for My Baby," *Photoplay* 25 (June 1944), pp. 55, 85–86.

20. Rosalind Russell, "They Still Lie about Hollywood," *Look* 15 (3 July 1951), pp. 36–43.

21. "Model Mothers: Family Poses of Some Professional Beauties," *Life*, 22 May 1944, pp. 65–70.

22. Frank McDonough, "Are Children Necessary?" *Better Homes and Gardens*, October 1944, p. 7.

23. *Penny Serenade*, 1941, written by Garson Kanin and Ruth Gordon, video from RSVP Movie Greats. Quotes taken from video, not screenplay.

24. Marynia Farnham and Ferdinand Lundberg, *The Modern Woman: The Lost Sex* (New York: Harper, 1947).

25. See Modell et al., "The Timing of Marriage in the Transition to Adulthood." The theme of parenthood was not present to the same extent in the movies of the 1920s, which focused more heavily on the couple, as did the fan magazines.

26. See Mark Crispin Miller, "Deride and Conquer," in Todd Gitlin, ed., *Watching Television* (New York: Pantheon Books, 1986), pp. 183–228, and James Gilbert, *Another Chance: Postwar America 1954–1985* (Chicago: Dorsey Press, 1986), pp. 64–66.

27. "The New American Domesticated Male," *Life* 36 (4 January 1954), pp. 42–45.

28. Quoted in Peter Filene, *Him/Her/Self: Sex Roles in Modern America*, 2nd ed. (Baltimore: Johns Hopkins University Press, 1986), pp. 172–173.

29. Andre Fontaine, "Are We Staking Our Future on a Crop of Sissies?" *Better Homes and Gardens*, December 1950, pp. 154–156.

30. Ibid., p. 156.

31. Samuel Middlebrook, "The Importance of Fathers," *Parents Magazine*, December 1947, pp. 28, 78.

32. Miriam Bergenicht, "A Build-up for Dad," *Parents Magazine*, June 1948, pp. 19, 88–99.

33. Advertisement in *Parents Magazine*, December 1947, p. 80; David R. Mace (Ph.D., professor of human relations, Drew University), "Fathers Are Parents, Too," *Woman's Home Companion*, June 1953, pp. 9, 11; and Clifford R. Adams (Ph.D., psychologist at Pennsylvania State University), "Making Marriage Work," *Ladies Home Journal*, October 1954, p. 41.

34. Nancy Cleaver, "Are You a Dud as a Dad?" *American Home*, August 1950, p. 21.

35. Chesser, *How to Make a Success of Your Marriage*, p. 27, and Farnham and Lundberg, *The Modern Woman*.

36. Research by Carl T. Javert, obstetrician of Cornell University Medical College, New York City, presented at the meeting of the American Academy of Obstetrics and Gynecology in Cincinnati, reported in "Fears and Babies," *Newsweek*, 28 December 1953, p. 49.

37. James Reed, *From Private Vice to Public Virtue: The Birth Control Movement and American Society since 1830* (New York: Basic Books, 1978), pp. 102, 144, 187.

38. Linda Gordon, *Woman's Body, Woman's Right: A Social History of Birth Control in America* (New York: Penguin Books, 1977), pp. 341–343.

39. Abraham Stone, "The Control of Fertility," *Scientific American*, April 1954, p. 31.

40. All quotes are from Gordon, *Woman's Body, Woman's Right*, pp. 347–349.

41. Reed, *From Private Vice to Public Virtue*, pp. 282–283.

42. As quoted in Gordon, *Woman's Body, Woman's Right*, p. 393.

43. "How to Plan a Family," *Ebony* magazine, July 1948, pp. 13–18, as quoted in "Case for Birth Control," *Newsweek*, 31 January 1955, pp. 60–61.

44. As quoted in "Birth Control—Or Not?" *Newsweek*, 4 August 1958, pp. 48–49. See also C. Thomas Dienes, *Law, Politics and Birth Control* (Urbana: University of Illinois Press, 1972), pp. 149–150, and Pascal Whelpton et al., *Fertility and Family Planning in the U.S.* (Princeton, N.J.: Princeton University Press, 1966), pp. 34, 303–304. For discussions of birth control used for population control, see Reed, *From Private Vice to Public Virtue*, Chapters 19, 21; Stone, "The Control of Fertility," pp. 31–33; and R. L. Meier, "Progress in Birth Control," *Nation*, 11 January 1958, pp. 29–32.

45. Birth control did not again become a contributing factor in the movement for women's liberation until the 1960s. See Gordon, *Woman's Body, Woman's Right*, Chapter 14.

46. "Birth Control Contest," *Time*, 5 March 1956, pp. 91–92. On the concern about the impact of contraception, see Martha Stuart and William T. Liu, eds., *The Emerging Woman: The Impact of Family Planning* (Boston: Little, Brown, 1970). The editors of this volume feared that fewer children would leave women with too much time on their hands; see p. vi.

47. The plan for a frightening pamphlet cover is documented in correspondence in ASHA papers.

48. Kinsey et al., *Sexual Behavior in the Human Female* (Philadelphia: W. B. Saunders, 1953), pp. 314–321; Kristin Luker, *Abortion and the Politics of Motherhood* (Berkeley: University of California Press, 1984), pp. 40–49; Dienes, *Law, Politics, and Birth Control*, p. 239; and Estelle B. Freedman and John D'Emilio, *Intimate Matters: A Social History of Sexuality in America* (New York: Harper & Row, 1988), Chapter 11.

49. R. Sauer, "Attitudes to Abortion in America, 1800–1973," *Population Studies* 28 (March 1974), pp. 53–67.

50. "Salve Killers," *Newsweek,* 18 October 1948, pp. 64, 66; "The Death of a Girl," *Time,* 26 September 1955, p. 72; "Torment," *Newsweek* (25 June 1956), pp. 28ff; and "The Case of the Violet Paste," *Time,* 18 October 1948, pp. 50ff.

51. See, for example, "A Reno for Abortions?" *Time,* 22 February 1954, pp. 66ff, and "The Wed and the Unwed," *Newsweek,* 7 April 1958, p. 92. See also Sauer, "Attitudes to Abortions in America." One dissenting voice was Edwin M. Schur, "The Abortion Racket: Product of a Laggard Law," *Nation,* 5 March 1955, pp. 199–201. On the declining number of approved therapeutic abortions, see Hartmann, *The Home Front and Beyond,* p. 172. See also Leslie J. Reagan, *When Abortion Was a Crime: Women, Medicine, and Law in the United States, 1867–1973* (Berkeley: University of California Press, 1998).

52. Computed from KLS items D44C23–D44C70; all concern pregnancy and birth information and preferences concerning number and spacing of children, use of birth control, and so on. D44C37 concerns "intentional termination of pregnancy." The Kinsey data reflect more abortions than the KLS data, but Kinsey's statistics included abortions performed when the women were not married as well as when they were, and the KLS respondents were asked only about abortions during marriage. See Kinsey et al., *The Sexual Behavior of the Human Female.*

53. "Family Planning," *Time,* 12 August 1957, p. 67, cited the survey by sociologist Ronald Freeman of the University of Michigan finding that even 87 percent of Roman Catholics surveyed reported using some form of birth control, many using "rhythm." See Whelpton et al., *Fertility and Family Planning in the U.S.,* pp. 350, 353. See also Lee Rainwater, *And the Poor Get Children: Sex, Contraception and Family Planning in the Working Class* (Chicago: Quadrangle Books, 1960).

54. Calculated from KLS items D44C23–D44C70, D46C40–D46C44.

55. Case 273, KLS.

56. Calculated from KLS items D44C49, D44C45, D44C36, D42C23, and D44C59, all pertaining to desired family size; D44C55, "Hopes or intentions to have more children than at present"; D44C65, "Reasons why smaller family desired"; D44C66, "Reasons why larger family desired."

57. Cases 75 and 290, KLS.

58. Cases 82 and 109, KLS.

59. Case 198, KLS.

60. Case 209, KLS.

61. John Campbell and John Modell, "Family Ideology and Family Values in the Baby Boom: A Secondary Analysis of the 1955 Growth of American Families Survey of Single Women," Technical Report No. 5 (Minneapolis: Family Study Center, University of Minnesota, 1984).

62. For discussions of the pronatalist ideology during these years, see Ellen Peck and Judith Senderowitz, eds., *Pronatalism: The Myth of Mom and Apple Pie* (New York: Thomas Y. Crowell, 1974), especially Judith Blake, "Coercive Pronatalism and American Population Policy," pp. 29–67, which examines the implicit ways in which public policies and professional assumptions fostered pronatalism.

63. Charles F. Westoff and Norman B. Ryder, *The Contraceptive Revolution* (Princeton, N.J.: Princeton University Press, 1977), pp. 338–339, 348–350.

64. Amram Scheinfeld, "Motherhood's Back in Style: The Case for Larger Families," *Ladies Home Journal*, September 1944, p. 136; Church, "Parents."

65. Nancy Pottishman Weiss, "Mother, the Invention of Necessity: Dr. Benjamin Spock's *Baby and Child Care*," *American Quarterly* 29 (Winter 1977), pp. 519–546.

66. Veroff et al., *The Inner American*, p. 22.

67. Carl C. Zimmerman and Lucius F. Cervantes, *Successful American Families* (New York: Pageant Press, 1960), defined success in terms of having children and rearing them to be educated. See my discussion in Chapter 4 of this volume.

68. Quoted by David Reisman in "The Found Generation," *American Scholar* 25 (Autumn 1956), pp. 421–436, and in Benita Eisler, *Private Lives: Men and Women of the Fifties* (New York: Franklin Watts, 1986), p. 4.

69. See, for example, James Gilbert, *A Cycle of Outrage: America's Reaction to the Juvenile Delinquent in the 1950s* (New York: Oxford University Press, 1986). Gilbert shows that during the 1950s, the media were blamed for fostering a peer-based youth culture that came between parents and children and led to juvenile delinquency.

Chapter 7: The Commodity Gap

1. William H. Whyte, Jr., "Budgetism: Opiate of the Middle Class," *Fortune*, May 1956, p. 133; Levitt quoted in Kenneth Jackson, *Crabgrass Frontier: The Suburbanization of the United States* (New York: Oxford University Press, 1985), p. 231.

2. See David Colker, "Building a 'Future' in 1948," *Los Angeles Times*, September 4, 1999, p. 1A. I am grateful to David Colker of the *Los Angeles Times*, who told me about this context and put me in touch with John Guedel. In a phone interview on July 13, 1999, John Guedel told me his version of the story. Guiliana Muscio, of the University of Padua, confirmed that the story of the Italian election is true. For other studies of American popular culture in the international context of the cold war, see Reinhold Wagnleitner and Elaine Tyler May, eds., *"Here, There, and Everywhere": The Foreign Politics of American Popular Culture* (Hanover, N.H.: University Press of New England, 2000).

3. Quotes from the debate in Moscow are from "The Two Worlds: A Day-Long Debate," *New York Times*, 25 July 1959, pp. 1, 3; "When Nixon Took on Khrushchev," a report on the meeting and the text of Nixon's address at the opening of the American National Exhibition in Moscow on 24 July 1959, printed in "Setting Russia Straight on Facts about the U.S.," *U.S. News and World Report*, 3 August 1959, pp. 36–39, 70–72; and "Encounter," *Newsweek*, 3 August 1959, pp. 15–19.

4. Letter to board of aldermen from Mayor Joseph Darst, 13 December 1951, Raymond Tucker Papers, Box 104, Special Collections, Olin Library, Washington University, St. Louis, Mo.

5. George H. Gallup, *The Gallup Poll, Public Opinion 1935–1971*, vol. 1: *1935–1948* (New York: Random House, 1972), p. 594; Hadley Cantril, ed., *Public Opinion, 1935–1946* (Princeton, N.J.: Princeton University Press, 1951), pp. 829, 831; and Susan Hartmann, *The Home Front and Beyond: American Women in the 1940s* (Boston: Twayne, 1982), p. 8.

6. George Katona, *The Mass Consumption Society* (New York: McGraw-Hill, 1964), pp. 14–15, and *The Powerful Consumer: Psychological Studies of the American Economy* (New York: McGraw-Hill, 1960), pp. 9–32; U.S. Bureau of the Census, *Historical Statistics of the United States, Colonial Times to 1970*, part 1 (Washington, D.C.: U.S. Government Printing Office, 1975), pp. 49, and 316–320; and Hartmann, *The Home Front and Beyond*, p. 8.

7. Katona, *The Powerful Consumer*, p. 27.

8. See Daniel Horowitz, *The Morality of Spending* (Baltimore: Johns Hopkins University Press, 1985), especially Chapter 8, for shifting ideas on spending in the 1930s.

9. Cantril, *Public Opinion*, pp. 1047–1048.

10. Katona, *The Powerful Consumer*, pp. 46, 156.

11. See Winifred D. Wandersee, *Women's Work and Family Values, 1920–1940* (Cambridge, Mass.: Harvard University Press, 1981), for a discussion of changing material expectations and the role of women's employment in family support. On the depression's legacy of employment for women, see S. Bennett and Glen Elder, Jr., "Women's Work in the Family Economy," *Journal of Family History* 4 (Summer 1979), pp. 153–176.

12. George Putnam, newscast in the documentary film by the Archives Project, *The Atomic Cafe*, 1982, Thorn Emi Video.

13. National Association of Savings Banks survey and Office of Civilian Requirements survey, cited in John Morton Blum, *V Was for Victory: Politics and American Culture during World War II* (New York: Harcourt Brace Jovanovich, 1976), pp. 100–101; Clifford Edward Clark, *The American Family Home, 1800–1960* (Chapel Hill: University of North Carolina Press, 1986), p. 195.

14. Clark, *American Family Home*, pp. 102–103.

15. Jackson, *Crabgrass Frontier*, pp. 231–232.

16. Clark, *The American Family Home*, p. 213; Jackson, *Crabgrass Frontier*, pp. 231–232, 249.

17. "Should-Must Cities Decentralize?" *Commonwealth*, 31 May 1948, quoted in John H. Mollenkopf, "The Postwar Politics of Urban Development," William K. Tabb and Larry Sawyers, eds., *Marxism and the Metropolis* (New York: Oxford University Press, 1978), p. 131.

18. Jackson, *Crabgrass Frontier*, pp. 11, 190–193, 203–218, and 283–295. On racial segregation and redlining in the postwar suburbs, see also Thomas Sugrue, *The Origins of the Urban Crisis: Race and Inequality in Postwar Detroit* (Princeton, N.J.: Princeton University Press, 2005); Robert O. Self, *American Babylon: Race and the Struggle for Postwar Oakland* (Princeton, N.J.: Princeton University Press, 2005); and Cynthia Mills

Richter, "Integrating the Suburban Dream: Shaker Heights, Ohio," Ph.D. Dissertation, University of Minnesota, 1999.

19. Clark, *The American Family Home*, pp. 221–233; Jackson, *Crabgrass Frontier*, Chapters 11, 12.

20. Katona *The Mass Consumption Society*, pp. 14–18, 265–273.

21. Jackson, *Crabgrass Frontier*, p. 235.

22. Clark, *The American Family Home*, p. 219.

23. Stuart Ewen, *Captains of Consciousness: Advertising and the Social Roots of the Consumer Culture* (New York: McGraw-Hill, 1976); George Lipsitz, "The Meaning of Memory: Family, Class and Ethnicity in Early Network Television Programs," *Cultural Anthropology* 1 (November 1986), pp. 355–387.

24. Clark, *The American Family Home*, pp. 198, 210–213, 236.

25. Ibid., pp. 210–213.

26. Herbert Gans, *The Levittowners: The Ways of Life and Politics in a New Suburban Community* (New York: Pantheon, 1967), pp. 163–165.

27. Ibid., pp. 153–155, 206–212, and Clark, *The American Family Home*, pp. 224–243.

28. Jackson, *Crabgrass Frontier*, pp. 235–243.

29. Calculated from KLS items D43C61, D45C34, D45C36, and D45C35, pertaining to income and debts.

30. Calculated from KLS items D43C62, D43C57, D43C56, D43C55, and D43C53, pertaining to expenditures for housing, cars, and installment buying.

31. Calculated from KLS items D43C63–D43C67, pertaining to factors most important in determining the way extra money was spent.

32. Elizabeth Long, *The American Dream and the Popular Novel* (Boston: Routledge & Kegan Paul, 1985), pp. 52–76. See also Sloan Wilson, *The Man in the Grey Flannel Suit* (New York: Simon & Schuster, 1955).

33. Cases 224, 250, 24, 237, 244, 72, KLS.

34. Case 153, KLS. The reader is again reminded that the names of the KLS respondents used in this chapter are the author's invention and that the KLS identified respondents only by case number. For a provocative discussion of the tensions in the male provider role that illuminates issues raised in this case, see Barbara Ehrenreich, *The Hearts of Men* (Garden City, N.Y.: Doubleday, 1983).

35. Case 109, KLS.

36. Cases 244 and 75, KLS.

37. Case 62, KLS.

Chapter 8: Hanging Together

1. Case 75, KLS. These quotes are from respondents to the Kelly Longitudinal Study (KLS). The KLS identified respondents only by case number. The names used in the chapter are my invention.

2. Case 198, KLS.

3. Case 75, KLS.

4. Andrew Cherlin, *Marriage, Divorce, Remarriage* (Cambridge, Mass.: Harvard University Press, 1981), p. 25. In the early part of the twentieth century, heightened expectations for marriage led to a rise in the divorce rate. See Elaine Tyler May, *Great Expectations: Marriage and Divorce in Post-Victorian America* (Chicago: University of Chicago Press, 1980).

5. Joseph Veroff et al., *The Inner American: A Self Portrait from 1957 to 1976* (New York: Basic Books, 1981), pp. 146–149.

6. Cases 273 and 116, KLS.

7. Case 264, KLS.

8. Case 289, KLS.

9. Case 198, KLS.

10. Case 297, KLS.

11. Calculated from KLS items D48C31, "Overall happiness in marriage," and D48C25 and D48C23, which concern regret and satisfaction, respectively; quote is from Veroff et al., *The Inner American*, pp. 141–142. See also Jessie Bernard, *The Future of Marriage* (New York: Bantam Books, 1972).

12. George Lipsitz, *Class and Culture in Cold War America: "A Rainbow at Midnight"* (South Hadley, Mass.: J. F. Bergin, 1982), p. 93.

13. Case 77, KLS.

14. Case 38, KLS.

15. Case 118, KLS.

16. Case 271, KLS.

17. Case 90, KLS.

18. Calculated from KLS items D46C51–D46C76 concerning marital adjustments, KLS.

19. "Being married" helped goal attainment: 78 percent women, 79 percent men. Spouse helped goal attainment: 78 percent men, 66 percent women; hindered: 9 percent women, 5 percent men. Calculated from KLS items D45C68 and D48C30, 1955 survey.

20. Calculated from KLS items D40C44, D40C48, and D40C43.

21. Calculated from KLS items D48C24, "Choice if had life to live over"; D48C25, "Regret of marriage"; and D48C26, "Consideration of separation or divorce from spouse."

22. Edmund Bergler (M.D.), *Divorce Won't Help* (New York: Harper, 1948), pp. vii–viii.

23. Robert M. Goldenson (Ph.D.), "Why Boys and Girls Go Wrong or Right," *Parents Magazine*, May 1951, p. 82.

24. Case 244, KLS.

CHAPTER 9: THE END OF CONTAINMENT

1. Letter to Betty Friedan, 21 January 1963, from New York City, in Friedan Manuscript Collection, Schlesinger Library Manuscript Collections, Radcliffe College, Cambridge, Mass., hereafter referred to as Friedan Letters. All names were removed from the letters in the files.

2. Betty Friedan, *The Feminine Mystique* (New York: Dell, 1963); Daniel Horowitz, *Betty Friedan and the Making of the Feminine Mystique: The American Left, the Cold War and Modern Feminism* (Boston: University of Massachusetts Press, 1998); *Ebony* photo editorial, "Goodbye Mammy, Hello Mom," *Ebony*, March 1947, pp. 36–37.

3. Letter dated 14 May 1963, from Brookline, Mass., Friedan Letters.

4. Letter dated 13 March 1963, from Ridgewood, N.J., Friedan Letters.

5. Letter dated 24 August 1963, from Pittsburgh, Pa., Friedan Letters.

6. Letter dated 21 January 1963, from New York City, Friedan Letters.

7. Letter dated 22 March 1963, from Little Silver, N.J., Friedan Letters.

8. Letter dated 13 November 1963, from New Haven, Conn., Friedan Letters.

9. Letter dated 9 March 1964, from South Carolina, Friedan Letters.

10. Letter dated 21 January 1963, from New York City; letter dated 19 May 1964, from Far Rockaway, N.Y.; letter dated 7 April 1963 (locale not given); letter dated 25 May 1963, from Litely, Pa.; letter dated 22 October 1963, from Cornell University, Ithaca, N.Y., Friedan Letters.

11. Letter dated 16 February 1965, from Pickering, Ontario, Friedan Letters.

12. Letter to a friend, 5 June 1963, in Oakland, Calif., sent to Friedan with a note.

13. Letter dated 21 January 1963, from New York City; letter dated 19 May 1964, from Far Rockaway, N.Y.; letter dated 1 September 1964, from Harrisburg, Pa.; letter dated 13 March 1963, from Ridgewood, N.J., Friedan Letters.

14. Letter dated 17 May 1963, from Sioux Falls, S.D., Friedan Letters.

15. Letter dated 23 April 1963, from Leicester, Mass., Friedan Letters.

16. Letter dated 4 August 1964, from Glen Ridge, N.J., Friedan Letters.

17. Letter dated 29 May 1964, from Folcroft, Pa., Friedan Letters.

18. Amy Swerdlow, "Ladies Day at the Capitol: Women Strike for Peace versus HUAC," *Feminist Studies* 8 (1982), pp. 493–520, and in Linda K. Kerber and Jane DeHart-Mathews, eds., *Women's America: Refocusing the Past*, 2nd ed. (New York: Oxford University Press, 1987), pp. 415–433; quote from *Newsweek* is on pp. 416–417.

19. Ibid.

20. Sara Evans, *Personal Politics: The Roots of Women's Liberation in the Civil Rights Movement and the New Left* (New York: Knopf, 1979), pp. 3–23, and Paul Boyer, *By the Bomb's Early Light: American Thought and Culture at the Dawn of the Atomic Age* (New York: Pantheon, 1985), pp. 352–367. On the influence of Women Strike for Peace on the Test Ban Treaty, see *Science*, 13 March 1970, p. 1476, cited in Swerdlow, "Ladies' Day at the Capitol," p. 418. On the veteran feminists, see Leila J. Rupp and Verta Taylor, *Survival in the Doldrums: The American Women's Rights Movement, 1945 to the 1960s* (New York: Oxford University Press, 1987). On the New Left and the SDS, see James

Miller, *"Democracy Is in the Streets": From Port Huron to the Siege of Chicago* (New York: Simon & Schuster, 1987), and Todd Gitlin, *The Sixties: Years of Hope, Days of Rage* (New York: Bantam Books, 1987).

21. Reviews of the film are in the *Dr. Strangelove* file, New York Public Library Theater Arts Collection, Lincoln Center, New York.

22. For a discussion of the rise of the new feminist movement, see Evans, *Personal Politics*. On changing goals, see Gilda F. Epstein and Arline L. Bronzaft, "Female Freshmen View Their Roles as Women," *Journal of Marriage and the Family* 34 (November 1972), pp. 671–684; Andrea Schlissel Goldberg and Samuel Shiftlett, "Goals of Male and Female College Students: Do Traditional Sex Differences Still Exist?" *Sex Roles* 7 (December 1981), pp. 1214–1222; Mirra Komarovsky, "Female Freshmen View Their Future: Career Salience and Its Correlates," *Sex Roles* 8 (March 1982), pp. 299–314; Esther R. Greenglass and Riva Devins, "Factors Related to Marriage and Career Plans in Unmarried Women," *Sex Roles* 8 (January 1982), pp. 57–71; and Beth Bailey, *Sex in the Heartland* (Cambridge, Mass.: Harvard University Press, 1999).

23. These opinion polls are documented in George H. Gallup, *The Gallup Poll: Public Opinion 1935–1971*, vols. 1, 2, 3 (New York, Random House, 1972). I am grateful to Omri Shochatovitz for categorizing these polls and organizing them in chronological order.

24. Ibid. See also Ellen Rothman, *Hands and Hearts: A History of Courtship in America* (New York: Basic Books, 1984), pp. 306–311.

25. U.S. Bureau of the Census, *Historical Statistics of the United States, Colonial Times to 1970*, part 1 (Washington, D.C.: U.S. Government Printing Office, 1975), pp. 19, 49, 64, 133, 134. The birthrate continued to fall for two decades; it reached a record low in 1986, according to a 1987 census report. See "U.S. Fertility Rate Dropped to Record Low in 1986," *Minneapolis Star and Tribune*, 10 June 1987, p. 11A.

26. U.S. Bureau of the Census, *Historical Statistics of the United States*, pp. 316–317.

27. Rothman, *Hands and Hearts*, pp. 306–311, and Greer Litton Fox, "Sex Role Attitudes as Predictors of Contraceptive Use among Unmarried University Students," *Sex Roles* 33 (1977), pp. 265–283. See also John H. Scarlett, "Undergraduate Attitudes toward Birth Control: New Perspectives," *Journal of Marriage and the Family* 34 (May 1972), pp. 312–322, and Ira E. Robinson and Davor Jedlicka, "Change in Sexual Attitudes and Behavior of College Students from 1965 to 1980: A Research Note," *Journal of Marriage and the Family* 44 (February 1982), pp. 237–240. It is also interesting to note that sexual activity between unmarried individuals continued to be considered "premarital," even though studies were conducted on an unmarried population that may not have been headed toward marriage. See, for example, Richard R. Clayton and Janet L. Bokemeier, "Premarital Sex in the Seventies," *Journal of Marriage and the Family* 42 (November 1980), pp. 759–775; B. K. Singh, "Trends in Attitudes toward Premarital Sexual Relations," *Journal of Marriage and the Family* 42 (May 1980), pp. 387–393; J. Richard Udry et al., "Changes in Premarital Coital Experience of Recent Decade-of-Birth Cohorts of Urban American Women," *Journal of Marriage and the Family*

37 (November 1975), pp. 783–787; and Ira L. Reiss et al., "Premarital Contraceptive Usage: A Study and Some Theoretical Explorations," *Journal of Marriage and the Family* 37 (August 1975), pp. 619–630.

28. *New York Times*, as quoted in Rothman, *Hands and Hearts*, pp. 309–310; Eleanor D. Macklin, "Nontraditional Family Forms: A Decade of Research," *Journal of Marriage and the Family* 42 (November 1980), pp. 905–922; Leslie D. Strong, "Alternative Marital and Family Forms: Their Relative Attractiveness to College Students and Correlates of Willingness to Participate in Nontraditional Forms," *Journal of Marriage and the Family* 40 (August 1978), pp. 493–503; Jessie Bernard, "Note on Changing Life Styles, 1970–1974," *Journal of Marriage and the Family* 37 (August 1975), pp. 582–593; "Living Together in College: Implications for Courtship," *Journal of Marriage and the Family* 43 (February 1981), pp. 77–83; Paul C. Glick and Graham B. Spanier, "Married and Unmarried Cohabitation in the United States," *Journal of Marriage and the Family* 42 (February 1980), pp. 19–30; Paul R. Newcomb, "Cohabitation in America: An Assessment of Consequences," *Journal of Marriage and the Family* 41 (August 1979), pp. 597–603; Judith L. Lyness et al., "Living Together: An Alternative to Marriage," *Journal of Marriage and the Family* 34 (May 1972), pp. 305–311; Alan E. Bayer and Gerald W. McDonald, "Cohabitation among Youth: Correlates of Support for a New American Ethic," *Youth and Society* 12 (June 1981), pp. 387–402; Paul C. Glick and Arthur J. Norton, "Marrying, Divorcing, and Living Together in the U.S. Today," *Population Bulletin* 32 (1977), pp. 3–39; and John D'Emilio, *Sexual Politics, Sexual Communities: The Making of the Homosexual Minority in the United States, 1940–1970* (Chicago: University of Chicago Press, 1983).

29. Graham B. Spanier and Frank F. Furstenberg, "Remarriage and Reconstituted Families," paper prepared for Ad Hoc Meeting on Separation, Divorce and Family Reconstitution organized by the Committee on Child Development Research and Public Policy of the National Academy of Sciences, Stanford, Calif., 15–16 April 1982, hereafter referred to as Ad Hoc Meeting at Stanford, 1982. For a comparison of attitudes, see Marilyn Yalom et al., "Women of the Fifties: Their Past Sexual Experiences and Current Sexual Attitudes in the Context of Mother/Daughter Relationships," *Sex Roles* 7 (September 1981), pp. 877–887.

30. Rothman, *Hands and Hearts*, pp. 306–311; U.S. Bureau of the Census, *Historical Statistics of the United States*, pp. 133, 134; Valerie Kincade Oppenheimer, "Structural Sources of Economic Pressure for Wives to Work: An Analytical Framework," *Journal of Family History* 4, 2 (June 1979), p. 195; and "U.S. Expecting Smaller Families, Waiting Longer to Have Children," *Family Planning Perspectives* 13 (July/August 1981), p. 191. On the family patterns of the baby boomers, see, for example, Landon Y. Jones, *Great Expectations: America and the Baby Boom Generation* (New York: Ballantine Books, 1981), Sar A. Levitan and Richard S. Belous, *What's Happening to the American Family?* (Baltimore: Johns Hopkins University Press, 1981), p. 43; A. Regula Herzog et al., "Paid Work, Child Care, and Housework: A National Survey of High School Seniors' Preferences for Sharing Responsibilities between Husband and Wife," *Sex Roles* 9

(January, 1983), pp. 109–135; and Andrew Cherlin and Pamela Barnhouse Walters, "Trends in United States Men's and Women's Sex-Role Attitudes, 1972–78," *American Sociological Review* 46 (1981), pp. 453–460.

31. Andrew Cherlin, "Postponing Marriage: The Influence of Young Women's Work Expectations," *Journal of Marriage and the Family* 42 (May 1980), pp. 355–365, and Stephany Stone Joy and Paula Sachs Wise, "Maternal Unemployment, Anxiety, and Sex Differences in College Students' Self-Descriptions," *Sex Roles* 9 (April 1983), pp. 519–525.

32. Thomas J. Espenshade, "Economic Consequences of Changing Family Structures for Children, Families, and Society," Ad Hoc Meeting at Stanford, 1982; Thomas J. Espenshade, "The Economic Consequences of Divorce," *Journal of Marriage and the Family* 41 (August 1979), pp. 615–625; Mary Corcoran, "The Economic Consequences of Marital Dissolution for Women in the Middle Years," *Sex Roles* 5 (March 1979), pp. 343–353; and Ruth A. Brandwein, Carol A. Brown, and Elizabeth Maury Fox, "Women and Children Last: The Social Situation of Divorced Mothers and Their Families," *Journal of Marriage and the Family* 36 (August 1974), pp. 498–514.

33. For an excellent study of this problem, see Lenore J. Weitzman, *The Divorce Revolution: The Unexpected Social and Economic Consequences for Women and Children in America* (New York: Free Press, 1985), especially pp. ix–xxiv; Michael Gordon, *The Nuclear Family in Crisis: The Search for an Alternative* (New York: Harper & Row, 1972); and Sara Yogev, "Do Professional Women Have Egalitarian Marital Relationships?" *Journal of Marriage and the Family* 43 (November 1981), pp. 865–871. On the persistence of patterns in the face of change, see Helena Znoniecka Lopata and Kathleen Fordham Norr, "Changing Commitments of American Women to Work and Family Roles," *Social Security Bulletin* 43 (June 1980), pp. 3–14; Benson Rosen et al., "Dual Career Marital Adjustment: Potential Effects of Discriminatory Managerial Attitudes," *Journal of Marriage and the Family* 37 (August 1975), pp. 565–572; and James W. Ramey, "Communes, Group Marriage, and the Upper-Middle Class," *Journal of Marriage and the Family* 34 (November 1972), pp. 647–655.

34. See Phyllis Schlafly, *Kissinger on the Couch* (New Rochelle, N.Y.: Arlington House, 1974), and Carol Felsenthal, *The Sweetheart of the Silent Majority: The Biography of Phyllis Schlafly* (New York: Doubleday, 1981). In a press conference in 1975, Schlafly called on Henry Kissinger to resign and return the Nobel Peace Prize he won in 1973 because he "signed away our right to defend ourselves against incoming missiles." See Eileen Shanahan, "Antifeminist Says U.S. Helps Equal Rights Group," *New York Times*, 5 June 1975, unpaginated clipping, Schlafly Biography File, Schlesinger Library, Radcliffe College, Cambridge, Mass. See also Lisa McGirr, *Suburban Warriors: The Origins of the New American Right* (Princeton, N.J.: Princeton University Press, 2002).

35. See Michael Rogin, *Ronald Reagan: The Movie and Other Episodes in Political Demonology* (Berkeley: University of California Press, 1987); Garry Wills, *Reagan's America: Innocents at Home* (Garden City, N.Y.: Doubleday, 1987), pp. 279–288; and

Susan Faludi, *Backlash: The Undeclared War against American Women* (New York: Doubleday, 1991).

36. For the new civil defense propaganda, see Robert Scheer, *With Enough Shovels: Reagan, Bush, and Nuclear War* (New York: Random House, 1982).

EPILOGUE: ECHOES OF THE COLD WAR

1. George W. Bush, remarks to airline employees, O'Hare Airport, 27 September 2001, White House press release, www.whitehouse.gov/news/releases/2001/09/20010927-1.html.

2. Much of the material in this epilogue is drawn from Elaine Tyler May, "Echoes of the Cold War: The Aftermath of September 11 at Home," in Mary Dudziak, ed., *September 11 in History: A Watershed Moment?* (Durham, N.C.: Duke University Press, 2003).

3. Peter Carlson, "America Gamely Stumbled Off to War," *Washington Post,* 7 December 2001, p. A01, and George W. Bush, "Address to a Joint Session of Congress and the American People," 20 September 2001, United States Capitol, Washington, D.C., White House press release, www.whitehouse.gov/news/releases/2001/09/20010920-8.html.

4. The Bush administration's proposal to drill for oil in the Arctic National Wildlife Refuge would reduce oil imports from the Middle East by only 4 to 5 percent, and not for at least ten years. See Frank Rich, "The Bush Doctrine, R.I.P.," *New York Times,* 13 April 2002, p. A17.

5. See Elaine Tyler May, *Homeward Bound: American Families in the Cold War Era* (New York: Basic Books, 1999).

6. Susan Baer and Ellen Gamerman, "Terrorism Strikes America," *Baltimore Sun,* 12 September 2001, p. 12A; Laurel J. Sweet and Kay Lazar, "Attack on America," *Boston Herald,* 12 September 2001, p. 032; and Mary Leonard, "Attack on America/Washington, D.C.: Center of Government Becomes a Ghost Town," *Boston Globe,* 12 September 2001, p. A2.

7. Rosie DiManno, "A Nation's Confidence Is among the Casualties," *Toronto Star,* 12 September 2001, p. B01.

8. Unsigned editorial approving the action, "Fighting Back: Congress Acts Quickly in War on Terror," *San Diego Union-Tribune,* 15 September 2001, p. B10.

9. See Marc Howard Ross, "The Political Psychology of Competing Narratives: September 11 and Beyond," in Craig Calhoun, Paul Price, and Ashley Timmer, eds., *Understanding September 11* (New York: New Press, 2002), pp. 303–320.

10. Quoted in Kevin Diaz, "Cynicism Is Out, Trust in Government Is In," *Minneapolis Star Tribune,* 23 October 2001, p. A11.

11. Michael S. Sherry, *In the Shadow of War* (New Haven, Conn.: Yale University Press, 1995), p. x; see also Andrew Bacevich, *The New American Militarism: How Americans Are Seduced by War* (New York: Oxford University Press, 2006).

12. Frank Rich, "The Wimps of War," *New York Times*, 30 March 2002, www.NYTimes.com; Michael R. Gordon, "U.S. Nuclear Plan Sees New Weapons and New Targets," *New York Times*, 10 March 2002, p. 1A+.

13. Aristide Zolberg (professor of political science, New School University), "Guarding the Gates in a World on the Move," Social Science Research Council, www.ssrc.org/sept11/essays/zolberg.htm; Ann McFeatters, "Bush Signs Anti-terror Bill; Says Tough Law Will Preserve Constitutional Rights," *Pittsburgh Post-Gazette*, 27 October 2001, p. A6; and Jacques Steinberg, "A Nation Challenged: The Students," *New York Times*, 12 November 2001, Section A, p. 1.

14. Quoted in Kevin Diaz, "Cynicism Is Out."

15. Frank Rich, "The Wimps of War."

16. Bill Carter, "TV Notes: Sponsors Defect," *New York Times*, 26 September 2001, Section E, p. 7; Sheryl McCarthy, "City College Officials Need an Education on Freedom," *Newsday*, 11 October 2001, p. A48; and Editorial, *Washington Post*, 29 September 2001, p. A26.

17. Martin J. Sherwin, "Tattletales for an Open Society," *The Nation*, 21 January 2002, p. 40.

18. See May, *Homeward Bound*.

19. Steve Samuel, "A Weak Spot: The Luggage Hold," *New York Times*, 11 October 2001, p. A25.

20. Andrew Clark, "When Sales Start to Flag: The American Consumer," *The Guardian* (London), 29 September 2001, p. 32.

21. Topps Enduring Freedom card packet, distributed by the Topps Company, Inc., Duryea, Pa.

22. Ann McFeatters, "Bush Signs Anti-terror Bill; Says Tough Law Will Preserve Constitutional Rights," *Pittsburgh Post-Gazette*, 27 October 2001, p. A6.

23. Unsigned editorial, "Pledge of Allegiance—Mandatory Recitation Unnecessary," *Minneapolis Star Tribune*, 18 March 2002, p. A12, and Anthony Lonetree and James Walsh, "State Senate Backs Pledge Bill," *Minneapolis Star Tribune*, 26 April 2002, p. A1.

24. Kevin Flynn and Jim Dwyer, "Fire Dept. Lapses on 9/11 Are Cited," *New York Times*, 3 August 2002, p. 1A, and Jim Dwyer, Kevin Flynn, and Ford Fessenden, "9/11 Exposed Deadly Flaws in Rescue Plan," *New York Times*, 11 July 2002, N.Y. Region, p. 1. These stories note that at least 121 firefighters in striking distance of safety died as a result of a lack of communication between the police and fire departments, and within the fire department.

25. Susan Faludi, *The Terror Dream: Fear and Fantasy in Post-9/11 America* (New York: Metropolitan Books, 2007).

26. Editorial, "Closing the Safety Gap," *Christian Science Monitor*, 11 October 2001, p. 8.

27. Donna Nebenzahl, "Getting Closer: Sept. 11 Affecting Personal Relations," *The Gazette* (Montreal), 11 October 2001, p. D1; Courtney Lingle and John Libid, "Marriage-License Requests Up," *Denver Post*, 10 October 2001, p. A-12; and Michael E.

Ruane, "A Wedding Out of Mourning: Like Many Touched by Attacks, Couple Changed Approach to Life after Sept. 11," *Washington Post*, 10 October 2001, p. B03.

28. Robert D. Putnam, "Bowling Together," *American Prospect*, 11 February 2002, www.prospect.org/print/V13/3/putnam-r.html.

29. "Hugging Up 76,000 Percent," *The Onion*, 26 September 2001.

30. Nicholas D. Kristof, "Chicks with Guns," *New York Times*, 8 March 2002, p. A23.

INDEX